Radiant Truths

Radiant Truths

Essential Dispatches,

Reports, Confessions, &

Other Essays on American Belief

EDITED AND INTRODUCED

BY JEFF SHARLET

Yale

UNIVERSITY PRESS

New Haven and London

Published with assistance from the foundation established in memory of Amasa Stone Mather of the Class of 1907, Yale College.

Yale University Press books may be purchased in quantity for educational, business, or promotional use. For information, please e-mail sales.press@yale.edu (U.S. office) or sales@yaleup.co.uk (U.K. office).

Designed by Sonia Shannon.
Set in Fournier type by Tseng Information Systems, Inc.
Printed in the United States of America.

Library of Congress Cataloging-in-Publication Data

Radiant truths : essential dispatches, reports, confessions, and other essays on American belief / [edited by] Jeff Sharlet.
pages cm
Includes bibliographical references.
ISBN 978-0-300-16921-8 (hardback)
1. United States — Religion. I. Sharlet, Jeff.
BL2525.R33 2014
200.973 — dc23
2013031982

A catalogue record for this book is available from the British Library.

This paper meets the requirements of ANSI/NISO Z39.48-1992 (Permanence of Paper).

10 9 8 7 6 5 4 3 2 1

For Roxana

CONTENTS

ACKNOWLEDGMENTS

First, the living: Thanks to Dennis Covington, Anne Fadiman, Michael Lesy, Francine Prose, John Jeremiah Sullivan, and Matthew Teague for sharing their work. Special thanks to Peter Manseau, with whom I've been in conversation about the documentation of other people's religions since 2000. As for the dead, I hope my celebration of their writing will be enough; but for good measure, thanks to their estates and executors.

An anthology such as this is the result of years of conversation with too many writers, scholars, and friends to name. As I look over the long list from which I drew up my table of contents, though, I'm compelled to thank at least Jeff Allred, my agent, Kathy Anderson, Patton Dodd, Omri Elisha, Donovan Hohn, Scott Korb, Bruce Lawrence, Marjorie Pryse, Bob Sharlet, Bob Smietana, Shalene Vasquez, Michael Vazquez, Diane Winston, JoAnn Wypijewski, and Angela Zito.

I've developed my thinking about both literary journalism and religion through two small publications, the New York University Center for Religion and Media's critical review *The Revealer* and *Killing the Buddha*, a literary journal. Among the wonderful editors I've worked with at those two publications are Garret Baer, Nicole Greenfield, Kathryn Joyce, Ashley Makar, Paul Morris, Quince Mountain,

Ann Neumann, Jay Rosen, Nathan Schneider, Meera Subramanian, and Brook Wilensky-Lanford.

This book began as a conversation with Yale University Press's wise, patient, and intellectually generous Jennifer Banks. I'm grateful as well to Dan Heaton, Heather Gold, and Melissa Flamson. The book emerges in its present form from a course I first taught at Dartmouth College in 2011. The students in that course played an important part in helping me decide what should—and should not—be included. Research assistants Emily LaFond, Kelsey Stimson, Lizzie Aviv, Ashley Ulrich, Hannah Jung, Sadia Hassan, and Madison Pauly helped me scan 150 years of literary journalism and make the selections included herein presentable. I'm grateful to my Dartmouth colleagues for making room for this strange, in-between genre, and to Adrian Randolph, associate dean of the faculty, Arts and Humanities, for facilitating my research for this book.

The MacDowell Colony provided me with a crucial respite from campus life during which to complete my introduction. I'm especially grateful to insights provided by my fellow residents Vanessa Hartmann, Joan Leegant, Alex Mar, Jenna Osman, and Matt Wray.

And no book in which I have any kind of involvement is complete without gratitude for Julie Rabig, a scholar, writer, and reader, and, lucky for me, my wife.

Radiant Truths

INTRODUCTION
This Mutant Genre

REAL TOADS

... nor till the autocrats among us can be
   "literalists of
   the imagination" — above
   insolence and triviality and can present

for inspection, "imaginary gardens with real toads
   in them," shall we have
it.[1]

The title of the 1919 poem by Marianne Moore from which I've borrowed these lines is "Poetry." But its paradox — *imaginary gardens with real toads in them* — is at the heart of literary journalism, the practice of using fictional techniques to write factual stories. This poem, for instance, is a fact, a real toad; my appropriation of it, my arrangement of the facts, is the garden.

Moore kept revising "Poetry" for five decades. The version she published in her 1967 *Complete Poems* did away with all of the above, leaving only three curmudgeonly lines.[2] (Strictures of copyright law

prevent me from quoting much more than "dislike it.") Does that era-
sure make the real toads as imaginary as the garden? I don't think so.
But then, I'm a believer: I believe in the so-called art of fact.

SOMETHING BROUGHT YOU HERE

Over the years I've written about churches, temples, and Buddhist
centers, reported on exorcisms (individual and group), prayer cells,
and prayer rallies, squinted at my notebook among thousands of teens
thrilling violently to the Book of Judges. There were quieter moments,
too: kitchen table shabbat takeout chicken with the last Yiddish writer;
late night mojitos with a born-again Bible editor considering rebirth,
third time's the charm; whiskey with Mormons; tea before a shrine to an
anarchist martyr's slingshot. I'm most interested in the subset of religion known as belief, and that interest sometimes leads me to people
who might reject the term *religion* altogether: I've marched in Spain
with Jewish-American veterans of the Abraham Lincoln Brigade,
whispered with cadres of the Revolutionary Communist Party (certain that any Brooklyn café I proposed for a meeting must be "wired"),
and steamed with "primitivists" who insisted on nudity as a precondi-
tion for our conversation, the better to be honest with one another. As
a writer I practice participant-observation, so, with as clear-as-can-
be disclaimers — "Look, I don't really share your beliefs . . ." — I've
often joined in. I've eaten holy dirt and shoveled it, too, wrestled with
"spiritual warriors," and prayed with actual warriors that Jesus should
grant them righteous aim. I've called down the moon with half-naked
witches and laid hands — spiritually speaking, of course — on whoever
asked me to do so, even knowing that my touch was most likely profane. "It's no accident that you came here," someone always tells me,
here being her church, his coven, their compound, the midnight mass
in the graveyard. "It's like something *brought* you here."

    If you write about religious people, even your friends may
start making certain assumptions about the state of your soul. That

is, they'll imagine that you're either a scholar or a seeker. That you write about religion for the sake of scientific inquiry or that you write about religion because you're searching for one. That you're devising a theory, or pursuing a process of elimination. That, sooner or later, you'll arrive at an answer.

I prefer the questions posed by anthropologist Angela Zito. "What does the term 'religion,' when actually used by people, out loud, *authorize* in the production of social life?" she asks in an essay called "Religion Is Media." *The production of social life* — that's the kind of phrase anthropologists use to draw attention to the ways in which we compose "the stories we tell ourselves in order to live," as literary journalist Joan Didion famously wrote in *The White Album.* We are so busy living these stories that we rarely consider their fabrication, a term I use literally: Every story is "made up," to the extent that stories exist only if we make them. "Most of us do not notice it happening," writes Zito, circling around the "it," a matter of "self-making" and meaning-finding with yet more questions she finds within that single word, *religion,* questions about remembering and forgetting, facts and fictions. What do we set in motion when we say *religion,* out loud? "What acts can then possibly be performed?" Zito asks. "What stories can be told?"[3]

The stories collected here, which are about what happens when we say "religion" out loud, begin with Walt Whitman at war and end with Francine Prose driven to tears by the sight of Whitman's words. A neat enough trick, but don't let it fool you. There's an argument to be made for the chronology of this book, and by God I'm going to make it, just as I'm going to apologize for all that is missing. (Sorry, Mormons!)* But periodization and demographic representation aren't my concern

*Apologies also to Roman Catholics (23.9 percent of the American population, according to the Pew Forum on Religion and Public Life), underrepresented here in terms of story selection, though maybe not in actual word count, or power of those words; and to Old Catholics, in all your fascinating retrenchist glory; and to Protestants, whose significant presence still does not equal your demographic profile (51.3 percent); and to American Muslims (0.7 percent, says Pew, a

here. I could murmur about religious pluralism or preach religious literacy—both really terrific, I wholeheartedly endorse them—but this book is not your key to either. This book is an anthology. A selection. Which is to say, as believers and unbelievers so often do, it's personal.

IN THE IMMEDIATE WORLD

"'For in the immediate world, everything is to be discerned, for him who can discern it,'" James Agee writes in his 1941 masterpiece of literary journalism *Let Us Now Praise Famous Men*, "and centrally and simply, without either dissection into science, or digestion into art, but with the whole of consciousness, seeking to perceive it as it stands: so that the aspect of a street in sunlight can roar in the heart of itself as a symphony, perhaps as no symphony can: and all of consciousness is shifted from the imagined, the revisive, to the effort to perceive simply the cruel radiance of what is."[4]

"Roar in the heart of itself as a symphony": That *is* the imagined, the revisive. We are as bound by the imagined as by the flesh, and "the cruel radiance of what is" includes metaphor, the translation of light into sound into language. Wendy Doniger, a historian of religion, a scholar of myth, points to the common roots of those two terms, *metaphor* and *translation:* "English derivatives from related Greek and Latin words for the same thing: 'bringing across.'" If too simple to serve as a definition of literary journalism, this formulation at least states its ambition: "bringing across."[5]

---

disputed number), though a major complication of widely held American conceptions of Islam is included herein; and to Orthodox Christians, Greek, Russian, or otherwise (you total 0.6 percent, says Pew); and to Hindus (0.4 percent), and to Jains, Sikhs, Zoroastrians, Jehovah's Witnesses, Baba Lovers, Five-Percenters, Twelve Tribers, Animists, Odinists, Scientologists, Unificationists, graduates of est and the Landmark Forum, Raelians, Pastafarians, and all those decreed by pollsters—with no justice—as "Other." May you nonetheless find some glimmer of yourselves in these pages.

Eugene Jolas, the editor of an influential early-twentieth-century journal called *transition*, wrote in 1935 of his desire for a new kind of writing. His description cuts close to that idea of "bringing across": "The literature of the future will probably express the irruption of the supernatural, the phantastic, the eternal, into quotidian life." Although he published mainly fiction and poetry, he was dismissive of such forms. "The short story, the novel, the poem, etc.," would not do. He proposed instead the "paramyth": "a phantasmagoric mixture of the poem in prose, the popular tale of folklore, the psychograph, the essay, the myth, the saga, the humoresque . . . a mirror of a four-dimensional universe."[6]

Literary journalism is something like that. The name itself is a mashup: *literary* and *journalism*, art, or that which critics call art, vs. antiart, belles lettres vs. the who-what-where-when-why. In 1887, the critic Matthew Arnold called such writing "a new journalism" — "full of ability, novelty, variety, sensation, sympathy, [and] generous instincts" — anticipating the name by which the genre would come to be known during the 1960s.[7] *New*, then, is too old. Some prefer the label *creative nonfiction*, the name with which the National Endowment for the Arts, beginning in the early 1980s, and the academy, even now, paper over discomfort with journalism, considered vocational, crass. *Creative nonfiction*, then, is a term of bureaucratic finesse, its adjective too vague, its noun a negation. There's the seemingly more modest *narrative nonfiction*, but its adjective too tightly dictates form. It excludes the fragment, the argument, the found and the collaged. There's a term, increasingly in vogue, which contains all of these: *lyric essay*. Pretty. But it lacks creative tension. "The lyric essay," writes its most nimble champion, John D'Agata, "doesn't care about figuring out why papa lost the family farm, or why mama took to drink. It's more interested in replicating the feeling of that experience rather than reporting it." But reportage *is* replication; and I'm more interested in "the feeling of that experience," including the foreclosure notice on papa's farm and the data points of mama's despair, than I am in excluding information for the sake of form.[8]

To be fair, D'Agata, writing with his former teacher Deborah Tall in 1997, defined the lyric essay only as a subgenre. And yet, within "creative nonfiction" as an academic field, the lyric essay so thoroughly displaced other possibilities that ten years later, D'Agata lamented the claims he'd made for the lyric essay at the expense of "memoir . . . criticism, journalism, all narratives, etcetera." That didn't mean he'd abandoned what he and Tall had termed the "primacy" of "artfulness." "Do we read nonfiction in order to receive information, or do we read it to experience art?" D'Agata asks in the introduction to his 2009 anthology, *The Lost Origins of the Essay*. In answer, he argues for a "clear objective": *art*, "an alternative to commerce." And yet, says the cliché of our digital age with at least some truth, information wants to be free; and art has ever been sold.[9]

Perhaps all we need is *essay*, or Michel de Montaigne's sixteenth-century *essai*—French for "attempt." Perhaps it is enough just to try. "A loose sally of the mind," Samuel Johnson famously defined the term in his eighteenth-century dictionary. "An irregular, undigested piece; not a regular and orderly composition." Such a definition has much to recommend it, not least its appeal to indigestion: an essay, we might say, is a piece of writing that doesn't go down easy. It's suitable fare only for those who can stomach contradictions, such as this one from the contemporary Belarusian literary journalist Svetlana Alexievich: "Art may lie but a document never does." That is, a document may be full of lies, but its existence is a fact. As soon as we present it, however, we're on the "irregular" terrain of art. It's from this difficult country that I've selected the essays, the documents, that in this volume I choose to call literary journalism. I looked for pieces that "essay" these contradictions, true tales that recognize that the wrinkle in any truth is always the truth teller herself, essays that attempt to become documents and take stock of their failures to completely do so as an inevitable part of the story.[10]

In 1926, a young critic named John Grierson translated the French term *documentaire,* which referred to travelogues — or, as he later put it, "shimmying exoticisms" — into a new English word, *documentary,* which he later defined as "creative treatment of actuality." He envisioned and went on to practice documentary film as an art comprising "the blazing fact of the matter," its poetic power derived from its faithfulness to observable reality. Fact — or, really the dream of fact, the ideal of perfect accuracy — redirects the artist's imaginative power from the skirmishes of genre toward the endless question of "what is," radiant or opaque or even shimmying. Fact liberates art from the requirement of form. The literary journalist need be loyal only to the facts as best he or she can perceive them. Not structure or antistructure or tradition or innovation. Only perception.[11]

BUT-BUT-BUT

I explain this to my students through a story about a collaborative piece I wrote with the novelist and literary journalist Peter Manseau. Our subject was the performance of a song. The facts of the situation were remarkable: A serial killer in a church van had murdered a young woman, a soloist in another church's choir. The killer had been caught and convicted. The victim's church declared "Victory Day," to be observed through the wearing of red, the color of the blood of the lamb. And, maybe, of the killer they wanted to see given the electric chair, a sentence they sang for with an old gospel standard, "Power in the Blood." Peter and I attended one of the killer's hearings. In Peter's first pass at the story, the killer wore a red suit to his hearing. Only, he hadn't. It'd been beige, a jumpsuit, prison-issue.

"Red is better," said Peter. He was then mainly a novelist.*

"But-but-but," I said, with great eloquence. What I meant to say

---

*He's still a novelist, but he's since become a scrupulously accurate literary journalist as well, a fact I note here with apologies to Peter for cherry picking a story from our collaboration in which I just happened to be right. Imaginary gardens, indeed!

was that red isn't better, it's only more symmetrical. It's a ready-made that never was, a symbolic reality dropped in rather than revealed. Such symbols, imagined but not perceived, obscure the smaller truths that constitute literary journalism.

We settled on this: "Every day of the trial he'd worn a new suit, but now he wore a prison-issue coverall, beige. It rounded his shoulders and made his chest look hollow, but still he smiled, even for the prosecutor, just as he had smiled at the reverend when the reverend had sat in the gallery, praying for justice and power and blood."[12] It was our fight over "red" that sent us back to our notebooks, where we discovered the smile.

Maybe the distinction is this: Fiction's first move is imagination; nonfiction's is perception. But the story, the motive and the doubt, everything we believe—what's *that?* Imagination? Or perception? Art? Or information? D'Agata achieves paradoxical precision when he half-jokingly proposes a broader possibility: "that genre known sometimes as 'something else.'"[13]

EVIDENCE OF THINGS UNSEEN

American and *religion* are no less problematic terms, a fact this book not only acknowledges but also embraces. It's a tight squeeze, too, and at times uncomfortably so. It's easy to argue that Ellen Willis's journey to Jerusalem in pursuit of a brother who has made aliyah is an extension of the American imagination, but my inclusion of Amy Wilentz's sojourn in Port-au-Prince pulls Haiti under the American banner. But so, too, does the long history of U.S. interference in the affairs of that nation, casting a heavy shadow over its religious life. *Religion,* meanwhile, as used by scholars, encompasses far more than this book could hope to, from the mundane to the supernatural, and at the same time, perhaps, less. Norman Mailer's epiphanies at the 1968 exorcism of the Pentagon are clearly as religious as they are political, but Meridel Le Sueur's tale of her conversion to the cause of a strike is so purely political that it becomes religious. The most uncomplicated, sincere expression of American religion to be found in what follows is that of a group of Hmong immigrants who don't distinguish between their spiritual practice and medicine. Religion, or science? Laotian, or American?

The argument I believe emerges from this collection of voices, this cacophony choir, is that this something-else genre, literary journalism, is uniquely well suited to the documentation and representation of the strange category of American religion. Americans worry over religion, argue about religion, tell stories about religion, not just because of our ambiguous First Amendment (which promises both freedom *of* and freedom *from* religion) but because American identity — and American democracy — depends on a constant renegotiation of terms. The problems inherent in attempting to speak about "American religion" are integral to the development of literary journalism — a genre with roots around the world and deep in the past but which came into its own here in the United States as those states sought to separate, notably in Walt Whitman's *Specimen Days*, one of the most splendidly misshapen testimonies of nineteenth-century American writing.

It's a hurdy-gurdy piece of work, lurching and swinging, tabulating and testifying with no concern for the conventions of structure. Whitman seeks a more sublime pattern, that of a reality in which the facts of darkness and light are topsy-turvy, at times black and white, at times interchangeable. "Following, I give some gloomy experiences," he warns in a note to the first page, and there is indeed gloom in his account of the Civil War, but breaking through the darkness every now and then there is also the moon. "So white, so marbly pure and dazzling, yet soft," Whitman writes in an entry titled "The White House by Moonlight": " — the White House of future poems, and of dreams and dramas, there in the soft and copious moon — the gorgeous front, in the trees, under the lustrous flooding moon, full of reality, full of illusion — "[14]

That paradox—"full of reality, full of illusion"—and the means
by which Whitman arrives at it—a self-conscious immersion in a light
that reveals even as it enchants—contains within it the dilemma of
documenting "things unseen." It might also be said to contain the
whole of literary journalism, a tightrope between "evidence"—the
first half of the Apostle Paul's formulation, the facts—and the imagination that conjures it into a story. The anthropologist Michael Taussig, who sometimes doubles as a literary journalist, expands on the
paradox in theoretical terms: "To see the myth in the natural and the
real in magic, to demythologize history and to reenchant its reified
representation: that is a first step."[15] Taussig is writing about Joseph
Conrad's 1902 novel *The Heart of Darkness*, but in this book that "first
step" belongs to Whitman, who forty years earlier sought a formless
form with which to represent what he experienced as the paradox of
civil war in America: the truths we hold to be self-evident, marching
against one another.

The rest of Whitman's note is an explanation of his method that is as
good a starting point for literary journalism as any I know:

> I commenced at the close of 1862, and continued steadily
> through '63, '64, and '65, to visit the sick and wounded
> of the army, both on the field and in the hospitals in and
> around Washington city. From the first I kept little note-
> books of impromptu jottings in pencil to refresh my mem-
> ory of names and circumstances, and what was specially
> wanted, &c. In these I brief'd cases, persons, sights, oc-
> currences in camp, by the bedside, and not seldom by the
> corpses of the dead. Some were scratch'd down from nar-
> ratives I heard and itemized while watching, or waiting,
> or tending somebody amid those scenes. I have dozens
> of such little note-books left, forming a special his-
> tory of those years, for myself alone, full of associations

never to be possibly said or sung. I wish I could convey
to the reader the associations that attach to these soil'd
and creas'd livraisons, each composed of a sheet or two
of paper, folded small to carry in the pocket, and fasten'd
with a pin. I leave them just as I threw them by after the
war, blotch'd here and there with more than one blood-
stain, hurriedly written, sometimes at the clinique, not
seldom amid the excitement of uncertainty, or defeat, or
of action, or getting ready for it, or a march. Most of the
pages . . . are verbatim copies of those lurid and blood-
smutch'd little note-books.[16]

In *Memoranda During the War*, the Civil War journal he self-
published before grafting it into *Specimen Days*, he calls these "the
convulsive memories."[17]

As Joan Didion writes in "On Keeping a Notebook": "It all
comes back."[18]

USUALLY LITERARY JOURNALISM

Usually literary journalism is defined by a list of techniques. In his
valuable anthology *The Literary Journalists*, Norman Sims offers "immersion," "structure," "accuracy," "voice," "responsibility," and "the
masks of men," or "symbolic realities," as literary journalist Richard
Rhodes puts it.[19] Tom Wolfe, in his anthology *The New Journalism*,
narrows it down to four: "scene-by-scene construction," "dialogue,"
"third-person point of view," and "status details," Wolfe's version of
Rhodes's symbolic realities. Wolfe's definition of "status details" is a
brilliant list of its own: "This is the recording of everyday gestures,
habits, manners, customs, styles of furniture, clothing, decoration,
styles of traveling, eating, keeping house, modes of behaving toward
children, servants, superiors, inferiors, peers, plus the various looks,
glances, poses, styles of walking and other symbolic details that might

exist within a scene."[20] That is, the metaphors of daily life, along with the literary techniques with which to render them as a story.

But it's not as simple as a method. Wolfe locates the origins of these "devices"—or, at least, their development into tools to be re-invented by literary journalists—in the nineteenth-century realist fic-tion of Balzac and Dickens, the "unique power" of which, he writes, is "variously known as its 'immediacy,' its 'concrete reality,' its 'emo-tional involvement,' its 'gripping' or 'absorbing' quality."[21] That tips the scales too far toward the fictive, plot-driven side of Whitman's for-mulation, "full of reality, full of illusion." The term *immediacy,* when applied to a story made up of printed words—literally mediation, these symbolic little squiggles of ink—is a deception, a veil that obscures the constructedness of the story, the quality of having been made.

Absorbing, a term better left to advertisements for paper towels, implies only a passive position for the reader, soaked up by illusion alone. That's neither realist fiction nor journalism, but rather what screenwriter Ed Burns, in an episode of the television series *The Wire*—the greatest Victorian novel of the twenty-first century—mocks as "the Dickensian aspect."[22] It's fact manipulated into sensation, sensa-tion stripped down to sentiment and dressed up again as a too-familiar tale. The results—the work of Wolfe's lesser imitators, fake memoirs, reality TV—are grotesques, reminders that literary journalism is not the product of a technique but the documentation of a tension between fact and art, what is and our expression of it.

Which returns me to Whitman. It's not Whitman's poetry but his meditation on the piety of the term *literary* that provides us with an essential clue to the creation—or creation myth, as the case may be—of literary journalism. Piety, so intimately bound up in our idea of religion, is ultimately a more fundamental term, broader than its col-loquial religious application. Piety is a form of gratitude, "the proper acknowledgment of the sources of our existence and progress through life," writes the philosopher Jeffrey Stout.[23] But it's more often aped. In religion we call this *sanctimony;* in literature, we call this, well, *litera-*

ture. Writing thought worthy of reverence unto segregation, shelved in big-box bookstores separately from the rabble of ordinary "fiction."

In *Democratic Vistas*, the long essay he published in 1870–71 as his prose companion to *Leaves of Grass*, Whitman searched for a more vibrant piety, a wisdom that could be kept alive without sacrificing democracy. He did not disown the past, he set it in motion, "all the best experience of humanity, folded, saved, freighted to us here" in the "tiny ships we call Old and New Testament, Homer, Eschylus, Plato, Juvenal, &c." Whitman loved the "old undying elements," but the art he dreamed of for America would "adjust them to new combinations," "into groups, unities, appropriate to the modern, the democratic, the west, and to the practical occasions and needs of our own cities, and of the agricultural regions." Art for farms; stories for new cities. A nationalist project, to be sure, but one for an imaginary nation.[24]

The democratic dilemma Whitman tried to solve was how to liberate his writing from piety's conventions without losing piety's wisdom. Pious in this true sense is how we might describe Whitman's own most undying elements — to me, his little ships are his prose, not his poetry, and, for all of *Democratic Vistas'* eclectic grandeur, his simpler experiments with description. The reports; the "blood-smutch'd notebooks," timeless because they are so "rooted in the invisible roots," in the specificity of time and place and actual people.[25] Whitman's clichés — his *other* paradox, magical universalism bound to racialized nationalism — intrude, but in his journalism they only shade the lens through which he looks. They don't curtail his vision, "the radiation of this truth," the generosity with which he attempted to see "what is."[26]

Whitman's poetry, with its impious rejection of form, gestures toward literary journalism. But has American literary poetry — until Whitman mostly bound by European forms, and afterward written and read for the most part within well-versed enclaves — ever been a really democratic medium? Our "chants democratic," for better and more often for worse, have been journalistic. Journalism supposes that you can understand a thing by going out and gathering facts about it; that you can, and more important, have a right to detect motive in others by asking them impertinent questions; that you are entitled to gather your facts and arrange them as you see fit and thus define the world. It's not social science. Journalism rejects any too-tight methodology and looks with some suspicion and regret on its own late–twentieth-century entombment within the academy as a discipline rather than a democratic practice.

Perhaps that formalization was inevitable, a calcification bound to settle into any practice that puts on objective airs. The idea of objective journalism — the *belief* that it is possible to stand apart from the world — cuts close to the more obviously religious doctrine of infallibility. And yet the collapse of the old business model of journalism, that of big, centralized media organizations supported by advertising, may also be restoring journalism's democratic impulses, returning the power of questioning to the curious and the untrained. Maybe that's why an undertaking such as this book seems to me timely.

But I'm not making a case for conventional journalism here, as it has been or could be. I said it's been the genre of our chants democratic mostly for the worse because it so often deliberately eschews wisdom as dangerous to the collection (or, really, cultivation) of facts. Which leads us to the creation of the compromise, arguably an American genre: literary journalism. To say that one adopts the techniques of fiction for the sake of a factual story — as contemporary literary journalists say they do, and as Whitman and other earlier writers simply did — is first to acknowledge previous form and second to say that there is something worth learning from it. Piety, in short, married to the deliberate impiety of journalism. Literary journalism, creative nonfiction, lyric essays, this mutant genre, can never be wholly democratic any more than it can be fully pious. It cannot be just one thing. "Not that half only, individualism, which isolates," writes Whitman, since "there is another half, which is adhesiveness or love, that fuses, ties, and aggregates."[27] Pulling apart, pulling close: The little ships are always moving, often in the "wrong" direction, away from plot and toward a story, trued, like a wheel, by the writer.

Which is why the "second step" in this book, after Whitman, belongs to Henry David Thoreau, who with Whitman is half of the hybrid creation of modern literary journalism. Not at Walden Pond, certain of nature's supremacy, but at his most un-Thoreauvian, hightailing it down from his aborted ascent of Mount Ktaadn, where his transcendentalism crashes into the cold hard stone of the mountaintop, and crying, not preaching, "Contact! Contact!" even as it overwhelms him. That "failure," literary journalism's only essential truth—the impossibility of perfect representation of reality, visible and otherwise—makes it uniquely suited for the subject of American religion, so often struggling to be one or the other, pious or democratic, communal or individual, rooted or transcendent. The story of this struggle is that of the selections I've made: American religion, a history in pieces.

1863/1882

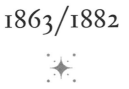

In the first excerpt that follows, a reconstructed account of a battle at Chancellorsville, Whitman poses himself a dilemma of genre rooted in reverence for his subjects. "Whoe'er can write the story?" he asks. "No history ever—no poem sings, no music sounds, those bravest men of all." Every literary journalist knows this. Sooner or later, if only for a short spell, writers must fall in love with their subjects. Heroes, villains, and ordinary people: They all become objects of obsessive fascination. It's that devotion that draws the writer's eye to the smallest of details, the facts that allow the writer to transcend his infatuation and to reconstruct human beings—not objects—as they were, or might have been, in a night battle.

In the second excerpt are a nurse's case studies, a pastor's notes, a clerk's recordings. They are pure journalism and at the end pure poetry, fused, just as Whitman's voice is with those around him.

WALT WHITMAN
From *Specimen Days*

But it was the tug of Saturday evening, and through the night and Sunday morning, I wanted to make a special note of. It was largely in the woods, and quite a general engagement. The night was very pleasant, at times the moon shining out full and clear, all Nature so calm in itself, the early summer grass so rich, and the foliage of the trees—yet there the battle raging, and many good fellows lying helpless, with new accessions to them, and every minute amid the rattle of muskets and crash of cannon, (for there was an artillery contest too,) the red life-blood oozing out from heads or trunks or limbs upon that green and dew-cool grass. Patches of the woods take fire, and several of the wounded, unable to move, are consumed—quite large spaces are swept over, burning the dead also—some of the men have their hair and beards singed—some, burns on their faces and hands—others holes burnt in their clothing. The flashes of fire from the cannon, the quick flaring flames and smoke, and the immense roar—the musketry so general, the light nearly bright enough for each side to see the other—the crashing, tramping of men—the yelling—close quarters—we hear the secesh yells—our men cheer loudly back, especially if Hooker is in sight—hand to hand conflicts, each side stands up to it, brave, determin'd as demons, they often charge upon us—a thousand deeds are done worth to write newer greater poems on—and still the woods on fire—still many are not only scorch'd—too many, unable to move, are burn'd to death.

Then the camps of the wounded—O heavens, what scene is this?—is this indeed *humanity*—these butchers' shambles? There are several of them. There they lie, in the largest, in an open space in the woods, from 200 to 300 poor fellows—the groans and screams—the odor of blood, mixed with the fresh scent of the night, the grass, the trees—that slaughter-house! O well is it their mothers, their sisters cannot see them—cannot conceive, and never conceiv'd, these things. One man is shot by a shell, both in the arm and leg—both are amputated—there lie the rejected members. Some have their legs blown off—some bullets through the breast—some indescribably horrid wounds in the face or head, all mutilated, sickening, torn, gouged out—some in the abdomen—some mere boys—many rebels, badly hurt—they take their regular turns with the rest, just the same as any—the surgeons use them just the same. Such is the camp of the wounded—such a fragment, a reflection afar off of the bloody scene—while over all the clear, large moon comes out at times softly, quietly shining. Amid the woods, that scene of flitting souls—amid the crack and crash and yelling sounds—the impalpable perfume of the woods—and yet the pungent, stifling smoke—the radiance of the moon, looking from heaven at intervals so placid—the sky so heavenly—the clear-obscure up there, those buoyant upper oceans—a few large placid stars beyond, coming silently and languidly out, and then disappearing—the melancholy, draperied night above, around. And there, upon the roads, the fields, and in those woods, that contest, never one more desperate in any age or land—both parties now in force—masses—no fancy battle, no semi-play, but fierce and savage demons fighting there—courage and scorn of death the rule, exceptions almost none.

What history, I say, can ever give—for who can know—the mad, determin'd tussle of the armies, in all their separate large and little squads—as this—each steep'd from crown to toe in desperate, mortal purports? Who know the conflict, hand-to-hand—the many conflicts in the dark, those shadowy-tangled, flashing moonbeam'd woods—the writhing groups and squads—the cries, the din, the cracking guns and pistols—the distant cannon—the cheers and calls and threats and awful music of the oaths—the indescribable mix—the officers' orders, persuasions, encouragements—the devils fully rous'd in human hearts—the strong shout, *Charge, men, charge*—the flash of the naked sword, and rolling flame and smoke? And still the broken, clear and clouded heaven   and still again the moonlight pouring silvery soft its radiant patches over all. Who paint the scene, the sudden partial panic of the afternoon, at dusk? Who paint the irrepressible advance of the second division of the Third corps, under Hooker himself, suddenly order'd up—those rapid-filing phantoms through the woods? Who show what moves there in the shadows, fluid and firm—to save, (and it did save,) the army's name, perhaps the nation? as there the veterans hold the field. (Brave Berry falls not yet—but death has mark'd him—soon he falls.) mark'd him—soon he falls.)

✦

A NEW YORK SOLDIER

This afternoon, July 22d, I have spent a long time with Oscar F. Wilber, company G, 154th New York, low with chronic diarrhœa, and a bad wound also. He asked me to read him a chapter in the New Testament. I complied, and ask'd him what I should read. He said, "Make your own choice." I open'd at the close of one of the first books of the evangelists, and read the chapters describing the latter hours of Christ, and the scenes at the crucifixion. The poor, wasted young man ask'd me to read the following chapter also, how Christ rose again. I read very slowly, for Oscar was feeble. It pleased him very much, yet the

tears were in his eyes. He ask'd me if I enjoy'd religion. I said, "Perhaps not, my dear, in the way you mean, and yet, may-be, it is the same
thing." He said, "It is my chief reliance." He talk'd of death, and said he
did not fear it. I said, "Why, Oscar, don't you think you will get well?"
He said, "I may, but it is not probable." He spoke calmly of his condition. The wound was very bad, it discharg'd much. Then the diarrhœa
had prostrated him, and I felt that he was even then the same as dying.
He behaved very manly and affectionate. The kiss I gave him as I was
about leaving he return'd fourfold. He gave me his mother's address,
Mrs. Sally D. Wilber, Alleghany post-office, Cattaraugus county, N.Y.
I had several such interviews with him. He died a few days after the
one just described.

HOME-MADE MUSIC

August 8th. — To-night, as I was trying to keep cool, sitting by a
wounded soldier in Armory-square, I was attracted by some pleasant singing in an adjoining ward. As my soldier was asleep, I left him,
and entering the ward where the music was, I walk'd half-way down
and took a seat by the cot of a young Brooklyn friend, S.R., badly
wounded in the hand at Chancellorsville, and who has suffer'd much,
but at that moment in the evening was wide awake and comparatively
easy. He had turn'd over on his left side to get a better view of the
singers, but the mosquito-curtains of the adjoining cots obstructed the
sight. I stept round and loop'd them all up, so that he had a clear show,
and then sat down again by him, and look'd and listen'd. The princi-
pal singer was a young lady-nurse of one of the wards, accompanying
on a melodeon, and join'd by the lady-nurses of other wards. They
sat there, making a charming group, with their handsome, healthy
faces, and standing up a little behind them were some ten or fifteen
of the convalescent soldiers, young men, nurses, & c., with books in
their hands, singing. Of course it was not such a performance as the
great soloists at the New York opera house take a hand in, yet I am not

sure but I receiv'd as much pleasure under the circumstances, sitting
there, as I have had from the best Italian compositions, express'd by
world-famous performers. The men lying up and down the hospital,
in their cots, (some badly wounded — some never to rise thence,) the
cots themselves, with their drapery of white curtains, and the shadows down the lower and upper parts of the ward; then the silence of
the men, and the attitudes they took — the whole was a sight to look
around upon again and again. And there sweetly rose those voices up
to the high, whitewash'd wooden roof, and pleasantly the roof sent it
all back again. They sang very well, mostly quaint old songs and de-
clamatory hymns, to fitting tunes. Here, for instance:

> My days are swiftly gliding by, and I a pilgrim stranger,
> Would not detain them as they fly, those hours of toil and
> danger;
> For O we stand on Jordan's strand, our friends are
> passing over,
> And just before, the shining shore we may almost
> discover.
>
> We'll gird our loins my brethren dear, our distant home
> discerning,
> Our absent Lord has left us word, let every lamp be
> burning,
> For O we stand on Jordan's strand, our friends are
> passing over,
> And just before, the shining shore we may almost
> discover.

1864

Henry David Thoreau's writing was as deeply stained by experience as Whitman's, but while Whitman found democratic transcendence among even the most broken, the naturalist often preferred to transcend other people altogether. Most famously at Walden Pond, but more intriguingly as he neared the top of Maine's tallest mountain, Ktaadn. There Thoreau hoped to commune with his natural divine. As he left his companions behind on the mountainside in the excerpt below, he seemed to have his story already written. But the encounter that followed didn't go as he hoped. The jolting terror of his response to what he found near the peak is one of the most electric statements of the uncertainty that would come to mark the literary journalism of phenomena beyond the known world.

HENRY DAVID THOREAU
From *The Maine Woods*

At length we reached an elevation sufficiently bare to afford a view of the summit, still distant and blue, almost as if retreating from us. A torrent, which proved to be the same we had crossed, was seen tumbling down in front, literally from out of the clouds. But this glimpse at our whereabouts was soon lost, and we were buried in the woods again. The wood was chiefly yellow birch, spruce, fir, mountain-ash, or round-wood, as the Maine people call it, and moose-wood. It was the worst kind of traveling; sometimes like the densest scrub-oak patches with us. The cornel, or bunch-berries, were very abundant, as well as Solomon's seal and moose-berries. Blueberries were distributed along our whole route; and in one place the bushes were drooping with the weight of the fruit, still as fresh as ever. It was the seventh of September. Such patches afforded a grateful repast, and served to bait the tired party forward. When any lagged behind, the cry of "blueberries" was most effectual to bring them up. Even at this elevation we passed through a moose-yard, formed by a large flat rock, four or five rods square, where they tread down the snow in winter. At length, fearing that if we held the direct course to the summit, we should not find any water near our camping-ground, we gradually swerved to the west, till, at four o'clock, we struck again the torrent which I have mentioned, and here, in view of the summit, the weary party decided to camp that night.

While my companions were seeking a suitable spot for this purpose, I improved the little daylight that was left in climbing the mountain alone. We were in a deep and narrow ravine, sloping up to the clouds, at an angle of nearly forty-five degrees, and hemmed in by walls of rock, which were at first covered with low trees, then with impenetrable thickets of scraggy birches and spruce-trees, and with moss, but at last bare of all vegetation but lichens, and almost continually draped in clouds. Following up the course of the torrent which occupied this—and I mean to lay some emphasis on this word *up*— pulling myself up by the side of perpendicular falls of twenty or thirty feet, by the roots of firs and birches, and then, perhaps, walking a level rod or two in the thin stream, for it took up the whole road, ascending by huge steps, as it were, a giant's stairway, down which a river flowed, I had soon cleared the trees, and paused on the successive shelves, to look back over the country. The torrent was from fifteen to thirty feet wide, without a tributary, and seemingly not diminishing in breadth as I advanced; but still it came rushing and roaring down, with a copious tide, over and amidst masses of bare rock, from the very clouds, as though a water-spout had just burst over the mountain. Leaving this at last, I began to work my way, scarcely less arduous than Satan's anciently through Chaos, up the nearest, though not the highest peak. At first scrambling on all fours over the tops of ancient black spruce-trees, (*Abies nigra*), old as the flood, from two to ten or twelve feet in height, their tops flat and spreading, and their foliage blue and nipt with cold, as if for centuries they had ceased growing upward against the bleak sky, the solid cold. I walked some good rods erect upon the tops of these trees, which were overgrown with moss and mountain-cranberries. It seemed that in the course of time they had filled up the intervals between the huge rocks, and the cold wind had uniformly

leveled all over. Here the principle of vegetation was hard put to it.
There was apparently a belt of this kind running quite round the mountain, though, perhaps, nowhere so remarkable as here. Once, slump-
ing through, I looked down ten feet, into a dark and cavernous region,
and saw the stem of a spruce, on whose top I stood, as on a mass of
coarse basket-work, fully nine inches in diameter at the ground. These
holes were bears' dens, and the bears were even then at home. This was
the sort of garden I made my way *over*, for an eighth of a mile, at the
risk, it is true, of treading on some of the plants, not seeing any path
through it — certainly the most treacherous and porous country I ever
travelled.

> "——nigh founder'd, on he fares,
> Treading the crude consistence, half on foot,
> Half flying."

But nothing could exceed the toughness of the twigs, — not one snapped
under my weight, for they had slowly grown. Having slumped, scram-
bled, rolled, bounced, and walked, by turns, over this scraggy country,
I arrived upon a side-hill, or rather side-mountain, where rocks, gray,
silent rocks, were the flocks and herds that pastured, chewing a rocky cud
at sunset. They looked at me with hard gray eyes, without a bleat or a low.
This brought me to the skirt of a cloud, and bounded my walk that night.
But I had already seen that Maine country when I turned about, waving,
flowing, rippling, down below.

When I returned to my companions, they had selected a camping-
ground on the torrent's edge, and were resting on the ground; one was
on the sick list, rolled in a blanket, on a damp shelf of rock. It was a
savage and dreary scenery enough; so wildly rough, that they looked
long to find a level and open space for the tent. We could not well camp
higher, for want of fuel; and the trees here seemed so evergreen and
sappy, that we almost doubted if they would acknowledge the influence of fire; but fire prevailed at last, and blazed here, too, like a good
citizen of the world. Even at this height we met with frequent traces

of moose, as well as of bears. As here was no cedar, we made our bed of coarser feathered spruce; but at any rate the feathers were plucked from the live tree. It was, perhaps, even a more grand and desolate place for a night's lodging than the summit would have been, being in the neighborhood of those wild trees, and of the torrent. Some more aerial and finer-spirited winds rushed and roared through the ravine all night, from time to time arousing our fire, and dispersing the embers about. It was as if we lay in the very nest of a young whirlwind. At midnight, one of my bedfellows, being startled in his dreams by the sudden blazing up to its top of a fir-tree, whose green boughs were dried by the heat, sprang up, with a cry, from his bed, thinking the world on fire, and drew the whole camp after him.

In the morning, after whetting our appetite on some raw pork, a wafer of hard bread, and a dipper of condensed cloud or water-spout, we all together began to make our way up the falls, which I have described; this time choosing the right hand, or highest peak, which was not the one I had approached before. But soon my companions were lost to my sight behind the mountain ridge in my rear, which still seemed ever retreating before me, and I climbed alone over huge rocks, loosely poised, a mile or more, still edging toward the clouds— for though the day was clear elsewhere, the summit was concealed by mist. The mountain seemed a vast aggregation of loose rocks, as if sometime it had rained rocks, they lay as they fell on the mountain sides, nowhere fairly at rest, but leaning on each other, all rocking-stones, with cavities between, but scarcely any soil or smoother shelf. They were the raw materials of a planet dropped from an unseen quarry, which the vast chemistry of nature would anon work up, or work down, into the smiling and verdant plains and valleys of earth. This was an undone extremity of the globe; as in lignite we see coal in the process of formation.

At length I entered within the skirts of the cloud which seemed forever drifting over the summit, and yet would never be gone, but was generated out of that pure air as fast as it flowed away; and when, a quarter of a mile further, I reached the summit of the ridge, which those who have seen in clearer weather say is about five miles along, and contains a thousand acres of table-land, I was deep within the hostile ranks of clouds, and all objects were obscured by them. Now the wind would blow me out a yard of clear sunlight, wherein I stood; then a gray, dawning light was all it could accomplish, the cloud-line ever rising and falling with the wind's intensity. Sometimes it seemed as if the summit would be cleared in a few moments and smile in sunshine: but what was gained on one side was lost on another. It was like sitting in a chimney and waiting for the smoke to blow away. It was, in fact, a cloud-factory,—these were the cloud-works, and the wind turned them off done from the cool, bare rocks. Occasionally, when the windy columns broke in to me, I caught sight of a dark, damp crag to the right or left; the mist driving ceaselessly between it and me. It reminded me of the creations of the old epic and dramatic poets, of Atlas, Vulcan, the Cyclops, and Prometheus. Such was Caucasus and the rock where Prometheus was bound. Æschylus had no doubt visited such scenery as this. It was vast, Titanic, and such as man never inhabits. Some part of the beholder, even some vital part, seems to escape through the loose grating of his ribs as he ascends. He is more lone than you can imagine. There is less of substantial thought and fair understanding in him, than in the plains where men inhabit. His reason is dispersed and shadowy, more thin and subtile like the air. Vast, Titanic, inhuman Nature has got him at disadvantage, caught him alone, and pilfers him of some of his divine faculty. She does not smile on him as in the plains. She seems to say sternly, why came ye here before your time? This ground is not prepared for you. Is it not enough that I smile in the valleys? I have never made this soil for thy feet, this air for thy breathing, these rocks for thy neighbors. I cannot pity nor fondle thee here, but forever relentlessly drive thee hence to where I *am* kind. Why seek me where I have not called thee, and then complain because you find me but a stepmother? Shouldst thou freeze or starve, or shudder thy life away, here is no shrine, nor altar, nor any access to my ear.

"Chaos and ancient Night, I come no spy
With purpose to explore or to disturb
The secrets of your realm, but * * *
* * * * * * * as my way
Lies through your spacious empire up to light."

The tops of mountains are among the unfinished parts of the globe, whither it is a slight insult to the gods to climb and pry into their secrets, and try their effect on our humanity. Only daring and insolent men, perchance, go there. Simple races, as savages, do not climb mountains—their tops are sacred and mysterious tracts never visited by them. Pomola is always angry with those who climb to the summit of Ktaadn.

According to Jackson, who in his capacity of geological surveyor of the state, has accurately measured it—the altitude of Ktaadn is 5,300 feet, or a little more than one mile above the level of the sea—and he adds, "It is then evidently the highest point in the State of Maine, and is the most abrupt granite mountain in New England." The peculiarities of that spacious table-land on which I was standing, as well as the remarkable semicircular precipice or basin on the eastern side, were all concealed by the mist. I had brought my whole pack to the top, not knowing but I should have to make my descent to the river, and possibly to the settled portion of the state alone and by some other route, and wishing to have a complete outfit with me. But at length, fearing that my companions would be anxious to reach the river before night, and knowing that the clouds might rest on the mountain for days, I was compelled to descend. Occasionally, as I came down, the wind would blow me a vista open through which I could see the country eastward, boundless forests, and lakes, and streams, gleaming in the sun, some of them emptying into the East Branch. There were also new mountains in sight in that direction. Now and then some small bird of the sparrow family would flit away before me, unable to command its course, like a fragment of the gray rock blown off by the wind.

I found my companions where I had left them, on the side of the peak, gathering the mountain cranberries, which filled every crevice between the rocks, together with blueberries, which had a spicier flavor the higher up they grew, but were not the less agreeable to our palates. When the country is settled and roads are made, these cranberries will perhaps become an article of commerce. From this elevation, just on the skirts of the clouds, we could overlook the country west and south for a hundred miles. There it was, the State of Maine, which we had seen on the map, but not much like that, — immeasurable forest for the sun to shine on, that eastern *stuff* we hear of in Massachusetts. No clearing, no house. It did not look as if a solitary traveller had cut so much as a walking-stick there. Countless lakes, — Moosehead in the southwest, forty miles long by ten wide, like a gleaming silver platter at the end of the table; Chesuncook, eighteen long by three wide, without an island; Millinocket, on the south, with its hundred islands; and hundred others without a name; and mountains, also, whose names, for the most part, are known only to the Indians. The forest looked like a firm grass sward, and the effect of these lakes in its midst has been well compared by one who has since visited this same spot, to that of a "mirror broken into a thousand fragments, and wildly scattered over the grass, reflecting the full blaze of the sun." It was a large farm for somebody, when cleared. According to the Gazetteer, which was printed before the boundary question was settled, this single Penobscot county in which we were, was larger than the whole State of Vermont, with its fourteen counties; and this was only a part of the wild lands of Maine. We are concerned now, however, about natural, not political limits. We were about eighty miles as the bird flies from Bangor, or one hundred and fifteen as we had ridden, and walked, and paddled. We had to console ourselves with the reflection that this view was probably as good as that from the peak, as far as it went, and what were a mountain without its attendant clouds and mists? Like ourselves, neither Bailey nor Jackson had obtained a clear view from the summit.

Setting out on our return to the river, still at an early hour in the day, we decided to follow the course of the torrent, which we supposed to be Murch Brook, as long as it would not lead us too far out of our way. We thus travelled about four miles in the very torrent itself, continually crossing and recrossing it, leaping from rock to rock, and jumping with the stream down falls of seven or eight feet, or sometimes sliding down on our backs in a thin sheet of water. This ravine had been the scene of an extraordinary freshet in the spring, apparently accompanied by a slide from the mountain. It must have been filled with a stream of stones and water, at least twenty feet above the present level of the torrent. For a rod or two on either side of its channel, the trees were barked and splintered up to their tops, the birches bent over, twisted, and sometimes finely split like a stable-broom; some a foot in diameter snapped off, and whole clumps of trees bent over with the weight of rocks piled on them. In one place we noticed a rock two or three feet in diameter, lodged nearly twenty feet high in the crotch of a tree. For the whole four miles, we saw but one rill emptying in, and the volume of water did not seem to be increased from the first. We travelled thus very rapidly with a downward impetus, and grew remarkably expert at leaping from rock to rock, for leap we must, and leap we did, whether there was any rock at the right distance or not. It was a pleasant picture when the foremost turned about and looked up the winding ravine, walled in with rocks and the green forest, to see at intervals of a rod or two, a red-shirted or green-jacketed mountaineer against the white torrent, leaping down the channel with his pack on his back, or pausing upon a convenient rock in the midst of the torrent to mend a rent in his clothes, or unstrap the dipper at his belt to take a draught of the water. At one place we were startled by seeing, on a little sandy shelf by the side of the stream, the fresh print of a man's foot, and for a moment realized how Robinson Crusoe felt in a similar case; but at last we remembered that we had struck this stream on our way up, though we could not have told where, and one had descended into the ravine for a drink. The cool air above, and the continual bathing of our bodies in mountain water, alternate foot, sitz, douche, and plunge baths, made this walk exceedingly refreshing, and we had travelled only a mile or two after leaving the torrent, before every thread of our clothes was as dry as usual, owing perhaps to a peculiar quality in the atmosphere.

After leaving the torrent, being in doubt about our course, Tom threw down his pack at the foot of the loftiest spruce tree at hand, and shinned up the bare trunk some twenty feet, and then climbed through the green tower, lost to our sight, until he held the topmost spray in his hand.* McCauslin, in his younger days, had marched through the wilderness with a body of troops, under General Somebody, and with one other man did all the scouting and spying service. The General's word was: "Throw down the top of that tree," and there was no tree in the Maine woods so high that it did not lose its top in such a case. I have heard a story of two men being lost once in these woods, nearer to the settlements than this, who climbed the loftiest pine they could find, some six feet in diameter at the ground, from whose top they discovered a solitary clearing and its smoke. When at this height, some two hundred feet from the ground, one of them became dizzy, and fainted in his companion's arms, and the latter had to accomplish the descent with him, alternately fainting and reviving, as best he could. To Tom we cried, where away does the summit bear? where the burnt lands? The last he could only conjecture; he descried, however, a little meadow and pond, lying probably in our course, which we concluded to steer for. On reaching this secluded meadow, we found fresh tracks of moose on the shore of the pond, and the water was still unsettled

---

* "The spruce-tree," says Springer in '51, "is generally selected, principally for the superior facilities which its numerous limbs afford the climber. To gain the first limbs of this tree, which are from twenty to forty feet from the ground, a smaller tree is undercut and lodged against it, clambering up which the top of the spruce is reached. In some cases, when a very elevated position is desired, the spruce-tree is lodged against the trunk of some lofty pine, up which we ascend to a height twice that of the surrounding forest."

To indicate the direction of the pines, he throws down a branch, and a man at the ground takes a bearing. [Thoreau's note]

as if they had fled before us. A little further, in a dense thicket, we seemed to be still on their trail. It was a small meadow, of a few acres on the mountain side, concealed by the forest, and perhaps never seen by a white man before, where one would think that the moose might browse and bathe, and rest in peace. Pursuing this course, we soon reached the open land, which went sloping down some miles toward the Penobscot.

Perhaps I most fully realized that this was primeval, untamed, and forever untameable *Nature*, or whatever else men call it, while coming down this part of the mountain. We were passing over "Burnt Lands," burnt by lightning, perchance, though they showed no recent marks of fire, hardly so much as a charred stump, but looked rather like a natural pasture for the moose and deer, exceedingly wild and desolate, with occasional strips of timber crossing them, and low poplars springing up, and patches of blueberries here and there. I found myself traversing them familiarly, like some pasture run to waste, or partially reclaimed by man; but when I reflected what man, what brother or sister or kinsman of our race made it and claimed it, I expected the proprietor to rise up and dispute my passage. It is difficult to conceive of a region uninhabited by man. We habitually presume his presence and influence everywhere. And yet we have not seen pure Nature, unless we have seen her thus vast, and drear, and inhuman, though in the midst of cities. Nature was here something savage and awful, though beautiful. I looked with awe at the ground I trod on, to see what the Powers had made there, the form and fashion and material of their work. This was that Earth of which we have heard, made out of Chaos and Old Night. Here was no man's garden, but the unhandselled globe. It was not lawn, nor pasture, nor mead, nor woodland, nor lea, nor arable, nor waste-land. It was the fresh and natural surface of the planet Earth, as it was made forever and ever, — to be the dwelling of man, we say, — so Nature made it, and man may use it if he can. Man was not to be associated with it. It was Matter, vast, terrific, — not his Mother Earth that we have heard of, not for him to tread on,

or be buried in, — no, it were being too familiar even to let his bones
lie there — the home this of Necessity and Fate. There was there felt
the presence of a force not bound to be kind to man. It was a place for
heathenism and superstitious rites, — to be inhabited by men nearer of
kin to the rocks and to wild animals than we. We walked over it with a
certain awe, stopping from time to time to pick the blueberries which
grew there, and had a smart and spicy taste. Perchance where *our* wild
pines stand, and leaves lie on their forest floor in Concord, there were
once reapers, and husbandmen planted grain; but here not even the
surface had been scarred by man, but it was a specimen of what God
saw fit to make this world. What is it to be admitted to a museum, to
see a myriad of particular things, compared with being shown some
star's surface, some hard matter in its home! I stand in awe of my body,
this matter to which I am bound has become so strange to me. I fear
not spirits, ghosts, of which I am one, — *that* my body might, — but I
fear bodies, I tremble to meet them. What is this Titan that has possession of me? Talk of mysteries! — Think of our life in nature, — daily to
be shown matter, to come in contact with it, — rocks, trees, wind on
our cheeks! the *solid* earth! the *actual* world! the *common sense! Contact!
Contact! Who are we? where are we?*

1869

Thoreau, encountering the divine on Ktaadn, was a tragedian; Mark Twain, discovering its absence on a "pleasure-excursion to the Holy Land," gives us farce. He wasn't the first to see that territory in such a light. "The whole thing is half melancholy, half farcical," Herman Melville wrote of an 1857 journey to Jerusalem. "Like all the rest of the world."

Farce may be funny, but it's as often as not a variety of grief. *The Innocents Abroad, Or the New Pilgrim's Progress,* Twain's 1869 account of a cruise around the world to what was then Palestine — originally published in New York and San Francisco newspapers — contains more passages of unvarnished anger than any of his fictions. After pages of bemusement, that anger is almost a relief, Twain's wit giving way to a desire for meaning and a fury at its desecration, whether at the hands of his American fellow travelers — literally dismantling ancient architecture for souvenirs — or through the fly-cursed poverty endured by so many of Palestine's inhabitants: "The ring of the horses' hoofs roused the stupid population, and they all came trooping out — old men and old women, boys and girls, the blind, the crazy, and the crippled, all in ragged, soiled and scanty raiment, and all abject beg-

gars by nature, instinct and education. How the vermin-tortured vaga-
bonds did swarm!"

If it were nothing but that, it would be no less didactic than
the travel literature Twain skewers throughout *Innocents Abroad*. But
Twain's anger isn't the opposite of satire, it's essential to it, the emotion
that makes his mockery more than contempt. Whenever his disgust
threatens to consume him, he slips sideways into a joke or a sketch, a
scene, a moment of comedy in which more often than not he's complicit.

An amiable sort such as young Jack, his favorite traveling companion, sees that as good humor. I think it's empathy, flickering in a
comic gale that's not always kind. We might call that uneasy combination the instability principle of literary journalism. Like Whitman, like
Thoreau, Twain as literary journalist refuses to resolve his story neatly.
The facts of the Holy Land, scripture, and a company of American pilgrims don't line up; they bump into each other, fall down, bonk each
other's noses, and haul themselves up for another attempt at getting
the story "right." That's a set-up, of course: the essential slapstick of
the nonfiction story.

MARK TWAIN
From *Innocents Abroad*

Gray lizards, those heirs of ruin, of sepulchres and desolation, glided in and out among the rocks or lay still and sunned themselves. Where prosperity has reigned, and fallen; where glory has flamed, and gone out; where beauty has dwelt, and passed away; where gladness was, and sorrow is; where the pomp of life has been, and silence and death brood in its high places, there this reptile makes his home, and mocks at human vanity. His coat is the color of ashes: and ashes are the symbol of hopes that have perished, of aspirations that came to nought, of loves that are buried. If he could speak, he would say, Build temples: I will lord it in their ruins; build palaces: I will inhabit them; erect empires: I will inherit them; bury your beautiful: I will watch the worms at their work; and you, who stand here and moralize over me: I will crawl over *your* corpse at the last.

A few ants were in this desert place, but merely to spend the summer. They brought their provisions from Ain Mellahah—eleven miles.

Jack is not very well to-day, it is easy to see; but boy as he is, he is too much of a man to speak of it. He exposed himself to the sun too much yesterday, but since it came of his earnest desire to learn, and to make this journey as useful as the opportunities will allow, no one seeks to discourage him by fault-finding. We missed him an hour from the camp, and then found him some distance away, by the edge of a brook, and with no umbrella to protect him from the fierce sun. If he had been used to going without his umbrella, it would have been well enough, of course; but he was not. He was just in the act of throwing a clod at a mud-turtle which was sunning itself on a small log in the brook. We said:

"Don't do that, Jack. What do you want to harm him for? What has he done?"

"Well, then, I won't kill him, but I ought to, because he is a fraud."

We asked him why, but he said it was no matter. We asked him why, once or twice, as we walked back to the camp, but he still said it was no matter. But late at night, when he was sitting in a thoughtful mood on the bed, we asked him again and he said:

"Well, it don't matter; I don't mind it now, but I did not like it to-day, you know, because *I* don't tell any thing that isn't so, and I don't think the Colonel ought to, either. But he did; he told us at prayers in the Pilgrims' tent, last night, and he seemed as if he was reading it out of the Bible, too, about this country flowing with milk and honey, and about the voice of the turtle being heard in the land. I thought that was drawing it a little strong, about the turtles, any how, but I asked Mr. Church if it was so, and he said it was, and what Mr. Church tells me, I believe. But I sat there and watched that turtle nearly an hour to-day, and I almost burned up in the sun; but I never heard him sing. I believe I sweated a double handful of sweat — I *know* I did — because it got in my eyes, and it was running down over my nose all the time; and you know my pants are tighter than any body else's — Paris fool-ishness — and the buckskin seat of them got wet with sweat, and then got dry again and began to draw up and pinch and tear loose — it was awful — but I never heard him sing. Finally I said, This is a fraud —

that is what it is, it is a fraud—and if I had had any sense I might have known a cursed mud-turtle couldn't sing. And then I said, I don't wish to be hard on this fellow, and I will just give him ten minutes to commence; ten minutes—and then if he don't, down goes his building. But he *didn't* commence, you know. I had staid there all that time, thinking may be he might, pretty soon, because he kept on raising his head up and letting it down, and drawing the skin over his eyes for a minute and then opening them out again, as if he was trying to study up something to sing, but just as the ten minutes were up and I was all beat out and blistered, he laid his blamed head down on a knot and went fast asleep."

"It *was* a little hard, after you had waited so long."

"I should think so. I said, Well, if you won't sing, you shan't sleep, any way; and if you fellows had let me alone I would have made him shin out of Galilee quicker than any turtle ever did yet. But it isn't any matter now—let it go. The skin is all off the back of my neck."

About ten in the morning we halted at Joseph's Pit. This is a ruined Khan of the Middle Ages, in one of whose side courts is a great walled and arched pit with water in it, and this pit, one tradition says, is the one Joseph's brethren cast him into. A more authentic tradition, aided by the geography of the country, places the pit in Dothan, some two days' journey from here. However, since there are many who believe in this present pit as the true one, it has its interest.

It is hard to make a choice of the most beautiful passage in a book which is so gemmed with beautiful passages as the Bible; but it is certain that not many things within its lids may take rank above the exquisite story of Joseph. Who taught those ancient writers their simplicity of language, their felicity of expression, their pathos, and above all, their faculty of sinking themselves entirely out of sight of the reader and making the narrative stand out alone and seem to tell itself? Shakespeare is always present when one reads his book; Macaulay is present when we follow the march of his stately sentences; but the Old Testament writers are hidden from view.

If the pit I have been speaking of is the right one, a scene transpired there, long ages ago, which is familiar to us all in pictures. The sons of Jacob had been pasturing their flocks near there. Their father grew uneasy at their long absence, and sent Joseph, his favorite, to see if any thing had gone wrong with them. He traveled six or seven days' journey; he was only seventeen years old, and, boy like, he toiled through that long stretch of the vilest, rockiest, dustiest country in Asia, arrayed in the pride of his heart, his beautiful claw-hammer coat of many colors. Joseph was the favorite, and that was one crime in the eyes of his brethren; he had dreamed dreams, and interpreted them to foreshadow his elevation far above all his family in the far future, and that was another; he was dressed well and had doubtless displayed the harmless vanity of youth in keeping the fact prominently before his brothers. These were crimes his elders fretted over among themselves and proposed to punish when the opportunity should offer. When they saw him coming up from the Sea of Galilee, they recognized him and were glad. They said, "Lo, here is this dreamer—let us kill him." But Reuben pleaded for his life, and they spared it. But they seized the boy, and stripped the hated coat from his back and pushed him into the pit. *They* intended to let him die there, but Reuben intended to liberate him secretly. However, while Reuben was away for a little while, the brethren sold Joseph to some Ishmaelitish merchants who were journeying towards Egypt. Such is the history of the pit. And the self-same pit is there in that place, even to this day; and there it will remain until the next detachment of image-breakers and tomb-desecraters arrives from the *Quaker City* excursion, and they will infallibly dig it up and carry it away with them. For behold in them is no reverence for the solemn monuments of the past, and whithersoever they go they destroy and spare not.

Joseph became rich, distinguished, powerful—as the Bible expresses it, "lord over all the land of Egypt." Joseph was the real king, the strength, the brain of the monarchy, though Pharaoh held the title. Joseph is one of the truly great men of the Old Testament. And he was the noblest and the manliest, save Esau. Why shall we not say a good word for the princely Bedouin? The only crime that can be brought against him is that he was unfortunate. Why must every body praise Joseph's great-hearted generosity to his cruel brethren, without stint of fervent language, and fling only a reluctant bone of praise to Esau for his still sublimer generosity to the brother who had wronged him? Jacob took advantage of Esau's consuming hunger to rob him of his birthright and the great honor and consideration that belonged to the position; by treachery and falsehood he robbed him of his father's blessing; he made of him a stranger in his home, and a wanderer. Yet after twenty years had passed away and Jacob met Esau and fell at his feet quaking with fear and begging piteously to be spared the punishment he knew he deserved, what did that magnificent savage do? He fell upon his neck and embraced him! When Jacob — who was incapable of comprehending nobility of character — still doubting, still fearing, insisted upon "finding grace with my lord" by the bribe of a present of cattle, what did the gorgeous son of the desert say?

"Nay, I have enough, my brother; keep that thou hast unto thyself!"

Esau found Jacob rich, beloved by wives and children, and traveling in state, with servants, herds of cattle and trains of camels — but he himself was still the uncourted outcast this brother had made him. After thirteen years of romantic mystery, the brethren who had wronged Joseph, came, strangers in a strange land, hungry and humble, to buy "a little food"; and being summoned to a palace, charged with crime, they beheld in its owner their wronged brother; they were trembling beggars — he, the lord of a mighty empire! What Joseph that ever lived would have thrown away such a chance to "show off?" Who stands first — outcast Esau forgiving Jacob in prosperity, or Joseph on a king's throne forgiving the ragged tremblers whose happy rascality placed him there?

Just before we came to Joseph's Pit, we had "raised" a hill, and there, a few miles before us, with not a tree or a shrub to interrupt

the view, lay a vision which millions of worshipers in the far lands of
the earth would give half their possessions to see — the sacred Sea of
Galilee!

Therefore we tarried only a short time at the pit. We rested the
horses and ourselves, and felt for a few minutes the blessed shade
of the ancient buildings. We were out of water, but the two or three
scowling Arabs, with their long guns, who were idling about the place,
said they had none and that there was none in the vicinity. They knew
there was a little brackish water in the pit, but they venerated a place
made sacred by their ancestor's imprisonment too much to be willing
to see Christian dogs drink from it. But Ferguson tied rags and handkerchiefs together till he made a rope long enough to lower a vessel
to the bottom, and we drank and then rode on; and in a short time we
dismounted on those shores which the feet of the Savior have made
holy ground.

At noon we took a swim in the Sea of Galilee — a blessed privilege in this roasting climate — and then lunched under a neglected old
fig-tree at the fountain they call Ain-et-Tin, a hundred yards from
ruined Capernaum. Every rivulet that gurgles out of the rocks and
sands of this part of the world is dubbed with the title of "fountain,"
and people familiar with the Hudson, the great lakes and the Missis-
sippi fall into transports of admiration over them, and exhaust their
powers of composition in writing their praises. If all the poetry and
nonsense that have been discharged upon the fountains and the bland
scenery of this region were collected in a book, it would make a most
valuable volume to burn.

During luncheon, the pilgrim enthusiasts of our party, who had
been so light-hearted and happy ever since they touched holy ground
that they did little but mutter incoherent rhapsodies, could scarcely
eat, so anxious were they to "take shipping" and sail in very person
upon the waters that had borne the vessels of the Apostles. Their
anxiety grew and their excitement augmented with every fleeting moment, until my fears were aroused and I began to have misgivings that

in their present condition they might break recklessly loose from all considerations of prudence and buy a whole fleet of ships to sail in instead of hiring a single one for an hour, as quiet folk are wont to do. I trembled to think of the ruined purses this day's performances might result in. I could not help reflecting bodingly upon the intemperate zeal with which middle-aged men are apt to surfeit themselves upon a seductive folly which they have tasted for the first time. And yet I did not feel that I had a right to be surprised at the state of things which was giving me so much concern. These men had been taught from infancy to revere, almost to worship, the holy places whereon their happy eyes were resting now. For many and many a year this very picture had visited their thoughts by day and floated through their dreams by night. To stand before it in the flesh — to see it as they saw it now — to sail upon the hallowed sea, and kiss the holy soil that compassed it about: these were aspirations they had cherished while a generation dragged its lagging seasons by and left its furrows in their faces and its frosts upon their hair. To look upon this picture, and sail upon this sea, they had forsaken home and its idols and journeyed thousands and thousands of miles, in weariness and tribulation. What wonder that the sordid lights of work-day prudence should pale before the glory of a hope like theirs in the full splendor of its fruition? Let them squander millions! I said — who speaks of money at a time like this?

In this frame of mind I followed, as fast as I could, the eager footsteps of the pilgrims, and stood upon the shore of the lake, and swelled, with hat and voice, the frantic hail they sent after the "ship" that was speeding by. It was a success. The toilers of the sea ran in and beached their barque. Joy sat upon every countenance.

"How much? — ask him how much, Ferguson! — how much to take us all — eight of us, and you — to Bethsaida, yonder, and to the mouth of Jordan, and to the place where the swine ran down into the sea — quick! — and we want to coast around every where — every where! — all day long! *I* could sail a year in these waters! — and tell him we'll stop at Magdala and finish at Tiberias! — ask him how much? — any thing — any thing whatever! — tell him we don't care what the expense is!" [I said to myself, I knew how it would be.]

Ferguson — (interpreting) — "He says two Napoleons — eight dollars."

One or two countenances fell. Then a pause.

"Too much! — we'll give him one!"

I never shall know how it was — I shudder yet when I think how the place is given to miracles — but in a single instant of time, as it seemed to me, that ship was twenty paces from the shore, and speeding away like a frightened thing! Eight crestfallen creatures stood upon the shore, and O, to think of it! this — this — after all that overmastering ecstasy! Oh, shameful, shameful ending, after such unseemly boasting! It was too much like "Ho! let me at him!" followed by a prudent "Two of you hold him — one can hold me!"

Instantly there was wailing and gnashing of teeth in the camp. The two Napoleons were offered — more if necessary — and pilgrims and dragoman shouted themselves hoarse with pleadings to the retreating boatmen to come back. But they sailed serenely away and paid no further heed to pilgrims who had dreamed all their lives of some day skimming over the sacred waters of Galilee and listening to its hallowed story in the whisperings of its waves, and had journeyed countless leagues to do it, and — and then concluded that the fare was too high. Impertinent Mohammedan Arabs, to think such things of gentlemen of another faith!

Well, there was nothing to do but just submit and forgo the privilege of voyaging on Genessaret, after coming half around the globe to taste that pleasure. There was a time, when the Savior taught here, that boats were plenty among the fishermen of the coasts — but boats and fishermen both are gone, now; and old Josephus had a fleet of men-of-war in these waters eighteen centuries ago — a hundred and thirty bold canoes — but they, also, have passed away and left no sign. They battle here no more by sea, and the commercial marine of Galilee numbers only two small ships, just of a pattern with the little skiffs the disciples knew. One was lost to us for good—the other was miles away and far out of hail. So we mounted the horses and rode grimly on toward Magdala, cantering along in the edge of the water for want of the means of passing over it.

How the pilgrims abused each other! Each said it was the other's fault, and each in turn denied it. No word was spoken by the sinners—even the mildest sarcasm might have been dangerous at such a time. Sinners that have been kept down and had examples held up to them, and suffered frequent lectures, and been so put upon in a moral way and in the matter of going slow and being serious and bottling up slang, and so crowded in regard to the matter of being proper and always and forever behaving, that their lives have become a burden to them, would not lag behind pilgrims at such a time as this, and wink furtively, and be joyful, and commit other such crimes—because it would not occur to them to do it. Otherwise they would. But they did do it, though—and it did them a world of good to hear the pilgrims abuse each other, too. We took an unworthy satisfaction in seeing them fall out, now and then, because it showed that they were only poor human people like us, after all.

So we all rode down to Magdala, while the gnashing of teeth waxed and waned by turns, and harsh words troubled the holy calm of Galilee.

1894

"A veritable page torn from the book of life," William T. Stead calls this story of a prostitute, "a human document." The setting is Chicago, "the imperial City of the boundless West" — a designation granted by a labor leader quoted on page one of Stead's 1894 study of vice, *If Christ Came to Chicago!* There's a ponderous subtitle — *A Plea for the Union of All Who Love in the Service of All Who Suffer* — and you might also want to skim through the first few pages of what follows, the better to get to the good bits, which are also the awful bits, a story Stead meant to be harrowing. He swoops in from the mythic plane of these opening pages to the material world of a "sporting house" — a brothel — and from there into the intimate life of a "_____" (his "phrase," that long blank space; he won't use the word he means, *whore*) called Maggie Darling.

Stead was an oddity among the moralists of his age, a Bible thumper who founded a journal dedicated to spiritualism and the paranormal, an antivice crusader comfortable enough in the company of sex workers to gather stories such as Maggie Darling's. That's why I think the best way to read this account, to understand it as Stead wants us to, is to skip straight to Maggie's tale, about two pages in, and then return to the preaching with which Stead introduces it. His moralistic preamble is leaden to our ears; but as the passion that propels Stead beyond the conventions of his day, aesthetically as well as morally, it's worth almost as much as his fine-grained rendering in miniature of the life of "the woman-Christ" Maggie Darling. The marriage of reformism to narrative here is not so much old-fashioned as simply more plainly joined than in contemporary literary journalism, a genre that remains rife with would-be do-gooders seduced by stories.

Stead's contemporaries accused him throughout his storied career of sensationalism, of importing into the respectable press the style and subject matter of working-class rags. Even worse, said some, his journalism was American in tone, "a New Journalism," in the disdainful words of Matthew Arnold. To a conservative such as Arnold, "new" was no more a compliment than the "democracy" to which he compared this journalistic development. Both New Journalism and "the democracy," he wrote, were almost admirable in their "ability, novelty, sensation, sympathy, generous instincts," but were as a result "featherbrained." Perhaps Arnold feared that the desire for contact with the realness of things that he and others saw as sensationalism would prove revolutionary. And so it did, in literary terms if not the political ones of which Stead dreamed. Stead wanted "government by journalism"; instead, he helped make a democracy of stories.

WILLIAM T. STEAD
Maggie Darling

Christ was a man. It is therefore easier to conceive of him as a pilgrim tramp, footsore and hungry, resting his weary limbs among the bums in the police station, than to conceive of his marred image in a female shape. But the woman-Christ like the child-Christ, either as the Christ of the Dolorous Way or as the redeeming and regenerating Savior, is a conception which must never be lost sight of.

The Christian Church, which for more than a thousand years has consecrated its proudest temples to the memory of the Magdalen, is a witness throughout the ages to the indestructibility of the divine element in every woman even when she has sunk so low as to make merchandise of her sex. The image of God in woman remains indefaceable even when in Lecky's words, which it is important to read without a shudder, she becomes "the eternal Priestess of Humanity blasted for the sins of the people." But although the publicans and harlots in his time welcomed the wandering eccentric from Nazareth, who shared their meals and sympathised with their sorrows, the conventional sentiment of this day would stand aghast at any such intermingling of the Messiah with the lost woman whom He came to seek and to save.

In Chicago some people have gone even further. One of the most zealous and faithful of the saintly and devoted women who have dedicated their lives to the service of the fallen told me with a heart sore with the anguish of thwarted sympathy, that so far from her efforts being supported by the Church, they were regarded as a development not to be encouraged.

"It was this way," she said. "I have given myself up to this work. I visited constantly in the levee and knew most of these women as friends. Now and then I would come upon one or another girl who would long to escape from her sad life. When I found such I took them into my own house, loved them, labored with them, and I rejoice to know that several of them became happy and converted Christians. I was pleased, my pastor was pleased. The penitent Magdalens were received into the church, and we were glad to see their simple faith and Christian life. But a deputation of the leading residents and church officers waited upon my pastor to protest against this kind of thing. They did not want their daughters to associate with harlots even though they were repentant. Besides the presence of these women would lower the character of the neighbourhood and the social standing of the church."

"That is incredible," I said abruptly, "to wish to close the doors of Christ's Church on the penitent Magdalen — that would be not the act of Christian but of the devil!"

"It was what they did," said my friend. "Fortunately my pastor is a good Christian and he refused to yield one single jot to the pressure brought to bear upon him. But the opposition was great. The respectability of the church must not be endangered by the admission of lost women, even when they have been found and are anxiously and prayerfully seeking to enter into the fold."

Here was a revelation indeed! Such a church may be respectable as Thurtell the murderer was declared to be respectable — because he kept a gig; but its respectability will not save it from going down, with all its conventionalities, into perdition, nor will it have far to go. For the abode of such is nigh unto the gates of Hell.

Swinburne's bitter lines come back to me as I listened to this good woman's story of some Chicago Christians, and heard its confirmation from others in churches.

> "Surely your race it was that He
> Beholding in Gethsemane,
> Bled the red bitter sweat of shame,
> Knowing the name of Christian should
> Mean to men evil and not good."

And assuredly in the long roll of the anti-Christian acts of the conventional church there is no blacker record than that which deals with the lost women of our streets. Nothing can exceed in revolting injustice the conventional mode of treating the weaker and the most tempted as a moral leper, while her guiltier partner occupies the highest places in the synagogue.

Justice is at least as holy a thing as charity, and the injustice of the world's judgment which the church has countersigned is as loathsome as the selfish immorality of the man which it condones as a kind of offset to the Draconian severity with which it avenges the faults of the weaker sinner.

The lost women, these poor sisters of Christ Jesus, the images in which we have fashioned a womanhood first made in the image of God, are as numerous in Chicago as in any other great city. The silent vice of capitals abounds here at least to the same extent that it prevails in other cities of the million class. Where there are a million inhabitants it is probably an under estimate if it is assumed that there must be at least a thousand women who make their living, not intermittently but constantly, by means of prostitution. These regulars of the army of vice constitute the solid core or nucleus of a host far more numerous of irregulars, who, either from love of license or from need of money, give way to a temptation which is always at hand. The inmates of the sporting house, so called, are probably not one-tenth of the total number of women who regard their sex as legitimate merchandise.

Both sporting houses and "roomers" may be found in all parts of the city, but there is no section in which they are so concentrated as in the district between Harrison and Polk, and between Clark and Dearborn Streets. It was there, in the center of the heart of Chicago, that I found Maggie Darling in the house of Madame Hastings.

Madame Hastings is a familiar figure in the alsatia of more than one city. She is famous in Chicago courts as having been the defendant in the case which led to the practical ruling that the police could not arrest any one they pleased on a warrant made out against those mythical personages, Richard Roe or John Doe. Before she contested that case, strange though it may appear to those who are unfamiliar with the Turkish methods of Chicago "justice," a policeman armed with a warrant charging Richard Roe with an offence against the law could, on the strength of the document, arrest anybody at his own sovereign will and pleasure. Mary Hastings, being raided on such a warrant, appealed to the higher court, which, as to be expected, promptly decided against the validity of the Richard Roe warrant, and Mary's name became famous in a leading case.

Apart from this excursion into the law-making region, Madame inspired some awe, if not respect, by the vengeance she wreaked upon certain police officers, who, having a grudge against her, smashed her furniture during her enforced absence from her property. She reported them to Mayor Harrison in person, and their offence being proved, three policemen and one sergeant were dismissed [from] the force; from which it may be seen that the name and fame of Mary Hastings are as familiar to the administration as to the lawyer. Her establishment is not a very large one beside the double house of Vina Fields, which almost immediately adjoins it, and the extensive premises of Carrie Watson on Clark Street. Madame Hastings' house is rather crowded when it contains twelve girls. Madame, who is Belgian, bred and born, owns another house at 2004 Dearborn Street, and in course of a somewhat adventurous career has seen much of the seamy side of life, both married and single, in Canada and the United States. She has plied her calling in Toronto, in British Columbia, in Denver, Portland, Oregon, in San Francisco, and has a wide and varied experience with the police wherever she has wandered. In San Francisco, she was in prison for six months for conduct too scandalous even for Californians. On the whole she has the greatest terror of the police of the Dominion. "When the English say you're to git, you've just got to git and that's all there is to it," she said mournfully, "you can't do anything with them; with our police it is different."

Of which there is no doubt. For as big Pat the Tarrier, the policeman, went his rounds in Fourth Avenue, he seldom failed to look in upon Madame at supper-time, or indeed, at any time when he felt thirsty. Pat was one of the four custodians of law and order whom it was necessary for Madame to square. The relations between the sporting houses and the police on their beats is intimate, not to say friendly. The house is at the absolute mercy of the officer, who can ruin its business by simply keeping it under constant observation, or he can, if he pleases, have it "pulled" every day in the week if his moral sense or his desire for vengeance should so prompt. The keeper of the house, if she is to live and thrive, must make friends with the policeman, and there is usually not the least difficulty in doing so. Tariffs vary in Fourth Avenue as in Washington, but Madame had succeeded in securing virtual protection at a blackmail scale of 2 dollars, 50 cents per officer per week with free drinks, and occasional meals whenever the "cop" felt hunger or thirst. As there were four of them on duty, two by day and two at night, and they were often thirsty, it may be taken that this police "protection" cost the house 15 dollars a week or 750 dollars a year — an irregular license fee paid to private constable for liberty to carry on. This of course does not include the further fees levied by superior officers, the fines, the money paid to bailsmen, and other incidental expenses, which fall heavy upon the houses of ill-fame.

"Ye ould _____s," said the Tarrier, one evening, as he marched in at the back door, "and wat kind o' soup hev ye's to-day? An' shure, and pass me the whusky, and for shame to ye, Maggie," he added, seeing one of the girls emptying a wine-glass, "for shame to ye, to think that ye are Oirish and a-drinking wine! It's whusky ye should drink."

He was not an ill-natured man, was Pat, and as he sat down and drank the whisky and tasted the soup in the midst of the scantily attired women, his good-nature beamed on his fat face and he became confidential:

"Now, I's tellin' ye," he said. "Be sure and look out, for I am going on another beat for the next month, and the cops that's coming are mean divils, and if ye don't take care it's pulled ye'll be, so look out for yourselves."

Sure enough, the next day there was a new patrolman on the beat, and the girls were more cautious in their hustling. The routine of the day at Madame Hastings was monotonous enough. In the morning, just before twelve, the coloured girl served cocktails to each of the women before they got up. After they dressed, they took another refresher, usually absinthe. At breakfast they had wine. Then the day's work began. The girls sat in couples at the windows, each keeping watch in the opposite direction. If a man passed they would rap at the window and beckon him to come in. If a policeman appeared, even if it were their fat friend, the curtains would be drawn and all trace of hustling would disappear. But before the officer was out of sight the girls would be there again. They went on duty fifteen minutes at a time. Every quarter of an hour they were relieved, until dinnertime. At five they dined, and then the evening's business began, with more drinking at intervals, all night through, to the accompaniment of piano-playing with occasional step-dancing, and adjournments more or less frequent, as customers were more or less plentiful. About four or five in the morning, when they were all more or less loaded with drink, they would close the doors and go to sleep. Next day it would begin again, the same dull round of drink and hustling, debauch and drink. A dismal, dreary, monotonous existence broken only by quarrelling and the constant excitement supplied by the police.

For a day or two the girls were discreet, but finding no harm came they relapsed a little, and "Redhead," the new policeman, saw them hustling at the window. So a warrant was sworn out at the police station and at five o'clock at night a posse of nine policemen sallied forth to "pull" Mary Hastings. The pulling of a house of this description is one of the favourite entertainments of the district. It attracts the floating and resident population as much as a first-class funeral draws the crowd in a country town. All unsuspecting the fate in store for them, the girls were preparing to sit down to dinner. Maggie was mixing the absinthe when the bell rang. Bohemian Mary — for here, as elsewhere in Chicago, there are people of all nationalities under heaven — opened the door. A policeman placed his foot so the door could not be closed in his face and demanded Madame. When she came he produced his warrant and eight other officers filed into the house. Every door was guarded. There was no escape. Had there been but a few minutes warning the girls could have fled down the trap doors prepared for such an event, which led to the cellar from whence they could escape to a friendly saloon which frequently received them into its hospitable shelter. But it was too sudden. "Oh _____!" said Maggie, running up stairs, "we're pulled!" "Yes," said the officer, "and you'd better dress yourselves and make ready to go off to the station."

As Maggie was hastily putting on her dress one of the officers who had followed her to her bedroom touched her on the shoulder. "Would you mind making a date with me?" he said. The girl's appearance pleased him. "And though he was on pleasure bent," like John Gilpin, "he had a frugal mind." Policemen get their women cheap, and when you are arresting a woman she cannot haggle about terms. So Maggie said, "For sure." "Well," he said, "I am on Clark, can I meet you there some day next week?" "Certainly," she replied, "send me a message making the date and it will be all right."

By this time they were getting ready to start. Madame had thrust a roll of 300 dollar bills into her stocking. The girls, not less mindful of contingencies, had stuffed into their stocking small bottles of whisky and cigarettes and made ready to accompany their captors. There were six altogether. The housekeeper, the cook, and one of the girls, a newcomer who was passed off as a servant, remained behind. Madame and her family of five stepped out amid the curious crowd which watched for the patrol waggon. "It makes a girl feel cheap," said Maggie, "let's start for the station." No sooner said than done. Bohemian Mary set off at a run followed by her cursing, panting custodian; then came the other girls, while Madame brought up the rear. It was no new thing to her. The house had been pulled only two months before, and it was all in a day's work.

When they arrived at the police station they were taken downstairs and locked up all together in one of the iron barred cells. The police found a bottle of wine in a French girl's stocking and drank its contents to the immense indignation of its owner, who gave him in her own vocabulary "blue blazes." He only looked and laughed. "Here's to your health, Frenchie!" said the policemen as he drank the last drop. Madame in the meantime had despatched a trusty messenger for a bondsman, and as soon as he arrived she was bailed out. The girls in the cell amused themselves with shouting and singing, and cursing and drinking, while Maggie and another tested their agility by climbing like monkeys up the iron bars of their grated door.

It was more like a picnic than an imprisonment. They had drink and cigarettes and company. They were as noisy and more lively and profane than if they had been at home.

In about an hour Madame bailed them all out, putting up 10 dollars for their punctual appearance at the police court on Monday morning. Then the half dozen, more drunk than when they were pulled, sallied out in triumph and resumed business as usual in the old premises as if nothing had happened.

Fix or six hours afterwards, about midnight, I made Maggie Darling's acquaintance. I had been around several of the houses asking their keepers and their inmates to attend my meeting at the Central Music Hall the following day. A strange pilgrimage that was from house to house, to discuss what Christ would think of it, with landladies whose painted damsels in undress, were lounging all around! At last, well on to midnight, I came to Madame Hastings. The excitement of the "pulling" was still visible; Madame was indignant. She knew who it was that had put the "cops" on to her, and she cursed them accordingly. Maggie was flushed and somewhat forward; both her eyes were blacked, the result of a fight with a French inmate of the house.

"I don't want anything," I said to Maggie. "Why can you not talk decently once in a while? Sit down and let us have a good talk."

Maggie looked at me half incredulously, and then sat down.

"I want you to come to my meeting to-morrow night," I said, "at Central Music Hall."

"Yes," she said, "what kind of a meeting is it?"

"Oh, quite a new kind of meeting," I answered. "I am to speak on what Christ would think of all this, and I want you to know it all, to come to the meeting."

Maggie became serious; a dreamy look came over her face.

Then she said, "Oh, Christ! He's all right. It's the other ones, that's the devil." Then she stopped. "It's no use," she added, shortly.

"What's no use?" I asked, and after a time she told me the story which I repeated in brief at Central Music Hall next day.

It was a grim story; commonplace enough and yet as tragic as life, that was told to me at midnight in that tawdry parlour. The old Jezebel flitted in and out superintending her business; the jingling piano was going in the next room, where girls were dancing, and the air was full of the reek of beer and tobacco. Maggie spoke soberly, in an undertone so that Madame might not hear what she was saying. Her narrative, which she told without any pretence, or without any appeal for sympathy or for help, seemed a microcosm of the history of the human race. The whole of the story was there; from the Fall to the Redemption; from the Redemption to the Apostasy of the Church, and the blighting of the hopes of mankind. I give it here as a page, soiled and grimy it may be, but nevertheless a veritable page torn from the book of life. Maggie Darling is a human document in which is recorded the ruin of one of the least of those of the brethren of Christ. It illustrates many things in our social organisation, from the ruthless sacrifice of childhood, due to the lack of factory laws, to the murderous brutality of conventional Christianity, aping the morality without the heart of its Lord.

"No," said Maggie, coldly. "It's no use! Don't commence no religion on me. I've had enough already. Are you a Catholic?"

"Why?" I asked. "No, I am not a Catholic."

"I'm glad," she said, "you're not a Catholic. I have no use for Catholics. Least of all for Irish Catholics. I will never go near any of them anymore, and if I could do them any harm, I would travel a thousand miles to do it."

Maggie was excited and troubled. Something in the past seemed to harass her, and her language was more vigorous than can be quoted here. After a little she became more restrained, and by degrees I had her whole history.

She was born of Irish-American parents, in Boston, in 1870. Her father was a carpenter by trade. Her mother died when Maggie was a mere child. Shortly after her death the family crossed the continent to California, where her father married again. He was a drunkard, a gambler, and a violent tempered man, much given to drinking, and inclined to treat his children with great brutality. Maggie, after spending a year or two in a convent school in San Francisco, left before she had learned either to read or write, and began to make her own living, at nine years of age. She was employed in a shoe factory, where she made from 4 dollars 50 cents to 7 dollars a week at piecework. There were several children of only seven years of age in the factory. These infants were employed in picking shavings. They started work at six o'clock in the morning, had half an hour for dinner, and were dismissed at five. At the factory Maggie learned to read out of the newspapers, by the aid of her companions, and when she was eleven was sufficiently smart to obtain a situation as companion and reader to an old lady, who was an invalid, at 15 dollars a month and her board. The place was comfortable. She remained there until she was eighteen.

From that situation she went as chambermaid to a private family in Golden Gate Avenue. She was eighteen, full of vigour and gaiety. She was brunette with long dark hair, a lively disposition, and with all the charming audacity and confidence of inexperience. She fell in love. The man was older than she, and for a time she was as happy as most young people in their first dream. Of course she was going to be married. If only the marriage day would come! But there are twenty-four hours in every day, and seven days in every week. Her betrothed, not less impatient, hinted that after all they were already united, why could they not anticipate the ceremony. Did she not trust him? He swore that it was all right, that everybody did it, and they would be so much more to each other?

But why repeat the oft-told story? At first Maggie would not listen to the suggestion. But after a time when he pressed her and upbraided her and declared that she could not love him if she did not trust him, she went the way of many thousands, only to wake as they have done with the soft illusion dissipated by the terrible reality of motherhood drawing near, with no husband to be a father to her child. When she told him of her condition, he said that it was all right; they must get married directly. If she would leave her place and meet him next day, at the corner of a certain street, he would take her to a church and they would be married. In all trusting innocence, relying upon his word, she gave up her situation, put up such things as she could carry, and went next day to the trysting-place. Of course the man was not there. After waiting till heartsick she went to make inquiries; she soon discovered the fatal truth. Her lover was a married man, and he had skipped the town followed by the brother of another of his victims.

Imagine her position! She had exactly fifteen cents in her pocket. If she had gone home her father, fierce and irascible as he usually was, would have thought little of killing the daughter who had brought disgrace upon the family. She dared not return to her old situation which she had left so suddenly. She had no character from her mistress and no references. Besides in six months she would be confined. What was she to do?

Her position is one in which some thousands of young women find themselves all over the world at this very moment. She was in the position of Eve after she had eaten the fruit and had been cast out of the Garden of Eden. It is a modern version of the Fall, and as the Fall led down to destruction, so it was with Maggie Darling. She seemed to be shut up to sin. She wandered about the town seeking work. Finding none all that day she walked about in the evening. She kept walking aimlessly on and on, until night came and she was afraid. When it was quite dark and she found a quiet corner she crouched upon a doorstep and tried to sleep. What was she to do? She was lonely and miserable; every month her trouble would grow worse. Where could she hide? She dozed off, only to awaken with a start. No one was near; she tried to sleep again. Then she got up and walked a little and rested again. When morning came she was tired out and wretched. Then she remembered the address of a girl she knew who was living in the neighbourhood. She hunted her up and was made welcome. But her friend had no money. For one night she sheltered her, but all her efforts to find work were in vain.

What was to be done? On the third day she and her friend met a man who asked them if they wanted a job. They answered eagerly, yes. He gave them the address of a lady who he thought could give them something to do. They went there and found it was a house of ill-fame. The woman took them in and told them they might stay. Maggie hesitated. But what was she to do? She had lost her character and her place, and she had no friends. Here she could at least get food and shelter, and remain till her baby was born. It seemed as if she were driven to it. She said to herself that she could not help it, and so it came to pass that Maggie came upon the town.

Two years she remained there, making the best of it. Her baby fortunately died soon after it was born, and she continued to tread the cinder path of sin alone. This went on for three years, and then there dawned upon her darkened life a real manifestation of redeeming love. One day when she had a fit of the blues, a young man came into the house. He was very young, not more than twenty. Something in her appearance attracted him, and when they were alone he spoke to her so kindly that she marvelled. She told him how wretched she was, and he, treating her as if she were his own sister, encouraged her to hope for release. "Take this," he said, as he left her, giving her five dollars. "Save up all you can until you can pay off your debts and then we will get you out of this."

He came again, and yet again, always treating her in the same brotherly fashion, giving her five dollars every time, and never asking anything in return. After she had saved up sufficient store to pay off that debt to the landlady, which hangs like a millstone round the neck of the unfortunate, her young friend told her that he had talked to his mother and his sister, and that as soon as she was ready they would be delighted to take her into their home until such time as they could find her a situation. Full of delight at the unexpected deliverance, Maggie made haste to leave. The young man's mother was as good as her word. In that home she found a warm welcome, and a safe retreat. Maggie made great efforts to break off the habit of swearing, and although she every now and then would make a bad break, she made such progress that at length it was deemed safe and prudent to let her take a place as a general servant. The short stay in that Christian home had been to her as a glimpse into an opening paradise. Hope sprang up once more in the girl's breast. She would be an honest woman once again. Thus, as we have seen her reproduce the Fall, so we see the blessed work of the Redeemer. Now we have to see the way in which his people, "the other ones," as she called them, shuddering, fulfilled their trust.

Maggie went to a situation in Oakland, Alameda Co., Cal. Her new mistress was a Mrs. M'D_____, an Irish Catholic of very devout disposition. She was general servant at 10 dollars a month. She worked hard, and gave every satisfaction. Even the habit of profanity seemed to have been conquered. Gradually the memory of her past life with its hideous concomitants was becoming faint and dim, when suddenly the past was brought back to her with a shock. She was serving at table when she suddenly recognised in one of the guests a man who had been a customer in the old house. She felt as if she were going to drop dead when she recognised him, but she said nothing. The "gentleman," however, was not so reticent. "Where did you get that girl from?" he asked Mr. M'D_____. "Get her," said Mr. M'D_____; "why she's a servant in our house." "Servant," sneered her guest; "I know her. She is a _____ from San Francisco."

How eternally true are Lowell's lines:

> Grim-hearted world, that look'st with Levite eyes
>> On those poor fallen by too much faith in man,
> She that upon thy freezing threshold lies,
>> Starved to more sinning by thy savage ban,
> Seeking that refuge because foulest vice
>> More God-like than thy virtue is, whose span
> Shuts out the wretched only, is more free
> To enter Heaven than thou wilt ever be!

> Thou wilt not let her wash thy dainty feet
>> With such salt things as tears, or with rude hair
> Dry them, soft Pharisee, *that sitt'st at meat*
>> *With him who made her such, and speak'st him fair,*
> Leaving God's wandering lamb the while to bleat
>> Unheeded, shivering in the pitiless air:
> Thou hast made prisoned virtue show more wan
> And haggard than a vice to look upon.

But in this case it was even worse. The lamb which had sought shelter was driven back into the wilderness.

Mr. M'D_____ would not believe it, but said he would tell

his wife. Mrs. M'D_____ at once sent for Maggie. "If only I'd been cute," said she to me when telling the story, "I would have denied it, and they would have believed me. But I thought I had broken with all that, and that I had to tell the truth. So I owned up and said yes, it was true, I had been so, but that I had reformed, and had left all that kind of life. But the old woman, d_____ her! She would listen to nothing. 'Faith, she would not have the disgrace of having a _____ in her house!' —that was all she said."

"Have you anything against me?" said Maggie. "Have I not done your work for you ever since I came?"

"No," was the reply, "I have nothing against you, but I cannot have a person of your character in my house. You must go."

Maggie implored her to give her a chance. "You are a Catholic," she said; "will you not give me a helping hand?"

"No," was the inexorable reply. "That does not matter. I cannot have a _____ in my house."

Feeling as if she were sinking in deep water, Maggie fell on her knees sobbing bitterly and begged her for the love of God to have mercy on her, and at least to give her a recommendation, so that she might get another place.

It was no use. "I cannot do that, for if anything went wrong I would be to blame for it."

"Well, then," said Maggie, "at least give me a line saying that for the four months I have been here I have worked to your satisfaction."

"No," said she.

"The old hound!" exclaimed Maggie to me. "My God, if ever I get the chance I'll knife the old she-devil. Yes, if I swing for it. What does it matter? She's blasted my life. When I saw it was all no use, I lost all heart and all hope, and I gave up there and then. There's no hope for such as me. No, I had my chance and she spoiled it. God d_____n her for a blasted old hypocrite. And now it is no use. No use, never any more. I have taken dope, I drink. I'm lost. I'm only a _____. I shall never be anything else. I'm far worse than ever I was, and am going to the devil as fast as I can. It's no use. But _____ _____ me to blue blazes if ever I come within a thousand miles of that old fiend if I don't knife her, if I swing for it. When I think what I might have been but for her! Oh, Christ!" she cried, "what have they done with my life?"

What indeed? After the Fall the Redemption, after the Redemption the Apostasy, and now, as the result, one of

"The images ye have made of Me!"

1898

"I hate the professional newspaper man," wrote Lincoln Steffens, Abraham Cahan's editor at the *New-York Commercial Advertiser,* where "Dead After Purim" appeared. The year before, the *New York Times* had added the boast "All the News That's Fit to Print" to its front page, and the term "yellow journalism" came into popular usage. Steffens envisioned a third way, and to get there he wanted reporters interested in "mood as well as sense." Cahan was his man.

Cahan's first language was Yiddish, Hebrew his second, Russian his third. And then there was English. He'd arrived in New York in 1882 with little more than a mouthful. Fourteen years later, in 1896, he published a novel called *Yekl: A Tale of the New York Ghetto.* That was his credential. Steffens told his reporters they could write however they liked. Fiction would be fine. Cahan chose fact. In Yiddish — the language to which he'd ultimately return at the *Jewish Daily Forward,* or פֿאָרווערטס, as, by his own (accurate) account, "the best foreign language editor in the United States" — Cahan prescribed. In English he described. Not just the surfaces, but the religious and mythic undercurrents, the eddy and swirl of emotion and circumstance — and, as in what follows, the reconstructed realities, plural, of a man's last day.

Cahan's best work may have been the unbylined short sketches he wrote for newspapers, forgotten for nearly a century until a historian named Moses Rischin combed through archives for a brilliant collection, *Grandma Never Lived in America,* itself now largely forgotten too. They're brief, a moment, maybe a scene, little more. But as Cahan reveals in "Dead After Purim," there's depth even within small spaces, room enough to fall.

ABRAHAM CAHAN
Dead After Purim

Harris Freedman of 28 Orchard Street celebrated Purim like the good, pious Jew that he was. His religion bids the sons of Israel make merry on the fourteenth of Adar, and he did. In the morning he attended the reading of the Book of Esther at the synagogue. Willy, his twelve-year-old boy, Purim rattle in hand, was with him, and every time the Master Reader called out Haman's full name, Harris nudged the little fellow not to miss his chance. "Give it to him, my child!" he would say. "Make it hot for the enemy of the Jews, my darling." And as Willy's rattle joined the deafening noises around, Harris looked on beamingly and rubbed his hands for delight.

The dinner and the three-cornered Purim cakes, full of poppy seeds and covered with honey, were more than satisfactory. Harris had given gifts to the poor, according to the Book of Esther, and interchanged presents and felicitations with his friends. When night fell it found him in the best of spirits. He was pleased with the world, with his faith, with his family, with himself. He was ready for the great feast.

"Rosy," he said to his daughter, a comely damsel of nineteen Purims, "go and fetch your married sister, with her husband, and your married brother, with his wife. Purim does not take place every day. I want all my children at my table. Let it be a Purim feast worthy of a king."

Accordingly, Harris's married children, Joe and Bertha, came with their little families: Willy and Rosy joined them, and, with Harris at the head of the table in the front room on the second floor, and with Mrs. Freedman hovering about between the table and the kitchen stove, the picture was as Purim-like as it could be. The supper, if possible, was still better than the dinner; the *Hamantaschen* (Purim cakes) were the best Willy had ever tasted, and there was wine with which to get so drunk as to "confound Mordecai with Haman." Harris looked at his family, drank a toast to his happiness, and sang Purim song after Purim song. The Chaldaic words were Greek to him, but he knew that they spoke of the downfall of the enemies of Israel, and the melody was so dear—the same which his father had sung in Poland when Harris was as big as Willy—and his heart was thrilling and thrilling and tears of joy welled up in his eyes.

It was midnight when the little gathering broke up.

"It is late. We must go to work tomorrow," said Joe.

"Yes, my son," Harris seconded. "You must go to work and I must get up to see that the hands have something to do." For Freedman was a boss, a "kneepants" maker, with a small sweatshop, employing two machines, at 96 Canal Street. "Well, thanked be God for His mercy," he said, rising from the table. "May we be together next year, my children."

"Amen, thou Lord of the Universe!" Mrs. Freedman whispered, lifting her eyes to heaven. And ten minutes later the little apartment was immersed in sleep, Willy sharing the cot in the front room with his father, as usual.

At 10 o'clock this morning there was a crowd of people in front of the house at 28 Orchard Street. A gaunt patriarch was jingling a tin box half filled with coins, as he called out to the passersby in sepulchral tones, "Alms, deliver from death! Alms, deliver from death!" The tin box was filling up rapidly. Housewife after housewife on her way to the market stopped to put down her basket, drop a nickel and to say, devoutly: "Blessed be the true Judge!"

In the little courtyard within, a knot of men and women stood around two pools of blood. Some of the women were wringing their hands and crying bitterly as they looked, while one middle-aged man with enormous red sidelocks was murmuring psalms.

From the hallways on the second floor came the heartrending sobs of Willy.

"What's the matter, sonny?"

"Oh, my papa! He was such a good papa!" the boy answered. "I did not even hear him get up. Oh *papale, papale,* dear!" He relapsed into half Yiddish.

A pretty young girl who stood swaying to and fro in mute despair was pointed out as Rosy.

"She is a *kalle* [betrothed]," whispered the informant, "and she had some money saved from her work for a marriage portion, but her father borrowed it all for his shop, and as things went wrong with him and he could not raise the sum, he took it so close to heart that he committed suicide. He was the best father you ever saw."

Inside the house a bundle wrapped up in a white sheet lay on the floor. Three candlesticks, each with a lighted candle in it, stood on a chair at the head of this bundle. The room was full of old Jews — members of the Synagogue, "Men of Sochachov," to which Freedman had belonged, for like the other members he hailed from Sochachov, in Poland.

"The coroner? No," said one of the old men, tearfully, in answer to the question. "We have sent for a doctor to have the body examined. You see, if it is the case of suicide we have no right to bury him in a *talith** and *tachrichim* [burial clothes] nor to perform any of the rites.

---

* Prayer shawl. — *Ed.* [Note added by original editor, who also supplied the bracketed definitions elsewhere in the essay.]

Poor Harris! He was a good man, and I hope it will prove to have been an accident, so that we can bring him to the 'Burial of Israel.'"

Presently Dr. Alexander Rosenthal of 89 Henry Street made his appearance, and with his hat on like the rest knelt down and unwrapped the bundle, revealing the remains of Freedman all covered with blood. The old Jews looked on anxiously. "No fracture anywhere. Only the nose is broken. He could not have flung himself from the roof. I don't think it is a case of suicide."

"Of course it is not. He was a sickly man," somebody interposed. "He had frequent fainting spells. He must have dropped dead. So we can bury him like a Jew, Doctor?"

"I think so."

"A good year upon you!" the men of Sochachov shouted, in grim triumph, while through the open window could be heard the mournful jingle of the tin box and the solemn monotone of "Alms, deliver from death! Alms, deliver from death!"

1903

"The mysterious throbbing of the life that is inner and under." That, by her account, was what most interested Sara Jeannette Duncan. Yet she wrote mostly about manners. For her surface *was* depth. You can see it in the opening lines of "The Ordination of Asoka," published in *Harper's* magazine in 1903: "My invitation came from Oo-Dhamma-Nanda. That was his name 'in religion.'" Almost a complete story unto itself. An invitation, a stranger who is not what he seems, the gentle mockery of pretension.

But Oo-Dhamma-Nanda, an Irishman ordained as a Buddhist monk at a time when such a conversion was still remarkable enough to justify a magazine story, was not pretending. "Yes," Duncan reflects, "he was like them." *Them* — the story is racist, alert to imaginary distinctions between "one's own race" and the Burmese, bemused, too, by the "spiritualized" Irishness of Oo-Dhamma-Nanda. Duncan herself was a Canadian, married to an Englishman — she published the piece as Mrs. Everard Cotes, wife of a man identified in the story only as "the Stoic" — living in India, her reputation made by an autobiographical novel called *An American Girl in London*. She got her start in New Orleans, rose at the *Washington Post*, and is remembered now, if at all, for a satirical novel of provincial Ontario life called *The Im-perialist,* a story of the world she'd left behind. She understood dis-placement, reinvention, and the undercurrents that carry the past into the present. She could be cruel and funny and forgiving at the same time. "Nearly as good as 'Mark Twain,'" noted a contemporary critic. Sometimes better.

Henry James, whom she considered a peer, did not get the joke. Her writing, he told her, lacked the "bony structure and palpable, as it were, tense cord" that would result in a necessary "direction *and march of the subject.*" She lingered too long in that "mysterious throb-bing." No surprise to James: "It's the frequent fault of women's work," he consoled.

It's also why I've included Duncan's "Asoka" rather than a piece of James's rigidly certain *American Scene,* published two years later. In his nonfiction, James knew what he knew and marched his prose along accordingly. Not so Duncan, whose empathy surpasses her sar-casm and undermines her bigotry. "What I longed to get some inkling of," she writes of the Irishman, "was whether through mysticism and mortification he had really attained, even momentarily, another plane of existence."

No mystic herself, she could only observe. The result is a small comedy of manners, in which "the inner and the under" are hinted at but never fully revealed. That's the subtle trick of the story: Mrs. Ever-ard Cotes knew what she could not know.

SARA JEANNETTE DUNCAN
The Ordination of Asoka

My invitation came from Ou-Dhamma-Nanda. That was his name "in religion." Earlier he had been indicated by another, which implied, to those who knew it, an Irish diver employed in the pearl fisheries of Ceylon. But since the pearl-diver had gone forever, so, naturally, had his patronymic. There remained a priest of the yellow robe of Buddha called Ou-Dhamma-Nanda — "Lord of the Law of Happiness." He himself chose the designation, he told me. "You were not afraid," I said, "of such a name?"

"Oh, not at all," he replied. "I thought I'd like it."

He sat looking at me steadily and quietly, under the punkha in my friend's drawing-room, from which one saw the evening light upon the Irrawaddy. His head was shaved, his bare feet were crossed on the floor. He was plentifully swathed in his saffron habiliments, but the upper one fell like a plaid, leaving the right arm and shoulder uncovered. It was curiously repellent, that bare arm and shoulder; it expressed a detachment that was almost an indecency. I found myself staring at it with unforgivable rudeness.

It had been hard to know exactly what to expect, hard to give any definition to one's vision of a man of one's own race dedicated to a religious ideal of the East. I had seen many priests of Buddha, poonghees — in throngs, in companies, or solitary upon the highways, humble and contemplative, holding their great palm-leaf fans between their eyes and temptation — he would not, I thought, be like those. But he was curiously like them. His shaven head was as disconcertingly smooth, the sun had tanned his skin almost as dark as an olive. In his eyes, which were blue, sat the same look of withdrawal and of concentration, as if his spirit, intent upon inner examination, had turned its back upon the world. When he spoke or answered it looked over its shoulder. And all with the strangest Hibernian echo, not only in his voice, but on his long upper lip, in the way his eyes darkened when he smiled —

Yes, he was like them. Every morning, for three years, he had taken the *thabeik,* the begging-bowl, and gone out barefooted, bareheaded, past the little bamboo houses of the people, collecting his daily food, asking nothing, rejecting nothing, saying no word of thanks, a mute opportunity for good works. Every day for three years he had eaten but twice, at nine and at noon, and gone to bed fasting to preserve the innocence of his dreams. Every day for three years he had walked with downcast eyes fixed never more than six feet in front of him, telling upon his rosary, "I worship the Buddha; I worship the Law; I worship the Assembly," and hundreds of times every day had he whispered to himself, "Aneissa, dokka, anatta" — "Misery, pain, illusion" — when perhaps the sun was bright upon the padowk flowers, or the women laughed much at the well. He was vowed to no possessions, no desires; as he ate he assured himself that he took food to sustain the body only, and found a sin in its savor, making no haste at his meal, and always leaving, moreover, a mouthful upon the plate. He drank from his own primitive filter that he might not even take life invisible, and always he meditated upon the Law. I knew that he had done these things and many others that belonged to the part he had chosen. It was plain from his face that he had done them.

It was bound to be a catechism, and the results were bound to be meager. The mere spectacle of him was too dramatic, too absorbing—the wide gulf he had stepped across on the bridge of his yellow robe. It was as though I hailed him, with my questions, from the other side, as if he shouted to answer me, though his voice was soft and his speech illiterate. That was extraordinary, his ignorant manner of speaking, quite discounted and, as it were, neutralized, by the refinement he had gathered somewhere—not in Dublin.

I asked him, of course, what determined him to the rule and the order he had adopted. He answered me carefully, picking his words; and though the brogue was thick upon them, I suspected that it was nothing to the richness that he suppressed.

"It first came before me, as you may say, in Ceylon. I studied it a bit there, and then I came up here to Burma to one of these kyaungs, which is Burmese for monasteries, and the priests they tuk me in hand and learned me till I was already to enter the priesthud meself."

It was quite like that. But he seemed to have no more relation to his language than to any other circumstance of the life he had discarded.

"Do you read Pali?" I asked.

"I do not—yet. The sacred texts has got to be expounded to me. It's th' new letters of th' alphabet that comes hard to me—them an' the new language together. The other priests"—he smiled gently—"has got the start o' me there. They learned it as boys, here in the kyaungs."

I wondered whether I had ever before heard a creature from my own side of the world admit, for any purpose or under any circumstances, that an Oriental had "got the start" of him. This was humility indeed, astonishing and curiously sweet.

"You are the first European, are you not, to become a Buddhist priest in Burma?"

"I am," he said, and just for an instant the old Adam looked out of his eyes in a ray of vanity. But he lowered them at once, and when he looked up again it was veiled. What I longed to get some inkling of was whether through mysticism and mortification he had really attained, even momentarily, another plane of experience; there was no reason, after all, why this should be contradicted by a brogue. I made a cautious approach.

"Do you meditate much?" I asked.

"Not so much as some. There's some that does nothing else."

"Then what—" I paused, being troubled for words. He, too, looked troubled, as if definition were an exercise for which he felt himself ill-equipped.

"Well, I keep the rules, amountin' to two hundred and twenty-seven"—he looked at me as much as to say, "That's *some*thing"—"and I travel around whenever I can do anny good against the missionaries—"

"The Christian missionaries?"

"The same. I have nothing to say against Christianity, but it doesn't do here in Burma. I judge by results. I know the people that's Buddhists, and the people that's taken up with Christianity. It means that they're worse than they were before—they've got no religion. Buddhyism," he laid down with explanatory emphasis, "teaches them annyhow to lead good lives. Buddhyism is misunderstud. The Christian is apt to take it for idolatry."

"One does sometimes, even in Calcutta, hear the image of the Buddha described as a Burmese idol," I conceded.

"Well, there now," said Oo-Dhamma-Nanda.

It was in no way my desire that our interview should assume a disputatious character, and silence fell between us. Only for a moment, but it was long enough to convince me that Oo-Dhamma-Nanda would be the easiest person to be silent with I had ever met. He simply retreated from his bodily presence, which became at once as unembarrassing as a piece of furniture. Looking at him, I felt that the essence of what he had acquired, of what laid on him that eloquent difference, was still to defeat me. I grasped at the inevitable question. "Can you tell me what Nirvana is?" I asked.

His eyes darkened again with his spiritualized Irish smile. "I don't know as I could explain it, but if I maybe could, ye wouldn't understand," he said. "One thing's certain, it don't mean annihilation."

"If any teach Nirvana is to cease,
Say unto such they lie;
If any teach Nirvana is to live,
Say unto such they err."

I quoted, and Oo-Dhamma-Nanda said, "That's about it."

"Are you happy?" I ventured.

"That's none o' my business," he replied, and then as if to soften this asperity, he added, "Happiness in Buddhism is different to happiness outside of it. Ye wouldn't understand."

I had a sense of compunction when he went on to say that if he might get his umbrella, which he had left at the back of the house, he would like to go now—a discreet idea that perhaps his happiness was none of my business, either. Something like apology trembled on my lips, but I am afraid I forgot it when he told me that the second induction of a European into the Buddhist priesthood would take place the next morning at nine o'clock, "there or thereabouts," and that I might come and see it if I liked. After all, to a person who had relinquished not only the world, but his birthright in it, what was an apology?

The kyaung stood back from the road under trees, as Burmese monasteries always do. They were beating a gong in front of it at nine o'clock next morning; but they beat a gong so often in Burma, and for reasons so obscure, that it mingles with the barking of the pariahs, and the cawing of the crows, and falls upon alien ears, dulled into a kind of constant accompaniment to life. It would not have called us, the Stoic and me; but we knew the address. The Stoic is an Administrator; let him go at that. He is captive to the service of this gentle country and his far-off King; he would call himself a Pagoda Slave, but that is too cruel a term even for bondage like his. Besides, I am not sure that the Stoic finds no hidden bliss in putting up with it.

The monastery was built of brown unpainted teak. It stood on piles and looked sleepily at a radiant world from under its many high-pitched roofs; its appearance was rickety. As we climbed the outer staircase, Oo-Dhamma-Nanda appeared at the door of the landing. He explained genially that all was not yet ready; I believe they were shaving the candidate. The place was full of Burmans, both priests and the laity, full of talk and laughter and cheerful bustling. The candidate was abandoning the garments of this world. Would we wait? Wouldn't we! But if we might have a couple of chairs under the mahogany-tree furthest from the gong, we thought we would prefer to wait there.

They brought us chairs, the laity, detailed in two comely Burmese maidens, each with a rose above her ear, each in a fresh pink silk tamein and spotless white jacket. Then they brought a table and spread a cloth upon it, and on this they set forth madeira-cake and a plate of those terrible little Italian confections, mostly of almond paste, which lure us in the East, and to these they added long glasses and a bottle of cider.

"Oh, Stoic," said I, "behold your breakfast," but he only smiled indulgently and cut the madeira-cake. There are stoics who regard the feelings of other people even before the repress their own. A gay-colored group gathered at a respectful distance to watch our enjoyment of the feast, and among them was a little Burmese boy. I hope it was not very wrong; I beckoned to the little Burmese boy, who came willingly.

An idea seized one of the rose-decked maidens; she fled away as fast as her tightly wrapped petticoat would permit, and presently reappeared with two large brimming cups of tea. "The intention is excellent," remarked the Stoic, "but the milk is of the bazar," and he said something in Burmese which meant, I believe, that we were the kind of people who never drank tea. They received this with perfectly cheerful understanding; but they began to think of other things, and to run into the monastery and get them—pink lemonade and chocolates. We could only submit, passively, and the Stoic ate everything he could. Time passed, and without intermission they beat the gong.

"Do you realize," I said, "that we are taking part in a feast to celebrate the relapse of a Christian into paganism?"

"Let us hope," replied the Stoic, "that he will make a good pagan."

"It is a strange change."

"'The universe is transformation, life is opinion,'" quoted the Stoic.

"But whence this opinion?" I begged to know. "What wandering current from the heart of an exotic ideal thrilled Oo-Dhamma-Nanda and bade him follow? It must have had to penetrate so much."

"Perhaps he worships his dæmon. Perhaps, unknown to his kind, he has always worshipped it. Buddhism provides generously for that. We of the West worship our activity, or our ambition, or our sense of beauty; we never worship our dæmons. And to do it in real comfort you must make your body a negation, and dress it contemptuously in yellow cotton, and obey the Law."

"Oh," I said. There was no time to say more; it was ten o'clock, and midway on the grass between us and the monastery appeared Oo-Dhamma-Nanda, beckoning.

Most of the assemblage had drawn to one side of the room, and there it crouched on the floor upon its heels. On a mat before the people sat the old *Sadow*, the abbot. He had the most benevolent face I have ever seen in the world; his eyes wandered about him as if they dreaded meeting pain, and he smiled constantly, as water will ever ripple. It was as if he wished to ward off sadness with his smile. I watched it, fascinated, for a long time, wondering if he succeeded. A younger priest hovered about him, others huddled in the background. There was not a semblance of order; quite as many Burmans, men and women, were walking about and talking as were sitting in rows on the floor. The women specially bustled and laughed at the other side of the room, bending over baskets of eatables, not in any way humbled by the occasion, rather in their way mistresses of it. The room was divided by a long row of pagoda-shaped lacquered *ók*, which cover the food offerings to the priests. I saw no furniture except the couple of chairs which were found for the Stoic and me, and the table which pursued us from outside, to be immediately placed at our elbows, laden with fresh confections. A few Chinamen mingled with the Burmans, and many in whom the races were plainly blended. Oo-Dhamma-Nanda moved among them with lifted, anxious eyebrows; his glance was deprecating when it fell on us, but we could not be sure whether we were the subjects or the objects of his apology. The place was open all round; we could see through the wooden lattices the sun flaming on the trees outside. From mid-roof hung the ghost of a once marvelous dragon-lantern, torn and tarnished. Sparrows had built in it and flew constantly in and out, adding their tribute to the festival. It seemed, as it hung there, a type of nugatory incarnations. "Yet we," said the Stoic, "perpetually ask for truth, and always the sparrows build."

Then, while we all still talked and feasted, from an inner room appeared the candidate. He was dressed in robes of the priestly cut, but they were all white, and he stood in them a bent old man. His shaven head was as white as his garments, and so was his skin; his deep-set timid eyes had speculation and shrewdness in them; his nose was sharply aquiline, his lips tightly drawn. Surely, one thought, it was late. He desired to find peace and to annihilate sorrow, but would there be time? His steps could be so few upon the way; would the journey be worth the departure?

They all looked upon him kindly as he came forward among them, but the chatter did not cease until Oo-Dhamma-Nanda, through an interpreter, demanded silence. Then there was something like it, and the scattered groups melted upon the floor. The candidate was guided forward and shown where to kneel down. He carried his yellow robes in his arms, awkwardly. The officiating priest stood over him, the old abbot fixed his benignant gaze on him. The candidate kneeling, lifted his head and looked up at them, with affection and confidence and docility and submission, between man and man indeed a curious regard — across this gulf of race and tradition . . . how is one to write of the strange pang it brought? Out of the attitude, the delicate profile thrown back, the look of exaltation chosen and conviction desired, flashed a seizing resemblance. I looked at the Stoic and he at me. Together we ejaculated, "Cardinal Newman!" The image was the merest kaleidoscopic suggestion of dissolving circumstance, which immediately carried it away, but on the illusory scene of things we saw it for an instant painted before us.

The officiating priest began to speak, and the candidate repeated after him these things in Pali, addressing the abbot: "Grant me leave to speak. Lord, graciously grant me admission to deacon's orders. Lord, I pray for admission as a deacon. Again, Lord, I pray for admission as a deacon. A third time, Lord, I pray for admission as a deacon. In compassion for me, Lord, take these yellow robes and let me be ordained, in order to the destruction of all sorrow, and in order to the attainment of Nirvana."

This prayer he also repeated three times. Leaning forward, the abbot took the bundle of robes and gently threw a band about the candidate's neck, thus formally clothing him, I suppose, with righteousness. At this the candidate again retired with the priest. Some circumstance attended his going; they made way for him. He moved bent and rigid and slow from among us — a corpse in its grave-clothes he strangely seemed, going with volition to its burial. In the inner room, we learned, he changed into the yellow livery, saying after the priest: "In wisdom I put on the robes, as a protection against cold, as a protection against heat, as a protection against gadflies and mosquitoes, wind and sun and the touch of serpents, and to cover nakedness — that is, I wear them in all humility, for use only, and not for ornament or show."

Again he came out and knelt before the abbot: "Lord, I pray for the refuges and the precepts."

"*Buddham sáranam gacchámi; Dhammam sáranam gacchámi; Sangham sáranam gacchámi,*"* sonorously repeated the priest, and quaveringly the old man said it after him. He stumbled over some of the words — there was pathos here — and the cadence he gave to some did not satisfy the priest, so that, looking up like a child, he was obliged to say them several times. The words of the precepts were harder still — that by which he vowed to abstain from beautifying his person with garlands contained twenty syllables — and here the candidate often broke down, shaking a discouraged head. The dignity and the solemnity fled away from him; he became only a bewildered old man, a puppet in a play which it was doubtful whether he wholly understood. The kindly eyes of the abbot alone redeemed the situation, and the devotion of an old Burmese woman who stretched out joined hands before this miracle, with a flower in them.

There was still the selection of a name, the new name on the old tombstone of an Englishman. This, according to the usage, was at the candidate's choice, several being submitted to him. It was plainly an interesting moment; the old abbot leaned forward and whispered, the officiating priest bent down, and the others drew around; even the audience — should I say the congregation? — gathered closer, freely offering suggestions, and Oo-Dhamma-Nanda hovered over all. "Oo-Sri-Visuddha," "Venerable Lord of Purity"; "Oo-Candimâ," "Lord of the Moon"; "Oo-Dhamma-Sami," "Lord of the Written Law" — should it be any of these? The candidate hesitated; his fancy was not caught. "Oo-Asoka!" contributed an intelligent layman in a queue, smiling broadly ("That chap," said the attentive Stoic to me, "is a clerk in the Finance Department"), and the old man turned at the suggestion. "I've heard of Asoka," said he, vacillating. Oo-Dhamma-Nanda settled it. "Cahl him Asoka," said he with authority, and it was agreed.

"Do you like your name?" asked an English-speaking Burman,

* "I put my trust in Buddha; I put my trust in the Law; I put my trust in the Priesthood." [Duncan's note]

good-naturedly. "Oh, it's a nice name," quavered the old man, "but I'm not equal to Asoka."

I think they scamped the service; we were in Lower Burma, where orthodoxy, of late years, has suffered some dilution; but it had at least one feature super-added to the ritual of Shin-Gautama. Oo-Dhamma-Nanda, through an interpreter, addressed the assemblage. He held up his bare arm and they listened, many of them devoutly; the old woman still stretched out her flower. For that instant he was the pictorial priest, all to them that he could ever be. Then—ah me!—then he spoke. Alas, he addressed them as "Ladies and Gentlemen"; he made them a speech. It was about "the work," the work of the Society for the Propagation of Buddhism, of which Oo-Dhamma-Nanda appeared to be a cornerstone. "The object of this soci'ty," said he, "is that we should spread Buddhyism in all people whatsoever color they are." He spoke slowly, with his fingers joined at the tips, and at the end of every sentence he swayed forward on his toes and back—he might have been a ward politician addressing a crowd in the interests of Tammany. He referred to the newly-made deacon—"this gentleman who ye see here with the specs"—as the society's ripest fruit. He made the inevitable appeal for support. "They say union is stren'th," said he. He related, with modesty, some of his own exploits in defense of the indigenous faith. He had shut up no less than three mission stations, he told us, mainly by force of public argument, and he gave us details of one polemical struggle in which the missionary was fairly routed in the eyes of the audience, because he was unable to produce "anny sort of proof" for the story of Joshua and the sun. He was modest, but he also gloried. "If anny one gives throuble on these subjects," said he, "just you refer him to me. I don't think there'll be much more anxiety for public controversy so long as I'm around."

"It's Buddhyism cum shillalah," whispered the Stoic; and indeed the simple grotesqueness of it did appear. But the same flash showed Oo-Dhamma-Nanda in plainer revelation—his Western energy in full fling, all his vigor going out to preserve and proselytize, a figure of absurd and inconsistent violence vainly trying to merge itself in the great placid passive army of the yellow-robed. It proclaimed the compromise by which the spirit of the East might be brought to inhabit the blood of the West. The interpreter forged along, and the good Burmans, some of them large subscribers to the "Society," listened without obvious exultation, but appreciative and gratified. It was really not unlike a missionary-meeting at home; one saw the same depressed interest and respectful attention to the laborer returned from heathen vineyards. If the ladies had worn bonnets, the resemblance would have been complete.

One thing remained to finish the ordination of Asoka; he was to taste at once the essence of the abandonment of the body, to know without delay the new strange carelessness for the morrow which he was pledged to entertain. The priests put his begging-bowl into his hands and sent him among the women at the other side of the room. They heaped it heartily, one after another, with good things, rice and cakes fried in butter and condiments, putting in their packages with many jokes among themselves. Oo-Asoka, who moved gravely upon his quest, looked a little dazed at the laughter. . . .

We went down with the crowd, which showed as perfunctory a spirit as ever issued from a Broadway church. Nor did it lack its touch of cynicism, which came from the subordinate official in the queue, and was addressed to a paddy-broker in a checked silk petticoat. The clerk clapped the broker upon his fat shoulder. "'They are happy men,'" said he, smiling jovially, "'whose natures sort with their vocations.'"

My Stoic lifted his eyebrows. "Bacon!" said he — "Bacon — the ruffian!"

1916

What follows is mutant work indeed, and not just because it revolves around a "Devil Baby" who begins as a rumor, a fiction, and by the end has become . . . something else. Jane Addams seems to have intended a traditional essay from on high, peering down at women in the grip of "primitive" beliefs; by the end, she is among them. As in life: Addams was a reformer, one of the greatest of American history, a rich woman who moved to Chicago's slums and there established Hull House, a home and a community center for the poor, especially poor women. *For* the poor and *with* them; what began as paternalism became solidarity.

That's not a bad model for the evolution of literary journalism. It's easy, for instance, to draw a line from William T. Stead's portrait of a prostitute in "Maggie Darling" to Addams's picture of suffering women in "The Devil Baby at Hull-House," originally published in the *Atlantic Monthly*. Stead, if we forgive him his preliminary sermons, is best understood as a storyteller, gathering fact and detail and stringing them together into a tale with a beginning, a middle, and an end. Addams gathers facts and sets them free, and then follows them back into the lives of the women around her. She draws conclusions and then walks away from the easel. There is no "march of the subject," as Henry James would have it, in "The Devil Baby of Hull-House." Rather, despite Addams's own throat clearing—there's plenty of that, the formal gestures of a writer close to the great pragmatist philosophers of the day, including Henry James's brother William—the method of this piece is that of slow immersion into a worldview, a different way of knowing. It's a vision one can grasp only from within a Venn diagram of the urban poor, from within the overlap of ethnic and religious boundaries, a community of women in which the devil-baby makes sense—in which the devil baby is real.

JANE ADDAMS
The Devil Baby at Hull-House

The knowledge of the existence of the Devil Baby burst upon the residents of Hull-House one day when three Italian women, with an excited rush through the door, demanded that he be shown to them. No amount of denial convinced them that he was not there, for they knew exactly what he was like, with his cloven hoofs, his pointed ears and diminutive tail; moreover, the Devil Baby had been able to speak as soon as he was born and was most shockingly profane.

The three women were but the forerunners of a veritable multitude; for six weeks the streams of visitors from every part of the city and suburbs to this mythical baby poured in all day long, and so far into the night that the regular activities of the settlement were almost swamped.

The Italian version, with a hundred variations, dealt with a pious Italian girl married to an atheist. Her husband vehemently tore a holy picture from the bedroom wall, saying that he would quite as soon have a devil in the house as that; whereupon the devil incarnated himself in her coming child. As soon as the Devil Baby was born, he ran about the table shaking his finger in deep reproach at his father, who finally caught him and in fear and trembling brought him to Hull-House. When the residents there, in spite of the baby's shocking appearance, wishing to save his soul, took him to church for baptism, they found that the shawl was empty and the Devil Baby, felling from the holy water, ran lightly over the backs of the pews.

The Jewish version, again with variations, was to the effect that the father of six daughters had said before the birth of a seventh child that he would rather have a devil in the house than another girl, whereupon the Devil Baby promptly appeared.

Save for a red automobile which occasionally figured in the story, and a stray cigar which, in some versions, the new born child snatched from his father's lips, the tale might have been fashioned a thousand years ago.

Although the visitors to the Devil Baby included people of every degree of prosperity and education, even physicians and trained nurses who assured us of their scientific interest, the story constantly demonstrated the power of an old wives' tale among thousands of people in modern society who are living in a corner of their own, their vision fixed, their intelligence held by some iron chain of silent habit. To such primitive people the metaphor apparently is still the very "stuff of life"; or, rather, no other form of statement reaches them, and the tremendous tonnage of current writing for them has no existence. It was in keeping with their simple habits that the reputed presence of the Devil Baby at Hull-House did not reach the newspapers until the fifth week of his sojourn — after thousands of people had already been informed of his whereabouts by the old method of passing news from mouth to mouth.

During the weeks of excitement it was the old women who really seemed to have come into their own, and perhaps the most significant result of the incident was the reaction of the story upon them. It stirred their minds and memories as with a magic touch; it loosened their tongues and revealed the inner life and thoughts of those who are so often inarticulate. These old women enjoyed a moment of triumph, as if they had made good at last and had come into a region of sanctions and punishments which they understood.

Throughout six weeks, as I went about Hull-House, I would hear a voice at the telephone repeating for the hundredth time that day, "No, there is no such baby"; "No, we never had it here"; "No, he couldn't have seen it for fifty cents"; "We didn't send it anywhere because we never had it"; "I don't mean to say that your sister-in-law lied, but there must be some mistake"; "There is no use getting up an excursion from Milwaukee, for there isn't any Devil Baby at Hull-House"; "We can't give reduced rates because we are not exhibiting anything"; and so on and on. As I came near the front door, I would catch snatches of arguments that were often acrimonious: "Why do you let so many people believe it, if it isn't here?" "We have taken three lines of cars to come, and we have as much right to see it as anybody else"; "This is a pretty big place, of course you could hide it easy enough"; "What are you saying that for—are you going to raise the price of admission?" We had doubtless struck a case of what the psychologists call the "contagion of emotion," added to that "aesthetic sociability" which impels any one of us to drag the entire household to the window when a procession comes into the street or a rainbow appears in the sky.

But the Devil Baby of course was worth many processions and rainbows, and I will confess that, as the empty show went on day after day, I quite revolted against such a vapid manifestation of an admirable human trait. There was always one exception, however: whenever I heard the high eager voices of old women, I was irresistibly interested and left anything I might be doing in order to listen to them.

II

Perhaps my many talks with these aged visitors crystallized thoughts and impressions that I had been receiving through years; or the tale itself may have ignited a fire, as it were, whose light illumined some of my darkest memories of neglected and uncomfortable old age, of old peasant women who had ruthlessly probed into the ugly depths of human nature in themselves and others. Many of them who came to see the Devil Baby had been forced to face tragic human experiences; the powers of brutality and horror had had full scope in their lives, and for years they had had acquaintance with disaster and death. Such old women do not shirk life's misery by feeble idealism, for they are long past the stage of make-believe. They relate without flinching the most hideous experiences. "My face has had this queer twist for now nearly sixty years; I was ten when it got that way, the night after I saw my father do my mother to death with his knife." "Yes, I had fourteen children; only two grew to be men and both of them were killed in the same explosion. I was never sure they brought home the right bodies." But even the most hideous sorrows which the old women related had apparently subsided into the paler emotion of ineffectual regret, after Memory had long done her work upon them; the old people seemed, in some unaccountable way, to lose all bitterness and resentment against life, or rather they were so completely without it that they must have lost it long since.

Perhaps those women, because they had come to expect nothing more from life and had perforce ceased from grasping and striving, had obtained, if not renunciation, at least that quiet endurance which allows the wounds of the spirit to heal. Through their stored-up habit of acquiescence, they vouchsafed a fleeting glimpse of that translucent wisdom so often embodied in old women, but so difficult to portray. I recall a conversation with one of them, a woman whose fine mind and indomitable spirit I had long admired; I had known her for years, and yet the recital of her sufferings, added to those the Devil Baby had already induced other women to tell me, pierced me afresh.

"I had eleven children, some born in Bohemia and some born here; nine of them boys; all of the children died when they were little, but my dear Liboucha, you know all about her. She died last winter in the insane asylum. She was only twelve years old when her father, in a fit of delirium tremens, killed himself after he had chased us around the room trying to kill us first. She saw it all; the blood splashed on the wall stayed in her mind the worst; she shivered and shook all that night through, and the next morning she had lost her voice, couldn't speak out loud for terror. After a while her voice came back, although it was never very natural, and she went to school again. She seemed to do as well as ever and was awful pleased when she got into High School. All the money we had, I earned scrubbing in a public dispensary, although sometimes I got a little by interpreting for the patients, for I know three languages, one as well as the other. But I was determined that, whatever happened to me, Liboucha was to be educated. My husband's father was a doctor in the old country, and Liboucha was always a clever child. I wouldn't have her live the kind of life I had, with no use for my mind except to make me restless and bitter. I was pretty old and worn out for such hard work, but when I used to see Liboucha on a Sunday morning, ready for church in her white dress with her long yellow hair braided round her beautiful pale face, lying there in bed as I was, being brought up a freethinker and needing to rest my aching bones for the next week's work, — I'd feel almost happy, in spite of everything.

"But of course no such peace could last in my life; the second year at High School, Liboucha began to seem different and to do strange things. You know the time she wandered away for three days and we were all wild with fright, although a kind woman had taken her in and no harm came to her. I could never be easy after that; she was always gentle, but she was awful sly about running away, and at last I had to send her to the asylum. She stayed there off and on for five years, but I saw her every week of my life and she was always company for me, what with sewing for her, washing and ironing her clothes, cooking little things to take out to her and saving a bit of money to buy fruit for her. At any rate, I had stopped feeling so bitter, and got some comfort out of seeing the one thing that belonged to me on this side of the water, when all of a sudden she died of heart failure, and they never took the trouble to send for me until the next day."

She stopped as if wondering afresh that the Fates could have been so casual, but with a sudden illumination, as if she had been awakened out of the burden and intensity of her restricted personal interests into a consciousness of those larger relations that are, for the most part, so strangely invisible. It was as if the young mother of the grotesque Devil Baby, that victim of wrong-doing on the part of others, had revealed to this tragic woman, much more clearly than soft words had ever done, that the return of a deed of violence upon the head of the innocent is inevitable; as if she had realized that, although she was destined to walk all the days of her life with that piteous multitude who bear the undeserved wrongs of the world, she would walk henceforth with a sense of companionship.

Among the visitors were pitiful old women who, although they had already reconciled themselves to much misery, were still enduring more. "You might say it's a disgrace to have your son beat you up for the sake of a bit of money you've earned by scrubbing, — your own man is different, — but I haven't the heart to blame the boy for doing what he's seen all his life; his father forever went wild when the drink was in him and struck me to the very day of his death. The ugliness was born in the boy as the marks of the devil was born in the poor child upstairs."

This more primitive type embodies the eternal patience of those humble toiling women who through the generations have been held of little value, save as their drudgery ministered to their men. One of them related her habit of going through the pockets of her drunken son every pay-day, and complained that she had never got so little as the night before, only twenty-five cents out of fifteen dollars he had promised for the rent long overdue. "I had to get that as he lay in the alley before the door; I couldn't pull him in, and the copper who helped him home left as soon as he heard me coming and pretended he didn't see me. I have no food in the house nor coffee to sober him up with. I know perfectly well that you will ask me to eat something here, but if I can't carry it home, I won't take a bite nor a sup. I have never told you so much before. Since once of the nurses said he could be arrested for my non-support, I have been awfully close-mouthed. It's the foolish way all the women in our street are talking about the Devil Baby that's loosened my tongue — more shame to me."

There are those, if possible more piteous still, who have become absolutely helpless and can therefore no longer perform the household services exacted from them. One last wish has been denied them. "I hoped to go before I became a burden, but it was not to be"; and the long days of unwonted idleness are darkened by the haunting fear that "they" will come to think the burden too heavy and decide that the poorhouse is "the best." Even then there is no word of blame for undutiful children or heedless grandchildren, for apparently all that is petty and transitory falls away from austere old age; the fires are burnt out, resentments, hatreds, and even cherished sorrows have become actually unintelligible. It is as if the horrors through which these old people had passed had never existed for them, and, facing death as they are, they seem anxious to speak only such words of groping wisdom as they are able.

This aspect of memory has never been more clearly stated than by Gilbert Murray in his *Life of Euripides*. He tells us that the aged poet, when he was officially declared to be one of "the old men of Athens," said, "Even yet the age-worn minstrel can turn Memory into song"; and the memory of which he spoke was that of history and tradition, rather than his own. The aged poet turned into song even the hideous story of Medea, transmuting it into "a beautiful remote song about far-off children who have been slain in legend, children who are now at peace and whose ancient pain has become part mystery and part music. Memory — that Memory who is the mother of the Muses — having done her work upon them."

The vivid interest of so many old women in the story of the Devil Baby may have been an unconscious, although powerful testi-

mony that tragic experiences gradually become dressed in such trappings in order that their spent agony may prove of some use to a world
which learns at the hardest; and that the strivings and sufferings of
men and women long since dead, their emotion no longer connected
with flesh and blood, are thus transmuted into legendary wisdom. The
young are forced to heed the warning in such a tale, although for the
most part it is so easy for them to disregard the words of the aged. That
the old women who came to visit the Devil Baby believed that the
story would secure them a hearing at home was evident, and as they
prepared themselves with every detail of it, their old faces shone with
a timid satisfaction. Their features, worn and scarred by harsh living,
even as effigies built into the floor of an old church become dim and
defaced by rough-shod feet, grew poignant and solemn. In the midst
of their double bewilderment, both that the younger generation were
walking in such stranger paths and that no one would listen to them,
for one moment there flickered up that last hope of a disappointed life,
that it may at least serve as a warning while affording material for ex-
citing narrations.

Sometimes in talking to one of them, who was "but a hair's
breadth this side of the darkness," one realized that old age has its own
expression for the mystic renunciation of the world. The impatience
with all non-essentials, the craving to be free from hampering bonds
and soft conditions, was perhaps typified in our own generation by
Tolstoï's last impetuous journey, the light of his genius for a moment
making comprehensible to us that unintelligible impulse of the aged.

Often, in the midst of a conversation, one of these touching old
women would quietly express a longing for death, as if it were a natural
fulfillment of an inmost desire. Her sincerity and anticipation were so
genuine that I would feel abashed in her presence, ashamed to "cling
to this strange thing that shines in the sunlight, and to be sick with love
for it." Such impressions were in their essence transitory, but one result from the hypothetical visit of the Devil Baby to Hull-House will,
I think, remain: a realization of the sifting and reconciling power in-

herent in Memory itself. The old women, with much to aggravate and little to soften the habitual bodily discomforts of old age, exhibited an emotional serenity so vast and reassuring that I found myself perpetually speculating as to how soon the fleeting and petty emotions which seem so unduly important to us now might be thus transmuted; at what moment we might expect the inconsistencies and perplexities of life to be brought under this appeasing Memory, with its ultimate power to increase the elements of Beauty and Significance and to reduce, if not to eliminate, stupidity and resentment.

III

As our visitors to the Devil Baby came day by day, it was gradually evident that the simpler women were moved not wholly by curiosity, but that many of them prized the story as a valuable instrument in the business of living.

The legend exhibited all the persistence of one of those tales which have doubtless been preserved through the centuries because of their taming effects upon recalcitrant husbands and fathers. Shamefaced men brought by their women-folk to see the baby but ill-concealed their triumph when there proved to be no such visible sign of retribution for domestic derelictions. On the other hand, numbers of men came by themselves. One group from a neighboring factory, on their "own time," offered to pay twenty-five cents, a half dollar, two dollars apiece to see the child, insisting that it must be at Hull-House because "the women folks had seen it." To my query as to whether they supposed we would exhibit for money a poor little deformed baby, if one had been born in the neighborhood, they replied, "Sure, why not?" and, "It teaches a good lesson, too," they added as an afterthought, or perhaps as a concession to the strange moral standards of a place like Hull-House. All the members in this group of hardworking men, in spite of a certain swagger toward one another and a tendency to bully the derelict showman, wore that hang-dog look betraying the sense of unfair treatment which a man is so apt to feel when his woman-kind makes an appeal to the supernatural. In their determination to see the child, the men recklessly divulged much more concerning their motives than they had meant to do, and their talk confirmed my impression that such a story may still act as a restraining influence in that sphere of marital conduct which, next to primitive religion itself, we are told, has always afforded the most fertile field for irrational tabus and savage punishments.

What story more than this could be calculated to secure sympathy for the mother of too many daughters, and contumely for the irritated father? The touch of mysticism, the supernatural sphere in which it was placed, would render a man perfectly helpless.

The story of the Devil Baby, evolved to-day as it might have been centuries before in response to the imperative needs of anxious wives and mothers, recalled the theory that woman first fashioned the fairy-story, that combination of wisdom and romance, in an effort to tame her mate and to make him a better father to her children, until such stories finally became a rude creed for domestic conduct, softening the treatment that men accorded to women.

These first pitiful efforts of women, so widespread and powerful that we have not yet escaped their influence, still cast vague shadows upon the vast spaces of life, shadows that are dim and distorted because of their distance origin. They remind us that for thousands of years women had nothing to oppose against unthinkable brutality save "the charm of words," no other implement with which to subdue the fiercenesses of the world about them.

During the weeks that the Devil Baby drew multitudes of visitors to Hull-House, my mind was opened to the fact that new knowledge derived from concrete experience is continually being made available for the guidance of human life; that humble women are still establishing rules of conduct as best they may, to counteract the base temptations of a man's world. Thousands of women, for instance, make it a standard of domestic virtue that a man must not touch his pay envelope, but bring it home unopened to his wife. High praise is contained in the phrase, "We have been married twenty years and he never once opened his own envelope"; or covert blame in the statement, "Of course he got to gambling; what can you expect from a man who always opens his own pay?"

The women are so fatalistically certain of this relation of punishment to domestic sin, of reward to domestic virtue, that when they talk about it, as they so constantly did in connection with the Devil Baby, it often sounds as if they were using the words of a widely known ritual. Even the young girls seized upon it as a palpable punishment, to be held over the heads of reckless friends. That the tale was useful was evidenced by many letters similar to the anonymous epistle here given.

> me and my friends we work in talor shop and when we are going home on the roby street car where we get off that car at blue island ave. we will meet some fellows sitting at that street where they drink some beer from pail. they keep look in cars all the time and they will wait and see if we will come sometimes we ill have to work, but they will wait so long they are tired and they dont care they get rest so long but a girl what works in twine mill saw them talk with us we know her good and she say what youse talk with old drunk man for we shall come to thier dance when it will be they will tell us and we should know all about where to see them that girl she say oh if you will go with them you will get devils baby like some other girls did who we knows. she say Jane Addams she will show one like that in Hull House if you will go down there we shall come sometime and we will see if that is trouth we do not believe her for she is friendly with them old men herself when she go out from her work they will wink to her and say something else to. We will go down and see you and make a lie from what she say.

IV

The story evidently held some special comfort for hundreds of forlorn women, representatives of that vast horde of the denied and pro-
scribed who had long found themselves confronted by those mysterious and impersonal wrongs which are apparently nobody's fault but
seem to be inherent in the very nature of things.

Because the Devil Baby embodied an undeserved wrong to a
poor mother, whose tender child had been claimed by the forces of
evil, his merely reputed presence had power to attract to Hull-House
hundreds of women who had been humbled and disgraced by their
children; mothers of the feeble-minded, of the vicious, of the criminal, of the prostitute. In their talk it was as if their long rôle of maternal apology and protective reticence has at last broken down; as if
they could speak out freely because for once a man responsible for an
ill-begotten child had been "met up with" and had received his deserts.
Their sinister version of the story was that the father of the Devil Baby
had married without confessing a hideous crime committed years before, thus basely deceiving both his innocent young bride and the good
priest who performed the solemn ceremony; that the sin had become
incarnate in his child which, to the horror of the young and trusting mother, had been born with all the outward aspects of the devil
himself.

As if drawn by a magnet, week after week, a procession of forlorn women in search of the Devil Baby came to Hull-House from
every part of the city, issuing forth from the many homes in which
dwelt "the two unprofitable goddesses, Poverty and Impossibility."
With an understanding quickened perhaps through my own acquaintance with the mysterious child, I listened to many tragic tales from
the visiting women: of premature, "because he kicked me in the side";
of children maimed and burned because "I had no one to leave them
with when I went to work." These women had seen the tender flesh
of growing little bodies given over to death because "he wouldn't let

me send for the doctor," or because "there was no money to pay for the medicine." But even these mothers, rendered childless through insensate brutality, were less pitiful than some of the others, who might well have cried aloud of their children as did a distracted mother of her child centuries ago, —

> That God should send this one thing more
> Of hunger and of dread, a door
> Set wide to every wind of pain!

Such was the mother of a feeble-minded boy who said, "I didn't have a devil baby myself, but I bore a poor 'innocent,' who made me fight devils for twenty-three years." She told of her son's experiences from the time the other little boys had put him up to stealing that they might hide in safety and leave him to be found with "the goods" on him, until, grown into a huge man, he fell into the hands of professional burglars; he was evidently the dupe and stool-pigeon of the vicious and criminal until the very day he was locked into the State Penitentiary. "If people played with him a little, he went right off and did anything they told him to, and now he's been set up for life. We call such innocents 'God's Fools' in the old country, but over here the Devil himself gets them. I've fought off bad men and boys from the poor lamb with my very fists; nobody ever came near the house except such like and the police officers who were always arresting him."

There were a goodly number of visitors, of the type of those to be found in every large city, who are on the verge of nervous collapse or who exhibit many symptoms of mental aberration and yet are sufficiently normal to be at large most of the time and to support themselves by drudgery which requires little mental effort, although the exhaustion resulting from the work they are able to do is the one thing from which they should be most carefully protected. One such woman, evidently obtaining inscrutable comfort from the story of the Devil Baby even after she had become convinced that we harbored no such creature, came many times to tell of her longing for her son who had

joined the army some eighteen months before and was stationed in
Alaska. She always began with the same words. "When spring comes
and the snow melts so that I know he could get out, I can hardly stand
it. You know I was once in the Insane Asylum for three years at a
stretch, and since then I haven't had much use of my mind except to
worry with. Of course I know that it is dangerous for me, but what can
I do? I think something like this: 'The snow is melting, now he could
get out, but his officers won't let him off, and if he runs away he'll be
shot for a deserter — either way I'll never see him again; I'll die without seeing him' — and then I begin all over again with the snow." After
a pause, she said, "The recruiting officer ought not to have taken him;
he's my only son and I'm a widow; it's against the rules, but he was so
crazy to go that I guess he lied a little. At any rate, the government has
him now and I can't get him back. Without this worry about him, my
mind would be all right; if he was here he would be earning money and
keeping me and we would be happy all day long."

Recalling the vagabondish lad who had never earned much
money and had certainly never "kept" his hard-working mother, I ventured to suggest that, even if he were at home, he might not have work
in these hard times, that he might get into trouble and be arrested, —
I did not need to remind her that he had already been arrested twice, —
that he was now fed and sheltered and under discipline, and I added
hopefully something about seeing the world. She looked at me out of
her withdrawn harried eyes, as if I were speaking a foreign tongue.
"That wouldn't make any real difference to me — the work, the money,
his behaving well and all that, if I could cook and wash for him; I don't
need all the money I earn scrubbing that factory; I only take bread and
tea for supper, and I choke over that, thinking of him."

V

A sorrowful woman clad in heavy black, who came one day, exhibited
such a capacity for prolonged weeping that it was evidence in itself

of the truth of at least half her statement, that she had cried herself to sleep every night of her life for fourteen years in fulfillment of a "curse" laid upon her by an angry man that "her pillow would be wet with tears as long as she lived." Her respectable husband had kept a shop in the Red Light district, because he found it profitable to sell to the men and women who lived there. She had kept house in the rooms "over the store," from the time she was a bride newly come from Russia, and her five daughters had been born there, but never a song to gladden her husband's heart.

She took such a feverish interest in the Devil Baby that when I was obliged to disillusion her, I found it hard to take away her comfort in the belief that the Powers that Be are on the side of the woman, when her husband resents too many daughters. But, after all, the birth of daughters was but an incident in her tale of unmitigated woe, for the scoldings of a disappointed husband were as nothing to the curse of a strange enemy, although she doubtless had a confused impression that if there was retribution for one in the general scheme of things, there might be for the other.

When the weeping woman finally put the events of her disordered life in some sort of sequence, it was clear that about fifteen years ago she had reported to the police a vicious house whose back door opened into her own yard. Her husband had forbidden her to do anything about it and had said that it would only get them into trouble, but she had been made desperate one day when she saw her little girl, then twelve years old, come out of the door, gleefully showing her younger sister a present of money. Because the poor woman had tried for ten years, without success, to induce her husband to move from the vicinity of such houses, she was certain that she could save her child by forcing out "the bad people" from her own door-yard. She therefore made her one frantic effort, found her way to the city hall, and there reported the house to the chief himself. Of course, "the bad people" "stood in with the police," and nothing happened to them except, perhaps, a fresh levy of blackmail; but the keeper of the house, beside himself with rage, made the dire threat and laid the curse upon her. In less than a year from that time he had enticed her daughter into a disreputable house in another part of the district. The poor woman, ringing one doorbell after another, had never been able to find her, but the girl's sisters, who in time came to know where she was, had been dazzled by her mode of life. The weeping mother was quite sure that two of her daughters, while still outwardly respectable and "working downtown," earned money in the devious ways which they had learned all about when they were little children, although for the past five years the now prosperous husband had allowed the family to live in a suburb where the two younger daughters were "growing up respectable."

At moments it seemed possible that these simple women, representing an earlier development, eagerly seized upon the story simply because it was primitive in form and substance. Certainly one evening a long-forgotten ballad made an unceasing effort to come to the surface of my mind, as I talked to a feeble woman who, in the last stages of an incurable disease from which she soon afterwards died, had been helped off the street-car in front of Hull-House.

The ballad tells that the lover of a proud and jealous mistress, who demanded as a final test of devotion that he bring her the heart of his mother, had quickly cut the heart from his mother's breast and impetuously returned to his lady bearing it upon a salver; but that, when stumbling in his gallant haste, he stooped to replace upon the silver plate his mother's heart which had rolled upon the ground, the heart, still beating with tender solicitude, whispered the hope that her child was not hurt.

The ballad itself was scarcely more exaggerated than the story of our visitor that evening, who had made the desperate effort of a journey from home in order to see the Devil Baby. I was familiar with her vicissitudes: the shiftless drinking husband and the large family of children, all of whom had brought her sorrow and disgrace; and I knew that her heart's desire was to see again before she died her youngest son, who was a life prisoner in the penitentiary. She was confident that the last piteous stage of her disease would secure him a week's parole, founding this forlorn hope upon the fact that "they sometimes let them out to attend a mother's funeral, and perhaps they'd let Joe come a few days ahead; he could pay his fare afterwards from the insurance money. It wouldn't have taken much to bury me."

Again we went over the hideous story. Joe had violently quarreled with a woman, the proprietor of the house in which his disreputable wife lived, because she withheld from him a part of his wife's "earnings," and in the altercation had killed her—a situation, one would say, which it would be difficult for even a mother to condone. But not at all: her thin gray face worked with emotion, her trembling hands restlessly pulled at her shabby skirt as the hands of the dying pluck at the sheets, but she put all the vitality she could muster in his defense. She told us he had legally married the girl who supported him, "although Lily had been so long in that life that few men would have done it. Of course such a girl must have a protector or everybody would fleece her; poor Lily said to the day of her death that he was the kindest man she ever knew, and treated her the whitest; that she herself was to blame for the murder because she told on the old miser, and Joe was so hot-headed she might have known that he would draw a gun for her." The gasping mother concluded, "He was always that handsome and had such a way. One winter when I was scrubbing in an office-building, I'd never get home much before twelve o'clock; but Joe would open the door for me just as pleasant as if he hadn't been waked out of a deep sleep."

She was so triumphantly unconscious of the incongruity of a sturdy son in bed while his mother earned his food, that her auditors said never a word, and in silence we saw a hero evolved before our eyes: a defender of the oppressed, the best beloved of his mother, who was losing his high spirits and eating his heart out behind the prison bars. He could well defy the world even there, surrounded as he was by that invincible affection which assures both the fortunate and unfortunate alike that we are loved, not according to our deserts, but in response to some profounder law.

This imposing revelation of maternal solicitude was an instance of what continually happened in connection with the Devil Baby. In the midst of the most tragic recitals there remained that something in the souls of these mothers which has been called the great revelation of tragedy, or sometimes the great illusion of tragedy — that which has power in its own right to make life acceptable and at rare moments even beautiful.

At least, during the weeks when the Devil Baby seemed to occupy every room in Hull-House, one was conscious that all human vicissitudes are in the end melted down into reminiscence, and that a metaphorical statement of those profound experiences which are implicit in human nature itself, however crude in form the story may be, has a singular power of healing the distracted spirit.

If it has always been the mission of literature to translate the particular act into something of the universal, to reduce the element of crude pain in the isolated experience by bringing to the sufferer a realization that his is but the common lot, this mission may have been performed through such stories as this for simple hard-working women, who, after all, at any given moment compose the bulk of the women in the world.

1925

H. L. Mencken, the most famous journalist of the early twentieth century, would rewrite this dispatch, first published in the *Baltimore Evening Sun*, as a slightly longer essay called "The Hills of Zion," published in a collection of his work. I chose the newspaper version because it is wonderful to imagine opening one's paper and finding, amid dehydrated accounts of city council scuffles and paving mishaps, some Huck Finn excitement: "We could scarcely distinguish the figure of the preacher; it was like looking down the tube of a dark field microscope. We got out of the car and sneaked along the edge of a mountain cornfield."

I also chose the newspaper version because of what became of that sentence, and others like it, in Mencken's overcooked revision: "We could distinguish the figure of the preacher only as a moving mote in the light: it was like looking down the tube of a dark-field microscope. Slowly and cautiously we crossed what seemed to be a pasture, and then we stealthily edged further and further. The light now grew larger and we could begin to make out what was going on. We went ahead on all fours, like snakes in the grass."

The piece as Mencken originally wrote it, "on a roaring hot Sunday afternoon in a Chattanooga hotel room, naked above the waist and with only a pair of BVDs below," was already a figure of gross but deliberate distortion. Mencken evokes a firelit Pentecostal camp meeting as close cousin to the satanic ritual encountered in the woods in Nathaniel Hawthorne's famous 1835 story "Young Goodman Brown." Like Hawthorne, Mencken means to spurn "Puritanism," which Mencken defines as "the haunting fear that someone, somewhere, may be happy." Where Hawthorne resorted to gothic horror, Mencken relies on ridicule. And in revision, the more the better, "motes," adverbs, snakes, and all. What's missing from the later version is this half-serious confession: "If I have made the tale too long, then blame the spirit of garrulity that is in the local air. Even newspaper reporters, down here, get some echo of the call."

H. L. MENCKEN
Yearning Mountaineers' Souls
Need Reconversion Nightly

Dayton, Tenn., July 13.—There is a Unitarian clergyman here from New York, trying desperately to horn into the trial and execution of the infidel Scopes. He will fail. If Darrow ventured to put him on the stand the whole audience, led by the jury, would leap out of the courthouse windows, and take to the hills. Darrow himself, indeed, is as much as they can bear. The whisper that he is an atheist has been stilled by the bucolic make-up and by the public report that he has the gift of prophecy and can reconcile Genesis and evolution. Even so, there is ample space about him when he navigates the streets. The other day a newspaper woman was warned by her landlady to keep out of the courtroom when he was on his legs. All the local sorcerers predict that a bolt from heaven will fetch him in the end. The night he arrived there was a violent storm, the town water turned brown, and horned cattle in the lowlands were afloat for hours. A woman back in the mountains gave birth to a child with hair four inches long, curiously bobbed in scallops.

The Book of Revelation has all the authority, in these theologi-

cal uplands, of military orders in time of war. The people turn to it for
light upon all their problems, spiritual and secular. If a text were found
in it denouncing the Anti-Evolution law, then the Anti-Evolution law
would become infamous overnight. But so far the exegetes who roar
and snuffle in the town have found no such text. Instead they have
found only blazing ratifications and reinforcements of Genesis. Darwin is the devil with seven tails and nine horns. Scopes, though he
is disguised by flannel pantaloons and a Beta Theta Pi haircut, is the
harlot of Babylon. Darrow is Beelzebub in person and Malone is the
Crown Prince Friedrich Wilhelm.

I have hitherto hinted an Episcopalian down here in the Coca-
Cola belt is regarded as an atheist. It sounds like one of the lies that
journalists tell, but it is really an understatement of the facts. Even a
Methodist, by Rhea county standards, is one a bit debauched by pride
of intellect. It is the four Methodists on the jury who are expected to
hold out for giving Scopes Christian burial after he is hanged. They all
made it plain, when they were examined, that they were free-thinking
and independent men, and not to be run amuck by the superstitions
of the lowly. One actually confessed that he seldom read the Bible,
though he hastened to add that he was familiar with its principles. The
fellow had on a boiled shirt and a polka dot necktie. He sits somewhat
apart. When Darrow withers to a cinder under the celestial blowpipe,
this dubious Wesleyan, too, will lose a few hairs.

Even the Baptists no longer brew a medicine that is strong
enough for the mountaineers. The sacrament of baptism by total immersion is over too quickly for them, and what follows offers nothing
that they can get their teeth into. What they crave is a continuous experience of the divine power, an endless series of evidence that the true
believer is a marked man, ever under the eye of God. It is not enough to
go to a revival once a year or twice a year; there must be a revival every
night. And it is not enough to accept the truth as a mere statement of
indisputable and awful fact: it must be embraced ecstatically and orgi-

astically, to the accompaniment of loud shouts, dreadful heavings and gurglings, and dancing with arms and legs.

This craving is satisfied brilliantly by the gaudy practices of the Holy Rollers, and so the mountaineers are gradually gravitating toward the Holy Roller communion, or, as they prefer to call it, the Church of God. Gradually, perhaps, is not the word. They are actually going in by whole villages and townships. At the last count of noses there were 20,000 Holy Rollers in these hills. The next census, I have no doubt, will show many more. The cities of the lowlands, of course, still resist, and so do most of the county towns, including even Dayton, but once one steps off the State roads the howl of holiness is heard in the woods, and the yokels carry on an almost continuous orgy.

A foreigner in store clothes going out from Dayton must approach the sacred grove somewhat discreetly. It is not that the Holy Rollers, discovering him, would harm him; it is simply that they would shut down their boiling of the devil and flee into the forests. We left Dayton an hour after nightfall and parked our car in a wood a mile or so beyond the little hill village of Morgantown. Far off in a glade a flickering light was visible and out of the silence came a faint rumble of exhortation. We could scarcely distinguish the figure of the preacher; it was like looking down the tube of a dark field microscope. We got out of the car and sneaked along the edge of a mountain cornfield.

Presently we were near enough to see what was going on. From the great limb of a mighty oak hung a couple of crude torches of the sort that car inspectors thrust under Pullman cars when a train pulls in at night. In their light was a preacher, and for a while we could see no one else. He was an immensely tall and thin mountaineer in blue jeans, his collarless shirt open at the neck and his hair a tousled mop. As he preached he paced up and down under the smoking flambeaux and at each turn he thrust his arms into the air and yelled, "Glory to God!" We crept nearer in the shadow of the cornfield and began to hear more of his discourse. He was preaching on the day of judgment.

The high kings of the earth, he roared, would all fall down and die; only the sanctified would stand up to receive the Lord God of Hosts. One of these kings he mentioned by name — the king of what he called Greece-y. The King of Greece-y, he said, was doomed to hell.

We went forward a few more yards and began to see the audience. It was seated on benches ranged round the preacher in a circle. Behind him sat a row of elders, men and women. In front were the younger folk. We kept on cautiously, and individuals rose out of the ghostly gloom. A young mother sat suckling her baby, rocking as the preacher paced up and down. Two scared little girls hugged each other, their pigtails down their backs. An immensely huge mountain woman, in a gingham dress cut in one piece, rolled on her heels at every "Glory to God." To one side, but half visible, was what appeared to be a bed. We found out afterward that two babies were asleep upon it.

The preacher stopped at last and there arose out of the darkness a woman with her hair pulled back into a little tight knot. She began so quietly that we couldn't hear what she said, but soon her voice rose resonantly and we could follow her. She was denouncing the reading of books. Some wandering book agent, it appeared, had come to her cabin and tried to sell her a specimen of his wares. She refused to touch it. Why, indeed, read a book? If what was in it was true then everything in it was already in the Bible. If it was false then reading it would imperil the soul. Her syllogism complete, she sat down.

There followed a hymn, led by a somewhat fat brother wearing silver-rimmed country spectacles. It droned on for half a dozen stanzas, and then the first speaker resumed the floor. He argued that the gift of tongues was real and that education was a snare. Once his children could read the Bible, he said, they had enough. Beyond lay only infidelity and damnation. Sin stalked the cities. Dayton itself was a Sodom. Even Morgantown had begun to forget God. He sat down, and the female aurochs in gingham got up.

She began quietly, but was soon leaping and roaring, and it was hard to follow her. Under cover of the turmoil we sneaked a bit closer.

A couple of other discourses followed, and there were two or three hymns. Suddenly a change of mood began to make itself felt. The last hymn ran longer than the others and dropped gradually into a monotonous, unintelligible chant. The leader beat time with his book. The faithful broke out with exultations. When the singing ended there was a brief palaver that we could not hear and two of the men moved a bench into the circle of light directly under the flambeaux. Then a half-grown girl emerged from the darkness and threw herself upon it. We noticed with astonishment that she had bobbed hair. "This sister," said the leader, "has asked for prayers." We moved a bit closer. We could now see faces plainly and hear every word.

What followed quickly reached such heights of barbaric grotesquerie that it was hard to believe it real. At a signal all the faithful crowded up the bench and began to pray — not in unison but each for himself. At another they all fell on their knees, their arms over the penitent. The leader kneeled, facing us, his head alternately thrown back dramatically or buried in his hands. Words spouted from his lips like bullets from a machine gun — appeals to God to pull the penitent back out of hell, defiances of the powers and principalities of the air, a vast impassioned jargon of apocalyptic texts. Suddenly he rose to his feet, threw back his head and began to speak in tongues — blub-blub-blub, gurgle-gurgle-gurgle. His voice rose to a higher register. The climax was a shrill, inarticulate squawk, like that of a man throttled. He fell headlong across the pyramid of supplicants.

A comic scene? Somehow, no. The poor half wits were too horribly in earnest. It was like peeping through a knothole at the writhings of a people in pain. From the squirming and jabbering mass a young woman gradually detached herself — a woman not uncomely, with a pathetic home-made cap on her head. Her head jerked back, the veins of her neck swelled, and her fists went to her throat as if she were fighting for breath. She bent backward until she was like half of a hoop. Then she suddenly snapped forward. We caught a flash of the whites of her eyes. Presently her whole body began to be convulsed — great convulsions that began at the shoulders and ended at the hips. She would leap to her feet, thrust her arms in air and then hurl herself upon the heap. Her praying flattened out into a mere delirious caterwauling, like that of a tomcat on a petting party.

I describe the thing as a strict behaviorist. The lady's subjective sensations I leave to infidel pathologists. Whatever they were they were obviously contagious, for soon another damsel joined her, and then another and then a fourth. The last one had an extraordinary bad attack. She began with mild enough jerks of the head, but in a moment she was bounding all over the place, exactly like a chicken with its head cut off. Every time her head came up a stream of yells and barkings would issue out of it. Once she collided with a dark, undersized brother, hitherto silent and stolid. Contact with her set him off as if he had been kicked by a mule. He leaped into the air, threw back his head and began to gargle as if with a mouthful of BB shot. Then he loosened one tremendous stentorian sentence in the tongues and collapsed.

By this time the performers were quite oblivious to the profane universe. We left our hiding and came up to the little circle of light. We slipped into the vacant seats on one of the rickety benches. The heap of mourners was directly before us. They bounced into us as they cavorted. The smell that they radiated, sweating there in that obscene heap, half suffocated us. Not all of them, of course, did the thing in the grand manner. Some merely moaned and rolled their eyes. The female ox in gingham flung her great bulk on the ground and jabbered an unintelligible prayer. One of the men, in the intervals between fits, put on spectacles and read his Bible.

Beside me on the bench sat the young mother and her baby. She suckled it through the whole orgy, obviously fascinated by what was going on, but never venturing to take any hand in it. On the bed just outside the light two other babies slept peacefully. In the shadows, suddenly appearing and as suddenly going away, were vague figures, whether of believers or of scoffers I do not know. They seemed to come and go in couples. Now and then a couple at the ringside would step back and then vanish into the black night. After a while some came back. There was whispering outside the circle of vision. A couple of Fords lurched up in the wood road, cutting holes in the darkness with their lights. Once some one out of sight loosed a bray of laughter.

All this went on for an hour or so. The original penitent, by this time, was buried three deep beneath the heap. One caught a glimpse, now and then, of her yellow bobbed hair, but then she would vanish again. How she breathed down there I don't know; it was hard enough ten feet away, with a strong five-cent cigar to help. When the praying brothers would rise up for a bout with the tongues their faces were streaming with perspiration. The fat harridan in gingham sweated like a longshoreman. Her hair got loose and fell down over her face. She fanned herself with her skirt. A powerful old gal she was, equal in her day to obstetrics and a week's washing on the same morning, but this was worse than a week's washing. Finally, she fell into a heap, breathing in great, convulsive gasps.

We tired of it after a while and groped our way back to our automobile. When we got to Dayton, after 11 o'clock—an immensely late hour in these parts—the whole town was still gathered on the courthouse lawn, hanging upon the disputes of theologians. The Bible champion of the world had a crowd. The Seventh Day Adventist missionaries had a crowd. A volunteer from faraway Portland, Ore., made up exactly like Andy Gump, had another and larger crowd. Dayton was enjoying itself. All the usual rules were suspended and the curfew bell was locked up. The prophet Bryan, exhausted by his day's work for Revelation, was snoring in his bed up the road, but enough volunteers were still on watch to keep the battlements manned.

Such is human existence among the fundamentalists, where children are brought up on Genesis and sin is unknown. If I have made the tale too long, then blame the spirit of garrulity that is in the local air. Even newspaper reporters, down here, get some echo of the call.

Divine inspiration is as common as the hookworm. I have done my best to show you what the great heritage of mankind comes to in regions where the Bible is the beginning and end of wisdom, and the mountebank Bryan, parading the streets in his seersucker coat, is pointed out to sucklings as the greatest man since Abraham.

1934

Earlier the same year that Meridel Le Sueur published "I Was Marching" in a Communist monthly called the *New Masses,* she published another, equally radical essay called "Women Are Hungry" in the *American Mercury,* Mencken's magazine, then under the editorship of a Menckenite named Paul Palmer. Mencken had little use for democracy and less for communism. Le Sueur was a Communist. She was also a brilliant writer, at her best in the nonfiction writing her comrades called "three-dimensional reporting"—the new journalism of the Great Depression. The 1930s were bad years for almost everything but art and revolution. They were especially good years for documentary prose, with writers such as Ernest Hemingway, Richard Wright, Dorothy Day, and Langston Hughes conducting experiments in the *New Masses.*

Le Sueur's is one of the most interesting, an attempt to retain the intimacy of subjectivity even while transcending what another radical writer of those years, Josephine Herbst, called the "constricted I." The "constricted I" refers to the first person as means and end, yes, but also to the placid assumptions of writers looking at that which is different from them and seeing in it nothing but exoticism and anecdote.

Herbst proposed a religious solution: "communion." Le Sueur comes close to achieving it.

It's a cliché to say that communism was just a religion by another name. It wasn't; it isn't. But for writers such as Le Sueur, steeped as she was in what she called the "Puritanism" of her forebears, the equally utopian dreams of anarchists such as Emma Goldman (with whom she briefly lived in a commune), and the carnal mysticism of writers such as D. H. Lawrence (whose erotically explicit fiction she credits with saving her life), the line between ideology and theology blurred. Thank God. It was her insistence that writers must write out of "chaotic dark," toward a dream "that did not yet exist," that led to the creation of her most famous essay—famous, that is, among the small circle of those who remember such gorgeously lunatic writers— "I Was Marching."

MERIDEL LE SUEUR
I Was Marching

MINNEAPOLIS, 1934

I have never been in a strike before. It is like looking at something that is happening for the first time and there are no thoughts and no words yet accrued to it. If you come from the middle class, words are likely to mean more than an event. You are likely to think about a thing, and the happening will be the size of a pin point and the words around the happening very large, distorting it queerly. It's a case of "Remembrance of Things Past." When you are in the event, you are likely to have a distinctly individualistic attitude, to be only partly there, and to care more for the happening afterwards than when it is happening. That is why it is hard for a person like myself and others to be in a strike.

Besides, in American life, you hear things happening in a far and muffled way. One thing is said and another happens. Our merchant society has been built upon a huge hypocrisy, a cut-throat competition which sets one man against another and at the same time an ideology mouthing such words as "Humanity," "Truth," the "Golden Rule," and such. Now in a crisis the word falls away and the skeleton of that action shows in terrific movement.

For two days I heard of the strike. I went by their headquarters, I walked by on the opposite side of the street and saw the dark old building that had been a garage and lean, dark young faces leaning from the upstairs windows. I had to go down there often. I looked in. I saw the huge black interior and live coals of living men moving restlessly and orderly, their eyes gleaming from their sweaty faces.

I saw cars leaving filled with grimy men, pickets going to the line, engines roaring out. I stayed close to the door, watching. I didn't go in. I was afraid they would put me out. After all, I could remain a spectator. A man wearing a polo hat kept going around with a large camera taking pictures.

I am putting down exactly how I felt, because I believe others of my class feel the same as I did. I believe it stands for an important psychic change that must take place in all. I saw many artists, writers, professionals, even business men and women standing across the street, too, and I saw in their faces the same longings, the same fears.

The truth is I was afraid. Not of the physical danger at all, but an awful fright of mixing, of losing myself, of being unknown and lost. I felt inferior. I felt no one would know me there, that all I had been trained to excel in would go unnoticed. I can't describe what I felt, but perhaps it will come near it to say that I felt I excelled in competing with others and I knew instantly that these people were NOT competing at all, that they were acting in a strange, powerful trance of movement *together*. And I was filled with longing to act with them and with fear that I could not. I felt I was born out of every kind of life, thrown up alone, looking at other lonely people, a condition I had been in the habit of defending with various attitudes of cynicism, preciosity, defiance, and hatred.

Looking at that dark and lively building, massed with men, I knew my feelings to be those belonging to disruption, chaos, and disintegration and I felt their direct and awful movement, mute and powerful, drawing them into a close and glowing cohesion like a powerful conflagration in the midst of the city. And it filled me with fear and awe and at the same time hope. I knew this action to be prophetic and indicative of future actions and I wanted to be part of it.

Our life seems to be marked with a curious and muffled violence over America, but this action has always been in the dark, men and women dying obscurely, poor and poverty-marked lives, but now from city to city runs this violence, into the open, and colossal happenings stand bare before our eyes, the street churning suddenly upon the pivot of mad violence, whole men suddenly spouting blood and running like living sieves, another holding a dangling arm shot squarely off, a tall youngster, running, tripping over his intestines, and one block away, in the burning sun, gay women shopping and a window dresser trying to decide whether to put green or red voile on a mannequin.

In these terrible happenings you cannot be neutral now. No one can be neutral in the face of bullets.

The next day, with sweat breaking out on my body, I walked past the three guards at the door. They said, "Let the women in. We need women." And I knew it was no joke.

At first I could not see into the dark building. I felt many men coming and going, cars driving through. I had an awful impulse to go into the office which I passed, and offer to do some special work. I saw a sign which said "Get your button." I saw they all had buttons with the date and the number of the union local. I didn't get a button. I wanted to be anonymous.

There seemed to be a current, running down the wooden stairs, towards the front of the building, into the street, that was massed with people, and back again. I followed the current up the old stairs packed closely with hot men and women. As I was going up I could look down and see the lower floor, the cars drawing up to await picket call, the hospital roped off on one side.

Upstairs men sat bolt upright in chairs asleep, their bodies flung in attitudes of peculiar violence of fatigue. A woman nursed her baby. Two young girls slept together on a cot, dressed in overalls. The voice of the loudspeaker filled the room. The immense heat pressed down from the flat ceiling. I stood up against the wall for an hour. No one paid any attention to me. The commissary was in back and the women came out sometimes and sat down, fanning themselves with their aprons and listening to the news over the loudspeaker. A huge man seemed hung on a tiny folding chair. Occasionally some one tiptoed over and brushed the flies off his face. His great head fell over and the sweat poured regularly from his forehead like a spring. I wondered why they took such care of him. They all looked at him tenderly as he slept. I learned later he was a leader on the picket line and had the scalps of more cops to his name than any other.

Three windows flanked the front. I walked over to the windows. A red-headed woman with a button saying "Unemployed Council" was looking out. I looked out with her. A thick crowd stood in the heat below listening to the strike bulletin. We could look right into the windows of the smart club across the street. We could see people peering out of the windows half hidden.

I kept feeling they would put me out. No one paid any attention. The woman said without looking at me, nodding to the palatial house, "It sure is good to see the enemy plain like that." "Yes," I said. I saw that the club was surrounded by a steel picket fence higher than a man. "They know what they put that there fence there for," she said. "Yes," I said. "Well," she said, "I've got to get back to the kitchen. Is it ever hot!" The thermometer said ninety-nine. The sweat ran off us, burning our skins. "The boys'll be coming in," she said, "for their noon feed." She had a scarred face. "Boy, will it be a mad house!" "Do you need any help?" I said eagerly. "Boy," she said, "some of us have been pouring coffee since two o'clock this morning, steady, without no let-up." She started to go. She didn't pay any special attention to me as an individual. She didn't seem to be thinking of me, she didn't seem to see me. I watched her go. I felt rebuffed, hurt. Then I saw instantly she didn't see me because she saw only what she was doing. I ran after her.

✦

I found the kitchen organized like a factory. Nobody asks my name. I am given a large butcher's apron. I realize I have never before worked anonymously. At first I feel strange and then I feel good. The forewoman sets me to washing tin cups. There are not enough cups. We have to wash fast and rinse them and set them up quickly for buttermilk and coffee as the line thickens and the men wait. A little shortish man who is a professional dishwasher is supervising. I feel I won't be able to wash tin cups, but when no one pays any attention except to see that there are enough cups I feel better.

The line grows heavy. The men are coming in from the picket line. Each woman has one thing to do. There is no confusion. I soon learn I am not supposed to help pour the buttermilk. I am not supposed to serve sandwiches. I am supposed to wash tin cups. I suddenly look around and realize all these women are from factories. I know they have learned this organization and specialization in the factory. I look at the round shoulders of the woman cutting bread next to me and I feel I know her. The cups are brought back, washed and put on the counter again. The sweat pours down our faces, but you forget about it.

Then I am changed and put to pouring coffee. At first I look at the men's faces and then I don't look any more. It seems I am pouring coffee for the same tense, dirty sweating face, the same body, the same blue shirt and overalls. Hours go by, the heat is terrific. I am not tired. I am not hot. I am pouring coffee. I am swung into the most intense and natural organization I have ever felt. I know everything that is going on. These things become of great matter to me.

Eyes looking, hands raising a thousand cups, throats burning, eyes bloodshot from lack of sleep, the body dilated to catch every sound over the whole city. Buttermilk? Coffee?

"Is your man here?" the woman cutting sandwiches asks me.

"No," I say, then I lie for some reason, peering around as if looking eagerly for someone, "I don't see him now."

But I was pouring coffee for living men.

For a long time, about one o'clock, it seemed like something was about to happen. Women seemed to be pouring into headquarters to be near their men. You could hear only lies over the radio. And lies in the papers. Nobody knew precisely what was happening, but everyone thought something would happen in a few hours. You could feel the men being poured out of the hall onto the picket line. Every few minutes cars left and more drew up and were filled. The voice at the loudspeaker was accelerated, calling for men, calling for picket cars.

I could hear the men talking about the arbitration board, the truce that was supposed to be maintained while the board sat with the Governor. They listened to every word over the loudspeaker. A terrible communal excitement ran through the hall like a fire through a forest. I could hardly breathe. I seemed to have no body at all except the body of this excitement. I felt that what had happened before had not been a real movement, these false words and actions had taken place on the periphery. The real action was about to show, the real intention.

We kept on pouring thousands of cups of coffee, feeding thousands of men.

The chef with a woman tattooed on his arm was just dishing the last of the stew. It was about two o'clock. The commissary was about empty. We went into the front hall. It was drained of men. The chairs were empty. The voice of the announcer was excited. "The men are massed at the market," he said. "Something is going to happen." I sat down beside a woman who was holding her hands tightly together, leaning forward listening, her eyes bright and dilated. I had never seen her before. She took my hands. She pulled me towards her. She was crying. "It's awful," she said. "Something awful is going to happen. They've taken both my children away from me and now something is going to happen to all those men." I held her hands. She had a green ribbon around her hair.

The action seemed reversed. The cars were coming back. The announcer cried, "This is murder." Cars were coming in. I don't know how we got to the stairs. Everyone seemed to be converging at a menaced point. I saw below the crowd stirring, uncoiling. I saw them taking men out of cars and putting them on the hospital cots, on the floor. At first I felt frightened, the close black area of the barn, the blood, the heavy moment, the sense of myself lost, gone. But I couldn't have turned away now. A woman clung to my hand. I was pressed against the body of another. If you are to understand anything you must understand it in the muscular event, in actions we have not been trained for. Something broke all my surfaces in something that was beyond horror and I was dabbing alcohol on the gaping wounds that buckshot makes, hanging open like crying mouths. Buckshot wounds splay in the body and then swell like a blow. Ness, who died, had thirty-eight slugs in his body, in the chest and in the back.

The picket cars keep coming in. Some men have walked back from the market, holding their own blood in. They move in a great explosion, and the newness of the movement makes it seem like something under ether, moving terrifically towards a culmination.

From all over the city workers are coming. They gather outside in two great half-circles, cut in two to let the ambulances in. A traffic cop is still directing traffic at the corner and the crowd cannot stand to see him. "We'll give you just two seconds to beat it," they tell him. He goes away quickly. A striker takes over the street.

Men, women, and children are massing outside, a living circle close packed for protection. From the tall office building business men are looking down on the black swarm thickening, coagulating into what action they cannot tell.

We have living blood on our skirts.

That night at eight o'clock a mass meeting was called of all labor. It was to be in a parking lot two blocks from headquarters. All the women gather at the front of the building with collection cans, ready to march to the meeting. I have not been home. It never occurs to me to leave. The twilight is eerie and the men are saying that the chief of police is going to attack the meeting and raid headquarters. The smell of blood hangs in the hot, still air. Rumors strike at the taut nerves. The dusk looks ghastly with what might be in the next half hour.

"If you have any children," a woman said to me, "you better not go." I looked at the desperate women's faces, the broken feet, the torn and hanging pelvis, the worn and lovely bodies of women who persist under such desperate labors. I shivered, though it was 96 degrees and the sun had been down a good hour.

The parking lot was already full of people when we got there and men swarmed the adjoining roofs. An elegant cafe stood across the street with water sprinkling from its roof and splendidly dressed men and women stood on the steps as if looking at a show.

The platform was the bullet-riddled truck of the afternoon's fray. We had been told to stand close to this platform, so we did, making the center of a wide massed circle that stretched as far as we could see. We seemed buried like minerals in a mass, packed body to body. I felt again that peculiar heavy silence in which there is the real form of the happening. My eyes burn. I can hardly see. I seem to be standing like an animal in ambush. I have the brightest, most physical feeling with every sense sharpened peculiarly. The movements, the masses that I see and feel I have never known before. I only partly know what I am seeing, feeling, but I feel it is the real body and gesture of a future vitality. I see that there is a bright clot of women drawn close to a bullet-riddled truck. I am one of them, yet I don't feel myself at all. It is curious, I feel most alive and yet for the first time in my life I do not feel myself as separate. I realize then that all my previous feelings have been based on feeling myself separate and distinct from others and now I sense sharply faces, bodies, closeness, and my own fear is not my own alone, nor my hope.

The strikers keep moving up cars. We keep moving back together to let cars pass and form between us and a brick building that flanks the parking lot. They are connecting the loudspeaker, testing it. Yes, they are moving up lots of cars, through the crowd and lining them closely side by side. There must be ten thousand people now, heat rising from them. They are standing silent, watching the platform, watching the cars being brought up. The silence seems terrific like a great form moving of itself. This is real movement issuing from the close reality of mass feeling. This is the first real rhythmic movement I have ever seen. My heart hammers terrifically. My hands are swollen and hot. No one is producing this movement. It is a movement upon which all are moving softly, rhythmically, terribly.

No matter how many times I looked at what was happening I hardly knew what I saw. I looked and I saw time and time again that there were men standing close to us, around us, and then suddenly I knew that there was a living chain of men standing shoulder to shoulder, forming a circle around the group of women. They stood shoulder to shoulder slightly moving like a thick vine from the pressure behind, but standing tightly woven like a living wall, moving gently.

I saw that the cars were now lined one close fitted to the other with strikers sitting on the roofs and closely packed on the running boards. They could see far over the crowd. "What are they doing that for?" I said. No one answered. The wide dilated eyes of the women were like my own. No one seemed to be answering questions now. They simply spoke, cried out, moved together now.

The last car drove in slowly, the crowd letting them through without command or instruction. "A little closer," someone said. "Be sure they are close." Men sprang up to direct whatever action was needed and then subsided again and no one had noticed who it was. They stepped forward to direct a needed action and then fell anonymously back again.

We all watched carefully the placing of the cars. Sometimes we looked at each other. I didn't understand that look. I felt uneasy. It was as if something escaped me. And then suddenly, on my very body, I knew what they were doing, as if it had been communicated to me from a thousand eyes, a thousand silent throats, as if it had been shouted in the loudest voice.

THEY WERE BUILDING A BARRICADE.

Two men died from that day's shooting. Men lined up to give one of them a blood transfusion, but he died. Black Friday, men called the murderous day. Night and day workers held their children up to see the body of Ness who died. Tuesday, the day of the funeral, one thousand more militia were massed downtown.

It was still over ninety in the shade. I went to the funeral parlors and thousands of men and women were massed there waiting in the terrific sun. One block of women and children were standing two hours waiting. I went over and stood near them. I didn't know whether I could march. I didn't like marching in parades. Besides, I felt they might not want me.

I stood aside not knowing if I would march. I couldn't see how they would ever organize it anyway. No one seemed to be doing much.

At 3:40 some command went down the ranks. I said foolishly at the last minute, "I don't belong to the auxiliary—could I march?" Three women drew me in. "We want all to march," they said gently. "Come with us."

The giant mass uncoiled like a serpent and straightened out ahead and to my amazement on a lift of road I could see six blocks of massed men, four abreast, with bare heads, moving straight on and as they moved, uncoiled the mass behind and pulled it after them. I felt myself walking, accelerating my speed with the others as the line stretched, pulled taut, then held its rhythm.

Not a cop was in sight. The cortege moved through the stop-and-go signs, it seemed to lift of its own dramatic rhythm, coming from the intention of every person there. We were moving spontaneously in a movement, natural, hardy, and miraculous.

We passed through six blocks of tenements, through a sea of grim faces, and there was not a sound. There was the curious shuffle of thousands of feet, without drum or bugle, in ominous silence, a march not heavy as the military, but very light, exactly with the heart beat.

I was marching with a million hands, movements, faces, and my own movement was repeating again and again, making a new movement from these many gestures, the walking, falling back, the open mouth crying, the nostrils stretched apart, the raised hand, the blow falling, and the outstretched hand drawing me in.

I felt my legs straighten. I felt my feet join in that strange shuffle of thousands of bodies moving with direction, of thousands of feet, and my own breath with the gigantic breath. As if an electric charge had passed through me, my hair stood on end. I was marching.

1935

✦

I'm tempted to end this parade of tales here, with this story. "Hoodoo," as Hurston explains in an earlier chapter of *Mules and Men*, her underappreciated 1935 masterpiece, is how black people in Louisiana referred in her time to what white people called "voodoo." What I'd like to call this piece is "The Great Exception." It's the exception to the earnest rule of 1930s documentary realism. Or maybe, if it didn't sound like a term of financial chicanery, I'd call it "The Full Realization." Because this is a story of crossing over. Not of conversion. It's not a simple story of one thing, a writer, becoming another, a believer. It's a story of one thing, a writer, crossing over, still a writer, into the country, the territory, the swamp of the believers. That's what makes Hurston so astonishing. She crossed over and kept herself intact. "Full of reality, full of illusion," as Whitman wrote. That double vision, like W. E. B. DuBois's "double consciousness," wasn't just a metaphor for Hurston. "A pair of eyes," she writes, describing her double identity as a writer/hoodoo doctor following the initiation rite described below, "was painted on my cheeks as a sign that I could see in more ways than one." Painted on her cheeks! With paint! The mark, made.

That's what we're in this for. Not the mark but the vision. To learn "to see in more ways than one." That's why we chase after literary journalism, the hybrid genre, the monster genre—half-report, half-story; half-ethnography, half-magic.

ZORA NEALE HURSTON
Hoodoo

Now I was in New Orleans and I asked. They told me Algiers, the part of New Orleans that is across the river to the west. I went there and lived for four months and asked. I found women reading cards and doing mail order business in names and insinuations of well known factors in conjure. Nothing worth putting on paper. But they all claimed some knowledge and link with Marie Leveau. From so much of hearing the name I asked everywhere for this Leveau and everybody told me differently. But from what they said I was eager to know to the end of the talk. It carried me back across the river into the Vieux Carré. All agreed that she had lived and died in the French quarter of New Orleans. So I went there to ask.

I found an oil painting of the queen of conjure on the walls of the Cabildo, and mention of her in the guide books of New Orleans, but I did a lot of stumbling and asking before I heard of Luke Turner, himself a hoodoo doctor, who says that he is her nephew.

When I found out about Turner, I had already studied under five two-headed doctors and had gone thru an initiation ceremony with each. So I asked Turner to take me as a pupil. He was very cold. In fact he showed no eagerness even to talk with me. He feels sure of his powers and seeks no one. He refused to take me as a pupil and in addition to his habitual indifference I could see he had no faith in my sincerity. I could see him searching my face for whatever was behind what I said. The City of New Orleans has a law against fortune tellers, hoodoo doctors and the like, and Turner did not know me. He asked me to excuse him as he was waiting upon someone in the inner room. I let him go but I sat right there and waited. When he returned, he tried to shoo me away by being rude. I stayed on. Finally he named an impossible price for tuition. I stayed and dickered. He all but threw me out, but I stayed and urged him.

I made three more trips before he would talk to me in any way that I could feel encouraged. He talked about Marie Leveau because I asked. I wanted to know if she was really as great as they told me. So he enlightened my ignorance and taught me. We sat before the soft coal fire in his grate.

"Time went around pointing out what God had already made. Moses had seen the Burning Bush. Solomon by magic knowed all wisdom. And Marie Leveau was a woman in New Orleans.

"She was born February 2, 1827. Anybody don't believe I tell the truth can go look at the book in St. Louis Cathedral. Her mama and her papa, they wasn't married and his name was Christophe Glapion.

"She was very pretty, one of the Creole Quadroons, and many people said she would never be a hoodoo doctor like her mama and her grandma before her. She liked to go to the balls very much where all the young men fell in love with her. But Alexander, the great two-headed doctor, felt the power in her and so he tell her she must come to study with him. Marie, she rather dance and make love, but one day a rattlesnake come to her in her bedroom and spoke to her. So she went to Alexander and studied. But soon she could teach her teacher and the snake stayed with her always.

"She has her house on St. Anne Street and people come from the ends of America to get help from her. Even Queen Victoria ask her help and send her a cashmere shawl with money also.

"Now, some white people say she hold hoodoo dance on Congo Square every week. But Marie Leveau never hold no hoodoo dance. That was a pleasure dance. They beat the drum with the shin bone of a donkey and everybody dance like they do in Hayti. Hoodoo is private. She give the dance the first Friday night in each month and they have crab gumbo and rice to eat and the people dance. The white people come look on, and think they see all, when they only see a dance.

"The police hear so much about Marie Leveau that they come to her house in St. Anne Street to put her in jail. First one come, she stretch out her left hand and he turn round and round and never stop until some one come lead him away. Then two come together—she put them to running and barking like dogs. Four come and she put them to beating each other with night sticks. The whole station force come. They knock at her door. She know who they are before she ever look. She did work at her altar and they all went to sleep on her steps.

"Out on Lake Pontchartrain at Bayou St. John she hold a great feast every year on the Eve of St. John's, June 24th. It is Midsummer Eve, and the Sun give special benefits then and need great honor. The special drum be played then. It is a cowhide stretched over a half-barrel. Beat with a jaw-bone. Some say a man but I think they do not know. I think the jawbone of an ass or a cow. She hold the feast of St. John's partly because she is a Catholic and partly because of hoodoo.

"The ones around her altar fix everything for the feast. Nobody see Marie Leveau for nine days before the feast. But when the great crowd of people at the feast call upon her, she would rise out of the waters of the lake with a great communion candle burning upon her head and another in each one of her hands. She walked upon the waters to the shore. As a little boy I saw her myself. When the feast was over, she went back into the lake, and nobody saw her for nine days again.

"On the feast that I saw her open the waters, she looked hard at me and nodded her head so that her tignon shook. Then I knew I was called to take up her work. She was very old and I was a lad of seventeen. Soon I went to wait upon her Altar, both on St. Anne Street and her house on Bayou St. John's.

"The rattlesnake that had come to her a little one when she was also young was very huge. He piled great upon his altar and took nothing from the food set before him. One night he sang and Marie Leveau called me from my sleep to look at him and see. 'Look well, Turner,' she told me. 'No one shall hear and see such as this for many centuries.'

"She went to her Great Altar and made great ceremony. The snake finished his song and seemed to sleep. She drove me back to my bed and went again to her Altar.

"The next morning, the great snake was not at his altar. His hide was before the Great Altar stuffed with spices and things of power. Never did I know what become of his flesh. It is said that the snake went off to the woods alone after the death of Marie Leveau, but they don't know. This is his skin that I wear about my shoulders whenever I reach for power.

"Three days Marie, she set at the Altar with the great sun candle burning and shining in her face. She set the water upon the Altar and turned to the window, and looked upon the lake. The sky grew dark. The lightning raced to the seventeen quarters of the heavens and the lake heaved like a mighty herd of cattle rolling in a pasture. The house shook with the earth.

"She told me, 'You are afraid. That is right, you should fear. Go to your own house and build an altar. Power will come.' So I hurried to my mother's house and told them.

"Some who loved her hurried out to Bayou St. John and tried to enter the house but she try hard to send them off. They beat upon the door, but she will not open. The terrible strong wind at last tore the house away and set it in the lake. The thunder and lightning grow greater. Then the loving ones find a boat and went out to where her house floats on one side and break a window to bring her out, but she begs, 'NO! Please, no,' she tell them. 'I want to die here in the lake,' but they would not permit her. She did not wish their destruction, so she let herself be drawn away from her altar in the lake. And the wind, the thunder and lightning, and the water all ceased the moment she set foot on dry land.

"That night she also sing a song and is dead, yes. So I have the snake skin and do works with the power she leave me."

"How did Marie Leveau do her work?" I asked, feeling that I had gotten a little closer to him.

"She go to her great Altar and seek until she become the same as the spirit, then she come out into the room where she listens to them that come to ask. When they finish she answer them as a god. If a lady have a bad enemy and come to her she go into her altar room and when she come out and take her seat, the lady will say to her:

"'Oh, Good Mother. I come to you with my heart bowed down and my shoulders drooping, and my spirits broken; for an enemy has sorely tried me; has caused my loved ones to leave me; has taken from me my worldly goods and my gold; has spoken meanly of me and caused my friends to lose faith in me. On my knees I pray to you, Good Mother, that you will cause confusion to reign in the house of my enemy and that you will take their power from them and cause them to be unsuccessful.'

"Marie Leveau is not a woman when she answer the one who ask. No, She is a god, yes. Whatever she say, it will come so. She say:

"'Oh, my daughter, I have heard your woes and your pains and tribulations, and in the depth of the wisdom of the gods I will help you find peace and happiness.

"'It is written that you will take of the Vinagredes Four Volle* for him, and you will dip into it a sheet of pure parchment paper, and

---

* Four Thieves Vinegar. [All notes in this essay are Hurston's.]

on this sheet you will write the names of your enemies and send it to the house of your enemies, tightly sealed with the wax of a porcupine plant.

"'Then when the sun shall have risen and gone down three times, you will take of the water of Mars, called War Water, and in front of the house of your enemy you will sprinkle it. This you will do as you pass by. If it be a woman, you will take the egg of a guinea fowl, and put it into the powder of the fruit of cayenne and the dust of Goofer,* and you will set it on the fire in your own house and in clear water from the skies you will boil it until it shall be hard. This you will do so that there shall be no fruit from her womb.

"'And you shall take of the Damnation Powders, two drachmas, and of the water powders, two drachmas and make a package of it and send it to the home of the one who has spoken badly of you and has treated you mean, so that damnation and trouble shall be on the head of your enemy and not on you.

"'You will do this so that you will undo your enemies and you will take the power to harm you away from your enemies.

"'Oh daughter, go you in peace and do the works required of you, so that you will have rest and comfort from your enemies and that they will have not the power to harm you and lower you in the sight of your people and belittle you in the sight of your friends. So be it.'"

By the time that Turner had finished his recitation he wasn't too conscious of me. In fact he gave me the feeling that he was just speaking, but not for my benefit. He was away off somewhere. He made a final dramatic gesture with open hands and hushed for a minute. Then he sank deeper into himself and went on:

"But when she put the last curse on a person, it would be better if that man was dead, yes."

With an impatient gesture he signaled me not to interrupt him.

"She set the altar for the curse with black candles that have

---

* Dirt taken out of a grave.

been dressed in vinegar. She would write the name of the person to be cursed on the candle with a needle. Then she place fifteen cents in the lap of Death upon the altar to pay the spirit to obey her orders. Then she place her hands flat upon the table and say the curse-prayer.

"'To The Man God: Oh great One, I have been sorely tried by my enemies and have been blasphemed and lied against. My good thoughts and my honest actions have been turned to bad actions and dishonest ideas. My home has been disrespected, my children have been cursed and ill-treated. My dear ones have been backbitten and their virtue questioned. O Man God, I beg that this that I ask for my enemies shall come to pass:

"'That the South wind shall scorch their bodies and make them wither and shall not be tempered to them. That the North wind shall freeze their blood and numb their muscles and that it shall not be tempered to them. That the West wind shall blow away their life's breath and will not leave their hair grow, and that their finger nails shall fall off and their bones shall crumble. That the East wind shall make their minds grow dark, their sight shall fail and their seed dry up so that they shall not multiply.

"'I ask that their fathers and mothers from their furtherest generation will not intercede for them before the great throne, and the wombs of their women shall not bear fruit except for strangers', and that they shall become extinct. I pray that the children who may come shall be weak of mind and paralyzed of limb and that they themselves shall curse them in their turn for ever turning the breath of life into their bodies. I pray that disease and death shall be forever with them and that their worldly goods shall not prosper, and that their crops shall not multiply and that their cows, their sheep, and their hogs and all their living beasts shall die of starvation and thirst. I pray that their house shall be unroofed and that the rain, the thunder and lightning shall find the innermost recesses of their home and that the foundation shall crumble and the floods tear it asunder. I pray that the sun shall not shed its rays on them in benevolence, but instead it shall beat down on them and burn them and destroy them. I pray that the moon shall not give them peace, but instead shall deride them and decry them and cause their minds to shrivel. I pray that their friends shall betray them and cause them loss of power, of gold and of silver, and that their enemies shall smite them until they beg for mercy which shall not be given them. I pray that their tongues shall forget how to speak in sweet words, and that it shall be paralyzed and that all about them will be desolation, pestilence and death. O Man God, I ask you for all these things because they have dragged me in the dust and destroyed my good name; broken my heart and caused me to curse the day that I was born. So be it.'"

Turner again made that gesture with his hands that meant the end. Then he sat in a dazed silence. My own spirits had been falling all during the terrible curse and he did not have to tell me to be quiet this time. After a long period of waiting I rose to go. "The Spirit say you come back tomorrow," he breathed as I passed his knees. I nodded that I had heard and went out. The next day he began to prepare me for my initiation ceremony, for rest assured that no one may approach the Altar without the crown, and none may wear the crown of power without preparation. *It must be earned.*

And what is this crown of power? Nothing definite in material. Turner crowned me with a consecrated snake skin. I have been crowned in other places with flowers, with ornamental paper, with cloth, with sycamore bark, with egg-shells. It is the meaning, not the material that counts. The crown without the preparation means no more than a college diploma without the four years' work.

This preparation period is akin to that of all mystics. Clean living, even to clean thoughts. A sort of going to the wilderness in the spirit. The details do not matter. My nine days being up, and possessed of the three snakeskins and the new underwear required, I entered Turner's house as an inmate to finish the last three days of my novitiate. Turner had become so sure of my fitness as a hoodoo doctor that he would accept no money from me except what was necessary to defray the actual cost of the ceremony.

So I ate my final meal before six o'clock of the evening before and went to bed for the last time with my right stocking on and my left leg bare.

I entered the old pink stucco house in the Vieux Carré at nine o'clock in the morning with the parcel of needed things. Turner placed the new underwear on the big Altar; prepared the couch with the snake-skin cover upon which I was to lie for three days. With the help of other members of the college of hoodoo doctors called together to initiate me, the snake skins I had brought were made into garments for me to wear. One was coiled into a high headpiece — the crown. One had loops attached to slip on my arms so that it could be worn as a shawl, and the other was made into a girdle for my loins. All places have significance. These garments were placed on the small altar in the corner. The throne of the snake. The Great One* was called upon to enter the garments and dwell there.

I was made ready and at three o'clock in the afternoon, naked as I came into the world, I was stretched, face downwards, my navel to the snake skin cover, and began my three day search for the spirit that he might accept me or reject me according to his will. Three days my body must lie silent and fasting while my spirit went wherever spirits must go that seek answers never given to men as men.

I could have no food, but a pitcher of water was placed on a small table at the head of the couch, that my spirit might not waste time in search of water which should be spent in search of the Power-Giver. The spirit must have water, and if none had been provided it would wander in search of it. And evil spirits might attack it as it wandered about dangerous places. If it should be seriously injured, it might never return to me.

---

* The Spirit.

For sixty-nine hours I lay there. I had five psychic experiences and awoke at last with no feeling of hunger, only one of exaltation.

I opened my eyes because Turner called me. He stood before the Great Altar dressed ceremoniously. Five others were with him.

"Seeker, come," Turner called.

I made to rise and go to him. Another laid his hand upon me lightly, restraining me from rising.

"How must I come?" he asked in my behalf.

"You must come to the spirit across running water," Turner answered in a sort of chant.

So a tub was placed beside the bed. I was assisted to my feet and led to the tub. Two men poured water into the tub while I stepped into it and out again on the other side.

"She has crossed the dangerous stream in search of the spirit," the one who spoke for me, chanted.

"The spirit does not know her name. What is she called?"

"She has no name but what the spirit gives."

"I see her conquering and accomplishing with the lightning and making her road with thunder. She shall be called the Rain-Bringer."

I was stretched again upon the couch. Turner approached me with two brothers, one on either side of him. One held a small paint brush dipped in yellow, the other bore one dipped in red. With ceremony Turner painted the lightning symbol down my back from my right shoulder to my left hip. This was to be my sign forever. The Great One was to speak to me in storms.

I was now dressed in the new underwear and a white veil was placed over my head, covering my face, and I was seated in a chair.

After I was dressed, a pair of eyes was painted on my cheeks as a sign that I could see in more ways than one. The sun was painted on my forehead. Many came into the room and performed ceremonial acts, but none spoke to me. Nor could I speak to them while the veil covered my face. Turner cut the little finger of my right hand and caught the gushing blood in a wine cup. He added wine and mixed it with the blood. Then he and all the other five leaders let blood from themselves also and mixed it with wine in another glass. I was led to drink from the cup containing their mingled bloods, and each of them in turn beginning with Turner drank mine. At high noon I was seated at the splendid altar. It was dressed in the center with a huge communion candle with my name upon it set in sand, five large iced cakes in different colors, a plate of honeyed St. Joseph's bread, a plate of serpent-shaped breads, spinach and egg cakes fried in olive oil, breaded Chinese okra fried in olive oil, roast veal and wine, two huge yellow bouquets, two red bouquets and two white bouquets and thirty-six yellow tapers and a bottle of holy water.

Turner seated me and stood behind me with his ceremonial hat upon his head, and the crown of power in his hand. "Spirit! I ask you to take her. Do you hear me, Spirit? Will you take her? Spirit, I want you to take her, she is worthy!" He held the crown poised above my head for a full minute. A profound silence held the room. Then he lifted the veil from my face and let it fall behind my head and crowned me with power. He lit my candle for me. But from then on I might be a candle-lighter myself. All the candles were reverently lit. We all sat down and ate the feast. First a glass of blessed oil was handed me by Turner. "Drink this without tasting it." I gulped it down and he took the glass from my hand, took a sip of the little that remained. Then he handed it to the brother at his right who did the same, until it went around the table.

"Eat first the spinach cakes," Turner exhorted, and we did. Then the meal began. It was full of joy and laughter, even though we knew that the final ceremony waited only for the good hour of twelve midnight.

About ten o'clock we all piled into an old Studebaker sedan — all but Turner who led us on a truck. Out Road No. 61 we rattled until a certain spot was reached. The truck was unloaded beside the road and sent back to town. It was a little after eleven. The swamp was dismal and damp, but after some stumbly walking we came to a little glade deep in the wood, near the lake. A candle was burning at each of the four corners of the clearing, representing the four corners of the world and the four winds. I could hear the occasional slap-slap of the water. With a whispered chant some twigs were gathered and tied into a broom. Some pine straw was collected. The sheets of typing paper I had been urged to bring were brought out and nine sheets were blessed and my petition written nine times on each sheet by the light from a shaded lantern. The crate containing the black sheep was opened and the sheep led forward into the center of the circle. He stood there dazedly while the chant of strange syllables rose. I asked Turner the words, but he replied that in good time I would know what to say. It was not to be taught. If nothing came, to be silent. The head and withers of the sheep were stroked as the chanting went on. Turner became more and more voluble. At last he seized the straw and stuffed some into the sheep's nostrils. The animal struggled. A knife flashed and the sheep dropped to its knees, then fell prone with its mouth open in a weak cry. My petition was thrust into its throat that he might cry it to the Great One. The broom was seized and dipped in the blood from the slit throat and the ground swept vigorously — back and forth, back and forth — the length of the dying sheep. It was swept from the four winds toward the center. The sweeping went on as long as the blood gushed. Earth, the mother of the Great One and us all, has been appeased. With a sharp stick Turner traced the outline of the sheep and the digging commenced. The sheep was never touched. The ground was dug from under him so that his body dropped down into the hole. He was covered with nine sheets of paper bearing the petition and the earth heaped upon him. A white candle was set upon the grave and we straggled back to the road and the Studebaker.

I studied under Turner five months and learned all of the Leveau routines; but in this book all of the works of any doctor cannot be given. However, we performed several of Turner's own routines.

Once a woman, an excited, angry woman, wanted something done to keep her husband true. So she came and paid Turner gladly for his services.

Turner took a piece of string that had been "treated" at the altar and gave it to the woman.

"Measure the man where I tell you. But he must never know. Measure him in his sleep then fetch back the string to me."

The next day the woman came at ten o'clock instead of nine as Turner had told her, so he made her wait until twelve o'clock, that being a good hour. Twelve is one of the benign hours of the day while ten is a malignant hour. Then Turner took the string and tied nine knots in it and tied it to a larger piece of string which he tied about her waist. She was completely undressed for the ceremony and Turner cut some hair from under her left armpit and some from the right side of the groin and put it together. Then he cut some from the right arm pit and a tuft from the left groin and it was all placed on the altar, and burned in a votive light with the wish for her husband to love her and forget all others. She went away quite happy. She was so satisfied with the work that she returned with a friend a few days later.

Turner, with this toothless mouth, his Berber-looking face, said to the new caller:

"I can see you got trouble." He shivered. "It is all in the room. I feel the pain of it; Anger, Malice. Tell me who is this man you so fight with?"

"My husband's brother. He hate me and make all the trouble he can," the woman said in a tone so even and dull that it was hard to believe she meant what she said. "He must leave this town or die. Yes, it is much better if he is dead." Then she burst out, "Yeah, he should be dead long time ago. Long before he spy upon me, before he tell lies, lies, lies. I should be very happy for his funeral."

"Oh I can feel the great hate around you," Turner said. "It follow you everywhere, but I kill nobody, I send him away if you want so he never come back. I put guards along the road in the spirit world, and these he cannot pass, no. When he go, never will he come back to New Orleans. You see him no more. He will be forgotten and all his works."

"Then I am satisfied, yes," the woman said. "When will you send him off?"

"I ask the spirit, you will know."

She paid him and he sent her off and Turner went to his snake altar and sat in silence for a long time. When he arose, he sent me out to buy nine black chickens, and some Four Thieves Vinegar.* He himself went out and got nine small sticks upon which he had me write the troublesome brother-in-law's name—one time on each stick. At ten that night we went out into the small interior court so prevalent in New Orleans and drove nine stakes into the ground. The left leg of a chicken was tied to each stake. Then a fire was built with the nine sticks on which the name had been written. The ground was sprinkled all over with the Four Thieves Vinegar and Turner began his dance. From the fire to the circle of fluttering chickens and back again to the fire. The feathers were picked from the heads of the chickens in the frenzy of the dance and scattered to the four winds. He called the victim's name each time as he whirled three times with the chicken's head-feathers in his hand, then he flung them far.

The terrified chickens flopped and fluttered frantically in the dim firelight. I had been told to keep up the chant of the victim's name in rhythm and to beat the ground with a stick. This I did with fervor and Turner danced on. One by one the chickens were seized and killed by having their heads pulled off. But Turner was in such a condition with his whirling and dancing that he seemed in a hypnotic state. When the last fowl was dead, Turner drank a great draught of wine and sank before the altar. When he arose, we gathered some ashes from the fire and sprinkled the bodies of the dead chickens and I was told to get out the car. We drove out one of the main highways for a mile and threw one

* A conjure mixture.

of the chickens away. Then another mile and another chicken until the nine dead chickens had been disposed of. The spirits of the dead chickens had been instructed never to let the trouble-maker pass inward to New Orleans again after he had passed them going out.

One day Turner told me that he had taught me all that he could and he was quite satisfied with me. He wanted me to stay and work with him as a partner. He said that soon I would be in possession of the entire business, for the spirit had spoken to him and told him that I was the last doctor that he would make; that one year and seventy-nine days from then he would die. He wanted me to stay with him to the end. It has been a great sorrow to me that I could not say yes.

1953

"Artists in Uniform" originally appeared in the March 1953 issue of *Harper's* magazine as "Artists in Uniform: A Story by Mary McCarthy." Almost a year later, in the February 1954 edition of the magazine, McCarthy, a novelist and essayist today remembered best for her *Memoirs of a Catholic Schoolgirl*, published an addendum. An essay of its own, actually, called "Settling the Colonel's Hash." In it she addresses the questions sent to her by readers about "the chief moral or meaning" of the original piece, in which McCarthy describes her encounter with an anti-Semitic colonel and the lunch at which he orders hash. The hash, she explains, is not a symbol of anything; it's what the colonel ordered. And there are nuns in the piece because there were nuns on the train she shared with the colonel, and the "Mary McCarthy" in the story is depicted as wearing a green dress because McCarthy wore a green dress. That is all.

That's true only if there's no deeper level to our experience of the world than what you see. But "Artists in Uniform," a study of perception and its faults, suggests otherwise. McCarthy repeatedly emphasizes the colonel's "hawklike" face, first as expressive of his cruel manner, then as a contrast to the dull limits of his understanding.

Meanwhile, she worries that he'll see her green dress as a symbol of bohemianism that will undermine the cool reason of her case against anti-Semitism. She then frets that her alleged bohemianism does, in fact, undermine her cool reason. She works herself up to a theological fervor in her arguments with the colonel only to collapse into confused disbelief. What if the colonel's anti-Semitism isn't a matter of "religion"? What if her "anti-anti-Semitism" is its own kind of religious conviction?

Asking these questions, and answering them in the form of a story in which "the chief interest," she later wrote, "lay in the fact that it happened," goes to the essence of the fiction of literary nonfiction. "Fiction," after all, means "to arrange." McCarthy takes the facts of her encounter and arranges them. She does not make them up. She did wear a green dress. But she tells us about this dress, and then tells us again, shows it to us through her eyes and through her imagination of the colonel's perception. Likewise the colonel's ideas about Jews. He actually said these awful things. But the story is McCarthy's arrangement of the colonel's utterance of the words and of her changing perception of their meaning. That is, what they mean to the colonel and what they mean to her and what they might mean to you, the reader, observing the pair at lunch, McCarthy with her face "like a map of Ireland" and the colonel with his hash, between them a cloud of perception and misperception they both label "the Jews."

MARY McCARTHY
Artists in Uniform

The Colonel went out sailing,
He spoke with Turk and Jew . . .

"Pour it on, Colonel," cried the young man in the Dacron suit excitedly, making his first sortie into the club-car conversation. His face was white as Roquefort and of a glistening, cheese-like texture; he had a shock of tow-colored hair, badly cut and greasy, and a snub nose with large gray pores. Under his darting eyes were two black craters. He appeared to be under some intense nervous strain and had sat the night before in the club car drinking bourbon with beer chasers and leafing magazines which he frowningly tossed aside, like cards into a discard heap. This morning he had come in late, with a hangdog, hangover look, and had been sitting tensely forward on a settee, smoking cigarettes and following the conversation with little twitches of the nose and quivers of the body, as a dog follows a human conversation, veering its mistrustful eyeballs from one speaker to another and raising its head eagerly at its master's voice. The Colonel's voice, rich and light and plausible, had in fact abruptly risen and swollen, as he pronounced his last sentence. "I can tell you one thing," he said harshly. "They weren't named Ryan or Murphy!"

A sort of sigh, as of consummation, ran through the club car. "Pour it on, Colonel, give it to them, Colonel, that's right, Colonel," urged the young man in a transport of admiration. The Colonel fingered his collar and modestly smiled. He was a thin, hawklike, black-haired handsome man with a bright blue bloodshot eye and a well-pressed, well-tailored uniform that did not show the effects of the heat — the train, westbound for St. Louis, was passing through Indiana, and, as usual in a heat-wave, the air-conditioning had not met the test. He wore the Air Force insignia, and there was something in his light-boned, spruce figure and keen, knifelike profile that suggested a classic image of the aviator, ready to cut, piercing, into space. In base fact, however, the Colonel was in procurement, as we heard him tell the mining engineer who had just bought him a drink. From several silken hints that parachuted into the talk, it was patent to us that the Colonel was a man who knew how to enjoy this earth and its pleasures: he led, he gave us to think, a bachelor's life of abstemious dissipation and well-rounded sensuality. He had accepted the engineer's drink with a mere nod of the glass in acknowledgment, like a genial Mars quaffing a libation; there was clearly no prospect of his buying a second in return, not if the train were to travel from here to the Mojave Desert. In the same way, an understanding had arisen that I, the only woman in the club car, had become the Colonel's perquisite; it was taken for granted, without an invitation's being issued, that I was to lunch with him in St. Louis, where we each had a wait between trains — my plans for seeing the city in a taxicab were dashed.

From the beginning, as we eyed each other over my volume of Dickens ("*The Christmas Carol?*" suggested the Colonel, opening relations), I had guessed that the Colonel was of Irish stock, and this, I felt, gave me an advantage, for he did not suspect the same of me; strangely so, for I am supposed to have the map of Ireland written on my features.

In fact, he had just wagered, with a jaunty, sidelong grin at the mining engineer, that my people "came from Boston from way back," and that I — narrowed glance, running, like steel measuring-tape, up and down my form — was a professional sculptress. I might have laughed this off, as a crudely bad guess like his *Christmas Carol*, if I had not seen the engineer nodding gravely, like an idol, and the peculiar young man bobbing his head up and down in mute applause and agreement. I was wearing a bright apple-green raw silk blouse and a dark-green rather full raw silk skirt, plus a pair of pink glass earrings; my hair was done up in a bun. It came to me, for the first time, with a sort of dawning horror, that I had begun, in the course of years, without ever guessing it, to look irrevocably Bohemian. Refracted from the three men's eyes was a strange vision of myself as an artist, through and through, stained with my occupation like the dyer's hand. All I lacked, apparently, was a pair of sandals. My sick heart sank to my Ferragamo shoes; I had always particularly preened myself on being an artist in disguise. And it was not only a question of personal vanity — it seemed to me that the writer or intellectual had a certain missionary usefulness in just such accidental gatherings as this, if he spoke not as an intellectual but as a normal member of the public. Now, thanks to the Colonel, I slowly became aware that my contributions to the club-car conversation were being watched and assessed as coming from *a certain quarter*. My costume, it seemed, carefully assembled as it had been at an expensive shop, was to these observers simply a uniform that blazoned a caste and allegiance just as plainly as the Colonels' khaki and eagles. "*Gardez*," I said to myself. But as the conversation grew tenser and I endeavored to keep cool, I began to writhe within myself, and every time I looked down, my contrasting greens seemed to be growing more and more lurid and taking on an almost menacing light, like leaves just before a storm that lift their bright undersides as the air becomes darker. We had been speaking, of course, of Russia, and I had mentioned a study that had been made at Harvard of political attitudes among Iron Curtain refugees. Suddenly, the Colonel had smiled. "They're pretty

Red at Harvard, I'm given to understand," he observed in a comfortable tone, while the young man twitched and quivered urgently. The
eyes of all the men settled on me and waited. I flushed as I saw myself
reflected. The woodland greens of my dress were turning to their com-
plementary red, like a color-experiment in psychology or a traffic light
changing. Down at the other end of the club car, a man looked up from
his paper. I pulled myself together. "Set your mind at rest, Colonel," I
remarked dryly. "I know Harvard very well and they're conservative
to the point of dullness. The only thing crimson is the football team."
This disparagement had its effect. "So . . . ?" queried the Colonel.
"I thought there was some professor. . . ." I shook my head. "Absolutely not. There used to be a few fellow-travelers, but they're very
quiet these days, when they haven't absolutely recanted. The general
atmosphere is more anti-Communist than the Vatican." The Colonel
and the mining engineer exchanged a thoughtful stare and seemed to
agree that the Delphic oracle that had just pronounced knew whereof
it spoke. "Glad to hear it," said the Colonel. The engineer frowned and
shook his fat wattles; he was a stately, gray-haired, plump man with
small hands and feet and the pampered, finical tidiness of a small-town
widow. "There's so much hearsay these days," he exclaimed vexedly.
"You don't know *what* to believe."

I reopened my book with an air of having closed the subject and read a
paragraph three times over. I exulted to think that I had made a modest contribution to sanity in our times, and I imagined my words pyra-
miding like a chain letter—the Colonel telling a fellow-officer on the
veranda of a club in Texas, the engineer halting a works-superintendent
in a Colorado mine shaft: "I met a woman on the train who claims . . .
Yes, absolutely . . ." Of course, I did not know Harvard as thoroughly
as I pretended, but I forgave myself by thinking it was the convention
of such club-car symposia in our positivistic country to speak from
the horse's mouth.

Meanwhile, across the aisle, the engineer and the Colonel con-

tinued their talk in slightly lowered voices. From time to time, the
Colonel's polished index-fingernail scratched his burnished black head
and his knowing blue eye forayed occasionally toward me. I saw that
still I was a doubtful quantity to them, a movement in the bushes, a
noise, a flicker, that was figuring in their crenelated thought as "she."
The subject of Reds in our colleges had not, alas, been finished; they
were speaking now of another university and a woman faculty-member
who had been issuing Communist statements. This story somehow, I
thought angrily, had managed to appear in the newspapers without my
knowledge, while these men were conversant with it; I recognized a
big chink in the armor of my authority. Looking up from my book, I
began to question them sharply, as though they were reporting some
unheard-of natural phenomenon. "When?" I demanded. "Where did
you see it? What was her name?" This request for the professor's name
was a headlong attempt on my part to buttress my position, the implication being that the identities of all university professors were known
to me and that if I were but given the name I could promptly clarify the
matter. To admit that there was a single Communist in our academic
system whose activities were hidden from me imperiled, I instinctively
felt, all the small good I had done here. Moreover, in the back of my
mind, I had supreme confidence that these men were wrong: the story,
I supposed, was some tattered piece of misinformation they had picked
up from a gossip column. Pride, as usual, preceded my fall. To the
Colonel, the demand for the name was not specific but generic: what
kind of name was the question he presumed me to be asking. "Oh," he
said slowly with a luxurious yawn, "Finkelstein or Fishbein or Fein-
stein." He lolled back in his seat with a side glance at the engineer, who
deeply nodded. There was a voluptuary pause, as the implication sank
in. I bit my lip, regarding this as a mere diversionary tactic. "Please!"
I said impatiently. "Can't you remember exactly?" The Colonel shook
his head and then his spare cheekbones suddenly reddened and he
looked directly at me. "I can tell you one thing," he exclaimed irefully.
"They weren't named Ryan or Murphy."

The Colonel went no further; it was quite unnecessary. In an instant, the young man was at his side, yapping excitedly and actually picking at the military sleeve. The poor thing was transformed, like some creature in a fairy tale whom a magic word releases from silence. "That's right, Colonel," he happily repeated. "I know them. *I* was at Harvard in the business school, studying accountancy. I left. I couldn't take it." He threw a poisonous glance at me, and the Colonel, who had been regarding him somewhat doubtfully, now put on an alert expression and inclined an ear for his confidences. The man at the other end of the car folded his newspaper solemnly and took a seat by the young man's side. "They're all Reds, Colonel," said the young man. "They teach it in the classroom. I came back here to Missouri. It made me sick to listen to the stuff they handed out. If you didn't hand it back, they flunked you. Don't let anybody tell you different." "You are wrong," I said coldly, and closed my book and rose. The young man was still talking eagerly, and the three men were leaning forward to catch his every gasping word, like three astute detectives over a dying informer, when I reached the door and cast a last look over my shoulder at them. For an instant, the Colonel's eye met mine, and I felt his scrutiny processing my green back as I tugged open the door and met a blast of hot air, blowing my full skirt wide. Behind me, in my fancy, I saw four sets of shrugging brows.

In my own car, I sat down, opposite two fat nuns, and tried to assemble my thoughts. I ought to have spoken, I felt, and yet what could I have said? It occurred to me that the four men had perhaps not realized why I had left the club car with such abruptness: was it possible that they thought I was a Communist, who feared to be unmasked? I spurned this possibility, and yet it made me uneasy. For some reason, it troubled my *amour-propre* to think of my anti-Communist self living on, so to speak, green in their collective memory as a Communist or fellow traveler. In fact, though I did not give a fig for the men, I hated the idea, while a few years ago I should have counted it a great joke. This, it seemed to me, was a measure of the change in the social climate. I had always scoffed at the notion of liberals "living in fear" of political demagoguery in America, but now I had to admit that if I was not fearful, I was at least uncomfortable in the supposition that anybody, anybody whatever, could think of me, precious me, as a Communist. A remoter possibility was, of course, that back there my departure was being ascribed to Jewishness, and this too annoyed. I am in fact a quarter Jewish, and though I did not "hate" the idea of being taken for a Jew, I did not precisely like it, particularly under these circumstances. I wished it to be clear that I had left the club car for intellectual and principled reasons; I wanted those men to know that it was not I, but my principles, that had been offended. To let them conjecture that I had left because I was Jewish would imply that only a Jew could be affronted by an anti-Semitic outburst; a terrible idea. Aside from anything else, it voided the whole concept of transcendence, which was very close to my heart, the concept that man is more than his circumstances, more even than himself.

However you looked at the episode, I said to myself nervously, I had not acquitted myself well. I ought to have done or said something concrete and unmistakable. From this, I slid glassily to the thought that those men ought to be punished, the Colonel, in particular, who occupied a responsible position. In a minute, I was framing a businesslike letter to the Chief of Staff, deploring the Colonel's conduct as unbecoming to an officer and identifying him by rank and post, since unfortunately I did not know his name. Earlier in the conversation, he had passed some comments on "Harry" that bordered positively on treason, I said to myself triumphantly. A vivid image of the proceedings against him presented itself to my imagination: the long military tribunal with a row of stern soldierly faces glaring down at the Colonel. I myself occupied only an inconspicuous corner of this tableau, for, to tell the truth, I did not relish the role of the witness. Perhaps it would be wiser to let the matter drop . . . ? We were nearing St. Louis now; the Colonel had come back into my car, and the young accountant had followed him, still talking feverishly. I pretended not to see them and turned to the two nuns, as if for sanctuary from this world and its hatreds and revenges. Out of the corner of my eye, I watched the Colonel, who now looked wry and restless; he shrank against the windows as the young man made a place for himself amid the Colonel's smart luggage and continued to express his views in a pale breathless voice. I smiled to think that the Colonel was paying the piper. For the Colonel, anti-Semitism was simply an aspect of urbanity, like a knowledge of hotels or women. This frantic psychopath of an accountant was serving him as a nemesis, just as the German people had been served by their psychopath, Hitler. Colonel, I adjured him, you have chosen, between him and me; measure the depth of your error and make the best of it! No intervention on my part was now necessary; justice had been meted out. Nevertheless, my heart was still throbbing violently, as if I were on the verge of some dangerous action. What was I to do, I kept asking myself, as I chatted with the nuns, if the Colonel were to hold me to that lunch? And I slowly and apprehensively resolved this question, just as though it were a matter of the most serious import. It seemed to me that if I did not lunch with him — and I had no intention of doing so — I had the dreadful obligation of telling him why.

He was waiting for me as I descended the car steps. "Aren't you coming to lunch with me?" he called out and moved up to take my elbow. I began to tremble with audacity. "No," I said firmly, picking up my suitcase and draping an olive green linen duster over my arm. "I can't lunch with you." He quirked a wiry black eyebrow. "Why not?" he said. "I understood it was all arranged." He reached for my suitcase. "No," I said, holding on to the suitcase. "I can't." I took a deep breath. "I have to tell you. I think you should be *ashamed* of yourself, Colonel, for what you said in the club car." The Colonel stared; I mechanically waved for a red-cap, who took my bag and coat and went off. The Colonel and I stood facing each other on the emptying platform. "What do you mean?" he inquired in a low, almost clandestine tone. "Those anti-Semitic remarks," I muttered, resolutely. "You

ought to be *ashamed*." The Colonel gave a quick, relieved laugh. "Oh,
come now," he protested. "I'm sorry," I said. "I can't have lunch with
anybody who feels that way about the Jews." The Colonel put down
his attaché-case and scratched the back of his lean neck. "Oh, come
now," he repeated, with a look of amusement. "You're not Jewish, are
you?" "No," I said quickly. "Well, then . . ." said the Colonel, spreading his hands in a gesture of bafflement. I saw that he was truly surprised and slightly hurt by my criticism, and this made me feel wretch-
edly embarrassed and even apologetic, on my side, as though I had
called attention to some physical defect in him, of which he himself
was unconscious. "But I might have been," I stammered. "You had
no way of knowing. You oughtn't to talk like that." I recognized, too
late, that I was strangely reducing the whole matter to a question of
etiquette: "Don't start anti-Semitic talk before making sure there are
no Jews present." "Oh, hell," said the Colonel, easily. "I can tell a Jew."
"No, you can't," I retorted, thinking of my Jewish grandmother, for
by Nazi criteria I was Jewish. "Of course I can," he insisted. "So can
you." We had begun to walk down the platform side by side, disput-
ing with a restrained passion that isolated us like a pair of lovers. All
at once, the Colonel halted, as though struck with a thought. "What
are you, anyway?" he said meditatively, regarding my dark hair, green
blouse, and pink earrings. Inside myself, I began to laugh. "Oh," I said
gaily, playing out the trump I had been saving, "I'm Irish, like you,
Colonel." "How did you know?" he said amazedly. I laughed aloud. "I
can tell an Irishman," I taunted. The Colonel frowned. "What's your
family name?" he said brusquely. "McCarthy." He lifted an eyebrow,
in defeat, and then quickly took note of my wedding ring. "That your
maiden name?" I nodded. Under this peremptory questioning, I had
the peculiar sensation that I get when I am lying: I began to feel that
"McCarthy" was a nom de plume, a coinage of my artistic personality.
But the Colonel appeared to be satisfied. "Hell," he said, "come on to
lunch, then. With a fine name like that, you and I should be friends."
I still shook my head, though by this time we were pacing outside the

station restaurant; my baggage had been checked in a locker; sweat was running down my face and I felt exhausted and hungry. I knew that I was weakening and I wanted only an excuse to yield and go inside with him. The Colonel seemed to sense this. "Hell," he conceded. "You've got me wrong. I've nothing against the Jews. Back there in the club car, I was just stating a simple fact: you won't find an Irishman sounding off for the Commies. You can't deny that, can you?"

His voice rose persuasively; he took my arm. In the heat, I wilted and we went into the air-conditioned cocktail lounge. The Colonel ordered two old-fashioneds. The room was dark as a cave and produced, in the midst of the hot midday, a hallucinated feeling, as though time had ceased, with the weather, and we were in eternity together. As the Colonel prepared to relax, I made a tremendous effort to guide the conversation along rational, purposive lines; my only justification for being here would be to convert the Colonel. "There *have* been Irishmen associated with the Communist party," I said suddenly, when the drinks came. "I can think of two." "Oh, hell," said the Colonel, "every race and nation has its traitors. What I mean is, you won't find them in numbers. You've got to admit that the Communists in this country are 90 per cent Jewish." "But the Jews in this country aren't 90 per cent Communist," I retorted.

As he stirred his drink, restively, I began to try to show him the reasons why the Communist movement in America had attracted such a large number, relatively, of Jews; how the Communists had been anti-Nazi when nobody else seemed to care what happened to the Jews in Germany; how the Communists still capitalized on a Jewish fear of fascism; how many Jews had become, after Buchenwald, traumatized by this fear. . . .

But the Colonel was scarcely listening. An impatient frown rested on his jaunty features. "I don't get it," he said slowly. "Why should you be for them, with a name like yours?" "I'm *not* for the Communists," I cried, "I'm just trying to explain to you —" "For the

Jews," the Colonel interrupted, irritable now himself. "I've heard of such people but I never met one before." "I'm not 'for' them," I protested. "You don't understand. I'm not for *any* race or nation. I'm against those who are against them." This word, *them*, with a sort of slurring circle drawn round it, was beginning to sound ugly to me. Automatically, in arguing with him, I seemed to have slipped into the Colonel's style of thought. It occurred to me that a defense of the Jews could be a subtle and safe form of anti-Semitism, an exercise of patronage: as a rational Gentile, one could feel superior both to the Jews and the anti-Semites. There could be no doubt that the Jewish question evoked a curious stealthy lust or concupiscence. I could feel it now vibrating between us over the dark table. If I had been a good person, I should unquestionably have got up and left.

"I don't get it," repeated the Colonel. "How were you brought up? Were your people this way too?" It was manifest that an odd reversal had taken place: each of us regarded the other as "abnormal" and was attempting to understand the etiology of a disease. "Many of my people think just as you do," I said, smiling coldly. "It seems to be a sickness to which the Irish are prone. Perhaps it's due to the potato diet," I said sweetly, having divined that the Colonel came from a social stratum somewhat lower than my own.

But the Colonel's hide was tough. "You've got me wrong," he reiterated, with an almost plaintive laugh. "I don't dislike the Jews. I've got a lot of Jewish friends. Among themselves, they think just as I do, mark my words. I tell you what it is," he added ruminatively, with a thoughtful prod of his muddler, "I draw a distinction between a kike and a Jew." I groaned. "Colonel, I've never heard an anti-Semite who didn't draw that distinction. You know what Otto Kahn said? 'A kike is a Jewish gentleman who has just left the room.'" The Colonel did not laugh. "I don't hold it against some of them," he persisted, in a tone of pensive justice. "It's not their fault if they were born that way. That's what I tell them, and they respect me for my honesty. I've had a lot of discussions; in procurement, you have to do business with

them, and the Jews are the first to admit that you'll find more chis-
elers among their race than among the rest of mankind." "It's not a
race," I interjected wearily, but the Colonel pressed on. "If I deal with
a Jewish manufacturer, I can't bank on his word. I've seen it again and
again, every damned time. When I deal with a Gentile, I can trust him
to make delivery as promised. That's the difference between the two
races. They're just a different breed. They don't have standards of honesty, even among each other." I sighed, feeling unequal to arguing the
Colonel's personal experience.

"Look," I said, "you may be dealing with an industry where the
Jewish manufacturers are the most recent comers and feel they have
to cut corners to compete with the established firms. I've heard that
said about Jewish cattle-dealers, who are supposed to be extra sharp.
But what I think, really, is that you notice it when a Jewish firm fails to
meet an agreement and don't notice it when it's a Yankee." "Hah," said
the Colonel. "They'll tell you what I'm telling you themselves, if you
get to know them and go into their homes. You won't believe it, but
some of my best friends are Jews," he said, simply and thoughtfully,
with an air of originality. "They may be *your* best friends, Colonel," I
retorted, "but you are not theirs. I defy you to tell me that you talk to
them as you're talking now." "Sure," said the Colonel, easily. "More
or less." "They must be very queer Jews you know," I observed tartly,
and I began to wonder whether there indeed existed a peculiar class of
Jews whose function in life was to be "friends" with such people as the
Colonel. It was difficult to think that all the anti-Semites who made the
Colonel's assertion were the victims of a cruel self-deception.

A dispirited silence followed. I was not one of those liberals who
believed that the Jews, alone among peoples, possessed no characteris-
tics whatever of a distinguishing nature—this would mean they had no
history and no culture, a charge which should be leveled against them
only by an anti-Semite. Certainly, types of Jews could be noted and
patterns of Jewish thought and feeling: Jewish humor, Jewish ratio-
nality, and so on, not that every Jew reflected every attribute of Jewish

life or history. But somehow, with the Colonel, I dared not concede that there was such a thing as a Jew: I saw the sad meaning of the assertion that a Jew was a person whom other people thought was Jewish.

Hopeless, however, to convey this to the Colonel. The desolate truth was that the Colonel was extremely stupid, and it came to me, as we sat there, glumly ordering lunch, that for extremely stupid people anti-Semitism was a form of intellectuality, the sole form of intellectuality of which they were capable. It represented, in a rudimentary way, the ability to make categories, to generalize. Hence a thing I had noted before but never understood: the fact that anti-Semitic statements were generally delivered in an atmosphere of profundity. Furrowed brows attended these speculative distinctions between a kike and a Jew, these little empirical laws that you can't know one without knowing them all. To arrive, indeed, at the idea of a Jew was, for these grouping minds, an exercise in Platonic thought, a discovery of essence, and to be able to add the great corollary, "Some of my best friends are Jews," was to find the philosopher's cleft between essence and existence. From this, it would seem, followed the querulous obstinacy with which the anti-Semite clung to his concept; to be deprived of this intellectual tool by missionaries of tolerance would be, for persons like the Colonel, the equivalent of Western man's losing the syllogism: a lapse into animal darkness. In the club car, we had just witnessed an example: the Colonel with his anti-Semitic observation had come to the mute young man like the paraclete, bearing the gift of tongues.

Here in the bar, it grew plainer and plainer that the Colonel did not regard himself as an anti-Semite but merely as a heavy thinker. The idea that I considered him anti-Semitic sincerely outraged his feelings. "Prejudice" was the last trait he could have imputed to himself. He looked on me, almost respectfully, as a "Jew lover," a kind of being he had heard of but never actually encountered, like a centaur or a Siamese twin, and the interest of relating this prodigy to the natural state

of mankind overrode any personal distaste. There I sat, the exception
which was "proving" or testing the rule, and he kept pressing me for
details of my history that might explain my deviation in terms of the
norm. On my side, of course, I had become fiercely resolved that he
would learn nothing from me that would make it possible for him to
dismiss my anti-anti-Semitism as the product of special circumstances:
I was stubbornly sitting on the fact of my Jewish grandmother like a
hen on a golden egg. I was bent on making *him* see himself as a monster, a deviation, a heretic from Church and State. Unfortunately, the
Colonel, owing perhaps to his military training, had not the glimmer-
ing of an idea of what democracy meant; to him, it was simply a slogan
that sometimes useful in war. The notion of an ordained inequality was
to him "scientific."

"Honestly," he was saying in lowered tones, as our drinks were
taken away and the waitress set down my sandwich and his corned-
beef hash, "don't you, brought up the way you were, feel about them
the way I do? Just between ourselves, isn't there a sort of inborn feeling of horror that the very word, Jew, suggests?" I shook my head,
roundly. The idea of an *innate* anti-Semitism was in keeping with the
rest of the Colonel's thought, yet it shocked me more than anything
he had yet said. "No," I sharply replied. "It doesn't evoke any feeling
one way or the other." "Honest Injun?" said the Colonel. "Think back;
when you were a kid, didn't the word, Jew, make you feel sick?" There
was a dreadful sincerity about this that made me answer in an almost
kindly tone. "No, truthfully, I assure you. When we were children, we
learned to call the old-clothes man a sheeny, but that was just a dirty
word to us, like 'Hun' that we used to call after workmen we thought
were Germans."

"I don't get it," pondered the Colonel, eating a pickle. "There
must be something wrong with you. Everybody is born with that feeling. It's natural; it's part of nature." "On the contrary," I said. "It's
something very unnatural that you must have been taught as a child."
"It's not something you're *taught*," he protested. "You must have

been," I said. "You simply don't remember it. In any case, you're a man now; you must rid yourself of that feeling. It's psychopathic, like that horrible young man on the train." "You thought he was crazy?" mused the Colonel, in an idle, dreamy tone. I shrugged my shoulders. "Of course. Think of his color. He was probably just out of a mental institution. People don't get that tattletale gray except in prison or mental hospitals." The Colonel suddenly grinned. "You might be right," he said. "He was quite a case." He chuckled.

I leaned forward. "You know, Colonel," I said quickly, "anti-Semitism is contrary to the Church's teaching. God will make you do penance for hating the Jews. Ask your priest; he'll tell you I'm right. You'll have a long spell in Purgatory, if you don't rid yourself of this sin. It's a deliberate violation of Christ's commandment, 'Love thy neighbor.' The Church holds that the Jews have a sacred place in God's design. Mary was a Jew and Christ was a Jew. The Jews are under God's special protection. The Church teaches that the millennium can't come until the conversion of the Jews; therefore, the Jews must be preserved that the Divine Will may be accomplished. Woe to them that harm them, for they controvert God's Will!" In the course of speaking, I had swept myself away with the solemnity of the doctrine. The Great Reconciliation between God and His chosen people, as envisioned by the Evangelist, had for me at that moment a piercing majestic beauty, like some awesome Tintoretto. I saw a noble spectacle of blue sky, thronged with gray clouds, and a vast white desert, across which God and Israel advanced to meet each other, while below in hell the demons of disunion shrieked and gnashed their teeth.

"Hell," said the Colonel, jovially. "I don't believe in all of that. I lost my faith when I was a kid. I saw that all this God stuff was a lot of bushwa." I gazed at him in stupefaction. His confidence had completely returned. The blue eyes glittered debonairly; the eagles glittered; the narrow polished head cocked and listened to itself like a trilling bird. I was up against an airman with a bird's-eye view, a man who

believed in nothing but the law of kind: the epitome of godless ma-
terialism. "You still don't hold with that bunk?" the Colonel inquired
in an undertone, with an expression of stealthy curiosity. "No," I confessed, sad to admit to a meeting of minds. "You know what got me?"
exclaimed the Colonel. "That birth-control stuff. Didn't it kill you?"
I made a neutral sound. "I was beginning to play around," said the
Colonel, with a significant beam of the eye, "and I just couldn't take
that guff. When I saw through the birth-control talk, I saw through the
whole thing. They claimed it was against nature, but I claim, if that's
so, an operation's against nature. I told my old man that when he was
having his kidney stones out. You ought to have heard him yell!" A
rich, reminiscent satisfaction dwelt in the Colonel's face.

 This period of his life, in which he had thrown off the claims of
the spiritual and adopted a practical approach, was evidently one of
those "turning points" to which a man looks back with pride. He lingered over the story of his break with church and parents with a curious
sort of heat, as though the flames of old sexual conquests stirred within
his body at the memory of those old quarrels. The looks he rested on
me, as a sharer of that experience, grew more and more lickerish and
assaying. "What got *you* down?" he finally inquired, settling back in
his chair and pushing his coffee cup aside. "Oh," I said wearily, "it's a
long story. You can read it when it's published." "You're an author?"
cried the Colonel, who was really very slow-witted. I nodded and the
Colonel regarded me afresh. "What do you write? Love stories?" He
gave a half-wink. "No," I said. "Various things. Articles. Books. High-
browish stories." A suspicion darkened in the Colonel's sharp face.
"That McCarthy," he said. "Is that your pen name?" "Yes," I said,
"but it's my real name too. It's the name I write under *and* my maiden
name." The Colonel digested this thought. "Oh," he concluded.

 A new idea seemed to visit him. Quite cruelly, I watched it take
possession. He was thinking of the power of the press and the indiscre-
tions of other military figures, who had been rewarded with demotion.

The consciousness of the uniform he wore appeared to seep uneasily into his body. He straightened his shoulders and called thoughtfully for the check. We paid in silence, the Colonel making no effort to forestall my dive into my pocketbook. I should not have let him pay in any case, but it startled me that he did not try to do so, if only for reasons of vanity. The whole business of paying, apparently, was painful to him: I watched his facial muscles contract as he pocketed the change and slipped two dimes for the waitress onto the table, not daring quite to hide them under the coffee cup—he had short-changed me on the bill and the tip, and we both knew it. We walked out into the steaming station and I took my baggage out of the checking locker. The Colonel carried my suitcase and we strolled along without speaking. Again, I felt horribly embarrassed for him. He was meditative, and I supposed that he too was mortified by his meanness about the tip.

"Don't get me wrong," he said suddenly, setting the suitcase down and turning squarely to face me, as though he had taken a big decision. "I may have said a few things back there about the Jews getting what they deserved in Germany." I looked at him in surprise; actually, he had not said that to me. Perhaps he had let it drop in the club car. "But that doesn't mean I approve of Hitler." "I should hope not," I said. "What I mean is," said the Colonel, "that they probably gave the Germans a lot of provocation, but that doesn't excuse what Hitler did." "No," I said, somewhat ironically, but the Colonel was unaware of anything satiric in the air. His face was grave and determined; he was sorting out his philosophy for the record. "I mean, I don't approve of his methods," he finally stated. "No," I agreed. "You mean, you don't approve of the gas chamber." The Colonel shook his head very severely. "Absolutely not! That was terrible." He shuddered and drew out a handkerchief and slowly wiped his brow. "For God's sake," he said, "don't get me wrong. I think they're human beings." "Yes," I assented, and we walked along to my track. The Colonel's spirits lifted, as though, having stated his credo, he had both got himself in line with his public policy and achieved an autonomous thought. "I mean," he resumed, "you may not care for them, but that's not the same as killing them, in cold blood, like that." "No, Colonel," I said.

He swung my bag onto the car's platform and I climbed up behind it. He stood below, smiling, with upturned face. "I'll look for your article," he cried, as the train whistle blew. I nodded, and the Colonel waved, and I could not stop myself from waving back at him and even giving him the corner of a smile. After all, I said to myself, looking down at him, the Colonel was "a human being." There followed one of those inane intervals in which one prays for the train to leave. We both glanced at our watches. "See you some time," he called. "What's your married name?" "Broadwater," I called back. The whistle blew again. "Brodwater?" shouted the Colonel, with a dazed look of unbelief and growing enlightenment: he was not the first person to hear it as a Jewish name, on the model of Goldwater. "B-r-o-a-d," I began, automatically, but then I stopped. I disdained to spell it out for him: the victory was his. "One of the chosen, eh?" his brief grimace commiserated. For the last time, and in the final fullness of understanding, the hawk eye patrolled the green dress, the duster, and the earrings; the narrow flue of his nostril contracted as he curtly turned away. The train commenced to move.

1962

Another encounter, another meeting of two souls like and unlike each other. This time the narrator is James Baldwin, one of the great novelists of the twentieth century and also one of its most crucial essayists. "Down at the Cross," first published in two parts in the *New Yorker* in 1962 and then in his landmark 1963 book *The Fire Next Time,* merits the term *prophetic,* if we take the philosopher Cornel West's definition: "To prophesy is not to predict an outcome but rather to identify concrete evils." That's Baldwin's "Down at the Cross," an essay that encompasses Harlem and Chicago, Europe's then still-recent wars and the "African kings and heroes" of the moment in which Baldwin wrote—the beginning of the end of colonialism. Not just overseas, but at home, too.

Baldwin begins with himself at age fourteen, undergoing "a prolonged religious crisis." He considers the meaning of the term *religion.* "To state it in another, more accurate way, I became, during my fourteenth year, for the first time in my life, afraid—afraid of the evil within me and afraid of the evil without." That fear drove him to the church, where he became a boy preacher, and then away from it, where he became the writer we meet here—the writer whose prophetic power is so evident that he is invited to share a stage on television with Malcolm X. Following the appearance, Elijah Muhammad, leader of the Nation of Islam, for which Malcolm X was then a spokesman, summons Baldwin to dinner at his Chicago mansion.

Elijah Muhammad was a prophet in a different sense, speaking not of this world but of one he says once was and is still to come. Baldwin's prophetic speech is that of doubts and questions; Muhammad's is one of certainty and answers. Baldwin isn't having them. Then again, he won't dismiss them altogether. He grants the beauty of Muhammad's table, bathed in a light he remembers from childhood, "encountered later only in one's dreams." But his wits don't abandon him. He lays out the Nation of Islam's theology of "white devils" and "tricknology" on its own seemingly alien terms, only to turn it around, revealing it as a version of the truth, the brutal facts of African-American life that allow Baldwin "to glimpse dimly what may now seem to be a fantasy, although, in an age so fantastical, I would hesitate to say precisely what a fantasy is."

JAMES BALDWIN
From "Down at the Cross"

I was frightened, because I had, in effect, been summoned into a royal presence. I was frightened for another reason, too. I knew the tension in me between love and power, between pain and rage, and the curious, the grinding way I remained extended between these poles — perpetually attempting to choose the better rather than the worse. But this choice was a choice in terms of a personal, a private better (I was, after all, a writer); what was its relevance in terms of a social worse? Here was the South Side — a million in captivity — stretching from this doorstep as far as the eye could see. And they didn't even read; depressed populations don't have the time or energy to spare. The affluent populations, which should have been their help, didn't, as far as could be discovered, read, either — they merely bought books and devoured them, but not in order to learn: in order to learn new attitudes. Also, I knew that once I had entered the house, I couldn't smoke or drink, and I felt guilty about the cigarettes in my pocket, as I had felt years ago when my friend first took me into his church. I was half an hour late, having got lost on the way here, and I felt as deserving of a scolding as a schoolboy.

The young man who came to the door—he was about thirty, perhaps, with a handsome, smiling face—didn't seem to find my lateness offensive, and led me into a large room. On one side of the room sat half a dozen women, all in white; they were much occupied with a beautiful baby, who seemed to belong to the youngest of the women. On the other side of the room sat seven or eight men, young, dressed in dark suits, very much at ease, and very imposing. The sunlight came into the room with the peacefulness one remembers from rooms in one's early childhood—a sunlight encountered later only in one's dreams. I remember being astounded by the quietness, the ease, the peace, the taste. I was introduced, they greeted me with genuine cordiality and respect—and the respect increased my fright, for it meant that they expected something of me that I knew in my heart, for their sakes, I could not give—and we sat down. Elijah Muhammad was not in the room. Conversation was slow, but not as stiff as I had feared it would be. They kept it going, for I simply did not know which subjects I could acceptably bring up. They knew more about me, and had read more of what I had written, than I had expected, and I wondered what they made of it all, what they took my usefulness to be. The women were carrying on their own conversation, in low tones; I gathered that they were not expected to take part in male conversations. A few women kept coming in and out of the room, apparently making preparations for dinner. We, the men, did not plunge deeply into any subject, for, clearly, we were all waiting for the appearance of Elijah. Presently, the men, one by one, left the room and returned. Then I was asked if I would like to wash, and I, too, walked down the hall to the bathroom. Shortly after I came back, we stood up, and Elijah entered.

I do not know what I had expected to see. I had read some of his speeches, and had heard fragments of others on the radio and on television, so I associated him with ferocity. But, no—the man who came into the room was small and slender, really very delicately put together, with a thin face, large, warm eyes, and a most winning smile. Something came into the room with him—his disciples' joy at seeing

him, his joy at seeing them. It was the kind of encounter one watches
with a smile simply because it is so rare that people enjoy one another. He teased the women, like a father, with no hint of that ugly
and unctuous flirtatiousness I knew so well from other churches, and
they responded like that, with great freedom and yet from a great and
loving distance. He had seen me when he came into the room, I knew,
though he had not looked my way. I had the feeling, as he talked and
laughed with others, whom I could only think of as his children, that
he was sizing me up, deciding something. Now he turned toward me,
to welcome me, with that marvelous smile, and carried me back nearly
twenty-four years, to that moment when the pastor had smiled at me
and said, "Whose little boy are you?" I did not respond now as I had responded then, because there are some things (not many, alas!) that one
cannot do twice. But I knew what he made me feel, how I was drawn
toward his peculiar authority, how his smile promised to take the burden of my life off my shoulders. *Take your burdens to the Lord and leave
them there.* The central quality in Elijah's face is pain, and his smile is
a witness to it—pain so old and deep and black that it becomes personal and particular only when he smiles. One wonders what he would
sound like if he could sing. He turned to me, with that smile, and said
something like "I've got a lot to say to *you,* but we'll wait until we sit
down." And I laughed. He made me think of my father and me as we
might have been if we had been friends.

In the dining room, there were two long tables; the men sat at
one and the women at the other. Elijah was at the head of our table,
and I was seated at his left. I can scarcely remember what we ate, except that it was plentiful, sane, and simple—so sane and simple that it
made me feel extremely decadent, and I think that I drank, therefore,
two glasses of milk. Elijah mentioned having seen me on television
and said that it seemed to him that I was not yet brainwashed and was
trying to become myself. He said this in a curiously unnerving way,
his eyes looking into mine and one hand half hiding his lips, as though
he were trying to conceal bad teeth. But his teeth were not bad. Then I

remembered hearing that he had spent time in prison. I suppose that I *would* like to become myself, whatever that may mean, but I knew that Elijah's meaning and mine were not the same. I said yes, I was trying to be me, but I did not know how to say more than that, and so I waited.

Whenever Elijah spoke, a kind of chorus arose from the table, saying "Yes, that's right." This began to set my teeth on edge. And Elijah himself had a further, unnerving habit, which was to ricochet his questions and comments off someone else on their way to you. Now, turning to the man on his right, he began to speak of the white devils with whom I had last appeared on TV: What had they made *him* (me) feel? I could not answer this and was not absolutely certain that I was expected to. The people referred to had certainly made me feel exasperated and useless, but I did not think of them as devils. Elijah went on about the crimes of white people, to this endless chorus of "Yes, that's right." Someone at the table said, "The white man sure *is* a devil. He proves that by his own actions." I looked around. It was a very young man who had said this, scarcely more than a boy—very dark and sober, very bitter. Elijah began to speak of the Christian religion, of Christians, in the same soft, joking way. I began to see that Elijah's power came from his single-mindedness. There is nothing calculated about him; he means every word he says. The real reason, according to Elijah, that I failed to realize that the white man was a devil was that I had been too long exposed to white teaching and had never received true instruction. "The so-called American Negro" is the only reason Allah has permitted the United States to endure so long; the white man's time was up in 1913, but it is the will of Allah that this lost black nation, the black men of this country, be redeemed from their white masters and returned to the true faith, which is Islam. Until this is done—and it will be accomplished very soon—the total destruction of the white man is being delayed. Elijah's mission is to return "the so-called Negro" to Islam, to separate the chosen of Allah from this doomed nation. Furthermore, the white man knows his history, knows himself to be a devil, and knows that his time is running out, and all

his technology, psychology, science, and "tricknology" are being expended in the effort to prevent black men from hearing the truth. This
truth is that at the very beginning of time there was not one white
face to be found in all the universe. Black men ruled the earth and the
black man was perfect. This is the truth concerning the era that white
men now refer to as prehistoric. They want black men to believe that
they, like white men, once lived in caves and swung from trees and
ate their meat raw and did not have the power of speech. But this is
not true. Black men were never in such a condition. Allah allowed the
Devil, through his scientists, to carry on infernal experiments, which
resulted, finally, in the creation of the Devil known as the white man,
and later, even more disastrously, in the creation of the white woman.
And it was decreed that these monstrous creatures should rule the
earth for a certain number of years—I forget how many thousand,
but, in any case, their rule now is ending, and Allah, who had never
approved of the creation of the white man in the first place (who knows
him, in fact, to be not a man at all but a devil), is anxious to restore the
rule of peace that the rise of the white man totally destroyed. There is
thus, by definition, no virtue in white people, and since they are another creation entirely and can no more, by breeding, become black
than a cat, by breeding, can become a horse, there is no hope for them.

There is nothing new in this merciless formulation except the
explicitness of its symbols and the candor of its hatred. Its emotional
tone is as familiar to me as my own skin; it is but another way of saying that *sinners shall be bound in Hell a thousand years.* That sinners
have always, for American Negroes, been white is a truth we needn't
labor, and every American Negro, therefore, risks having the gates
of paranoia close on him. In a society that is entirely hostile, and, by
its nature, seems determined to cut you down—that has cut down so
many in the past and cuts down so many every day—it begins to be
almost impossible to distinguish a real from a fancied injury. One can
very quickly cease to attempt this distinction, and, what is worse, one
usually ceases to attempt it without realizing that one has done so. All

doormen, for example, and all policemen have by now, for me, become exactly the same, and my style with them is designed simply to intimidate them before they can intimidate me. No doubt I am guilty of some injustice here, but it is irreducible, since I cannot risk assuming that the humanity of these people is more real to them than their uniforms. Most Negroes cannot risk assuming that the humanity of white people is more real to them than their color. And this leads, imperceptibly but inevitably, to a state of mind in which, having long ago learned to expect the worst, one finds it very easy to believe the worst. The brutality with which Negroes are treated in this country simply cannot be overstated, however unwilling white men may be to hear it. In the beginning—and neither can this be overstated—a Negro just cannot *believe* that white people are treating him as they do; he does not know what he has done to merit it. And when he realizes that the treatment accorded him has nothing to do with anything he has done, that the attempt of white people to destroy him—for that is what it is—is utterly gratuitous, it is not hard for him to think of white people as devils. For the horrors of the American Negro's life there has been almost no language. The privacy of his experience, which is only beginning to be recognized in language, and which is denied or ignored in official and popular speech—hence the Negro idiom—lends credibility to any system that pretends to clarify it. And, in fact, the truth about the black man, as a historical entity and as a human being, *has* been hidden from him, deliberately and cruelly; the power of the white world is threatened whenever a black man refuses to accept the white world's definitions. So every attempt is made to cut that black man down— not only was made yesterday but is made today. Who, then, is to say with authority where the root of so much anguish and evil lies? Why, then, is it not possible that all things began with the black man and that he was perfect—especially since this is precisely the claim that white people have put forward for themselves all these years? Furthermore, it is now absolutely clear that white people are a minority in the world—so severe a minority that they now look rather more like an invention—and that they cannot possibly hope to rule it any longer. If this is so, why is it not also possible that they achieved their original dominance by stealth and cunning and bloodshed and in opposition to the will of Heaven, and not, as they claim, by Heaven's will? And if *this* is so, then the sword they have used so long against others can now, without mercy, be used against them. Heavenly witnesses are a tricky lot, to be used by whoever is closest to Heaven at the time. And legend and theology, which are designed to sanctify our fears, crimes, and aspirations, also reveal them for what they are.

I said, at last, in answer to some other ricocheted questions, "I left the church twenty years ago and I haven't joined anything since." It was my way of saying that I did not intend to join their movement, either.

"And what are you now?" Elijah asked.

I was in something of a bind, for I really could not say—could not allow myself to be stampeded into saying—that I was a Christian. "I? Now? Nothing." This was not enough. "I'm a writer. I like doing things alone." I heard myself saying this. Elijah smiled at me. "I don't, anyway," I said, finally, "think about it a great deal."

Elijah said, to his right, "I think he ought to think about it *all* the deal," and with this the table agreed. But there was nothing malicious or condemnatory in it. I had the stifling feeling that *they* knew I belonged to them but knew that I did not know it yet, that I remained unready, and that they were simply waiting, patiently, and with assurance, for me to discover the truth for myself. For where else, after all, could I go? I was black, and therefore a part of Islam, and would be saved from the holocaust awaiting the white world whether I would or no. My weak, deluded scruples could avail nothing against the iron word of the prophet.

I felt that I was back in my father's house—as, indeed, in a way, I was—and I told Elijah that I did not care if white and black people married, and that I had many white friends. I would have no choice, if it came to it, but to perish with them, for (I said to myself, but not to

Elijah), "I love a few people and they love me and some of them are
white, and isn't love more important than color?"

Elijah looked at me with great kindness and affection, great pity,
as though he were reading my heart, and indicated, skeptically, that I
might have white friends, or think I did, and they *might* be trying to be
decent — now — but their time was up. It was almost as though he were
saying, "They had their chance, man, and they goofed!"

And I looked around the table. I certainly had no evidence to
give them that would outweigh Elijah's authority or the evidence of
their own lives or the reality of the streets outside. Yes, I knew two or
three people, white, whom I would trust with my life, and I knew a
few others, white, who were struggling as hard as they knew how, and
with great effort and sweat and risk, to make the world more human.
But how could I say this? One cannot argue with anyone's experience
or decision or belief. All my evidence would be thrown out of court as
irrelevant to the main body of the case, for I could cite only exceptions.
The South Side proved the justice of the indictment; the state of the
world proved the justice of the indictment. Everything else, stretching back throughout recorded time, was merely a history of those exceptions who had tried to change the world and had failed. Was this
true? *Had* they failed? How much depended on the point of view?
For it would seem that a certain category of exceptions never failed
to make the world worse — that category, precisely, for whom power
is more real than love. And yet power *is* real, and many things, including, very often, love, cannot be achieved without it. In the eeriest
way possible, I suddenly had a glimpse of what white people must go
through at a dinner table when they are trying to prove that Negroes
are not subhuman. I had almost said, after all, "Well, take my friend
Mary," and very nearly descended to a catalogue of those virtues that
gave Mary the right to be alive. And in what hope? That Elijah and the
others would nod their heads solemnly and say, at least, "Well, *she's* all
right — but the *others!*"

And I looked again at the young faces around the table, and

looked back and Elijah, who was saying that no people in history have ever been respected who had not owned their land. And the table said, "Yes, that is right." I could not deny the truth of this statement. For everyone else has, *is,* a nation, with a specific location and a flag — even, these days, the Jew. It is only "the so-called American Negro" who remains trapped, disinherited, and despised, in a nation that has kept him in bondage for nearly four hundred years and is still unable to recognize him as a human being. And the Black Muslims, along with many people who are not Muslims, no longer wish for a recognition so grudging and (should it ever be achieved) so tardy. Again, it cannot be denied that this point of view is abundantly justified by American Negro history. It is galling indeed to have stood so long, hat in hand, waiting for Americans to grow up enough to realize that you do not threaten them. On the other hand, how is the American Negro now to form himself into a separate nation? For this — and not only from the Muslim point of view — would seem to be his only hope of not perishing in the American backwater and being entirely and forever forgotten, as though he had never existed at all and his travail had been for nothing.

Elijah's intensity and the bitter isolation and disaffection of these young men and the despair of the streets outside had caused me to glimpse dimly what may now seem to be a fantasy, although, in an age so fantastical, I would hesitate to say precisely what a fantasy is. Let us say that the Muslims were to achieve the possession of the six or seven states that they claim are owed to Negroes by the United States as "back payment" for slave labor. Clearly, the United States would never surrender this territory, on any terms whatever, unless it found it impossible, for whatever reason, to hold it — unless, that is, the United States were to be reduced as a world power, exactly the way, and at the same degree of speed, that England has been forced to relinquish her Empire. (It is simply not true — and the state of her ex-colonies proves this — that England "always meant to go.") If the states were southern states — and the Muslims seem to favor this — then the borders of a hostile Latin America would be raised, in effect, to, say, Maryland. Of the American borders on the sea, one would face toward a powerless Europe and the other toward an untrustworthy and nonwhite East, and on the north, after Canada, there would be only Alaska, which is a Russian border. The effect of this would be that the white people of the United States and Canada would find themselves marooned on a hostile continent, with the rest of the white world probably unwilling and certainly unable to come to their aid. All this is not, to my mind, the most imminent of possibilities, but if I were a Muslim, this is the possibility that I would find myself holding in the center of my mind, and driving toward. And if I were a Muslim, I would not hesitate to utilize — or, indeed, to exacerbate — the social and spiritual discontent that reigns here, for, at the very worst, I would merely have contributed to the destruction of the house I hated, and it would not matter if I perished, too. One has been perishing here so long!

And what were they thinking around the table? "I've come," said Elijah, "to give you something which can never be taken away from you." How solemn the table became then, and how great a light rose in the dark faces! This is the message that has spread through streets and tenements and prisons, through the narcotics wards, and past the filth and sadism of mental hospitals to a people from whom everything has been taken away, including, most crucially, their sense of their own worth. People cannot live without this sense; they will do anything whatever to regain it. This is why the most dangerous creation of any society is that man who has nothing to lose. You do not need ten such men — one will do. And Elijah, I should imagine, has had nothing to lose since the day he saw his father's blood rush out — rush down, and splash, so the legend has it, down through the leaves of a tree, on him. But neither did the other men around the table have anything to lose. "Return to your true religion," Elijah has written. "Throw off the chains of the slavemaster, the devil, and return to the fold. Stop drinking his alcohol, using his dope — protect your women — and forsake the filthy swine." I remembered my buddies of years ago, in the hallways, with their wine and their whisky and their tears; in hallways still, frozen on the needle; and my brother saying to me once, "If Harlem didn't have so many churches and junkies, there'd be blood flowing in the streets." *Protect your women:* a difficult thing to do in a civilization sexually so pathetic that the white men's masculinity depends on a denial of the masculinity of blacks. *Protect your women:* in a civilization that emasculates the male and abuses the female, and in which, moreover, the male is forced to depend on the female's bread-winning power. *Protect your women:* in the teeth of the white man's boast "We figure we're doing you folks a favor by pumping some white blood into your kids," and while facing the southern shotgun and northern billy. Years ago, we used to say, "*Yes,* I'm black, goddammit, and I'm beautiful!" — in defiance, into the void. But now — now — African kings and heroes have come into the world, out of the past, the past that can now be put to the uses of power. And black has *become* a beautiful color — not because it is loved but because it is feared. And this urgency on the part of American Negroes is *not to be forgotten!* As they watch black men elsewhere rise, the promise held out, at last, that they may walk the earth with the authority with which white men walk, protected by the power that white men shall have no longer, is enough, and more than enough, to empty prisons and pull God down from Heaven. It has happened before, many times, before color was invented, and the hope of Heaven has always been a metaphor for the achievement of this particular state of grace. The song says, "I know my robe's going to fit me well. I tried it on at the gates of Hell."

It was time to leave, and we stood in the large living room, saying good night, with everything curiously and heavily unresolved. I could not help feeling that I had failed a test, in their eyes and in my own, or that I had failed to heed a warning. Elijah and I shook hands, and he asked me where I was going. Wherever it was, I would be driven there — "because, when we invite someone here," he said, "we take the responsibility of protecting him from the white devils until he gets wherever it is he's going." I was, in fact, going to have a drink with several white devils on the other side of town. I confess that for a fraction of a second I hesitated to give the address — the kind of address that in Chicago, as in all American cities, identified itself as a white address by virtue of its location. But I did give it, and Elijah and I walked out onto the steps, and one of the young men vanished to get the car. It was very strange to stand with Elijah for those few minutes, facing those vivid, violent, so problematic streets. I felt very close to him, and really wished to be able to love and honor him as a witness, an ally, and a father. I felt that I knew something of his pain and his fury, and, yes, even his beauty. Yet precisely because of the reality and the nature of those streets — because of what he conceived as his responsibility and what I took to be mine — we would always be strangers, and possibly, one day, enemies. The car arrived — a gleaming, metallic, grossly American blue — and Elijah and I shook hands and said good night once more. He walked into his mansion and shut the door.

1968

In 1968, the year *The Armies of the Night*—subtitled *History as Novel/The Novel as History*—appeared (first in *Harper's* magazine, then as a book), the poet Marianne Moore threw the ceremonial opening pitch of the season for the Yankees. A real poet, not a toad, in the imaginary garden of American baseball. Moore admired Mailer. Mailer admired Mailer, too. His presentation of himself as a character, referred to in the third person throughout *The Armies of the Night*, is grandiose, ironic, and absurd, a toad, indeed—they say he was beautiful, but for those of us who can only look at the pictures there's a squat little man with a satyr's curls. The garden of *Armies*, though, is a version of the real well suited to the flux of the times: a protest against the Vietnam War at which the Pentagon would be exorcised and levitated by the democratic imagination of the masses. Masses, that is, as ridiculously individualistic as Mailer.

Mailer won the Pulitzer Prize and the National Book Award for *The Armies of the Night*, reversing a critical slump that might be said to have extended as far back as the 1951 publication of his second novel, *The Barbary Coast*, panned as a disappointment following his 1948 bestseller *The Naked and the Dead*—a World War II novel that itself now seems a creaky collage of other people's styles and ideas. His fiction never equaled his nonfiction, never came close, a truth he winks at in *Armies* when the poet Robert Lowell tells Mailer he thinks he's "the finest journalist in America." Journalist? "There are days," Mailer responds, "when I think of myself as being the best writer in America."

Critics said that with *Armies* Mailer had invented a new genre, a nonfiction novel. Truman Capote, who'd published his true-crime blockbuster *In Cold Blood* two years previous, disagreed; *he'd* invented the new form.

Neither of them had, of course, but the belief that somebody had invented something—that literature could be new again—was enough to give the new "new journalism" a momentary imprimatur as possibly the future of American letters. That is, the kind of writing considered *serious*. Capote *was* serious. Mailer was, too, but in *Armies* he deliberately made it hard to take him seriously. Like Meridel Le Sueur, like Zora Neale Hurston, in this excerpt, from a chapter called "The Witches and the Fugs," Mailer takes the step Thoreau wouldn't. He crosses over.

And then he comes back. That's the real gift of *The Armies of the Night:* its double identity, the yin-yanged mind of its split-personalitied creator, bundled up in a fact and a fiction both of which were called "Mailer."

NORMAN MAILER

From *The Armies of the Night*

Since the parking lot was huge as five football fields, and just about empty, for they were the first arrivals, the terminus of the March was without drama. Nor was the Pentagon even altogether visible from the parking lot. Perhaps for that reason, a recollection returned to Mailer of that instant (alive as an open nerve) when they had seen it first, walking through the field, just after the March had left the road on the Virginia side of the Potomac; there, topping a rise, it appeared, huge in the near distance, not attractive. Somehow, Mailer had been anticipating it would look more impressive than its pictures, he was always expecting corporation land to surprise him with a bit of wit, an unexpected turn of architectural grace—it never did. The Pentagon rose like an anomaly of the sea from the soft Virginia fields (they were crossing a park), its pale yellow walls reminiscent of some plastic plug coming out of the hole made in flesh by an unmentionable operation. There, it sat, geometrical aura complete, isolated from anything in nature surrounding it. Eras ago had corporation land begun by putting billboards on the old post roads?—now they worked to clean them up—just as the populace had finally succeeded in depositing comfortable amounts of libido on highway signs, gasoline exhaust, and oil-stained Jersey macadam — now corporation land, here named Government, took over state preserves, straightened crooked narrow roads, put up government buildings, removed unwelcome signs till the young Pop eye of Art wept for unwelcome signs — where are our old friends? — and corporation land would succeed, if it hadn't yet, in making nature look like an outdoor hospital, and the streets of U.S. cities, grace of Urban Renewal, would be difficult to distinguish when drunk from pyramids of packaged foods in the aisles of a supermarket.

For years he had been writing about the nature of totalitarianism, its need to render populations apathetic, its instrument — the destruction of mood. Mood was forever being sliced, cut, stamped, ground, excised, or obliterated; mood was a scent which rose from the acts and calms of nature, and totalitarianism was a deodorant to nature. Yes, and by the logic of this metaphor, the Pentagon looked like the five-sided tip on the spout of a spray can to be used under the arm, yes, the Pentagon was spraying the deodorant of its presence all over the fields of Virginia.

The North Parking Lot was physically separated from the Pentagon by a wide four-lane highway. Corporate wisdom had been at work — they might have been rattling about in the vast and empty parking lot of a modern stadium when no game is being played. Being among the first hundred to arrive, they found themselves in a state of confusion. No enemy was visible, nor much organization. In the reaches of the parking lot where they had entered was some sort of crane, with what appeared to be a speaker's platform on the end of its arm, and that was apparently being gotten ready for more speeches. Lowell, Macdonald, and Mailer discussed whether to remain there. They were hardly in the mood for further addresses, but on the other hand, combat was getting nearer — one could tell by the slow contractions of the gut. It was not that they would lose their courage, so much as that it would begin to seep away; so the idea of listening to speeches was not intolerable. There would be at least company.

But a pleasant young woman accompanied by her child had come up to greet Lowell, and she now mentioned that the hippies were going to have a play at the other end of the parking lot and music seemed by far the better preparation for all battle, and music was indeed coming from that direction. So they set out, a modest group in the paved empty desert of the North Parking Area, and strolled toward the sounds of the band which were somehow medieval in sound, leaving behind the panorama of marchers slowly flowing in. On the way, they agreed again that they would be arrested early. That seemed the best way to satisfy present demands and still get back to New York in time for their dinners, parties, weekend parts. The desire to get back early is not dishonorable in Lowell and Macdonald; they had stayed on today, and indeed probably had come this far because Mailer had helped to urge them, but Mailer! with his apocalyptic visions at Lincoln Memorial and again on the March, his readiness to throw himself, breast against breast, in any charge on the foe, why now in such a rush? Did he not respect his visions?

Well the party that night looked to be the best coming up in some time; he simply hated to miss it. Besides, he had no position here; it was not his March on the Pentagon in conception or execution; he was hardly required to remain for days or even hours on the scene. His function was to be arrested — his name was expendable for the cause. He did not like the idea of milling about for hours while the fine line of earlier perception (and Vision!) got mucked in the general confusion. Besides, he was a novelist, and there is no procurer, gambler, adventurer or romantic lover more greedy for experience in great gouts — a part of the novelist wished to take the cumulative rising memories of the last three days and bring them whole, intact, in sum, as they stood now, to cast, nay — shades of Henry James — to *fling* on the gaming tables of life resumed in New York, and there amass a doubling and tripling again. He was in fact afraid that within the yawning mute concrete of the parking lot this day which had begun with such exultation would dissipate into leaderless armies wandering about, acting like clowns and fools before the face of the authority; or worse, raw massacres, something more than bones broken: actual disasters — that was also in the air. He did not know if he was secretly afraid too much would happen or too little, but one thing he knew he hated — that would be to wait, and wait again, and nerve up to the point of being arrested, and get diverted and wait again while the light of the vision went out of the day and out of his head until hungry and cold they would all shamble off shamefacedly to New York on a late plane, too late for everything all around. One could not do that to this day. Great days demanded as much respect as great nights — Victorian, no Edwardian, were Mailer's more courtly sentiments.

And in his defense, one decent motive. He had the conviction that his early arrest might excite others to further effort: the early battles of a war wheel on the hinge of their first legends — perhaps in his imagination, in lockstep to many a montage in many an old movie, saw the word going out from mouth to ear to mouth to ear, linking the troops — in fact cold assessment would say that was not an inaccurate expectation. Details later.

Yes, Mailer had an egotism of curious disproportions. With the possible exception of John F. Kennedy, there had not been a President of the United States nor even a candidate since the Second World War whom Mailer secretly considered more suitable than himself, and yet on the first day of a war which he thought might go on for twenty years, his real desire was to be back in New York for a party. Such men are either monumental fools or excruciatingly practical since it may be wise to go to every party you can if the war is to continue for two decades. Of course, the likelihood is that the government — old corporation land — knew very well how wise it was to forge an agreement in negotiation to stage (dump) the marchers on arrival in the North Area's parking — coming off the March and into the face of a line of troops at the Pentagon, Mailer along with a good many others would not have been diverted with thoughts of New York whereas the parking area was so large and so empty that any army would have felt small in its expanse.

Well, let us move on to hear the music. It was being played by the Fugs, or rather — to be scrupulously phenomenological — Mailer heard the music first, then noticed the musicians and their costumes, then recognized two of them as Ed Sanders and Tuli Kupferberg and knew it was the Fugs. Great joy! They were much better than the last time he had heard them in a grind-it-out theater on Macdougal Street. Now they were dressed in orange and yellow and rose colored capes and looked at once like Hindu gurus, French musketeers, and Southern cavalry captains, and the girls watching them, indeed sharing the platform with them, were wearing love beads and leather bells — sandals, blossoms, and little steel-rimmed spectacles abounded, and the music, no rather the play, had begun, almost Shakespearean in its sinister announcement of great pleasures to come. Now the Participant recognized that this was the beginning of the exorcism of the Pentagon, yes the papers had made much of the permit requested by a hippie leader named Abbie Hoffman to encircle the Pentagon with twelve hundred men in order to form a ring of exorcism sufficiently powerful to raise the Pentagon three hundred feet. In the air the Pentagon would then, went the presumption, turn orange and vibrate until all evil emissions had fled this levitation. At that point the war in Vietnam would end.

The General Services Administrator who ruled on the permit consented to let an attempt be made to raise the building ten feet, but he could not go so far as to allow the encirclement. Of course, exorcism without encirclement was like culinary art without a fire — no one could properly expect a meal. Nonetheless the exorcism would proceed, and the Fugs were to serve as a theatrical medium and would play their music on the rear bed of the truck they had driven in here at the end of the parking lot nearest to the Pentagon some hundreds of yards from the speaker's stand where the rally was to take place.

Now, while an Indian triangle was repeatedly struck, and a cymbal was clanged, a mimeographed paper was passed around to the Marchers watching. It had a legend which went something like this:

> October 21, 1967, Washington, D.C., U.S.A., Planet Earth
>
> We Freemen, of all colors of the spectrum, in the name of God, Ra, Jehovah, Anubis, Osiris, Tlaloc, Quetzalcoatl, Thoth, Ptah, Allah, Krishna, Chango, Chimeke, Chukwu, Olisa-Bulu-Uwa, Imales, Orisasu, Odudua, Kali, Shiva-Shakra, Great Spirit, Dionysus, Yahweh, Thor, Bacchus, Isis, Jesus Christ, Maitreya, Buddha, Rama do exorcise and cast out the EVIL which has walled and captured the pentacle of power and perverted its use to the need of the total machine and its child the hydrogen bomb and has suffered the people of the planet earth, the American people and creatures of the mountains, woods, streams, and oceans grievous mental and physical torture and the constant torment of the imminent threat of utter destruction.
>
> We are demanding that the pentacle of power once again be used to serve the interests of GOD manifest in the world as man. We are embarking on a motion which is millennial in scope. Let this day, October 21, 1967, mark the beginning of suprapolitics.
>
> By the act of reading this paper you are engaged in the Holy Ritual of Exorcism. To further participate focus your thought on the casting out of evil through the grace of GOD which is all (ours). A billion stars in a billion galaxies of space and time is the form of your power, and limitless is your name.

Now while the Indian triangle and the cymbal sounded, while a trumpet offered a mournful subterranean wail, full of sobs, and mahogany shadows of sorrow, and all sour groans from hell's dungeon, while finger bells tinkled and drums beat, so did a solemn voice speak something approximate to this: "In the name of the amulets of touching, seeing, groping, hearing and loving, we call upon the powers of the cosmos to protect our ceremonies in the name of Zeus, in the name of Anubis, god of the dead, in the name of all those killed because they do not comprehend, in the name of the lives of the soldiers in Vietnam who were killed because of a bad karma, in the name of sea-born Aphrodite, in the name of Magna Mater, in the name of Dionysus, Zagreus, Jesus, Yahweh, the unnamable, the quintessent finality of the Zoroastrian fire, in the name of Hermes, in the name of the Beak of Sok, in the name of scarab, in the name, in the name, in the name of the Tyrone Power Pound Cake Society in the Sky, in the name of Rah, Osiris, Horus, Nepta, Isis, in the name of the flowing living universe, in the name of the mouth of the river, we call upon the spirit . . . to raise the Pentagon from its destiny and preserve it."

Now spoke another voice. "In the name, and all the names, it is you."

Now the voice intoned a new chant, leaving the echo of the harsh invocation of all giants and thunders in the beat of cymbals, triangles, drums, leather bells, the sour anguish of a trumpet reaching for evil scurried through the tents of a medieval carnival.

Then all the musicians suddenly cried out: "Out, demons, out— back to darkness, ye servants of Satan—out, demons, out! Out, demons, out!"

Voices from the back cried: "Out! . . . Out! . . . Out! . . . Out!" mournful as the wind of a cave. Now the music went up louder and louder, and voices chanting, "Out, demons, out! Out, demons, out! Out, demons, out!"

He detested community sing—an old violation of his childhood had been the bouncing ball on the movie screen; he had wanted to watch a movie, not sing—but the invocation delivered some message to his throat. "Out, demons, out," he whispered, "out, demons, out." And his foot—simple American foot—was, of course, tapping. "Out, demons, out." Were any of the experts in the Pentagon now shuddering, or glory of partial unringed exorcism—even vibrating? Vibrating experts? "Out, demons, out! Out, demons, out!" He could hear Ed Sanders' voice, Ed of the red-gold head and red-gold beard, editor and publisher of a poetry magazine called *Fuck You*, renaissance conductor, composer, instrumentalist and vocalist of the Fugs, old protégé of Allen Ginsberg, what mighty protégés was Allen amassing. Sanders spoke: "For the first time in the history of the Pentagon there will be a grope-in within a hundred feet of this place, within two hundred feet. Seminal culmination in the spirit of peace and brotherhood, a real grope for peace. All of you who want to protect this rite of love may form a circle of protection around the lovers."

"Circle of protection," intoned another voice.

"These are the magic eyes of victory," Sanders went on. "Victory, victory for peace. Money made the Pentagon—melt it. Money made the Pentagon, melt it for love."

Now came other voices, "Burn the money, burn the money, burn it, burn it."

Sanders: "In the name of the generative power of Priapus, in the name of the totality, we call upon the demons of the Pentagon to rid themselves of the cancerous tumors of the war generals, all the secretaries and soldiers who don't know what they're doing, all the intrigue bureaucracy and hatred, all the spewing, coupled with prostate cancer in the deathbed. Every Pentagon general lying alone at night with a tortured psyche and an image of death in his brain, every general, every general lying alone, every general lying alone."

Wild cried followed, chants: "Out, demons, out! Out, demons, out! Out! out! out! Out, demons, out."

Sanders: "In the name of the most sacred of sacred names Xabrax Phresxner."

He was accompanied now by chants of, "hari, hari, hari, hari, rama, rama, rama, rama, Krishna, hari Krishna, hari, hari, rama, Krishna."

"Out, demons, out."

They all chanted: "End the fire and war, and war, end the plague of death. End the fire and war, and war, end the plague of death." In the background was the sound of a long sustained Ommmm.

On which acidic journeys had the hippies met the witches and the devils and the cutting edge of all primitive awe, the savage's sense of explosion — the fuse of blasphemy, the cap of taboo now struck, the answering roar of the Gods — for what was explosion but connections made at the rate of 10 to the 10th exponent of the average rate of a dialogue and its habitual answer — had all the TNT and nuclear transcendencies of TNT exploded some devil's cauldron from the past? — was the past being consumed by the present? by nuclear blasts, and blasts into the collective living brain by way of all exploding acids, opiums, whiskies, speeds, and dopes? — the past was palpable to him, a tissue living in the tangible mansions of death, and death was disappearing, death was wasting of some incurable ill. When death disappeared, there would be no life.

Morbid thoughts for the edge of battle, thoughts out alone without wings of whiskey to bring them back, but Mailer had made his lonely odyssey into the land of the witches, it had taken him through three divorces and four wives to decide that some female phenomena could be explained by no hypothesis less thoroughgoing than the absolute existence of witches. A lonely journey, taken without help from his old drugs, no, rather a distillate of his most difficult experience, and he had arrived at it in great secrecy, for quondam Marxist, nonactive editor of a Socialist magazine, where and how could he explain or justify a striking force of witches — difficult enough to force a Socialist eye to focus on what was existential. Now, here, after several years of the blandest reports from the religious explorers of LSD, vague Tibetan lama goody-goodness auras of religiosity being the only publicly announced or even rumored fruit from all trips back from the buried Atlantis of LSD, now suddenly an entire generation of acid-heads seemed to have said good-bye to easy visions of heaven, no, now the witches were here, and rites of exorcism, and black terrors of the

night—hippies being murdered. Yes, the hippies had gone from Tibet
to Christ to the Middle Ages, now they were Revolutionary Alche-
mists. Well, thought Mailer, that was all right, he was a Left Conservative himself. "Out, demons, out! Out, demons, out!"

"You know I like this," he said to Lowell. Lowell shook his head.
He looked not untroubled. "It was all right for a while," he said, "but
it's so damn repetitious."

And Macdonald had a harsh glee in his pale eye as if he were
half furious but half diverted by the meaninglessness of the repeti-
tions. Macdonald hated meaninglessness even more than the war in
Vietnam; on the other hand, he lived for a new critical stimulation:
here it might be.

But to Lowell it was probably not meaningless. No, probably
Lowell reacted against everything which was hypnotic in that music.
Even if much of his poetry could be seen as formal incantations, halfway houses on the road to hypnosis and the oceans of contemplation
beyond,

> O to break loose, like the chinook
> Salmon jumping and falling back,
> Nosing up the impossible
> Stone and bone-crushing waterfall—

yes, even if Lowell's remarkable sense of rhythm drew one deep into
the poems, nonetheless hypnotic they resolutely were not, for the language was particular, with a wicked sense of names, details, and places.

> . . . Remember playing
> Marian Anderson, Mozart's *Shepherd King,*
> *il re pastore?* Hammerheaded shark,
> the rainbow salmon of the world—your hand
> a rose . . . And at the Mittersill, you topped
> the ski-run . . .

Lowell's poetry gave one the sense of living in a well, the echoes were deep, and sound was finally lost in moss on stone; down there the light had the light of velvet, and the ripples were imperceptible. But one lay on one's back in this well, looking up at the sky, and stars were determinedly there at night, fixed points of reference; nothing in the poems ever permitted you to turn on your face and try to look down into the depths of the well, it was enough you were in the well—now, look up! The world dazzled with its detail.

Lowell, drawn to hypnosis, would resist it, resist particularly these abstract clackety sounds like wooden gears in a noisemaker, "Hari, hari, hari, hari, rama, rama, Krishna, hari, rama, Krishna," and the whoop of wild Indians in "out, demons, out!" Nothing was more dangerous to the poet than hypnosis, for the *style* of one's entrance to that plain of sleep where all ideas coalesced into one, was critical— enter by any indiscriminate route, "Om, Om, Om," and who knows what finely articulated bones of future prosody might be melted in those undifferentiated pots—no, Lowell's good poetry was a reconnaissance into the deep, and for that, pirate's patrols were the best— one went down with the idea one would come back with more, but one did not immerse oneself with open guru Ginsberg arms crying, "Baa, baa, slay this sheep or enrich it, Great Deep," no, one tiptoed in and made a raid and ideally got out good. Besides, the Fugs and Hindu bells and exorcisms via LSD were all indeed Allen Ginsberg's patch; poets respected each other's squatter's rights like Grenadiers before the unrolled carpet of the King.

But of course Lowell's final distaste was for the attraction itself of these sounds (which were incidentally lifting Mailer into the happiest sense of comradeship). Without a drink in him, he was nonetheless cheering up again at the thought of combat, and deciding it would be delightful to whack a barricade in the company of Ed Sanders with the red-gold beard who had brought grope-freak talk to the Village and always seemed to Mailer a little over-liberated, but now suitable, yes, the Novelist was working up all steam in the "Out, demons, out."

1970

Nineteen sixty-eight was also the year Garry Wills published in *Life* magazine the essay that would become "Whittier: First Day" in his brilliant 1970 study of America, liberalism, and original sin—as embodied in the personage of the thirty-seventh president—*Nixon Agonistes*. It's a finer-grained piece of work than *The Armies of the Night*, with a subtler understanding of religion—suburban as well as ecstatic—as the constant current that carries American politics along. Nixon is only a shadow here, barely a memory in Whittier, California, the hometown to which Wills travels to visit a church and Nixon's alma mater, Whittier College. Church and school, institutions of stability, here rendered as mildly devoted to things as they are, their people only dimly aware of what time it was, 1968, of the earth giving way beneath them. It's the extraordinary ordinariness of Wills's scenes, juxtaposed with flights not of fancy but of history and criticism, that make the reader tremble, too. It's the close-up and the long view blending together, the microscope and the telescope of myth, as historian of religion Wendy Doniger puts it. "But sometimes," she adds, "life itself is the text in which we read the myth of double vision."

GARRY WILLS
Whittier: First Day

When you are actually *in* America, America hurts.
—D. H. LAWRENCE

Nixon spent the last weekend before election 1968 in Los Angeles, at the posh tiered Century Plaza Hotel, site of a big demonstration and semiriot when President Johnson stayed there (we now have many such unmonumented battlefields). Nixon was resting, readying himself for the ordeal of the campaign's last hours — the election eve telethon; the long flight back on election day; then the eerie time he has known so often, waiting for the oracle that issues piecemeal from election booths to be put together, less and less enigmatic as the night passes, pronouncing his future.

He needed rest. He had been sliding, with quiet inevitability, down in the polls. Humphrey, who *could* not win a month ago, just *might* win now. There were hundreds of desperate last-minute plans to reverse this trend. Nixon was bombarded with them. Yet he sat there, shell-shocked. Back in New York, his strategists around John Mitchell

even considered accepting Humphrey's challenge to debate; one reason for dismissing the plan was Nixon's harried state. He was getting
irritable. He needed rest.

I decided to spend the two blank days of his rest in Whittier, the
hometown he would not be visiting this weekend. It takes a mere forty
minutes to get there when traffic is moving. Century City streets, with
extravagant astral names like Galaxy Boulevard, wind almost inevitably up onto Santa Monica Freeway, which arches one on a low tra-
jectory over the sunken metropolis. Los Angeles, thanks to earthquake
legislation, is literally a topless city. It grows by creeping through
valleys, up hills, stripping earth and then reclothing it in Western-
pastel, a muddied blend of low Spanish and low modern styles. Up
on the freeway, one crosses this discolored carpet of a town without
seeing much of it. Railings, poles, signs make a tunnel. Downtown
buildings are hidden by the placards that mark exits and bifurcations
and irrevocable chances to weave out of one freeway to another. But
these low buildings do not, as one might expect, leave a clear prospect
of sky. The gray morning thickness of air was cut by many lines, by
their nodes and carriers, joinings and dispersions—latticework pylons
lifting this network of wires. Lanes of traffic knot and ravel out beneath a tangle of the city's nerves. It is the dreary future of McLuhan's
vision—a quiver of disembodied awareness, signal and reception;
America fondly creates the entity she has praised for years as a "live
wire." This part of the country looks like a crush of people speeding
nowhere, a jam of signals saying nothing, a great human switchboard.
No wonder Nixon left it as soon as he could.

But the place he left as a boy was open land, haze of sun leaf-
sieved into lemons on Leffingwell's ranch, oranges on the Murphy
ranch, and—between the two, strategically placed to service workers
from both farms—the Nixon grocery store. I saw little of that agrarian
valley remaining as I came down off the throughway and went east out
of Whittier Boulevard, past the very small buildings and very large
signs that trigger America's bottomless lust for hamburgers. At Whit-

tier itself, I turned up the town's main street, which runs north toward a green side of mountain, under which Whittier College is sheltered. It seemed the place to begin.

But it was Sunday; perhaps no one would be on campus. Just before I reached the college, I saw the First Friends Church on my left, with people streaming into it. Outside, one of those black chinked signs under the glass, with white chips dropped into proper slots announcing the sermon: "The Christian and the Election." I pulled into a parking lot across the street, at the William Penn Hotel. I thought this might be Nixon's own church. Perhaps I could decide here, of all places, which man to vote for on Tuesday.

Not that I expected any candidate to be endorsed outright from the pulpit. Dr. Norman Vincent Peale merely made trouble for his friend, Dick Nixon, when he attacked Kennedy in 1960. Politics and religion are supposed to observe an oil-and-water compact in America. That is why priests at political demonstrations anger ladies on their street corners. When Kennedy said he would "do the right thing" and observe the neat division, he came as close as an American politician ever does to expressing the "true code of a gentleman." Nixon had to dissociate himself from Dr. Peale's charges. (So, in time, did Peale himself. He amiably pleaded that he had "never been too bright anyhow.")

First Friends, the largest Quaker church in the area, has a plain board meetinghouse air, but with boards cushioned and floor carpeted. Hardly Marble Collegiate, but verging on Wooden Collegiate. It has "stained-glass" windows — pale colored patterns of frame, niche, surrounding scrolls, with a large blank in the middle, watery cosmetics for some absent image.

My hope that this might be Nixon's boyhood church was soon dashed. That is a more austere affair further east on Whittier Boulevard, near the site of the Nixon store. But Nixon's relatives attend the downtown church — his Aunt Ollie is there this morning. And the pastor is an alumnus of Whittier College, as are most of the parish leaders.

If one is to find survivals from the old Whittier, there is no better place to look than at First Friends on a Sunday morning. Attendance was thin, and those present seemed well above average age, handsomely wrinkled (as by Norman Rockwell's undemanding pencil) — *survivors,* hardy and at peace. The balcony level was empty, but for a ten-year-old girl in a seizure of concentration. Her bright eyes traveled intent across the faces beneath her. She seemed to be studying, trying to read answers. She did not, however, look much toward the pastor, or seem to be heeding his words.

They were eminently unheedable. The Christian will vote for Christ, and find peace. The pastor's style is Preacher's Ingratiating, rhetorical equivalent of Wooden Collegiate — the chirpy persuasiveness that made Dr. Peale one of the "Twelve Best U.S. Salesmen" for 1954. This Quaker pastor looks like Harold Lloyd grown older and more poised, bewildered goggles turned now to twinkling beacon lights of brotherhood. Every few seconds, a kindly smile helps the glasses light parishioners on their way. He can hardly finish a statement without asking for agreement or some common ground of understanding. Anecdote: "I went on a train ride . . ." Solicitation: "Have you been on a train recently?" Anecdote: "The little boy ran away . . ." Solicitation: "Did you ever try to run away?" The rhetorical questions insinuate, as painlessly as possible, a moral tone into the congregation's daily concerns. It is the cheerleader tone of Nixon trying to slip a fast one by: "Incidentally, in mentioning Secretary Dulles, isn't it wonderful, finally, to have a Secretary of State who isn't taken in by the Communists, who stands up to them?"

If you vote for Christ, you will find peace. It is the message of Nixon's own spiritual guide, Dr. Peale, who offers us a babysitter God: "He just puts His big arms around everybody and hugs them up against Himself." A nonpolitical Nanny-God to protect us from Kennedys. But will He? There is a contradiction in the fact that Peale, arguing for separation of church and state, fending off Rome's threat to that separation, jumped *into* politics. Nor was it the first time. He caused a stir back in 1948 by advancing MacArthur for President (he likes to include, in his edifying stories of achievers-through-prayer, the feats of executive types among the military). Peale is not really concerned to keep religion out of politics. He wants to keep *other* religions out — every kind but his. As Donald Meyer puts it in *The Positive Thinkers,* Peale's constituency is that great middle class afflicted by anomie — the kind of people drawn to Wallace rallies. They have affluence without satisfaction, privilege without style — lives empty at the center, like the pastel windows in First Friends. They are not safe in their possessions, because they are not conscious of deserving them. They do not know why they gain or retain life's chromium graces; their own infidelity tortures them. To them Peale comes preaching acceptance. They have *not* failed themselves and their children. If they thought of themselves as failures, now they must think only of Peale's gratulatory maxims: "The Spirit Lifter that I read and committed today lies deeply imbedded in my mind. It is now sending off through my thoughts its healing, refreshing effects." Nineteenth-century Christianity urged the poor to learn contentment with their lack of money. Peale and his brethren must teach man to submit to wealth: "There was a time when I acquiesced in the silly idea that there is no relationship between faith and prosperity." A religion of the "deserving poor" has become the religion of the undeserving rich — for those uneasy because they no longer wear cloth coats.

To "vote for Christ" is to vote for oneself as Christ-like — a process of self-hypnosis that says the consumer life of middle America is, no matter what it seems, a godly life. But one can only learn such passivity toward affluence if the system blessing the nation is kept beyond question. If a man is always discussing the rules of the game, trying to change or improve them, he cannot relax into contentment with his lot. That is why Peale denounces "preachers offering intellectualized sermons on social problems." It distracts man from the search for inner joy to be always "fumbling with materialistic processes." The Pealite's main commerce with material things is peaceful enjoyment of them, putting off all doubt that they reflect God's blessing: "This world is somehow built on moral foundations. This . . . is the one lesson history teaches . . . The good never loses." Peale is the palliative that no longer served those flocking to Wallace speeches.

The little girl was right, then, to turn her eyes on the Norman Rockwell ladies. This congregation had not been summoned to accept Christ, but to accept itself. To accept itself accepting a world of sunny disorientation. The milky white center is reserved in these windows because *they,* the people, America's large blank center, are the object of their own cult. She would have to "make her decision" for — or against — them. Her problem was posed in the older women's somnolence, their wrinkles lightly penciled: would she soak up their nice thoughts, along with the sun; sweeten like an orange of this valley? It was easy, as I watched her puzzled face, to imagine Richard Nixon at her age, wondering if this world would hold him.

After his sermon, and a song, the pastor went outside where, along with his assistant, he greeted the line of parishioners with handshakes, one last twinkle of unobtrusive inspiration. As I waited to talk with him, various people came up to say hello: "I've never seen you here before. Is there something I can do for you?" "Friends" live up to their name. We talk about the Nixons, about the town, about its other Quaker church. I look over the pamphlets and bulletins — theological blandness, with one tart touch of politics, the Quaker antiwar movement (no mention of that in the sermon on Christians and the Election). The friendly bulletin has notes on the community: "On the day the Apollo [VII] blasted off, Mr. and Mrs. X also left the launching pad for Canada . . ." Perfect oneness with the culture. All systems go.

When the pastor has pumped and twinkled his last, he leads me into his study and starts changing. "Rams game, we'll just make it. Want to come?" I say I must work all day, in Whittier. He is too broadminded to resent such antisabbatarianism. It looks like a rainy November day for the game, he is pulling on heavy pants and a sweater — back to Harold Lloyd's college days. As he becomes less and less clerical, one with the culture around him, blasting off for the game, I watched the reverse of a process I had seen, six weeks earlier, in Chicago. During the Democratic Convention, a group of clergymen was formed to act as peacemakers in the streets. Not many Roman priests took part (Chicago's Cardinal — "Louisiana Fats" to his liberal critics — does not like "activists" in his diocese), but ministers and rabbis hunted up and wore Roman collars, with black suit and dickey: they wanted to be recognized as clergymen, men set apart from the rest of society. The collar would protect them (they hoped — vain hope) from Mayor Daley's Irish Catholic cops.

In a way, Peale had been right about Kennedy. (It was typical of him, when his stand became inconvenient, to call it wrong. One should accept oneself as "not too bright" when this reduces social friction.) He was right, as the women on Baltimore's street corner had been right. It was impossible to keep religion out of politics in the age of Billy Graham and Dr. Peale. Where they preach, from Nixon's elbow, acceptance, what is left for religion of a different sort but to preach rejection? And that will seem, to the goodhearted pastor and his assistant, an "un-American" thing — the suggestion that the consumer life is not necessarily godly.

Talbert Moorehead, already dressed for the Rams game, arrives to drive his pastor to the stadium. Moorehead was in the class just before Nixon's at Whittier, and he is happy to reminisce — how Nixon helped him with a speech, how Nixon founded the Orthogonians ("pigs" to the older society of Franklins — Moorehead was a Franklin), how he ran for Congress the first time with everybody helping stuff mail. I listen until kickoff time drags them away, then Moorehead invites me to his office the next day (it is just down the street, beside the Bank of America). When they leave, I go back to the William Penn for breakfast — the hotel is just one of many ways the town reminds itself of Quaker history — of Wales (Bryn Mawr Street), of New England (Whittier College, Greenleaf Avenue), of Philadelphia (the college's "Franklins" — though Ben makes a gamy addition here, as he did to

Sir William's "holy experiment" in the eighteenth century). There is a
Friends Avenue, a Quaker Maid Dairy.

In the hotel lobby, one office door is marked "Christology" — a
religious unity movement, the desk clerk explains. Leaflets give the
schedule for community events: among them, "Karate for Teenagers,
7:30–9:00 in Gunn Park." Back on the street, I pause at the window of
"The Beard," a boutique next to First Friends Church — silky mandarin
jackets with Maltese crosses on chains. The closest I had come, all that
Sunday morning, to reminders of the crucifixion.

Up Greenleaf, it is only a block to the college; the first building,
Mendenhall — which houses the president's office. No one is here Sunday; that gives me time to study a bulletin board with clippings about
Nixon. I find, later, that a second Nixon board was spattered with mud
one night ("By students?" I ask — "Who knows?" the answer) and had
to be moved inside the president's office. Over the mantel, in the open
hall of the building, is a quote from the school's namesake:

> Early hath Life's mighty question
> Thrilled within the heart of youth,
> With a deep and strong beseeching,
>   What and where is Truth?

Along with the school, the football team is named for the gentle abo-
litionist poet: "Tigers Beat Poets" goes a notice of last week's loss to
Occidental, as if announcing a brute fact of nature. The Quaker poet
was also a Republican, one of the party's earliest supporters, an elector
in the college that chose Lincoln. But his latter-day pupils are not true
to the poet's party. In a copy of the student paper (*Quaker Campus*), I
find a column urging Humphrey's election ("I have no particular love
for R.M.N.") and an editorial supporting Eugene McCarthy: "Nixon
. . . would lead without scruples or conscience . . . Nixon headed off
the stronger personality of Nelson Rockefeller by kissing elephant be-
hinds" (*O John!*). "For God's sake, forget the Pueblo" (*O Greenleaf!*).
"[America] is a sick, violent, racist society intent on destroying itself"

(*O Whittier!*). A student Human Rights Commission has been formed to make sure no Delano grapes shall make their way onto Campus Inn tables, that no housemothers shall enter a girl's room without search warrant ("things go on on this campus that are in violation of the law"). It is just as well Nixon aspired to the presidency of the United States. He could hardly succeed as president of Whittier College.

The college is small. The library, on crutch-shaped stilts of poured concrete, is Modern Campus Standard (except for the name, Bonnie Bell Wardman Library). The science building plants its concrete crutches on Hadley Field, where Nixon played guard as a Poet. I look for a place where Nixon might have spent his time, an old building—and stop by the oldest: Founders Hall. In front there is an "Orthogonian Pond" donated by the club's early members. This hall, built by pioneers in 1894, has on its second floor a large room, with a stage and rows of folding chairs, that served as chapel for services, auditorium for commencements, theater for plays and debates, and meeting-house for campus politics. Here was the hub of campus life when the campus was the hub of community life, when education was local and truly public—elocutionary, a matter of performance to meet local standards. Here Nixon's mother performed and graduated; and his cousin, Jessamyn West. Here he debated and acted, cried real effortful tears in *Bird in Hand,* and scored the large triumphs of a forensic senior year.

The place is ghosted with cobwebs and disanimated furniture—stuffed birds, science slides, the rags of curtain and scenery, things made for public theatrical life that all look dead in private. On the third floor, elocution is still taught; only now it is called "The Psychology of Persuasive Speech," and it uses tape recorders and the apparatus of McLuhan's age. The fourth floor has moldering stage costumes, out-of-date fedoras and silky gowns that seem to have starved on their hangers. The stairs that wind down have built-in benches at each landing—former "student centers." There is a time lag between this solid building and the new ones perched on stilts, as if ready to take off. The lag will be remedied one month after Nixon's election, when Founders Hall goes up in flames.

If Whittier life revolved around the second story of Founders Hall, the group that held this key piece of terrain was the "Literary Society" which, for Whittier, *was* a society. "Chief" Newman, full-blooded Indian who was football coach of the Poets, says, "When I came on the campus in 1929, the Franklins were the controlling force." Nixon, with Newman's help, changed that. "The Orthogonians became more aggressive, and began recruiting the best boys on campus." In the indulgent way of community colleges, which have near horizons populous with friendly onlookers, Franklins were the "brilliant" set at Whittier. There is no brilliance like a schoolboy's since it is all promise — a thing indefinite and opening out, therefore infinite. Every speech or poem is not so much a thing achieved as a harbinger. And this was, by most standards, the sphere Nixon belonged to. His grades were good, his debating excellent, his political skills already apparent. But there was, then as always, a deep distrust of brilliance in him. "I won my share of scholarships," he wrote later, "and of speaking and debating prizes in school, not because I was smarter but because I worked longer and harder than some of my gifted colleagues." Brilliance, like the hare, moves in spurts, unreliably over the long haul. Nixon would seek out the turtles, slower, methodical, more certain. He was first president of the Orthogonians. His uneasiness with brilliance he maintains to this day — the feelings that burst out when he talks about "intellectuals," standoffish Effinghams not at the mercy of Steadfast.

Some of this feeling undoubtedly comes from Nixon's sensitivity to the plight of the underdog, his genuine compassion. Talbert Moorehead, when he was running for class president, had to make a speech in that life-and-death arena of schoolboy hopes, the second floor of Founders, and he felt inadequate to the task. Nixon, without being told, sensed this, and took him aside. "I can still see him now, pacing up and down, telling me how to give a speech: 'You've got to find an issue and concentrate on *it*, not on yourself.' He was a great one for 'issues.'"

He found a number of issues that made him a leader — without making him, in the customary sense, popular. He was friendly with everyone, but he had no close friends or admiring circle. When he was not in class, he was at the store, working; and few boys remember going out there to see him (though they remember the large meals brought from the grocery and, in those Depression times, shared with others). He rose not so much by force of personality — he would have scorned the "buddy boy" approach, even if he were capable of it — as by finding the right issues.

Dancing, for instance — frowned on in this Quaker school. He won his race for president of the student body by promising to bring dances to the campus, though he himself did not attend them. His argument, made successfully to the trustees, was that it was better to have dancing under campus control than to let students seek it in the more sulphurous atmosphere of Los Angeles. Another campus "issue" was the annual bonfire, a point of class pride. Each year the fire was fueled with scrap wood topped by an outhouse. The competition was to see which senior chairman could top the pile of debris with the largest specimen — two-holer, say, or even three. Nixon scored an immense remembered triumph when his diligence turned up a four-holer. Picture the systematic intensity that went into this achievement. There is a Steward method at poker, a Chotiner method at elections, and a four-holer method in campusmanship. Show him the rules, and he will play your game, no matter what, and beat you at it. Because with him it is not a game.

But the greatest "issue" of his school days was the Orthogonians' undermining of the Franklins. The Franklins wore formal dress to their meetings and were literary. The Orthogonians were "common man" in style — and mainly made up of athletes. Chief Newman, the coach, claims he did not get involved in campus politics, and so cannot be included in the club's founders, but Moorehead claims everybody thought of the Orthogonians as "Chief Newman's boys." It is this tie, no doubt, and not the time he spent on the football bench, that makes Nixon feel so close, even now, to "the Chief." Football was also his way to remain "common" during his triumphs on the long debating tours of that time. He would not get trapped in the first-class lounge where Steadfast might make fun of his "snooty" ways.

That Sunday afternoon in Whittier, after talking to Mrs. Olive Marshburn (Aunt Ollie) and Mr. Merle West (Jessamyn's brother), I drove over to see the Chief. He lives in a fine suburban home on what used to be Murphy's ranch, the orange farm. He is slow in his movements and speech, firm, with the air of a chieftain, yet not haughty. "The Orthogonians kind of adopted me as a godfather." I asked if the stories about Nixon's tension before games were true—that he could not eat or sleep. "I guess so. He never spared himself. He used to take an awful lacing in scrimmage. He was tenacious as the dickens. When he got hold of something, he never let go." He was not much of an athlete, though? "No." Nixon was not only small, but clumsy. His wife recalls that he almost killed himself trying to rollerskate when they were first dating. Why, I asked the chief, did he keep trying so hard? "I guess he thought it was his duty. Everyone tried to do something for the team, then—even if it was only to work as manager, a thankless task. Hubert Perry, the son of the banker who got Dick into politics, was manager of the team in Dick's day. We used to empty the town on a football day. It was a smaller world, then. Less sophisticated. You can't get anybody to volunteer for manager anymore." According to one classmate, Richard Harris, Nixon's role was even more ignominious than the manager's: Nixon and Harris served as "cannon fodder" to the team; they were tackling dummies—part of a defense line against which the first string did its practicing. There were not many available for the varsity at Whittier—Nixon's freshman team was made up of eleven men, so injuries or substitutions were plainly impossible. The coach had to take what he could get in the way of a second eleven for the varsity, and Nixon and Harris were it. After all his effort, Nixon did not get a football letter in senior year.

There is a self-punishing side to Nixon that only makes sense back in what Newman calls that smaller, less sophisticated world. It was a world where men were supposed to strive and deserve, even if they did not succeed. It became fashionable, in the years after Nixon's crushing defeat of 1962, to ask what kept him running. It was the same thing that kept him on the football field, where he did not belong — the sacredness of running, the need to *deserve* luck eventually by showing the pluck that starts at the bottom and never quits. The titles of Horatio Alger stories are very eloquent: *Making His Way, Helping Himself, Struggling Upward, Bound to Rise*. The emphasis is not on having risen, but on rising. Luck comes to many, but only pluck turns luck into a molder of character. It is the code of Emerson: "Life only avails, not the having lived. Power ceases in the instant of repose."

Andrew Carnegie thought no men should inherit money. We should all start equal, so the man of worth can *prove* his worth. Alger actually accomplished this aim in fiction; he used the Victorian plot-device of putting an heir in rags — unconscious prince among the paupers — to make him earn, at the bottom, the fortune that was his by mere inheritance. The doctrine of equality is, in Carnegie's hands, a way of clearing the field for self-assertion. But if we are to start equal each generation, why not each year, or each day? If what one's father did in the last decade gives an unfair advantage in this decade, why does what I accomplished yesterday not give me an unfair advantage today?

The poisonous thing about Horatio Alger was not that he made men aim at wealth or success — he did not: the stories' idle rich "boys with kid gloves" stay richer, for the most part, than laborious rising heroes. The hero did not aim at success but at succeeding — that is, at character formation and "self-improvement." He was a martyr to duty — Lincoln and Wilson forging their souls and losing their cause.

The self-made man is the true American monster. The man who wants to make something outside himself—a chair, a poem, a million dollars—produces something. It can be praised or condemned; but it is "out there," a thing wrought or won or subdued, apart from the self. The *self*-maker, self-improving, is always a construction in progress. The man's product—his self—is never finished, not severed from him to stand on its own. He must ever be tinkering, improving, adjusting; starting over; fearful his product will get out of date, or rot in the storehouse. His lovingly worked stained window has, always, a white space at the center. To stand out "fair and square" is to stand out, by earned excellence, from the ranks of the common man. And to do that one must keep returning to the ranks, starting over. Found the Orthogonians, and when they become a fashionable society, found neo-Orthogonians—and so in an endless line of men rising but doomed to avoid having risen. (If one sheds the "Republican" cloth coat, does one not lose the Republicanism with it?)

Emerson, the Horatio Alger of the educated, felt this duty always to be starting over. He said one must become a child again each day— "unaffected, unbiased, unbribable, unaffrighted"—to achieve real independence, which is independence from one's past achievements and judgments, as well as from the rest of the race's opinions. It is not truth (the goal) Emerson is interested in, but *discovery* of truth (the process). Strike out on your own, he says, or "tomorrow a stranger will say with masterly good sense precisely what we have thought and felt all the time, and we shall be forced to take with shame our own opinion from another."

Nixon has this self-improving mania: the very choice of a framework for his book reflects it. As with most of his strategic decisions, the choice of an outline for *Six Crises* met several needs. First, it was another way to ride Ike's coattails—a citation shows he means people to think of *Eisenhower's Six Great Decisions* by Walter Bedell Smith. But, even beyond that choice, he had war-gamed the situation until he chose The Method for writing a book. On one hand, by focusing on a limited number of situations, rather than adopting the standard framework of autobiography, he could omit certain parts of his life entirely. The names of Helen Douglas and Joe McCarthy simply did not occur in the book. On the other hand, he can watch himself in action, and "improve" himself publicly, by the elocutionary method of that second-floor platform in Founders Hall. The book is a report card on the student's progress. Mistakes in one crisis are corrected in the next, as if we were moving from semester to semester, from one course to another. Here he is, moralizing, at the height of the fund trouble: "In such periods of intense preparations for battle, most individuals experience all the physical symptoms of tension — they become edgy and short-tempered, some can't eat, others can't sleep. I had experienced all these symptoms in the days since our train left Pomona. I had had a similar experience during the Hiss case." He still lives through that rough day before the football game. "But what I had learned was that feeling this way before a battle was not something to worry about — on the contrary, failing to feel this way would mean I was not adequately keyed up, mentally and emotionally, for the conflict ahead." One must not only try one's best, but be conscious of trying; not enough to win, you must deserve the victory; deserve it by suffering for it. Easy wins are somehow tainted — the meaningless prizes of the brilliant. "It is only when the individual worries about how he feels that such physical factors become signs of self-destruction rather than of creativity. Two of the most important lessons I have learned from going through the fire of decision is [*sic*] that one must know himself, be able to recognize his physical reactions under stress for what they are, and that he must never worry about the necessary and even healthy symptoms incident to creative activity." It becomes a matter of *health* to tense up, and to watch one's tenseness, parading these symptoms of effort as one boasts of a cloth coat, or of scholarships won without any special ability. Nothing is being given *him* on a silver platter. He is, Uriah-like, proud of his humble origin and great effort. No charisma here, or Kennedy charm; no decadent kid gloves.

This spirituality of improvement is like the self-consciousness of health faddists. True men of action, Chesterton argued, know that concentration on health is unhealthy: "Even if the ideal of such men were simply the ideal of kicking a man downstairs, they thought of the end like men, not of the process like paralytics. They did not say, 'Efficiently elevating my right leg, using, you will notice, the muscles of the thigh and calf, which are in excellent order, I —' Their feeling was quite different. They were so filled with the beautiful vision of the man lying flat at the foot of the staircase that in that ecstasy the rest followed in a flash." But the self-made man has to concentrate on the thing he is making, on his product and end and whole excuse — on himself. When Nixon writes that "adversity breaks the weak but makes the strong," he is not simply repeating a platitude. Making the self strong is the task proposed to man by the Whittier of his youth, by the moral old America of Emerson.

The true significance of nineteenth-century liberalism was not so much that products are tested on the open market of free enterprise, or that truth will triumph in the free market of the academy, as that man himself must be spiritually *priced*, must establish his value ("amount to something"), in each day's trading. To experience one's worth in the real testing place, in the active trading of today's market, is the sole aim of America's moral monsters. That is why Emerson trumpets the need to "bring the past for judgment into the thousand-eyed present and live ever in a new day . . . a true man belongs to no other time or place, but is the center of things." That is the spirit of Nixon's cult of crisis — his eagerness, always, to be "in the arena," his praise of others for being cool under pressure, for being "tested in the fires."

But what if, having entered the market, one's stock falls? Who or what is there to lend support in that case? The merit, for an Emerson, is all his own if he stands independent, freed of help from the centuries. And if the merit is each man's without debt, then the failure must be one's own as well. Nixon puts it this way: "Chief Newman, my football coach in college and a man who was a fine coach but an even more talented molder of character [that's the real game, all right, mold the self, make a new little free-standing Emerson], used to say: 'You must never be satisfied with losing. You must get angry, terribly angry, about losing. But the mark of a good loser [improve oneself even in defeat] is that he takes his anger out on himself [succeed at becoming a martyr, even if you do not succeed in the vulgar sense] and not on his victorious opponents or his team-mates [stand alone even in defeat, don't admit human needs, don't lean].'"

It is this morality of demonstrated daily desert—this meritocracy, with active trading in merits and demerits—that lies behind heartland America's hatred of welfare and relief and the systematic alleviation of poverty. The deserving rise; if the undeserving are also helped, what happens to the scoring in this game of spiritual effort and merit badges? The free-market of virtue and soul-making is destroyed by such "controls," such interference with incentive. Emerson knew this: "Your miscellaneous popular charities; the education at colleges of fools, the building of meetinghouses to the vain end to which many now stand; alms to sots, and the thousand-fold relief societies;—though I confess with shame I sometimes succumb and give the dollar, it is a wicked dollar, which by and by I shall have the manhood to withhold."

No wonder the victims of Whittier must collapse into Dr. Peale's smarmy embrace. What a grisly world our Emersons and Algers have bequeathed us from those days of literary and elocutionary societies, of calculating sermons about mastery of the soul. Think of the souls whose Dun & Bradstreet rating just keeps falling. That is when Peale must hurry in and tell men to accept themselves: "There are many people who simply can't have faith in God because they have no faith in themselves." How *can* they have, when the trading system for made and unmade selves has put a price tag on them? Therefore Peale and his associates "use psychiatry and psychology to help people love themselves." Put the brain to sleep; otherwise it can only whir end-

lessly on its pin. "Americans just buzz round like various sort of propellers, pinned down by their freedom and equality" — their freedom
to enter the market, their equality of opportunity, their chance to get
in on the trading.

Even one day in Whittier, spent imagining the America of Nixon's childhood, is suffocating. That world has a locker-room smell, of
spiritual athleticism. As I drove back toward Los Angeles that night,
along Whittier Boulevard, wide lane enscrolled on either side with
continuous neon scallops, the sulphur of Los Angeles seemed a better
thing to breathe than the muggy air, heavy with moral perspiring, of
Whittier.

1977

Beginning to See the Light, the collection of essays from which "Truth and Consequences" is excerpted, was out of print when I came across it in an artists' colony library committed to saving the work of everyone who'd ever been through there. It's criticism. Narrative criticism: responses to Dylan, Elvis, the Who, the Velvet Underground, and others that are also works of literary journalism, stories of experience fully sensual and fully intellectual at the same time. I'd never read anything like them. This was before I knew that Willis was one of the great rock writers of the sixties and seventies, easily as fabulous as Lester Bangs, Greil Marcus, and the rest of the men who became a canon. Willis wasn't included. First, because she was a woman. Second, because she demolished the fan boys' fetishization of authenticity, their obsession with the original blues and the bootleg riff, the esoteric over the democratic.

Her concern, she wrote in her introduction, wasn't purity, it was *liberation,* and she'd seize it wherever she could find it. "Why," she asked, "regard commercial art as intrinsically more compromised than art produced under the auspices of the medieval church, or aristocratic patrons? Art has always been in some sense propaganda for

ruling classes and at the same time a form of struggle against them. Art
that succeeds manages to evade or transcend or turn to its own purposes the strictures imposed on the artist; on the deepest level it is the
enemy of authority, as Plato understood."

"Next Year in Jerusalem," the essay from which "Truth and Consequences" is taken, is a twenty thousand–word investigation, originally produced under the auspices of *Rolling Stone,* of what it might
mean to Willis to become a religious Jew. Twenty thousand words!
About ordinary Jews, in a mass media magazine about pop culture.
This really was new journalism. Not that it came out of a vacuum.
Willis's deliberately plain prose echoes the reportage of Meridel Le
Sueur, another feminist writer for whom the ornamentation of literary fashion seemed an unnecessary, even dangerous, burden. And
what Willis describes in her introduction as her fundamental, animating quarrel with the "puritanical discomfort with the urge — whatever
form it takes — to gratification now" recalls the redeeming quality of
Mencken's rage against religion, his hatred of those he saw as the enemies of pleasure. Willis's antidote to that anger — "it is the longing for
happiness that is potentially radical," she writes, "while the morality
of sacrifice is an age-old weapon of rulers" — might almost have been
written by that Christian crusader W. T. Stead, the original "new journalist," in 1894.

What follows is this book's second trip to the Holy Land, with
Willis as a not-so-innocent abroad, immersing herself in the world of
her brother Mike, a once-secular Jew who has recently converted to
Orthodoxy.

ELLEN WILLIS
Truth and Consequences

"The first commandment," said Reb Noach, "is to know there is a God." We were resuming a conversation we had started a few days earlier. "The disease of Western thought," he had said then, "is: 'There is no absolute truth.' But it's intuitively obvious that either something is true or it isn't. Listen— 'There is no absolute truth.' 'Are you sure?' 'Yes.' 'Are you *absolutely* sure?'" I could afford to laugh. I believed something was true or it wasn't; I just didn't think we could know for sure which was which. "They call us fanatics. But a fanatic is someone who won't listen to reason. I say, let's reason together. Let's find a premise on which we can both agree, and reason from there. The purpose of reason," he had concluded, "is to get someone to the point where his intuition will say, 'Yes, you're right.'"

"*Know* there is a God," Reb Noach repeated. "Not 'have faith.' Understand! Reason! But reason can only tell you what you already know. It's a servant, like your hand." He held his hand out. "Hand! Come to my nose!" The hand did not move. "What's this? Revolution? Don't be silly! No, your hand acts on what you really want, not on what you say you want. Reason will tell you what you really know — what are *your* perceptions. Not other people's, not society's."

For the next hour or so, Reb Noach tried to persuade my intuition. If my father on his deathbed asked me to say a mourner's prayer for him, would I? Of course. If he asked me to say a bunch of nonsense syllables, would I? Probably not. Why not? What's the difference? Well, I think religious ritual is meaningful, worthy of respect; that doesn't mean it represents absolute truth. If someone ran in front of my car and I hit him, wouldn't I feel guilty, even if I couldn't possibly have stopped in time? Yes, I would. What did that tell me? "Even if it's not technically my fault, someone has suffered because of me. It's irrational, but I'd think, 'If I'd just done something different — taken the bus, stayed home. . . .'"

"The reason you would feel guilty," Reb Noach said, "is that it really *would* be your fault. If you hadn't done something wrong, God wouldn't have chosen you as the instrument of someone's death."

I appreciated Reb Noach's technique. I realized that I had, on occasion, used it myself. (Don't you and your husband both work? Suppose you lived with your sister, and you both worked, and she wanted you to cook dinner every night because she was tired — would you do it? Why not? Well, then, what's different about doing it for a man?) But my intuition was unconvinced. I still couldn't see the ultimate Reality as a being who cared, willed, intervened in our lives and — might as well bring it up — decreed separate functions for men and women.

"You don't think men and women are basically different?"

"*Basically*, no," I said. "*Basically*, I think we're all human beings."

"One of the craziest ideas in this crazy modern world," said Reb Noach, "is that men and women are the same. Men and women are two different species!"

I insisted that whatever the differences — and who could tell at this point which were inherent, which imposed by a patriarchal culture? — they did not require women to devote themselves to as many babies as chose to make their appearance. Reb Noach shook his head.

"Children are the greatest pleasure," he said, "but people today are so decadent they prefer their material comforts to children."

"It's not just material comfort!" I protested. "People have a right to some freedom — some time for themselves . . ."

"Decadence, Ellen. I'd have 50 children, a hundred. Every child is a lesson in love!"

"My parents aren't decadent! They've worked hard to bring up three children — to educate us all . . ."

Suddenly I found myself weeping.

"Ellen!" The rabbi's voice vibrated through me, alarmed, caring, soothing as a touch. "I'm not condemning *people!* Who knows who's better than who? I'm talking about actions. Mistakes, Ellen."

I wasn't sure why I was crying — except that if my middle-class family-centered parents could by any standard be accused of decadent behavior, then I was completely hopeless. My loss of control took me by surprise. I suppose it was my first overt symptom of culture shock.

How long was it since I'd landed at the airport — eight days? Nine? It felt much longer. My sense of time had changed, along with my perspective. I was, in crucial ways, an outsider — a reporter, at that — in a strange culture. Yet because I was Jewish, I was also family. Whatever anyone might think of me, whether I was religious or not, so long as I was living in the Orthodox community I was on some basic level accepted as part of it. And so I began, almost imperceptibly at first, to identify with that community and feel weirdly estranged from the secular world. I found myself thinking of non-religious people as "they." When I had an errand in downtown Jerusalem I felt assaulted by its frenetic, noisy, garish urbanness, by the crowds of Israelis who milled along Jaffa Road without a care for the subtleties of Jewish law.

Even the ever-present political tension began to seem part of that other world. A deep belief that God controls events tends to cool political fervor, and only a minority of Orthodox Israelis fit the stereotype of the militant religious nationalist; Mike and his friends were critical of the rabbinical establishment for what they saw as its readiness to bend the Torah to the demands of the state. I had arrived in Israel at a volatile time: Palestinian students had been demonstrating in the Old City; Israeli Arabs were protesting the expropriation of Arab land in the Galilee. I read about it all in the *Jerusalem Post*, feeling, absurdly, that Israeli politics had been much more vivid to me when I was in New York.

A religious universe enveloped me. I was surrounded by people who believed and, more important, lived that belief every minute. Conversation among Orthodox Jews never strays far from questions of ethics, points of law, one's religious activities; even small talk is inescapably religious: "I'm feeling better, *boruch Hashem!*"; "I ran into so-and-so on Shabbos"; "She's going to have a *milchig* [dairy] wedding." Orthodox life has its own special rhythm. There is the daily rhythm of prayer and the weekly rhythm of preparations for Shabbos: rushing to clean and cook before Friday sundown, when all work must be suspended; setting lights to go on and off automatically; taking turns showering, hoping the hot water won't run out; dressing up; lighting the Sabbath candles. There is Shabbos itself: making *Kiddush* (blessing and sharing wine); washing and breaking bread and sitting down to the traditional European-Jewish Friday night chicken dinner; the men going off to *shul* Saturday morning, coming home to a meal of *cholent*, a stew that is made before Shabbos and left simmering on the stove; studying, walking, visiting or napping in the afternoon; the light supper and finally the *havdalah* ("division") ceremony with which Shabbos ends.

Although the process was less dramatic, my immersion in Jewish life was having a far more potent effect on me than my confrontation with Jewish ideas. I could argue with ideas, but I could not, without being an abrasive nuisance, refuse to adapt, in important respects, to the customs of my hosts. On the most superficial level this meant not washing Abby and Sharon's dairy dishes in the meat sink, but it also meant shifting mental gears to participate in conversations that took a religious outlook for granted. Living with Orthodox Jews was like being straight at a party where everyone else is stoned; after a while, out of sheer social necessity, you find yourself getting a contact high.

There was, for instance, the afternoon I spent talking with Lorie and Frieda. Frieda had recruited Lorie for her *ba'al teshuva* organization; they were planning to go back to New York in July to get the project moving. I started giving advice. If they wanted young, educated women to take Judaism seriously, I argued, their organization would have to engage women's minds the way Aish HaTorah had engaged Mike's. That meant . . . and then I heard myself: I was telling them how to seduce me.

I had always thought of Orthodox Judaism as a refuge for compulsives: not only did its ubiquitous requirements and prohibitions seem to preclude spontaneity, but since the *halacha*, like any body of law that applies basic principles to specific situations, was open to interpretation, it provided endless opportunities for what outsiders would call hairsplitting. For example, it's Shabbos and Sharon and Abby have a problem: they have, as usual, left a kettle of boiling water on a burner they lit Friday afternoon, and now the flame has gone out. Is it permitted to switch the kettle to another lit burner? If the water has cooled off, heating it up again would violate the rule against cooking on Shabbos. If it's still hot, moving it should be okay. But it must have cooled off slightly. How hot does it have to be? Under the kettle, covering both burners, is a metal sheet, there as a reminder not to turn the flames up or down; does this make both flames one fire, which would mean that switching the kettle is allowed in any case? Abby, Sharon and Josh debated this issue for half an hour—it remained unresolved, and they did not move the kettle.

I understood now that to call this sort of behavior compulsive was to assume that religious observance was a distraction from life, while for believers it was the whole point; secular concerns were the distraction. If doing *mitzvos*—all of them, not just those you understood or liked — was the way to serve God, to connect with Reality, then it was crucial to do them exactly right. For the people around me Torah was not a straitjacket but a discipline, shaping and focusing their energies toward the only meaningful end. It was an arduous discipline, but one that was no more inherently compulsive than my own search for the precise adjective, or the care with which feminists analyzed the minutiae of sexual relationships.

And what was so sacred, anyway, about the arcane customs of my hyperurban, freelance existence? For all that I was so attached to it, I had to admit that it was, in the context of human history, more than a little strange. Sociologists liked to talk about how rootless and mobile Americans were, but most Americans at least had families. Despite my reluctance to assume the burdens of motherhood in a sexist society, it disturbed me to think that I would very likely never have children: I felt that child rearing, like working and loving, was one of the activities that defined humanness. Even my work — my excuse for so much of what I did or didn't do — sometimes struck me as ridiculous. What was the point of sitting home scratching symbols on paper, adding my babblings to a world already overloaded with information? And what of my belief in the supreme importance of connecting with Reality? Orthodox Jews acted on their version of that belief; did I? Well, there was my therapy. It occupied all of 45 minutes of my week — less time than it took me (speaking of compulsive rituals) to read the Sunday *Times*. Did I really have my priorities straight?

If my traumatic talk with Mike had shocked me into realizing that Judaism was a plausible intellectual system, living in Jerusalem was making me realize that Judaism was a plausible way of life. And that realization slid relentlessly into the next: that it was plausible even for me. My rapport with Abby and Sharon weakened my defenses against this frightening idea. I experienced Shimoni Street as a kind of halfway house. Much as I admired the rebbetzin, she was too unlike me to be a model. Lorie, in an entirely different way, was also from another world. But Abby and Sharon had the psychology of modern intellectual women. If they found Orthodox life exalting and full of purpose — if they had been exposed to the freedoms I had, yet did not feel deprived — perhaps I did not need those freedoms as much as I thought.

Yet even as I was drawn into the Orthodox subculture, I also resisted it. My resistance took an embarrassing form, it surfaced as a spoiled brat yelling, "I won't!" If I had come to Israel to experience Judaism, it made sense for me to try to observe Jewish law. I had resolved, for instance, to eat only kosher food during my stay. For a month this would scarcely be a major deprivation; I had stuck to reducing diets that required much more discipline. Yet I found that I couldn't keep away from the junk food stands on Jaffa Road; I stuffed myself with suspect brands of chocolate; under my modest dresses I was puffing out at a disquieting rate. Then there was the synagogue issue. Though communal prayer was not required of women, I felt that I should, at least once, attend services at an Orthodox shul. But I was afraid to face what I saw as the total humiliation of sitting upstairs in the women's section. Some journalist, I mocked myself. Lucky no one ever sent you to cover a war.

I began to realize that I was depressed. The weather, still wintry and raw, depressed me. The city itself depressed me, which was a surprise. On my first trip to Israel I had reacted very differently. I was not thinking about religion then; I was preoccupied with politics, war, history, the tragic clash of nationalism. But I had been awed by the radiance of Jerusalem. Perhaps it was just the combination of natural beauty and antiquity, but whatever holiness was, the city breathed it. Standing before the massive stones of the Western Wall, submerged in a crowd of people praying, I had felt the pain and ecstasy of millions of pilgrims course through me.

A friend had arranged for several members of our group to have Friday night dinner with a religious family, and all evening I felt the way I had at the Wall. Everything had a preternatural clarity and significance. When our host said the blessings over the bread and wine, I

marveled that I had been so obtuse as not to see. Blessing one's food —
appreciating the miracle of food — what could be more fitting? And
the whole idea of the Sabbath, one day a week when you were forbidden ordinary distractions and had to be alone with yourself and Reality
. . . I imagined myself back in New York City, spending a Saturday
without writing, eating in a restaurant, taking the subway; a whole day
with the phone off the hook and the record player silent. A fantasy, of
course, I could never live that way, didn't even want to, and yet I felt
a pang: isn't this what it's all about, the acid peace, the connection you
say you want, getting rid of all the noise?

Now, though I remembered those feelings, I couldn't recreate
them. I went to the Wall, saw weathered stone spattered with pigeon
droppings, left quickly because of the cold wind. And Shabbos, with
all its restrictions, was simply oppressive, like a tight girdle. "Last
time," said Mike, "you could be open to it because you weren't seriously thinking about it as a possibility."

It was during Shabbos, the second since I'd arrived, that my depression hit full force. A friend of Mike's had invited us for the weekend. He and his wife were warmly hospitable and I struggled guiltily
against my gloom. I felt suffocated by domesticity, by the children
calling for mommy, the men leaving for shul and the women staying
home, the men sitting at the table and the women carting away the
dishes. I wanted to tear off my itchy, constricting stockings. I wanted
to write in my notebook, turn on lights, eat without going through half
an hour of ritual first.

The next day I went to El Al to confirm my return reservation.
The flight I was booked on left April 22nd, but my excursion ticket was
good for two extra weeks if I wanted them and I figured it was time to
decide. I was always superstitious about switching flights; now, looking over the timetable, I felt irrationally certain that if I changed my
plans I would end up staying in Israel. *Something* would trap me here.
When Lorie first came to Jerusalem she had dreamed she was in prison,
supervised by a mean lady; she had wanted to get out, but by the time

they were ready to let her go, a month later, she loved it and wanted to stay. On the strength of that dream Lorie had decided to stay a month and, sure enough she was still here . . . This is ridiculous, I lectured myself. If you want to go you'll go; if you want to stay you'll stay; and if God is really controlling your life it's useless to second-guess Him. I debated staying at least a few extra days, but that would mean going through another Shabbos. I decided to stick with my original flight.

As soon as I left the office, a new wave of paranoia hit: God would punish me for my rotten attitude toward Shabbos. My plane would crash or be attacked by terrorists. *Mida k'neged mida* — measure for measure. Later that day, I realized I couldn't leave on April 22nd: it was the last day of Passover, and I had been invited to Reb Noach's. The prospect of having to change my reservation after all solidified my conviction that I would never make it back to the States. I had received a sign. There were no coincidences.

When I told Mike about my scheduling mix-up, he looked as if I'd punched him in the jaw. "You're leaving early," he said. "I thought you had six weeks."

"I planned on staying a month. I'm just doing what I was going to do all along."

"It's not just that. You want to leave because you're depressed. You're reacting exactly the same way I did."

My gut contracted.

"Mike, I'm not you. We may be alike in a lot of ways, but we're two different people." Under the panic I had to remember that, hold on to that. "If I want to go home I'm going home, and I'm not going to feel guilty about it."

"But you can't postpone these questions . . ." He shook his head. "When you first came, you were really relating to what was going on. Now I feel as if you've withdrawn."

"Do you really have to go back?" the rebbetzin asked. I had come over for another talk with Reb Noach.

"Theoretically," I said, "I could throw over my entire life and stay. But I don't want to."

"Do you think it's important to find out if there's a God?"

"Well . . ." Leave me alone! Get off my back!

"If there is, and we don't find out, are we culpable?"

I don't have to listen to this! It's brainwashing, that's what it is!

"I can find out in New York," I said.

"If I offered you a $200,000 business deal," Reb Noach put in, "you wouldn't say, 'I can make the same deal in America.' You'd say, 'Let's talk.'"

"I have a whole life to get back to," I insisted. "I *like* my life."

"Then you *won't* really try to find out," said the rebbetzin.

"I didn't say that."

"Well, will you?"

"I don't know," I said, feeling miserable.

I was not in the best mood to face Reb Noach. During our talks, he had been going through the proofs of God one by one. His theme this time was: "A design must have a designer." I had by now had this argument with several people. I still didn't buy it. Finally, Reb Noach said, "Ellen, think for a minute: is there a reason you don't want to believe the proofs?"

"Well, I can't deny that," I said. "I don't want to change my whole world view. But . . ."

"Look at it objectively! If you accept *one proof* it doesn't mean changing your whole world view."

"But I don't accept it. I don't see that the order in the universe has to be created by a personal God."

"There seems to be a wall here," said Reb Noach. "I don't want to pursue this unless you want to."

He started on another tack. "Why was the world created? For our pleasure. What is the one thing we are capable of doing? Seeking pleasure. So how can we go wrong? Insanity! Tell me — what's the opposite of pleasure?"

"Pain," I said.

"No! No! The opposite of pleasure is *comfort*. Pleasure *involves* pain. Decadence is opting for comfort. For example, what's more important, wisdom or money? Ask most people, they'll say 'wisdom.' 'Okay, stay here six months and I'll give you wisdom.' 'I can't—I have a job, a girlfriend, I'm supposed to take a vacation in the Greek islands.' 'Stay six months and I'll give you $20,000.' 'Fine!' 'What about your job, your girlfriend?' 'They'll wait.'

"The soul wants wisdom; the body wants money. The soul wants pleasure; the body wants comfort. And what's the highest pleasure? The aim of the soul? God, Ellen. That's real happiness—ecstasy, Ellen! Find out what you're living for! Take the pain—pleasure only comes with a lot of pain. I'm your friend—I'm with you. Give up your life of striving for success, for identity, your name up there . . ."

Unfair! "Do you really think I write just to get my name in print?"

"I think you do it to have an identity. To be 'a writer.'"

"I do like having that. But would you believe that I write mainly because I enjoy it, and I'm good at it, and"—defiantly—"I think it's useful work!"

"Shakespeare's okay," said Reb Noach, "but unless you know the real meaning of life, you're a zombie, a walking dead man. Find out what you're living for, Ellen. Clarity or death!"

There began to be moments—usually early in the morning, before I forced myself to get up and face the day—when I was more inclined than not to believe that it was all true, that I was only resisting because I couldn't stand the pain of admitting how wrong I was. *What about the prophecies* . . . and the way modern history seemed almost a conspiracy to drive the Jews back to Israel . . . and the Bible . . . Mike and I had been going over Genesis, along with the Rashi commentary, and I had had a sudden vision, like an acid flash, of a Garden, and a Presence . . . and my personality, my Sagittarian compulsion to aim straight at the cosmic bull's-eye . . . "*The blessing and curse of being a*

Jew," said Reb Noach, "*is that Jews are thirsty for God, for the absolute. A Jew can never have peace. Whatever he does he'll be the best at, whether it's being a radical or being a criminal. It's all misplaced searching for God. Every Jew is a neurotic . . .*"

And if I became religious, what would I do? Insanity, decadence, call it what you please, I could never be a traditional Jewish mother. But maybe I didn't have to be. Actually only men were subject to a specific mitzvah to marry and have children. And not everyone took the Weinbergs' hard line on procreation — according to one rabbi I'd met, a psychologist, the *halacha* permitted contraception when necessary to preserve a woman's health, including her emotional health. Nor were the role divisions in the family absolute, no law actually forbade women to work outside the home, or men to share housework. Even within the bounds of Judaism I could be a feminist of sorts, crusading for reforms like equal education, perhaps contesting the biased *halachic* interpretations of male rabbis. And my experience would put me in a unique position to reach women like me and bring them back.

In private I could have this fantasy, even take it seriously. Which would not stop me, an hour or a minute later, from getting into a furious argument with a man. It was one thing to consider the abstract possibility that women's role in Judaism was not inherently oppressive, another to live in a culture that made me feel oppressed. Once when Mike and I were dinner guests of another of his teachers I complained, "You know, it makes me feel like a servant when you sit there like a lump while I help serve and clean up."

"It isn't customary for the men to help," Mike said, "and if I got up I'd make everybody uncomfortable, including the women." He had a point — when in Rome and all that — but it was a point he was not exactly loath to make. The fact was that for Mike, moving from Western secular society to Orthodox Judaism had meant an increase in status and privilege; for me it meant a loss.

One night Mike and I got together with Dick Berger, one of his best friends at the yeshiva. Mike was very high on Dick, who, he said, was an unusually perceptive person with a gift for sensing someone's emotional blocks. He had been encouraging Mike to get more connected to his feelings. I had met Dick once and he had told me a little about himself. He had been a newspaper reporter in Pittsburgh, had written an unpublished novel, had been into psychedelics and Transcendental Meditation. Later he had told Mike that he felt I had seen him only as material for my article. I didn't think that was true, but I worried about it anyway. I hated it when people claimed to know my motives better than I did, but I always worried that they were right.

The conversation that night was pleasant enough until Dick and I got into an argument about men sharing child care. Dick suggested that 3,000 years of tradition shouldn't be tampered with, and I started getting angry in a way I knew from experience led to no good. Then he really pushed the wrong button.

"You're so emotional! Can't we talk about this objectively?"

"You're hardly being objective. It's in your interest as a man to think what you think."

"I'm feeling detached," Dick insisted. "By that I mean attached to my basic essence. You're reacting out of your conditioning in Western culture."

"You're reacting out of your male-supremacist prejudices, only you have 3,000 years of tradition on your side."

"But I'm not being aggressive and hostile—you are!"

"You can afford to be 'objective' and 'detached'! You're happy with the system—I'm the one who's being oppressed by it! Why shouldn't I be hostile—what right do you have to demand that we have this conversation on your terms . . ." My sentence went hurtling off into the inarticulate reaches of un-God-like rage.

Another time, another friend of Mike's: Harvey, a tall, dark, intense South African. "I'm not here because I want to be," he said. "I want freedom and money and the pleasures of the body. I was happy in my non-religious life—I miss it. But once you know there's a God . . ."

We started arguing about design and evolution. "Either there's a God," Harvey said, "or all this harmony and purpose is a coincidence."

"Those aren't the only possibilities . . ."

"And there are vast odds against coincidence. If you had a dart board that had lots of red and just a little white, where do you think your dart would hit?"

"That's a silly analogy," I said.

"What if you had to lay money on it?"

"I'm not going to play this game! It's ridiculous! It's irrelevant!"

"Answer me," the prosecutor insisted. "Would you bet on white or red?"

"I'm not Pascal!" I yelled. "And I'm not about to change my entire life because of some *abstract intellectual decision* about what the odds are on there being a God!"

"The Torah isn't only a carrot, you know. It's a stick, as well. There's punishment—you get cut off . . ."

And I'm not going to play your guilt game, either! You men are not going to cram your sexist religion down my throat!

There it was, the dirty little secret: I might be persuaded to return to Judaism—but not by a man. After one of our encounters, Reb Noach had declared, "You are emotionally committed to rebelling against the male sex!" He was right, of course, and in principle I agreed that one ought to be wary of such a priori commitments. But whenever I clashed with a man I seemed to end up with a renewed conviction that my rebellion was a matter of simple sanity. Men with their obnoxious head trips! Men with their "objectivity": "Let's discuss this rationally—should I remove my foot from your neck or shouldn't I?"

1987

Before Michael Lesy wrote the book from which this account of Orthodox Jewish ritual slaughters is drawn, *The Forbidden Zone,* he made five books about photographs. The first was called *Wisconsin Death Trip.* When I teach it, my students call it "the dead baby book." That's what many of the photographs depict: dead babies. Their parents would commission a photographer to make a record of the deceased, garlanded with flowers, cute as a button, propped up in a coffin. Such were the customs of Black River Falls, Wisconsin, "a typical little town" of the late nineteenth century. In *Death Trip,* Lesy let his arrangement of the photographs and his selections from a local paper, thick with infanticide, patricide, matricide, arson, ghosts, wells, and simple insanity, tell his story. In *The Forbidden Zone,* a series of encounters with people who deal with death, the words are Lesy's, but the questions he asks of and about his subjects are largely the same: "Why do they do what they do? How do they bear it? What do they know that the rest of us don't?"

To answer these questions, Lesy decides, he has to go where his subjects go. In one of the chapters that precedes "Shochets," Lesy describes a visit to a more common kind of slaughterhouse, in Omaha. It concludes with the author as killer: "Whatever had done it, I grabbed the gun, leaned down, and pressed it against the skull of the steer closest to me. The animal tossed its head to shake it loose. Its skull was as broad as my forearm, brown, muddy, and hard as stone. I leaned down, and as my weight balanced against the strength of the steer's neck, I squeezed the lever. The gun bounced up and back. The steer dropped away as if the ground had opened under it. 'Nothing to it,' I thought. 'As easy as hitting pop flies to the outfield.' Zeke grinned and nodded. 'Go for it,' he whooped. I leaned over to knock the second one. 'Sweet-fucking-Jesus,' I thought, and straightened up and shoved the gun back at him."

By then he's two chapters into his inquiry, already overwhelmed, and before he gets to the shochets there'll be a murder and the death of a teacher, a man to whom he'd hoped to turn for guidance through this "forbidden zone." "Just don't get too close to all that, Michael," the teacher tells him before he dies. "I can't avoid it," Lesy says. "I've got to get dirty." By the next page he's regretting that romanticism; the page after that, he's at his teacher's funeral. Oh, and the shochets. The religious part. They're there, too, but then every page of *The Forbidden Zone* is suffused with the stuff of religion, the Judaism he's born into, the Christianity in which he was schooled, and the rawest, pagan — prepagan — questions anyone can ask about suffering and death. That this person called Michael Lesy is asking these questions here is central to the story. His presence isn't an argument or a style, he's not a new journalist, flashing his id at the reader. He's a man who knows that the soul behind the camera matters as much to the picture as one before the lens. Like it or not, they're collaborators: complicit in the creation.

MICHAEL LESY
Shochets

Shochets are slaughterers, ritual slaughterers, Orthodox Jews who kill animals according to an ancient code that divides the world of flesh into things clean and unclean. The killing they do is religiously sanctioned, conducted according to an intricate set of laws that link men with God by sanctifying the most elemental acts. What they do is a sacrament, like the taking of bread and wine, a religious service commanded by God, that permits others to obey Him. From what I had read, a kosher kill is quicker and less painful than the one I'd seen in Omaha, done with a knife, not an air gun, done by hand, not with a machine. Its ritual protects the slaughterer from the moral consequences of what he does; its method spares the victim a painful death.

All this I wanted to believe, but not just because of what I'd learned when I was young. My Bar Mitzvah was far behind me, and all the books I'd since read about the secrets of Jewish mysticism and the ecstatic practices of Hasidism were just books. I was like the Jew in a story I'd once heard about the Holocaust: in one of the extermination camps, a pious rabbi and a Jew who was a Jew in name only became friends. One day, the time came for everyone to die: the guards herded a huge crowd of them out into the snow, marched them to a clearing, and told them to dig a pit. When the pit was dug, the guards said to them: "Listen to us: if you can jump across, we'll let you live; if you can't, we'll kill you." One by one, the men tried, and one by one they fell in and were shot. Finally it came time for the rabbi to try. Behind him, in line, stood the Jew. "It's impossible, I'll never make it," said the Jew. "Hold on to me," said the rabbi. "Close your eyes and we'll jump together." So together they jumped, and when the Jew opened his eyes, he and the rabbi were on the other side. "My God! How did we do it?" said the Jew. "It was simple," said the rabbi. "You held on to me, and I held on to my ancestors." Perhaps I'd lived too sweet and easy a life, but the death I'd caused in Omaha and the killings I'd seen in Florida had opened a pit in front of me. Perhaps I was more religious than the Jew in the story, but if I was to get across, I was going to need the help of a man who was devout.

Unfortunately, none of the rabbis I spoke with believed me. I told them I was a Jew, maybe not an Orthodox one, but I belonged to a congregation and observed the Commandments. None of that mattered. I told them where I was born, who my parents were, who my relatives were, where I'd studied. It made no difference: at best, I was a stranger; at worst, a troublemaker, maybe even — God forbid — a Jew who hated other Jews, a traitor, an apostate. They even had a name for such a person: an *apikoros* they called him. That sort of trouble they didn't need. So, Mr. Lesy, they said, good luck, but call someone else. Finally I did something sensible: two miles from my house was an Orthodox congregation. I went there, asked to see the rabbi, and explained. Until then, everything had happened on the telephone. This time the rabbi looked at me. Maybe he saw I was desperate, or maybe he saw I was just a harmless man in need of some help. He did what he could: he knew no *shochets* himself but there was a rabbi in New Jersey, he said, a man famous for his learning, an authority on the codes of *kashruth*, a scholar of the Law. This rabbi, this sage, supervised a kosher slaughterhouse. "Call him, use my name if it'll help." I called the rabbi and it did. He spoke like a man never contradicted. "If you want to come, I'll see you," he said. "But, as far as spending much time at the plant, that is impossible, impossible; the men cannot be distracted. They have enough to do; it is very serious; they have no time to talk to anyone. But if you come, I'll see you. I'll meet you at the plant. I'll show you that there is no pain. You'll see it; you'll be satisfied, and then you'll say goodbye." "Rabbi," I said, "it's very far for me to come for a short visit." "How long do you need to know that something is good?" he asked. "What is good is good. The longer you're here, it won't change. What are you asking me?" "I'm asking for more than a quick tour." "That's out of the question. If you want to come, all right, fine, we have nothing to hide. Otherwise, *sei gesund.*" "Whatever time you can spare, I'd be grateful." "Fine," he said. "I'll see you in a week, on Monday. When you know your flight, call my secretary. Sunday, before you come, call me at home: it's possible I may be out of the country. Otherwise, the plant is close to Newark Airport. You can take a cab."

The idea of stepping out of an airplane and into a slaughterhouse made me smile. "Something's better than nothing," I thought. "No matter what, I'll be able to visit Warren." Warren was Warren Susman, a professor of American history at Rutgers. Long ago, when I'd earned my doctorate, he'd been my teacher. Over the years we'd become friends, but Warren always remained the one who knew, and I the one who asked. What Warren knew were books. Great books, obscure books, remarkable books, trivial books. Warren was like the renegades at the end of Bradbury's *Fahrenheit 451*, the runaways who memorized and recited whole classics, except Warren was all of them combined, capable of citing anything and everything, not just author and publisher, but content, and not just content, but context, spinning it all out in an intellectual lacework that filled the air with references, quotations, allusions, footnotes, and asides. In front of a class, he sounded like a finely tuned small orchestra; alone in a room, he raced along like a string quartet. Four years before, he'd had a mas-

sive heart attack and barely survived. When he woke up, he discovered
that whatever had gone wrong had somehow freed him of the angina
pain that had tormented him. His near-death left him elated. During his convalescence, he watched television and read Sontag's *Illness
as Metaphor*. He displayed a copy of it on his nightstand, so he could
watch the faces of his visitors when they noticed it. Now he was out,
teaching and talking again, walking around in a body that might suddenly fail him, enjoying the risk. His father had been a cardiac invalid,
confined to the house, cooking and cleaning, while Warren's mother
ran the family business. Warren had inherited his father's heart, but he
refused to stay home and wait.

When I called to tell him I was coming to Newark to see a
slaughterhouse, he laughed. "The perfect place." He chuckled. "But
what on earth for?" I told him, and immediately he began to name
books. "Philippe Ariès, of course, and McNeill's *Plagues and Peoples*,
and certainly you ought to have a look at Hillman's *The Dream and the
Underworld*." "Wait, Warren, wait," I said. "It's gone beyond that." I
began to tell him what I'd seen. I told him of the medical pathology
lab and the homicide section. I told him about the evidence technicians
with their Super Glue, the black detective with his tape recording, and
all the others with their collection of color glossies. I described my
coincidences with the television, the overlaps between *A Night to Remember* and the cattle, and *Brainstorm* and the dead woman. I was
about to tell him what I'd done in Omaha, when I stopped myself.
"My God, Warren," I said. "I'm sorry. Maybe I shouldn't be talking
about this. Does it bother you? Shit! I'm sorry." "No, no, no, no, no,"
he trilled back. "It's *fascinating*. I don't know if that's a good sign about
me" — he laughed — "but it's *very* intriguing; it's so Kafkaesque. When
did you say you'd be in Newark?" "This Monday," I said. "Excellent,"
he said. "I'll be in Minneapolis over the weekend. I'm on a panel at the
Historical Convention. I'll be back Monday. You see your rabbi, and
we'll get together Tuesday." He paused. "Just don't get too close to all
that, Michael." "Oh, Warren," I said, "I can't avoid it. If I stay away,

nothing'll touch me, and if that happens, I can't write. I've got to get dirty." "Just be careful," he said. "Stay well," I said. "Take care," he replied and hung up.

That was Thursday. On Friday, I went to a bookstore and saw Warren's face staring out of the pages of a literary supplement. His publisher had just issued a collection of his essays, twenty years of pieces that had appeared in obscure foreign publications, scattered about in film quarterlies and scholarly journals, now drawn together in a collection that the reviewer called a monument of scholarship. I looked at Warren's picture. His beard had grown white, his face thinner, his forehead higher, his eyes more intent, his gaze more centered. He looked like a wise old man, a truth teller and a skeptic. "How wonderful," I thought. "Maybe he can tell me what all this means."

Saturday evening, a woman called to tell me that Warren had died in the middle of his speech. The funeral would be Monday, she said. "Will you be attending?" she asked. "I don't know," I said. "Damn!" I thought. "It's as if he wrote the script." Surrounded by colleagues, accompanied by friends, riding on a wave of good reviews, he'd stood before an audience eager to hear him. His words had come without effort, his comments articulate and erudite, his observations precise and witty. Then he'd taken a breath, collapsed, and died. Died in mid-sentence, in mid-thought. For an intellectual, not a bad way to go. Not like some terminal case, hooked up to a respirator, robbed of the power of speech. Not like his father, puttering around the house. I walked outside and looked at the night. "Ah, Warren," I thought, "you always were a good teacher: I call you to talk about death; you offer books; I counter with experience. For once I thought I had you. Then you went out and died." "Goddamn it," I said out loud, "I don't want to go to your goddamn funeral. I don't want to and I don't need to. You won't be there anyway. You already made your point: 'Don't wait; die while you're still alive.' Great. I get it: you had no choice. But school's out now." Then I got frightened. "You talk about coincidences," I thought. "The stuff on the tube was bad enough, but this—

what is this? You go out looking and it'll find you. You mess with this
and it'll crawl right up your leg. You should never have called him. You
asshole. Remember what you said? 'I'm interested in death.' What did
you think you were talking about? Some kind of idea? 'Don't get too
close,' he said. But you said you had to. As if you were an artist. How
romantic. You get any closer and it'll take you along. You only think
you know what you're doing."

Sunday morning, I woke up sure I wouldn't go. "I'll send a tele-
gram," I thought. "The work will be my tribute. I don't want to lose my
chance. I'll go see the rabbi." That evening, I called the rabbi at home.
His wife answered. I introduced myself. "I'm calling to confirm my
appointment." "Something's come up," she said. "Is the rabbi out of
the country?" I asked. "No," she said, "it's something personal." "Excuse me," I said, "but 'something personal'—what personal?" "His
sister," she said. "She's very sick. She's in a coma. It doesn't look good.
He's with her in the hospital. It happened this morning. It's impossible for him to see you." "I'm sorry," I said, "but is there some way for
me to see the plant without him?" "No, no," she said, "it's impossible.
I'm sorry. Call tomorrow." I said goodbye. "You've got the touch," I
thought. "You've done it now." I walked outside. "Okay, dumbo," I
said. "You get the message? You want it spelled out in flaming letters,
twelve feet high? Consider: a week ago you make plane reservations to
go see a slaughterhouse. Then you call Warren. You talk about death.
He says he'll be back Monday. He's right, except he's in a box. You get
scared; you back away. 'Work's the best tribute,' you say. Then you call
the rabbi: his sister's dying. You can't see him, but you still have the
plane reservations. You thought you made reservations to see a beef
kill. But you're wrong: the tickets were for your teacher's funeral. It's
Abraham and Isaac in reverse: a man instead of an animal. School's not
out. You still have some lessons to learn. You started asking questions
and now you don't have a choice. You're going to a funeral. Pay attention, you might learn something."

Monday morning I flew into Newark, took a train, then took a cab to the funeral home. There were a hundred people there when I arrived, and more coming. In the crowd of strangers, I recognized two men, both academics, colleagues of Warren. "He'd nearly died at the convention in Montreal," one said. "When?" I asked. "A couple months ago, but that was nothing: he was in the hospital just a few days before we left for Minneapolis. His doctor told him he was taking a chance, but that's what his life was: he'd been holding on for years, waiting for the odds to change for a quadruple bypass." Overhead, from speakers in the ceiling, music began to play, and the crowd began to move into the main parlor. I looked around: maybe 250 people, ambling into a large, low-ceilinged room, gray walls, off-white trim, pale blue carpet. Everyone found chairs, and there we sat for fifteen minutes, listening to the music, waiting. The sound that came through the speakers grew so faint and garbled that it was difficult to know what we were hearing. I turned to the man on my right. "Shostakovich?" I asked. He shook his head. "Beethoven's *Eroica*. Warren's favorite." I turned to the man on my left. "Shostakovich?" I asked. "No," he whispered. "Sousa. Warren loved it." I looked around for the coffin. There was a big flat table in the front of the room, but there was nothing on it. I turned to the man on my left. "Where's the body?" I asked. "He was cremated," he said. "What does that mean?" I thought. "Are they going to bring him in on a platter, in an urn, surrounded by lilies, when the music stops? What's going on?" Then I noticed a big, beautiful pitcher on a stand next to the old man who looked as if he was going to lead the service. "That's it. Warren's in there," I thought.

The old man stood up, poured himself a drink from the pitcher, and welcomed us. He paid his respects to Warren, then introduced the first of four other speakers. Each of them tried to recall Warren in such a way that the rest of us could see him and hear him one last time. One read a poem, one spoke of Warren as a friend, another of him as a teacher, another as a colleague. The air stayed empty; the room stayed quiet. No one carried in his ashes or called his soul back to life. The old man rose and thanked us; music came from the speakers again;

everyone stood up and began to move out the door. "Shit!" I thought. "Nothing happened. He's disappeared." I stared at the back of the suit jacket in front of me. Above us, the speakers went dead. We inched along. When the music began again, it was different. Maybe someone had changed the tape or changed the channel, but a new melody filled the room, loud enough to be heard clean and clear. It began as a simple organ solo, the tune of "My Country 'Tis of Thee." I smiled. "The perfect recessional for an American historian," I thought. But then it changed. It didn't stop after the first verse, or the second, or the third. The solo became an organ voluntary. I bent my head and listened. Each new refrain spun filigrees of sound around the old tune, each variation more exuberant and playful than the one before. The crowd came to a stop. I closed my eyes. Warren's mind took shape in the air above my head. It hovered just below the ceiling, then skipped across the room, as profligate but graceful, as inventive but true, as gay but serious as the music itself. The crowd crept forward again. Above them, the organ played and Warren danced. No one looked up. He'd been a brilliant man, entranced with the intricacies of this world. I'd loved him for that. I had tears in my eyes. As I reached the door, the music ended and Warren disappeared.

That evening, I called the rabbi's house. His wife answered. "His sister has died," she announced. "He has gone into mourning. In ten days, he can see you. We'll call you then. Goodbye." I knew I'd tripped a wire. "You're two for two," I thought. While the rabbi mourned, I waited in New York, counting the days. One morning, the phone rang: it was the editor of a literary magazine. Could I meet him for lunch? Of course, I said, but I was surprised. He and I had never met. We knew about each other. We'd exchanged letters about my work. He'd expressed an interest in perhaps publishing excerpts of it, but I'd never expected him to call. As I understood it, he was a man my age who'd made his reputation when he was the young executive editor at another magazine that published exposés about the Mafia, the CIA, and the assassination of Jack Kennedy. The fact that we'd lived through the same historical period was enough to guarantee us, if not a publishing relationship, then at least a decent lunch. At the proper time, I gave his name to the maître d' and was escorted to a table where a remarkably young-looking man rose to greet me. "Mike?" he said, extending his hand. "Alan?" I replied, wondering what I was doing there, dressed in a suit, with a smile on my face, halfway between a funeral and a slaughterhouse. We sat down and looked at each other. I wondered what he saw. I felt like the Sorcerer's Apprentice, dressed in robes that were too big for him, wearing a hat that made him look like a dunce, terrified he'd just unleashed a spell he couldn't control. The maître d' hadn't stopped me; Alan hadn't drawn back in horror. Whatever was happening to me wasn't visible. I looked across the table at him and was amazed. For a man close to forty, he didn't have a mark on him. Not a blemish, not a tear; his face was as perfect as a Dorian Gray; his manner as unaffected and fresh as Holden Caulfield's. I felt old and a little dirty.

We began by discussing flavored vodkas, then ordered a bottle of Chablis. He chose the venison; I decided on the salmon. "Well, Mike," he said, his voice casual but his gaze intent, "what have you learned so far?" He leaned back and looked at me like a buyer appraising a painting. I took a breath and lit a cigarette. A woman at the next table leaned over and said the smoke was endangering her health. I begged her pardon, and put out the cigarette. The editor was still sitting there, faintly smiling, waiting for an answer. I had no idea what he wanted to hear. None of what I'd seen was fit conversation for a decent restaurant. If my smoke offended the lady next door, only God knew what my words would do to anyone in range. I looked over Alan's head, down the length of the restaurant, full of chatter and bustle, to the front door. When I looked back, he was still waiting. I didn't want to offend him. He was paying the tab; the salads hadn't even arrived. If I told him the details, I might find myself sitting alone. He thought I was an author, a potential contributor—I felt like Calamity Jane. I looked at him. "'What have I learned?'" I said. "That's a good question, Alan."

I decided to keep it general. "You know, I've been riding around with homicide detectives in Florida for the past couple weeks. The place they're at's not like Miami or L.A.; it's a nice town, not too big, not too small. Most of the time, they deal with sort of petty stuff, rage and folly, that sort of thing. But every once in a while, every couple weeks, they deal with evil. Human evil. So, I guess, to begin with, to answer you, I'd say that's what I've learned: evil exists. Evil exists in the world; it's quantifiable and qualifiable; it's present, not historical, not remote. You don't have to read about it in the Holocaust, or take some plane to see it in Cambodia; it's tangible, like a rock, or a stone, or a piece of wood; it's . . ." As the waiter arranged a plate of hearts of palm in front of him, Alan said, "But isn't that all relative?" I closed my eyes and saw the Smothers Brothers combing the dead woman's pubic hair. "Relative?" I thought. "Evil? What did Alan think I was talking about? Breaking a publishing contract? Not meeting a deadline? He was talking about an idea, and I was talking about fact." I opened my eyes and saw him watching the woman at the next table. He grinned at me. "So," he said, "what else have you learned?" "What I've learned," I thought, "is to tell the difference between someone who's been around and someone who hasn't." I felt like a veteran talking to a rookie, except that the rookie might be paying for more than my tab. "What else?" I said. "Hard to say, Alan. Nothing much. The usual stuff. You know: life lives off death. That kind of thing. Nothing special. I'm working on it." "Well, good," he said. "Glad to hear it. Keep at it. We're anxious to have first look at it." Then he changed the subject to his Saab. The entrée came and we switched to repair rates for BMWs. Over coffee, we talked about handball.

Three days later, the rabbi's wife called; I could come if I wanted. "To the plant?" I asked. "No," she said, "to the yeshiva." "Excuse me," I said, "but what yeshiva?" "The rabbi's academy. He wants to meet you there." She told me the time and named the place.

To get there I had to take a bus. It lurched through the traffic on the interstate, past Newark Airport, a foot at a time. After an hour, the driver let off. On the map, the town was marked in capital letters, but all I could see was a drugstore, some gas stations, and six lanes of traffic. I crossed the road and began looking for the yeshiva. Every building I passed looked abandoned, without a tree or an upturned face. I kept walking until I came to what looked like a public high school. "Hebrew Academy" said the sign. Inside, the walls were noisy with children. I asked directions and found the office. When I gave my name to the secretary, a little sparrow of a man, hunched over an adding machine at a desk behind her, turned his neck to inspect me. While I waited, a Russian Jew walked in, waving a federal income-tax form. "This," he said in English, "this is what?" Then he switched to Yiddish and the little man at the adding machine rose to help, clucking like a mother hen. The secretary turned to me and said, "The rabbi will see you now." As I stood up, I saw him at the end of a short hallway, standing by the open door of his office. We shook hands. He was a handsome old man with a full white beard, a black skullcap on his head, dressed in a black suit so finely tailored, its lines so distinct, its color so deep, that, as he stood framed in the light, he looked like a Hebrew letter, freshly printed by a scribe. His eyes sparkled behind his spectacles. "Come in, come in," he said. He sounded happy to see me, as if I were some travel agent, come to confirm his vacation plans. As soon as he reached his desk and sat down, he grew serious. "This school," he said, spreading his hands, "I founded fifty years ago. It has risen from nothing. Now there are 750 students from kindergarten through high school." He looked at me. "Do you know what they study?" He didn't wait for an answer. "They study the meaning of being a Jew." He smiled and opened his hands. "So," he said, still looking at me, "what is it you want to learn?" "First," I said, "I must thank you for seeing me. I wish also to express my sympathy for your loss." He gave a curt nod. "I understand," I said, "that ritual slaughter sanctifies an elemental process, that it links what is below with what is above. With your permission, I'd like to witness it."

The rabbi closed his eyes and bent his head. His office was finely paneled, but it was empty except for a bookcase, a desk, and two chairs. Under the glass top of his desk, turned to the visitor, were black-and-white photographs of him standing with three other old men, all of them beaming at one another through their beards. The rabbi leaned toward me, his eyes still closed, his head cocked as if listening to my words. Then, with a jerk, he straightened up and nodded. "Very well," he said. He began to speak then, clearly but rapidly, always looking at me, his glance a test of my comprehension.

"You know, of course, that we are commanded to do this in Deuteronomy, where it is written, 'Thou shalt kill of thy herd and of thy flock, which the Lord hath given thee, as I have commanded thee.' What is important are the words 'as I have commanded.' There is a story about the Jewish people when we stood at the foot of Mt. Sinai. Perhaps you know it?" I opened my mouth, but he wasn't interested. "It is said that Ha Shem lifted the whole mountain in the air and held it over our heads. Then He said, 'Now you can choose. Either you can receive my Commandments and obey them and live. Or you can refuse them and die. Choose.'" The rabbi's eyes glinted. "So. We chose. We chose to live." He smiled, but it was a smile that could have cut glass. "You understand?" I nodded. He continued like a judge citing precedents.

"The laws governing the process of *shechita* have been elaborated in tractate Hullin of the Babylonian Talmud, then codified by Maimonides and Joseph Karo. *Shechita* consists of a single, *uninterrupted* cut by a knife across the animal's neck. The cut must be made at a certain point and no other; the knife must be twice as long as the neck is wide; the blade must be sharper than a scalpel, so sharp that if it cuts a man he cannot feel it—because, if a man can feel nothing, neither will a beast. The blade must be without a flaw; its edge must be perfect, since a nick or a tear is always more painful than a cut. The whole purpose is to kill the animal so swiftly that it feels no pain. No pain. That is the principle of *tza'ar ba'alei hayyim:* to avoid inflicting

pain on any living creature." I thought of the animals rearing and bellowing in Omaha. The rabbi went on.

"The law forbids an animal be killed in the presence of one that
has been slaughtered. And why? To spare it terror and humiliation.
The law demands that if, somehow, a wild beast is captured alive and
then slaughtered, its blood must be covered immediately. And why?
Why is this? Because to kill a wild animal that owes nothing to man is
more shameful than to kill one that has been raised by him and owes
him its life." "Shame?" I thought. The rabbi leaned over to the bookcase and took out a small black book. He shows the title to me: *Shechita: Religious, Historical, and Scientific Aspects.* "The goyim say we
are inhumane. Inhumane?? Listen carefully." He found his place and
read: "'The incision should be carried from the surface of the skin
down to, but not touching, the vertebrae. This necessarily includes the
severance of the trachea, esophagus, carotid arteries, jugular veins,
the pneumogastrics, and the main and upper cardiac branches of the
sympathetic nerves. Severing the carotids causes an immediate and
acute anemia of the brain, which is followed instantaneously by un-
consciousness.'" He closed the book and leaned back. "Do you know
what that means? It means that by the time the animal can feel pain, its
brain has been deprived of blood and oxygen and it has lost consciousness. All this must be done precisely, without hesitation. Because, if
there is a pause, or any sawing or any tearing or stabbing, or if the
stroke is too high or too low, or if the blade hits bone or is impeded in
any way—then the animal is unfit to eat. And why? Because it may
have died in pain."

He stood up. "Come. We'll go to the plant. You'll see with your
own eyes." There was nothing I could say. He had religion, law, and
medicine on his side. We walked out to the parking lot. I looked around
for his car. A Buick? A Chrysler? He walked over to a slate-blue Lincoln Continental, opened the door, and said, "Come!" I was on my
way to a slaughterhouse with a pious aristocrat. He drove well and

swiftly. I rested in the cushions and listened. "Once," he said, "I was called to testify about *shechita* in Washington. To prepare, I went to a plant where they killed pigs. I wanted to compare. It was a modern plant; the pigs rode up an escalator and at the top a man touched them on the head with an electric prod and they died — but if he didn't touch them in the right place, they screamed. They screamed. This they considered humane. This they ate." I remembered Omaha. The rabbi turned off into a warehouse district that looked as if it had been bombed from the air. Semis roared down whatever side of the road had the fewest craters. The Lincoln bounced along untouched, as if it had diplomatic plates. We pulled up in front of a plant old enough to have supplied beef to troops during the Civil War.

The rabbi jumped out of the car without a word, entered the plant, strode down a corridor and into an elevator. Men stood aside. I followed like an aide. We rode up to the manager's office and were given freshly laundered, newly ironed, light-blue lab coats. Then we went down to the kill floor. It was entirely different from Omaha. It was quieter. It was less congested. There were fewer men, fewer machines, more space, fewer animals. In Omaha, they'd killed 130 an hour. Here, maybe fifty. In Omaha, they'd been driven by the clock. Here they had a quota, but rushing things didn't help. Blacks dressed in bib aprons, boots, and hard hats did the heavy work. Government inspectors stood by, checking as they checked in Omaha, but scattered here and there beside the conveyor belts were bearded Orthodox Jews examining hearts, lungs, stomachs, livers, and spleens, looking for any of the dozens of defects that could have rendered an animal, even if properly killed, unfit to eat. Any evidence that it had been so injured or ill that it would have died in a year made it forbidden. As we passed them, the Jews looked up, smiled, and nodded their respects. The rabbi leaned toward me and spoke in my ear: "The Talmud says, 'The best of the butchers are associates of Amalek.' Do you know what that means?" I nodded. The Amalekites were the cruelest enemies of the ancient Jews. I would have said something, but I knew better. The rabbi answered himself. "It means that even the best butchers are merciless and unfeeling. That is why we require a man, if he is a *shochet*, to lead a blameless life. He must observe the Law; he must be moral. Otherwise, he might sink to such a level, because of his work, that he would become degraded, like a criminal, and whatever he did would be unfit. To be a *shochet* is not just to have a job; it is not just to work; it is a service: to be a *shochet*, a man must serve the Law and serve the Children of Israel." I thought of Omaha and Dwight the shitkicker and the Mexican with the ponytails and all the men standing around with their knives, stoned, drunk, or strung out, their faces slack, their eyes dull. I thought of McTier and his dirty jokes and what I'd done. The rabbi turned and led me across the floor to the kill.

The *shochet* looked up; the rabbi introduced me. The *shochet* nodded and handed the rabbi his knife. It was perhaps sixteen inches long, perhaps three inches wide, the blade as thin as a bread knife, the end squared off like a cleaver. The rabbi ran his thumbnail straight up it; then he turned the blade to the right and ran his nail down it; then he turned it to the left, and ran his nail up it again. He had inspected three of the blades' edges, but all I could wonder was why he hadn't sliced his thumb in half. He handed the knife back to the *shochet:* no nicks. The *shochet* ran his own thumbnail up and down it, nodded his respects, and then stepped back to the kill. The kill was unlike anything I'd ever seen. The animal to be killed had been driven down a chute, then around a corner, into a large metal pen. A black man stood to one side, on a raised platform by a console, operating a set of controls. When the animal entered the pen, the man pressed a button and closed the gate behind it. He touched another button and the gate pushed the animal forward. The animal couldn't see through either side of the pen, but in front of it was a heavily padded opening, about the same size as and at the same level as its head. Hemmed in by darkness, pressed from behind, it stuck its head through the hole to look out. As soon as it did, the man at the console pressed another set of buttons: all at once, the opening closed like a collar around the animal's neck; the back of the pen nudged it even farther forward, and the sides of the pen moved inward, to enclose it. The animal now stood with nowhere to go, staring straight ahead, looking at a blank plaster wall. It could still move its head a bit. To prevent even this, the operator pressed another button and a device that looked like a curved stirrup, made of smooth, tubular, stainless steel, rose underneath the animal's jaw, cupped its chin, and stretched its neck, so that its nose pointed 30 degrees in the air. The animal was still staring at a blank wall, but it was clearly uncomfortable. At that moment, the *shochet* stepped to the animal's side, the knife in his right hand, out of the animal's sight. What he did then looked like a man drawing a bow across a cello, forward, then back. The blade sliced up through the animal's neck to its spine as quickly as if it had sliced through a tomato. The *shochet*'s arm reached out then drew back. There was no noise. Blood spurted, then sprayed. The *shochet* ran his hand between the severed halves of the neck to be sure the cut was clean and complete. The animal stood, perfectly still, eyes open, for perhaps ten seconds. Then its knees buckled, and as they buckled, the man at the console released and opened the right side of the pen. As it collapsed, a gang of men shackled it, dragged it out, and hoisted it, head down, perhaps three feet above the tile floor. The *shochet* stepped back into a little room adjacent to the kill, washed his blade under running water, washed his hands and dried them, then ran his thumbnail along the blade, from its tip to its handle. The rabbi said goodbye. "See me in the office in twenty minutes," he said. I nodded, and he left me.

The *shochet* and I stood in the little room. He was a middle-aged man with a full gray beard and mild oval eyes. He watched me, calmly. Across from where he stood was a deep vat of hot water that held twenty knives, submerged in a rack, handles up, blunt ends down. "Are these yours?" I asked. "Some are; some belong to others." "By why are they here?" "To keep them ready; there's lye in the water to keep off the rust. When one gets dull, I have another." He stepped out for the next kill. It was just like the other: swift, sure, and quiet. In Omaha, the men had sworn and shouted; the animals had stumbled, kicked, snorted, and died bellowing; here, one animal at a time stood alone, stared at nothing, and died before it knew it.

The *shochet* stepped back into the room. There was enough time between kills for an interrupted conversation. He spoke to me as calmly, as untroubled as a man might chat with a stranger sitting in his kitchen over a cup of tea. His was sixty-three years old, he said. From Poland. He washed his hands. From a town called Pinsk. Now part of Russia. He dried them. He'd been born there, then come to America when he was five. He inspected the blade. How long had he been a *shochet?* I asked. For thirty-three years, he said. Twenty-two here; eleven years in Boston. Now his son was one. He stepped out for the next kill. When he stepped back, he said he'd have a break in six minutes and we could talk. Every hour, he said, they rested, to keep their hands steady. I thought about the frantic factory pace of the kill in Omaha. "A rest every hour for the sake of their hands?" I thought.

Soon, another *shochet* appeared and we left for the locker room. We sat on a bench. The *shochet* leaned back and closed his eyes; his hands lay palms down on his thighs. When he looked at me again, he said, "Do you know what they call the knife?" I remembered the rabbi and hesitated, but the *shochet* waited. "Yes," I said, "a *halef*." "Do you know what that means?" "No," I answered. "It means 'sharp-no-nick.' Literally, that's what it means. But also, it's called 'that-which-from-life-to-death-transforms.' The knife has physical properties and also nonphysical properties: it is a thing, a no-nick-sharp, but it also has the power to transform." I thought, then, of all the knives I'd seen in Omaha, and how, in the hands of the men there, they looked like weapons. The *halef* was a knife, many times sharper, many times deadlier than those other knives, but in the *shochet*'s hands it seemed like a wand or a bow of an instrument. "And what you do," I asked, "what do you call that?" "What I do is a mitzvah, like wearing tallis and tefillin. It is a duty. To fulfill it is a good deed." "But," I asked, "what about the killing? Isn't there a Commandment about that?" "For humans, yes, of course, certainly, but animals have no souls. If they had souls, to kill them would be a sin. Animals are living things; as such, they must be treated with respect, but they have no soul. A steer has more life in it than an apple, but if I went to a tree and picked an apple, it would be no sin. The same with an animal." I thought of McTier and his carrots. I wondered what the animals thought. I wondered what Lord Krishna would say. "Ha Shem gave Adam dominion over the beasts of the field, the fowl of the air, and the fish of the sea," said the *shochet*. "He gave man the right to kill certain of them, 'as I have commanded thee.' So this is what I do."

It was time for him to return to the kill. I thanked him and went to see the rabbi. "They could never sell this as a weekend sport for unhappy accountants," I thought. "There's too much talk of obedience and not enough rage and aggression. It's also more difficult than hitting pop flies to the outfield." I stepped in the elevator and pressed the button for the manager's office. "What an extraordinary set of circumstances," I thought. "In Omaha, the kill was rational and brutal. Here it's religious and humane. In Omaha, the animals and the men were both debased. Here the animals die one at a time, and the men keep clean with holy law." The rabbi was waiting for me and drove me to the train, where I said goodbye. "Warren and the rabbi," I thought. "Different teachers, same lesson. One kills, one dies. Maybe there's a way to do it that doesn't degrade you."

On the flight home, I looked out the window. "Precious but useless knowledge," I thought. "Your teacher's died, you've met the rabbi, you've had lunch with an editor. You know more than you did before, but it's tainted you. It's turned you into a magnet: you attract the darkness as the darkness attracts you. Meanwhile, people play handball and fret about their Saabs. Maybe there's a way to die that's good, and maybe there's a way to kill that's proper, but if that editor's any indication, for most people, what you've learned is nothing but a bunch of words." Three days later, my mother called. "Your father's had an accident," she said. "He was driving and he blacked out. The car's a total wreck. Thank God he didn't kill anyone. He's in the hospital. He wants you to come." I got on another plane. "Ah, Michael," I thought. "Three in a row? Is this what it's about? Warren wasn't enough? Are you trying to speed things up?"

I met my father's doctor in the corridor outside his room. "Your mother's just gone down to get a sandwich," he said. "What about my father?" I asked. "For now, he's okay. What he had was a transient ischemic attack; it's like a little stroke. He'll have to give up his driver's license and he'll have to be watched. This time, he was lucky; but it could happen again, any time. He could be walking and"—he snapped his fingers—"he could blank out and fall. This time he was wearing a seat belt, but next time he could be outside and hit something hard. We'll do some brain scans. He was very, very lucky." When I walked in, he was sitting up in bed, adhesive strips across the bridge of his nose, a gauze across his forehead. I kissed him. "The car's demolished," he said. "I don't remember what happened. I was driving, then, when I woke up, the police were there with an ambulance. The car hit a fire hydrant. It's finished. We'll have to buy a new one." "Forget the car," I said. "Thank God you're in one piece." "Mother will have to drive me from now on. I can't be trusted. I'll put a tremendous burden on her." He put his hands over his eyes. "Dad?" I said. He didn't answer. "Dad?" When he spoke, there were tears in his voice. "I only hope I go before your mother. There's no way to tell." I didn't know what to say. He went on, "Unless you do it mechanically—but that would bring disgrace on the family. I'd never do it." "My God!" I said. "What are you talking about? You had an accident. You're getting old. Mother will drive you. It's not the end of the world." He cupped his forehead in his hands. His shoulders trembled, then he wept. "Why does everything I do go wrong?" he said. I put my arms around him. I'd never held him like that. He'd never spoken like that. All my life, he'd acted as if he were perfect. All my life, I'd believed he was. He'd given advice, healed the sick, comforted the weak; I'd made mistakes, done wrong, and was ashamed. He'd been right; I'd been wrong; he'd been strong, I'd been weak. All my life, until now. Now he wept, and I hugged him. "Precious but useless knowledge," I thought. "Maybe I can use it."

For the next week, my mother and I sat and watched him try to recover. The accident had broken off bits and pieces of him we couldn't see. Arms stiff, legs stiff, fingers splayed, he slid one foot in front of the other, like a man afraid of slipping on an icy sidewalk. Sometimes he'd lean forward, then quickly lean back as if the room had suddenly tilted up, then down. Back and forth, from the bed to the window, he'd feel his way, one step at a time, as if afraid he might fall into a hole hidden under the carpet. When he ate, he ate in slow motion: first the fingers closed on the fork, then the hand raised it to his mouth, then the arm swung it toward his lips, the whole process like a crane lifting cargo into the bay of a freighter. Every gesture he made was tentative; every move, imprecise. Sometimes his words slurred; every once in a while, his mind lost itself. I sat like a man on a beach, watching a sand castle crumble. On the last day I was there, he asked me what I was writing. He'd asked that twice before, and each time I'd told him: a book about people who deal with death. Each time I'd told him, he'd listened but said nothing. This time, though, he replied. "Death means nothing for the people who die," he said. "It's like words on a blackboard: one minute they're written, the next minute they're erased. It's simple for people who die." His eyes were pale gray. "But for the people who live, it's not. They're the ones who do all the writing." "That's me," I said. I kissed him goodbye. He began to cry. "I won't see you again," he said.

I kissed him again. "You'll see me, you'll see me; stop this; you're still alive; stop crying, I'll see you again."

1989

The subject of this excerpt from *The Rainy Season*, Amy Wilentz's account of Haiti after the collapse of the American-backed dictatorship of Jean-Claude Duvalier, is religion and politics. Or maybe: religion *or* politics. Wilentz isn't certain. In her defense, nobody seems to be. Certainly not the rich Haitians with whom she shares a dinner of lobster and champagne and grasping attempts to comprehend "Titid" — "street urchin" — the diminutive Catholic priest who has become the sparkplug of the ongoing revolution. Nor, even, for that matter, Titid himself, Father Jean-Bertrand Aristide. We hear him preach as if he's sounding for depth, we see him smile over the Dechoukaj — the "uprooting," in metaphorical terms — of a Tonton Macoute, one of Duvalier's henchmen. The priest, in these pages, is not quite certain who he is becoming, what Haiti is becoming, and what the church will mean to it. He has not yet become president of Haiti, or been deposed, or restored by American troops, or sent again into exile, or returned. That is to come. For now we have a portrait of man as seen by others, all of them puzzled, which begins, "I couldn't tell what was happening." Wilentz doesn't need to "tell what was happening," only to show it shifting before her, religion and politics and all that those two terms can stand for twisting like a Möbius strip, one becoming the other, as each already was.

AMY WILENTZ
From *The Rainy Season*

I couldn't tell what was happening. I'd been back and forth to Haiti four or five times by now, but things were getting out of control, and I couldn't always understand what I saw. On the street outside St.-Jean-Bosco, Father Aristide's small yellow church, a crowd of five or six hundred had massed, carrying branches and beating on wooden blocks. I didn't see Aristide anywhere; this was unusual. Typically, the first thing you noticed when you came to St.-Jean-Bosco was Aristide — the priest who had lectured me after Duvalier fell — surrounded by a group of young people, talking. This time, Aristide didn't seem to be there. The crowd had just begun pouring into the churchyard through the gates. It was July 1987. Inside the churchyard, youths were chanting slogans and talking, shouting at one another. Everyone was looking around, they seemed to be trying to figure out what to do next. A man in a yellow tee shirt was carrying a long stick in his hand, hitting it hard over and over into his other palm, looking around. Three boys standing under a tree were rapping on blocks with short sticks, pounding out a loud, repetitive rhythm. They all seemed to be waiting for something, but they didn't have their bearings here. I didn't recognize any of them from my visits to the church. They weren't kids from St.-Jean-Bosco. They weren't Aristide's followers.

All at once, they began pressing into the hall that leads to the inner courtyard, a huge, urgent mass filing into a very narrow, dark hallway. The crush was hot and fast. If you didn't know the corridor, its small steps at the front and back, how smooth the surface of the dark floor, the twist near Aristide's office, you had little chance of making it those few feet without falling. A lot of people fell. When we emerged into the light of the courtyard, someone was already ringing the school bell. It was loud, insistent over the clattering of the wooden blocks, like an alarm. Something was happening farther on, but I couldn't see anything; I was lodged against a wall among the crowd. Suddenly they started surging back in the other direction, down toward the dark corridor from which we had just emerged.

I didn't want to go back down the black corridor with the huge hot crowd, but I went back. Once they started pushing, I had no choice. And then I saw the reason, which was a slight figure perched on the shoulders of some of the tallest young men in the crowd, looking precarious and fragile. It was Aristide, and he couldn't get his balance. They were trying to take him out into the street. The man with the stick was right beneath him, giving orders to the youths who were carrying him. Aristide was holding on to his glasses and hunching over, unhappy, uncomfortable, embarrassed. He was not in control, but there was nothing he could do about it. Each time he almost fell, the man with the stick raised it over the priest's head, and the others lifted him up again. He swayed up there on the youths' shoulders, and they swept forward. They were laughing, tossing him. He was like a puppet in their hands. They were throwing him among themselves like a little girl's floppy doll, paying no attention to his discomfort. Each time they came to a step, he had to crouch over at the last minute to avoid slamming his face into the ceiling.

"*Nou vle Titid*," the boys chanted, calling Aristide by his nickname that has connotations of cute littleness, as in *petit*. In French, *titi* is slang for "street urchin." We want Titid, the boys said. They had him.

When they finally squeezed out with him into the open, the man with the stick turned toward him again, to get a look at his prize in the sun. But Aristide had disappeared. The youths looked confused, almost frightened, as though he had disappeared into thin air. It took them a few seconds to realize he had dismounted, their burden had been so light. The man with the stick was screaming at them. They searched among themselves for the priest, pushing one another aside, but they couldn't find him. He had already escaped into his office, and then into the sacristy. The little street boys who lived under Aristide's protection in and around the churchyard had seen him flee. They were just a little smaller than he was and could see him better than the tall youths, but they weren't saying anything to the man with the stick. Instead, they mixed with this strange new crowd, possible targets for begging. Little, sinewy Waldeck, who was usually too busy playing cards or marbles to pay attention to the comings and goings at the church, was working the crowd, asking for pennies from them and dollars from me. I was white, he reasoned, and so I must be richer than the others. But the youths weren't interested in Waldeck and his begging. They were after Aristide.

"These guys are no good," Waldeck said, standing next to me and fiddling with his ragged shirt. "Give me five dollars," he said to me. I just looked at him.

The youths couldn't figure out where Aristide had gone. Angry, they started swarming into the church. They packed the place, all these young men with their angry faces and tee shirts with slogans from the students' federation and the peasants' collectives. In a short time, Aristide emerged. He had changed into his vestments. He was absolutely cool.

When he got to the microphone, the raucous crowd immediately quieted. He looked at them for a good long minute. They stayed silent.

"*Granmèt-la avèk nou,*" he said. The Lord be with you.

"*E avèk oumenm tou*," the boys gave the traditional response. And also with you.

"*Granmèt-la*," said Aristide for emphasis, "*avèk nou tout.*" The Lord be with all of you. He grasped the side of the table he stood behind. He still stared out into the crowd. He was trying to figure out who they were.

"*E avèk oumenm tou*," the youths responded, unsure.

"*Granmèt-la avèk nou tout.*" He seemed to be seeking reassurance in their voices.

"*E avèk oumenm tou*," they shouted, rising in their feet. "*E avèk oumenm tou.*"

Still he was not satisfied. But he told them, in a short, passionate sermon, to stand firm, to work against Duvalierism, that opposing Namphy's provisional military junta was holy work, that they themselves were holy.

"The last," he said later, "was questionable."

At the end of his talk, he asked them to join him in singing the "Dessalinienne," the country's national anthem. They all rose, raising their hands, as is the custom, in an approximation of the fascist salute, and sang the song, a stirring cross between the "Marseillaise" and the "Internationale." Waldeck filtered among them, still looking for funds. The priest disappeared.

The youths flowed out into the streets, with Waldeck and his pals trailing after them, but although they went around town past the National Palace, where they taunted the soldiers who were on guard, and over to the police station, where they made faces at the policemen and blocked police cars from moving, the authorities did not shoot. The youths wanted shooting, but they didn't get it. Not that day, anyway.

Back at the church, Aristide had a nervous prostration, and then a migraine. It was a nightmare, he said. He didn't know who those boys were, or who had sent them. Anyone could have paid them to come and start trouble. He hadn't recognized their faces. Who were they, and why had they come? Would he be blamed for their actions? He took to his bed, and his headache got worse.

When I first came back to St.-Jean-Bosco to meet Aristide again for the first time since Duvalier had left, I hardly remembered his face from that time when I had come by during the Dechoukaj in February 1986, and we had sat and talked inside the church courtyard with the guinea fowl waddling in the background. Yet Aristide's was not a face to forget: hollow-cheeked, goggle-eyed, wide-mouthed. The foreign journalists called him diminutive, bespectacled. "His Holiness," was the nickname Harry and the others used, though not in print. It was hard to believe that this small person who took up virtually no room at all could bring thousands of people to their feet and lead Port-au-Prince's slums with a wave of his hand.

As one of the few prominent people in Port-au-Prince who had stuck their necks out in Jean-Claude's waning days, publicly expressing the growing discontent and disgust with Duvalierism, Aristide had helped to create in the capital the same climate of unrest and protest that already existed in the countryside, and that made the dictator's departure necessary. By the end of Jean-Claude's days, Aristide was the most visible of the many young progressive priests and nuns — together called Ti Legliz, the Little Church — who had been organizing peasants and slum-dwellers in Haiti since the late 1970s.

The first time I met him, everything was chaotic and you couldn't talk to anyone for more than ten minutes before the excited crowds swept by. A few days later, Aristide said a historic mass in Gonaïves, where the Dechoukaj had begun in the fall of 1985 after three schoolchildren were shot dead by the Army. Some of the Haitian bishops were there in Gonaïves, lined up on their thrones inside the bizarre modern cathedral in the middle of the town square. The church was crammed and boiling hot, and Bishop Emmanuel Constant of Gonaïves was looking through his breviary, as though lost in study. No one in the noisy, excited church was paying attention to him, when silence suddenly began to fall over the jubilant crowd, first up front, and then slowly making its way over the congregants. Aristide in his white cassock had come to the pulpit, and he was simply standing there with his hands clasped, waiting for silence.

"It was the first time I had seen him," said a British journalist. "He looked just the way you would imagine a little black angel would look, you know, the one who is always left out of the paintings with all the little white angels. Transfixed, beatific. And childlike. I wouldn't have been surprised to see a halo form over that head, you would have thought it was just light and heat coming from his words. When he spoke, they all went wild."

Back in February 1986, Aristide had seemed like a radical participant in Duvalier's overthrow. When I met him again, half a year later, he was modulating. There was more sweetness, more common humanity, less vitriol. The sweetness, however, was not entirely believable, even with his famous angelic childlikeness. After all, sitting in a corner of his office was the life-sized effigy of a Tonton Macoute, and, as Aristide pointed out, the clothes were real, had once belonged to a real member of Duvalier's militia.

"We dechouked him," he told me.

"We?" I said. It sounded like an admission, coming from a priest.

"We, the people, I mean," he said, smiling.

It was raining again that night when I went to pick up my friend Charles, a Haitian mulatto I had met early in my stay. We were going up the hill to Pétionville for dinner. "It will just be small," said Jeanne, a friend of Charles's, when she called me. "Bring a date. Maybe Charles? I'm fixing lobster." This meant that Marianne, the woman who works in her kitchen and has the same name as Haiti's most popular margarine, would be making lobster. In Pétionville, when your mulatto host asks you if you want something to drink, and you say Coke, he says, "Well, I'll get it for you," and claps his hands. Then black Joseph or Marcel or Dieuseul appears in the doorway, and your host says, "A Coke for Mademoiselle."

Our car barely made it up the hill, twice we went backward when we meant to go forward, and Charles kept cursing the car and I kept hoping we wouldn't get a flat from all the tumbling rocks, because it was raining so hard. We couldn't see anything but our breath on the windows. Everything was black outside, probably the electricity had been cut. The only lights were our lights, until we got to the top of the hill, where everyone has his own generator, just in case. We drove down the residential streets of Pétionville. Even in the daytime, when it's not raining, you can see only the less expensive houses, because the rest of them sit behind high cement security walls. We honked out in front of Jeanne's gates (*la barrière*, Haitians call them, appropriately), and finally Joseph the *gardien* came and opened up, and we drove down the circular driveway to Jeanne and Sylvain's house. We parked under the dark, dripping bougainvillea. The spotlights were on above the terrace, and I could see Jeanne's three Dobermans pacing the top of the security wall.

"Pierrot, *encore du champagne pour ce côté de la table, non?*" says Jeanne. More champagne for this side of the table, and I look down at my lobster, its meat artistically removed from its shell, some delicate green beans arranged at its side, some delicately boiled potatoes nestled next to the beans, gold silverware. Pierrot is not in uniform — Haitian servants don't usually wear uniforms. He has on a dark polyester shirt with blue palm trees on it, and some old pants. Pierrot is the boyfriend of Marianne the cook, but Joseph the gardien is her real boyfriend. There are endless battles because of this, according to Jeanne. Someday soon, she will have to get rid of Pierrot. Jeanne likes to tell stories about the servants. Jeanne's servants like to tell stories about Jeanne. Jeanne told me she got Marianne from her mother ten years ago after her wedding, and now every time Jeanne has a man over during the day, Marianne reports back to Maman. "*Cela fait partie de la comédie, tu vois,*" Jeanne tells me. It's part of the game, you see.

The champagne that Pierrot pours is good, and it makes Jeanne more voluble than usual.

"But I don't understand," she says. "If the point of having elections is to elect someone who will continue the work of the junta, why have elections?" She points Pierrot to Charles's glass. "Why not just keep the junta? Besides," she says, laughing, "Sylvain knows Namphy." Her husband smiles.

"That wouldn't be democracy, my dear," Sylvain says. "Anyway, it's not what the Americans want. Besides, people need to think that they have elected their President. It will help the national spirit." He raises his eyebrows. Sylvain is always ironic. He learned it in France. He also drinks too much; he learned that in France, too.

"The Haitian people aren't that stupid, as you all know." This is Charles. Of course my date says the wrong thing. Everyone looks at everyone else except for Charles, and I look at my lobster.

"If they're not so stupid, why are they living the way they do?" This from a former government minister. His wife picks silently at her food. The former minister is having an affair with Jeanne, that's what Charles told me.

"Well, they seem to have figured *something* out," says Charles. "Look at the demonstrations. Look at Father Aristide." Charles spears a potato and eats it whole. I feel he is eating with too much enthusiasm. Jeanne is watching him.

"What do you mean, look at Aristide?" asks Sylvain. "There's not much to look at, really, is there?" he gazes around the table for approval, and gets some murmurs, but the guests seem to find the lobster more engrossing than the talk. Pierrot pours more champagne. During dinner, Charles and I keep one eye on Pierrot. He is our favorite this evening, dispelling tension wherever he goes. It's raining hard outside the patio where we are eating, a sheltered alcove in the garden. I can hear American voices on the cable television in the next room; the kids are probably watching *Dynasty*. Every so often, three little girls wearing white dresses come running into the dining room to ask Jeanne to settle a quarrel. Jeanne pats them. They speak half in English, half in French. They go to the Union School, with all the American Embassy kids, where Creole is forbidden.

Charles is still following the conversation. "What I mean is that Aristide is tapping the people's intelligence, and giving some kind of form to the ideas they have but can't really express." This is a long speech for Charles, who is also checking on Pierrot's whereabouts. His glass is empty.

"Aristide is a little dictator, in true Haitian style," says Sylvain. "A fascist in the making. Couldn't be plainer. And the only thing 'the people' know, the only 'idea' they have," he says, skewering a piece of lobster on the end of his gold fork and holding it in the air, "is that they'd like to be eating this." He waves the piece of pink meat around, pops it into his mouth, picks up his champagne, and takes a sip. "And with our bloody corpses at their feet, I might add."

"Sylvain," says Jeanne. She looks over at Pierrot, standing in the doorway. Pierrot speaks some French, as well as Creole.

"Sorry." Sylvain goes back to his plate. But he can't leave the subject alone. He looks up again at Charles. "But so, do you think that's the kind of 'idea' that Aristide is helping the people form? To kill us and eat our food? Clever little bastard, no? Kill them and eat their food."

"Right, and rape their wives and daughters and nationalize their businesses, and murder all white and light-skinned people," said my date. "I don't know, Sylvain, I think the guy is more moderate than that. I think he's talking about jobs and food, you're right about the food. But it doesn't seem that unreasonable. Anyway, he talks about forming alliances with the bourgeoisie."

"Not with *me*," says Sylvain. "I think he's preaching revolution. That's how the Nicaraguans got their revolution, by forming alliances with the bourgeoisie. You see how far *that* got them." He looks happy, he's finally said what he meant to say all along. Jeanne excuses herself and leaves the room with the smallest daughter tucked under her arm.

"Look, Charles, you want a revolution. You want to go live in La Saline with this priest? You want Aristide to decide where you eat and you live? You are us, Charles. What this priest calls 'the parasites.' Aristide would say, 'I'll take Charles's business. I'll live in Charles's house. I will take his girlfriend, his bank account. I will put him in prison. I will put him in Fort Dimanche.'"

"Sylvain!" Charles laughs. "You're being too dramatic. Aristide is the one who wants to *shut* Fort Dimanche."

"Well, some other place, then," Sylvain says. "Or he'll take you and turn you into a houseboy."

"You're exaggerating, just like the Americans."

"I don't think so," says Sylvain. "You can't be too careful with these popular leaders, even if they are priests. I always remember how scared my father was of Fignolé and his steamroller." Daniel Fignolé was a politician who rose to prominence in the late 1940s. He was feared by the elite for his following among Port-au-Prince's proletariat, whom he could bring out onto the streets at will. They were his *rouleau compresseur*, his steamroller.

"These rabble-rousers like Fignolé or this new one, they always appeal to the people's worst instincts," Sylvain want on. "Aristide, he appeals to their racism. You don't see any light faces in his congregation, have you noticed? He says the 'elite,' and they know that what he means is 'the mulattos.' Every day he's getting worse and worse. He'll have to shut up soon. He'll have to. Or be shut up. Pierrot, where is the champagne?" Sylvain looks around the table. "I mean, it can't go on like this, can it?"

On Mother's Day, a huge mass inside St.-Jean-Bosco, with little girls dressed in layers of lace, and boys in suits, and mothers everywhere in elaborate hats. The sun shining against the blue walls gives the church interior an otherworldly atmosphere, and little Aristide in his white robes looks like an angel at the altar. He is Titid today, making the congregation laugh, reaching out to them with his arms extended. Over and over, he has the children shout, as loud as they can, "*Mamamn, cheri, mwen renmen w.*" Mommy, darling, I love you. I feel uncomfortable in the heat and sentiment. It's like being inside a candy box. The kids are delighted, they shout and wave, and the mothers look sedate, pleased with themselves.

The text today is Jesus saying, "What is the Lord's, is mine, and what is mine is the Lord's." Since the Lord is Jesus' father and today is Mother's Day, Aristide extends the text to mothers as well. It seems trite, but he is happy, beaming down at his people, his face relaxed, talking as if he were simply in a room filled with friends.

Then, slowly, another Aristide emerges. Beads of sweat form on his high forehead, and his eyes focus on something farther away than the people in the front rows. His long fingers grasp the side of the altar table, and his body begins to sway. He stops talking, and begins preaching, prophesying. Mother's Day is a thing of the past. He takes the text and with some stunning leaps of logic and rhetorical twists, arrives at the conclusion that the only Christian way to run an economy is through communal property, since we are all, like Jesus, the children of the Lord, all brothers and sisters.

Once he is into his sermon, he is possessed, in part by the force of his own words, in part by the congregation's response. He hammers at the air, points his finger like a knife, solicits repetition first from one side of the church, then from the other, personally and by name attacks capitalism and with a brutal round of statistics shows what it does to the People of the Third World, lets fly with the words "communal," "in common," "community," without quite pronouncing that one similar word that the Well-Placed U.S. Embassy Official, an acquaintance of mine, is always waiting to hear from Aristide's lips. With a dismissive flick of one raised wrist, he tosses onto the heap of disposable Duvalierists the two men who lead the military junta. "Namphy." Flick. "Régala." Flick. The congregation roars, applauds, rises to its feet unbidden. He's on a real roll, repeating the adjectives that define an appropriate Haitian society: "Evangelical, popular, socialist." He says the three words again. The congregation says them. "Louder," he says. They say them louder. "Again," he says. They repeat the words.

He's like a little stick of dynamite, the energy of his gestures, his intense focus, his explosive bursts of eloquence, his devastating power. The congregation looks like a mirror of the priest: total concentration, rooted excitement. "Titid, Titid," the two young men next to me whisper in aroused unison. The girls watch the priest with their mouths open, their palms turned upward on their knees, their feet in and out of their too-tight high-heeled shoes. No one wants to miss a word. Scores of young men hold their tape recorders up toward the loudspeakers. Everyone wants to do exactly what Aristide tells them to do. When he asks them a question, you can almost hear them thinking, "What does he want us to say?" If, as they sometimes but rarely do, they give the wrong answer, he laughs, and says, "Wait, think," and explains better what the question means. Then he repeats it, and he gets the right answer. He always gets what he wants.

At the end of the sermon, the congregation crosses itself, Aristide looks down on them and pats his brow with a white handkerchief, and they begin to sing a St.-Jean-Bosco standard: "Satan Ale," or Satan, Get Lost. By Satan, in this context, they mean the regime. Aristide himself wrote the words. A few days later, when I go to visit the Well-Placed U.S. Embassy Official, I can hear Aristide's voice in the background, saying, "Evangelical, popular, socialist." It repeats the words over and over while I'm trying to do an interview. Afterward, I wander around the offices looking for that voice, which I can still hear. In a small room at the end of the hall, sitting at a small desk, I find an earnest-looking clerk, listening to a tape and translating. He tells me he translates Aristide's Sunday sermon every week.

1994

One of the great legends of literary journalism is the origin of Tom Wolfe's 1963 *Esquire* magazine essay "There Goes (Varoom! Varoom!) That Kandy-Kolored (Thphhhhhh!) Tangerine-Flake Streamline Baby (Rahghhh!) Around the Bend (Brummmmmmmmmmmmmmmmm) . . ." — that was the title — as nothing but a set of notes. He was blocked, goes the story, so he gathered them up and sent them off to his editor, Byron Dobell, who merely removed "Dear Byron" and called it an article.

Maybe the story is true. Maybe it's marketing. Either way, both ways, it echoes the anxiety of immediacy that so often defines writing about religion.

We don't usually connect *immediacy* to *media* — the former means the lack of the latter, which is a plural noun for all that stands in between you and reality. That includes TV and newspapers and magazines, of course, the stuff we're usually talking about when we talk about media. It also includes all the rituals and stories and ways of knowing we've devised to talk about what we think we know. Even talking is mediation. Religion, especially, is. But that's where it gets really tricky, because so much of religion as we commonly think of it is dedicated to *immediacy*. That is, unmediated encounters between a person and some kind of divine: conversations with God, speaking in tongues, the melting of the material implied by transubstantiation, the wafer as it is miracle-ized into the body of Christ, enlightenment, the condition called "spiritual but not religious." Immediacy. The idea is to cut away all the formalities, the forms, and get right to the thing itself.

Same deal with writing about religion that seeks to evoke such experiences. Same deal, for that matter, with most of literary journalism, a genre dedicated to the illusion that through ink on a page you can feel what it felt like to be in a war, or in love, or in the driver's seat of a kandy-kolored tangerine-flake streamline baby. The best work seeks to fulfill that ambition even as it acknowledges its impossibility. "Arguing with the Pope," by Barbara Grizzuti Harrison — a new journalist too smart, too candid, too *prickly,* to settle for illusion — is just such an effort. Like Wolfe, Harrison presents her account (in her case, of the pope's 1993 visit to Denver) as notes, a diary — an argument, indeed, and a messy one, stuffed with digressions and parentheticals. She gives us the *feeling* of argumentation as much as the argument itself. But feeling is not separated from intellect here. Harrison does not view spirit and its medium, flesh, as distinct. It's in that "coincidence of opposites," as Harrison puts it in another context, that the true potential of the genre is to be found.

BARBARA GRIZZUTI HARRISON
Arguing with the Pope

If some small mistake were made in doctrine, huge blunders might be made in human happiness. . . . A slip in the definitions might stop all the dances; might wither all the Christmas trees or break all the Easter eggs. . . . The Church had to be careful, if only that the world might be careless.

—G. K. CHESTERTON, *Orthodoxy*

I am Roman Catholic in the way my eyes are brown—it is not a condition from which I can, or wish to, escape. But from time to time my love for my Church is sorely tested, as it was when I went to Denver last summer to see the Pope (who had designated the week of August 11 to August 15 as World Youth Day). I had no way of knowing at the time that an encyclical—a pastoral letter to the whole Church, designed to protect the faithful from "fundamental error"—would soon be published. On October 5 the Pope issued the 179-page document called *Veritatis Splendor,* a remarkable and controversial document for which, it is clear to me now, the Denver convention was a kind of spiritual and tactical preparation.

In the event, the encyclical would ask and implacably answer questions I had brought with me to Denver (*Is it ever permitted to commit an act of lesser evil to prevent a larger evil?*), questions that had been the source of petty irritation, of bemused speculation, and also of anguish to me: questions about the place of the fractious Catholic Church in the technologized world; questions about my own place in the Church in which I, in jubilant belief and in sorrowful disbelief, profess to believe; questions about human sexuality; and questions, reflecting my own moral dilemmas, about the role of conscience in the affairs of the body.

The Church has always been at war with the world, which it simultaneously loves; it is in this coincidence of opposites that the spiritual wealth of the Church lies. I went to Denver to see — I needed to see, in the flesh — the demanding old Pope, a man wedded to the past, a man who calls the earth a "vast planet of tombs," and the buoyant young people in whom the future lives so vividly. Stasis and energy, the old and the young: perhaps another coincidence of opposites, two halves of the equation meeting and (like the lion and the lamb) providentially joining. One is sometimes immensely grateful to the Church for espousing eternal values and sometimes inclined to regard it as fossilized. One's equilibrium, such as it is, rests shakily on the apparent dichotomy of spirit and flesh . . . the instructive flesh.

I always feel that the real test of one's affections lies in the flesh, and in dreams (an alchemical combination): love is not disembodied. Dulled, abraded, snarled, and put-upon, true love is regenerated the moment one rests eyes upon the beloved; isn't it so? And answers that evade us in the light of day come to us in dreams that open or close the valves of our hearts.

One's heart is troubled: If only the Roman Catholic Church were not — with its witnesses and martyrs to social justice, and its prophets, its cranky and adorable saints, gorgeous and noble, sly and grand, its heroic go-to-church-every-Sunday foot soldiers — so wonderful. If only it were not so terrible, so stern (and simultaneously inane) in its

increasingly rabid insistence on absolute obedience to truth as truth is
defined by the Holy Father, and so terrible in its apparent determination to treat the human body as if it were a curse, particularly in view
of the fact that we are instructed to believe in the sanctity of matter, a teaching—thrilling, sane, and consummately logical—that de-
rives from the Incarnation, the enfleshment of God, a miracle that took
place in the body of a mortal woman.

My love for the Church has been informed in no small part by
the perception that it was a perversion of its articulated truths to regard the body as merely an envelope for the entrapped, laboring soul
and also, in great part, by the supremacy the Church has traditionally
accorded the role of conscience in the affairs of the body. . . . I went to
Denver with lucid dread.

Most Catholics I know well have a dense and complicated love
for the official, institutional Church; through their love run antipathies
and dissent (to say nothing of doubt) like a constant, low-grade fever.
When I was received into the Catholic Church, fifteen or so years ago
(odd that I shouldn't remember the date of my First Communion),
I used to feel vexation toward Catholics for whom the primary fact
about the Church was that it was "repressive." For "cultural Catholics" I had, I am not pleased to admit, disdain: one believed that the
Church was the channel for truth and grace, or one didn't. I have since
come to what may be a more sophisticated and is certainly a more liberal view: the Church is three-tiered. There is the official Church, the
loyal (troubled and sad and hopeful rather than bitterly angry) opposition, and radical reformers who wish to drastically reshape the institution's hierarchy.

I was baptized Roman Catholic. I became a Jehovah's Witness
when I was nine and remained one until I was twenty-two. (You cannot imagine the bliss of compressing the loneliness and horror of those
years into one sentence.) I symbolized my dedication to Jehovah's
Witnesses by immersion in water at a 1944 convention of Witnesses
in Buffalo. (There was a plague of caterpillars that year; they dropped,

fat and death-green and juicy, from the trees and writhed in the light
of street lamps; they fell, with soft little thumps and oily leavings, on
one's hair.)

For years I was told what friends I might have: no "worldly"
ones—that is to say, no one who wasn't a Jehovah's Witness in
good standing. I was told what music I might listen to: Beethoven,
"worldly" and syphilitic, might very well, I was given to understand,
be the deceptive and seductive voice of the devil, who stalked about
masked as an angel of light; I was twenty-three before I heard Bach's
Mass in B Minor for the first time. I was told what books I might read:
I read Salinger locked in an attic closet, crying for the joy of him. I
worked as a housekeeper at the world headquarters of Jehovah's Witnesses. I was told I was "too smart." I was told to remove my affections from the "worldly" object my love had, without the consent of
my will, sought out and sanctified (a schoolteacher, Arnold Horowitz);
I was instructed to rejoice in his destruction and the destruction of all
the wicked at a bloody and imminent Armageddon. (*"If thy right hand
offends thee, cut it off."*) I was nine when I started preaching from door
to door, miserable and arrogant, singular, a freak. I left Jehovah's Witnesses more than a decade later, when I understood that I could not
love and worship a God who was less compassionate than I. It came
down to two simple propositions: I could not believe in the intrinsic
wickedness of the world and the flesh; and God could not kill Arnold.

The official Roman Catholic Church, when I first came to it after
years in the desert of disbelief, was an absolute haven for me; I didn't
quarrel with it, precisely because I was told I *might* quarrel with it.
The Church offered me the freedom of the cloister: safety within defined parameters. I felt the space to be ample, the horizons limitless.
I loved the rambunctiousness of Catholics, their freedom to choose
and to tease, to question and to provoke; I loved the diversity within
the unity. I loved the sacramental life of the Church, the liturgy, the
community. By comparison with my apocalyptic religion, the Roman

Catholic Church was fireworks and a party, and I came to feel at home
in the wild and startling world I had been brought up to despise.

I brought this baggage—a lot of baggage—to World Youth
Day. I brought loathing for religious isolationism and the conviction
that my adolescent suffering lived on somewhere in my spirit and mar-
row, a toxin that had insinuated itself into my faith; I wanted to close
the circle of time and bring the past and the present into alignment and
into an apprehension of my faith.

What follows is a report from the front; and it is a report from
the interior.

AUGUST 9

Jet-lagged and wilted, I am sitting in the thick heat of the Sixteenth
Street Mall. No one is shopping; merchants are cranky; mounted
police—who outnumber pedestrians at the outdoor mall—look sober,
obsequious, and silly (rather, in their demotic scorn, like camels). In
a penumbra of shade I fiddle with food at a pizza boutique; nearby a
man stands with a cutout cardboard effigy of the Pope for anyone who
wishes to be photographed with a likeness of the Holy Father; there
are no takers.

Joslins Department store has announced 30 percent off silver and
gold crosses ($14.99–$350). Evangelist Richard Roberts has announced
a Miracle Healing Service to be held on Friday the thirteenth at Happy
Church on Orchard Road. The Reverend Maurice Gordon, pastor of
the Lovingway United Pentecostal Church, has placed an illuminated
sign on the façade of his building: ANTI-CHRIST COMING TO DENVER
IN AUGUST? Is the Pope the Antichrist? "He's on the shortlist, along
with the Dalai Lama," Rev. Gordon replies.

Breathing hard—Denver is 5,280 feet high, and we are warned
that it will take three or four days to get fully acclimated to the height
and the bone-dry heat—I pick up my official press-information loose-

leaf notebook from the press-registration desk of the 739-room Radisson Hotel, where I am staying, as are 550 other members of the press (altogether, 3,500 journalists registered). This simple chore is not entirely without muddying incident:

"You can't have your notebook yet. There's a misprint about St. Clare of Assisi."

"Yes, but I have to know where to go. . . . What's St. Clare got to do with it?"

Silence.

"Perhaps you could black out the stuff about St. Clare? Or rip out the page?" St. Clare is the patron saint of washerwomen and of television.

"No."

"Yes, but I really must go where the kids are. I long to . . ."

He relents. (The air is thin up here.) "All right," he says, "I can see you have a good heart." He can? How can he? I grind my teeth at this presumption. "Having a bad hair day?" a reporter from a regional Catholic paper asks, and I glare at her, dampening her beaming smile, poor thing; I feel myself to have been sufficiently commented upon. The red notebook, of Talmudic length and obscure detail (what are "pre-animation" programs?), serves me ill; by the end of Youth Day, the Grand Ballroom of the Radisson will be littered with unused notebooks, information having been gleaned chaotically from word of mouth and from local newspapers.

I am offered a book called *You Better Believe It: A Playboy-Turned-Priest Talks to Teens*, written by Father Ken Roberts, who, according to the accompanying promotional leaflet, "left the jet-setting life of an English playboy to become a Catholic priest."

I am handed a copy of the Benedictine Rule: "Prefer nothing whatever to Christ."

McNichols indoor stadium, where the kids are registering, shimmers in the hellish sun. Helicopters swarm overhead, their propellers slicing heat so tangible one feels one could carry it in a bucket. They are Marine helicopters, each equipped to hold twelve combat-ready servicemen, and they crisscross the unblemished sky, making landings and mock landings at adjoining Mile High Stadium: ugly apocalyptic insects, drowning thought. They are practicing for the arrival of the Pope on August 12 and the arrival of President Clinton, who is to greet him. With a sickening act of the imagination, I freeze the moment and see, in the sprawled bodies of travel-weary kids claiming their patches of shade and in the insistent stuttering whine of the big-bellied copters, a foretaste of war, an image of the destruction — the "civilization of death" — the Holy Father would come to Denver to decry. . . . The earth, the Pontiff once said, is "ever more a burial ground."

Exhaustion and adrenaline. Under tents people browse lazily among a hundred kinds of Church-sanctioned souvenirs: white foam miters; Miracle Mugs, which, empty, portray night in Denver under a black sky unenlivened by a yellow sickle moon — when the cups are filled with hot liquid, the scene changes stereoptically, and as the sun comes up so does a grinning Pontiff. They wear T-shirts on which are emblazoned HE WHO DIES WITH THE MOST TOYS — STILL DIES; GET A LIFE; HIS PAIN IS YOUR GAIN; IDAHO 'TATERS.

Inside McNichols participants queue for credentials and for housing assignments in dorms, parish houses, host-family homes, garages, and in a five-acre tent city in the southeast corner of Fitzsimons Army Medical Center (where there are no showers, no electricity, and no plumbing).

The youthful participants, 186,000 of them, have come from all over the world — Australia, Hong Kong, Sudan, Poland, Mexico, India, Pakistan, France, Italy, Turkey, Bosnia, Serbia, Haiti, Cambodia, Ukraine — for recommitment to the Church, an exercise in communal sanctity and activism and personal meditation and prayer. Seventy percent are from the United States. Cuba has two delegates; Nicaragua has 474. Some were self-selected. Some were chosen by their parishes and dioceses, others by Catholic organizations national and

international—Teens Encounter Christ, Catholic Charismatic Renewal, Catholic Boy Scouts, the Salesian Youth Movement—liberal
(the Maryknolls) and conservative (Opus Dei); they flew, they walked,
they came by bus and car, often at great personal expense and discomfort. They participated in walkathons and fastathons and lotteries to
get here.

They've come, one kid says, "to continue to grow each day in
holiness." The kid who says this is wearing a backpack and a money
belt, jeans and a WHITE SOX baseball cap; he is carrying a guitar, and
on his T-shirt are the words CHRIST'S COUNTERCULTURE. "And to
cruise girls?" I ask, emboldened by the sight of three lissome long-
haired beauties signing their names in Magic Marker, on the muscled
chest of a blond Californian giant.

"Yeah," he says shyly. "Yeah. Why not?"

Why not, indeed? One believes, if one is Catholic—one is
obliged to believe—in the sanctity of the flesh, the holiness of matter, the sacramental nature of the quotidian: we believe because God
became Man.

In the close air of the stadium, Mexican girls, hot, are singing
"California, Here We Come." (Why?) Puerto Ricans are chanting
"Puerto Rico! Puerto Rico! Puerto Rico!" popping their fingers, snap-
ping gum. Nuns are trying, with total lack of stereotypical severity, to
impose order while at the same time encouraging and sustaining good
cheer: a middle-aged nun joins a conga line; her feet are unversed but
her body is willing, and her veil flies and her crucifix swings in a wide
arc on her ample breast. Guys with cowboy shirts and girls with cowboy boots gravely execute a country line dance.

Thirty-seven years ago I attended religious conventions of Jehovah's Witnesses. How well I remember the delectable boy-girl tension
of those assemblies: sitting behind third base at Yankee Stadium looking across to the first-base stands, where I knew Dennis Gates sat,
wondering if he was scanning the stands for me; crossing my legs just

so, in case he was, primping my hair. We wore white gloves in those days and a cologne called Friendships Gardens; we danced the tango. Bob Schroeder took me for a walk in Central Park, and we looked deep into each other's eyes and talked about God, our eyes like fires in a dry thicket. At some point during the exceedingly invigorating God talk, I noticed Bob Schroeder was holding my hand. He blushed brick red. "It's just a hand," I said. "I'm just holding it," he said.

The question now reverberating in my head is relentless: Is there something aberrant about a young person's choosing, in 1993, to come to a religious convention? Chelsea would look at home here, and Amy Carter too, and so, for that matter, would George Stephanopoulos. These kids are no kookier, nerdier, weirder than kids one might find at any summer camp or on any college campus . . . and far less fanatical and obsessive than the kids at Woodstock, with which World Youth Day is constantly and tediously compared.

But: no premarital sex, no birth control, priestly celibacy — can they accept all this? If I am inclined to feel that the official post–Vatican II Church is profoundly anti-body (and I'm fifty-nine, for heaven's sake), what must these kids, hormones executing double somersaults in their veins, think?

A twenty-year-old from Oklahoma, still clothed in baby fat, earnestly informs me that sex is not a coarse act, not a matter of slippery heaving bodies and cracking bones. (He's a virgin; he should know.) A convert, he tells me the great thing about the Catholic Church is that it "puts its cards on the table . . . and then you dialogue . . . yin and yang," he says, losing me.

A young Guatemalan man who lives in South-Central L.A. and works in a gang mission tells me that "rhythm is a good birth-control method, if the man is disciplined enough." "And if he isn't?" The girls sitting around him on the brown grass outside McNichols giggle and throw their hands in the air.

Pretty Mary Margaret, pale — perhaps from an excess of piety,

perhaps from exhaustion—is jumpy, both drained and anticipatory;
she has just arrived on a three-day bus ride from Vancouver, and she
wants nothing so much as a shower. She is assigned to the Fitzsimons
center . . . where a cupful of water will have to suffice. "I'm going to
Mexico next year," she says, "so this is a kind of warm-up to all *that*
suffering." It is in my mind to tell her that she needn't court suffering
or flirt with it; it will come to her, in the fullness of time, unbidden and
quite soon enough . . . I censor my unkind words, but not my thoughts:
Mary Margaret, I think, will grow up to be the kind of Catholic I cannot abide. She will forever be offering her sufferings up to God (not a
bad idea in itself—suffering, like guilt, having to be put to some use,
given the remorselessness of its occurrence); and she will make a general pest and martyr of herself, a reproach to joy. She will create suffering in order to offer it up to God (to whom no gift is unacceptable),
when all she has to do (alas) is wait for it to visit her.

Sylvain, from France, who tells me that he is "here to be in
the light," says that "the set teachings of the Church are the ideal—
something we strive for but often don't reach. The Church is like a
great family, a refuge; it takes you in when you fail, when no one else
will—it has to."

In the afternoon, the International Youth Forum—an elite corps of
young people, 270 delegates from 101 countries presented by orga-
nizers as "the real working group" of the assembly, the "cream of
the crop," the "leaven of the loaf"—holds the first of two Vatican-
managed press conferences in the science building of Regis University.
In official press releases, there is familiar homiletic rhetoric about work
and family and thematic decrial of the "anti-life culture" of abortion,
euthanasia, AIDS, suicide . . . and, rather nicely, I think, the recognition that illiteracy is as much a threat to life as drugs and alcohol,
"because living is to have the capacity of understanding . . . to know
the truth and seek it, to prepare . . . for work that is dignified and for

an active participation in the life of the community." (*"In the beginning was the Word . . ."*)

Cardinal Eduardo Pironio, head of the Pontifical Council for the Laity, on the dais with three members of the Youth Forum, says, "This Forum must essentially be a Forum of grace, of sanctity, of transparency."

There is something about the word "transparency" that pierces my heart. In the Middle Ages, it was believed that sin made humans opaque; if one were without sin, one would be transparent, full of light. ("Like those anatomical models at Toys R Us," my boyfriend, a rascal, says.) Transparency (or candor, which, later, Denver Archbishop J. Francis Stafford was to urge upon youth): a radical openness to experience, a willingness to risk and to risk being seen—to risk being known in all one's dimensions—a welcomed and embraced vulnerability, the qualities of which Mary (to whose Immaculate Heart in 1984 the Holy Father entrusted the Soviet Union) is in Scripture the best and most revered example.

There is also, on the dais, an American resident of Rome, Joan Lewis, representing the Vatican Information Service. I ran into Ms. Lewis in the early Eighties, in Santa Susanna, the American church in Rome, which I regarded as a kind of curiosity: it seemed odd to me that anyone should want to chitchat with American government servants in heavenly Rome when one could be in the animating and intriguing company of Italian Catholics, who, for better or for worse, treat their churches like extensions of their living rooms. I have a clear picture of Ms. Lewis in the *cortile* of Santa Susanna, her loud voice—a voice straight from a Henry James novel, Henrietta Stackpole without largess of heart—pitilessly mocking the length of little Italian girls' skirts. (Girls' dresses fall to their ankles until the girls grow breasts, and then the skirts climb to their thighs; there is no logic in this—Roman logic defies comprehension but sometimes rewards intuition.) Now it falls to Ms. Lewis to introduce the panelists and to explain their mandate, which is to prepare and deliver to the Pope a "letter of purpose," the fruit of collegial workshop discussions, meditation, and prayer.

I ask His Eminence if I may sit in — quietly and unobtrusively — on some of the forum's workshops. I see ahead of me days of abstractions and propaganda, and I long for substance and exhilaration and healing. After all, this is a media event, and, after all, these young men and women are here, they say, to evangelize. So why don't they start with us, with the press, heathens one and all? But the rule is strict: members of the press are not to be admitted. "Do you think the youth would be comfortable with you in the room?" the cardinal says. I can't think why not. The cardinal's definition of youth is elastic: the youngest participant in the forum is fifteen-year-old Ijang Marysyilanus from Indonesia; the oldest is thirty-nine.

Cardinal Pironio's message to the forum is: "To live is to be happy and to pass on the happiness of having discovered Life to others." It occurs to me that it has been a long time since happiness has been a goal one hears spoken of with any ease; one hears about self-esteem and well-being, about sobriety and recovery and physical and mental fitness and okayness and wellness . . . and even about unhappiness — but happiness seems to have been shrunk and made to retreat into a closet, as if it were too wet, too unruly, too immodest, too enormous to be trotted out naked for the public gaze.

The panelists deplore dissent ("Certain things are settled and should be accepted"). "My people are just surviving," says Yvette, a young woman from Cameroon. "Do you think they care about women priests?" Women's ordination and clerical celibacy and abortion are problems "only for people outside the Church and for Americans. . . . There's no news in these issues." Yvette says it is impossible to entertain any notion of community that is not predicated upon absolute obedience to the Church.

I want, for any number of reasons, to cry.

"Love God and do as you please. . . . Have God in your heart — at

your court—in your ivory bed—under your rich robes—in the army—at banquets." —Blessed Ermengard, Duchess of Bretagne. How beautiful.

But *Love God and do as you please*, exquisite in its simplicity, could, by a sin-disordered mind and callous conscience, be read as: Do whatever the hell you feel like doing. Human nature is so "affected by sin," the voice of our conscience could be that of Cyndi Lauper masquerading as Renata Tebaldi. How do I know that I am not so riven and polluted by sin that I wouldn't know Truth if it bit my cheek?

I find myself in the familiar position of longing for the religious certainty that I simultaneously abjure; whereas for the members of the International Youth Forum, seventy-three-year-old Karol Wojtyla is Absolute and brother, Father and friend.

Twilight, and an end to enervating heat; I am made tranquil by the mountain-cool air. The kids, at dusk, are exuberant. Seeking one another's faces, hands, smiles, needing to hear their questions echoed and their answers echoed, needing to play and to pray in unison, they are gathered here in Civic Center Park (renamed, for the occasion, Celebration Plaza), a short walk from the Radisson and from the gilt-domed capitol. I find myself humming a song from an old movie called *State Fair*. There are booths offering literature—calls to vocation and to missionary work, information about Catholic colleges and universities. The grass, bordered with begonias and petunias, smells sweet. There are bratwurst vendors and Häagen-Dazs and Coke carts.

Two Italian priests, skirts hiked up, feet dangling in the reflecting pool, are smoking. One of them, in easy response to my curious glance, shrugs. "Ah," he says. "We smoke in Italy. Why? Because we know in our bones that we are mortal, and we believe in our hearts that we are immortal. You jog."

Later that night, in my room at the Radisson, superimposed on pay-TV (*Basic Instinct*) is an image I can't get out of my mind: a Mexican girl—hot, slutty-looking by any reasonable North American standards—kneeling bareheaded in the brutal coruscant sun, her hands folded in prayer, whispering (moaning) the rosary. Her chipped red fingernail polish.

(What will happen to her later? After prayers, under her sleeping bag in the garage-dorm she shares with boys and girls endowed, like her, with sanctity and sex, will she cuddle, will she flirt, will she snuggle with her fantasies of a lovely boy? Will she clutch her rosary to her breast? I look up "slut" on my Compaq computer's thesaurus; the only antonym it gives for "slut" is "virgin." *Pace papa.*)

No single image of the Pope stains my imagination; in the pictures I resurrect from memory he is virile, austere (pigeon-toed, hunched), old, detached, hammy, doomsday-sad, and totally lacking in the charisma he is said in abundance to have—in particular by television newspeople who disagree with all that he holds sacred, but won't let that stand in the way of their being charmed.

He has sent, in advance of his flying to them, a "message to the Youth of the World" (prefaced by the theme of the gathering, from the Gospel according to John: "I came that they might have life, and have it to the full"):

> *True and lasting unity . . . can only be achieved by building on the foundations of a common heritage of values accepted and shared by all, . . . respect for the dignity of the human person, a willingness to welcome life, the defence of human rights, and openness to transcendence and the realm of the spirit. . . .*

He inveighs against superficiality or despair and "the teachers of the 'fleeting moment,' who invite people to give free rein to every instinctive urge or longing, with the result that individuals fall prey to a sense of anguish and anxiety leading them to seek refuge in false artificial paradises."

Once he was a poet; and sometimes he gives one reason to remember this: just before he comes to Denver from Mexico, "the poor

South," he says, "will judge the rich North." He strikes me as northern in his (cool and tidy) temperament, not messily Mediterranean or
Latin. So, nice, therefore, to hear him speak a prose poem about the
untidy, unruly South, simultaneously meek and flamboyant, bowed-
down and noisy, the South that creates muddles and knows (because it
has had so much practice) how to live with tragedies. It is my peculiar
bigotry to believe that Roman Catholics are southern; Episcopalians
are northern.

The Pope calls the young people ambassadors, evangelizers . . .
and these words cause in me a little flurry of anxiety: I do not like to be
reminded that I was once a child evangelist; it frightens me.

AUGUST 10

The buzz in the Grand Ballroom, working space for reporters, who may
watch Youth Day events on a mammoth TV screen, is that a papal encyclical is in the works — rumored to be (though, as it happened, not)
infallible. For an encyclical to be infallible — immune from error — the
Pope must speak ex cathedra (the last infallible statement was made
in the late 1950s). The anticipation of an infallible encyclical designed
to protect the faithful from fundamental errors in faith and morals is
fraught with jittery excitement and alarm, particularly when the subject is human sexuality — which, according to the buzz, it is.

In one of the official press releases, we are told to expect the Pope
to address himself in Denver to what he calls "destructive criticism" of
the Church. How will he define "destructive"?

Buzz: There will, according to the encyclical, be a new litmus
test for the appointment of bishops: they must verbally condemn birth
control.

In the Sixties, following the bracing openness of Vatican II,
moral theologians were inclined to speak of sex not in absolute but
in relative terms (in Vatican-speak, they were informed by "propor-

tionalism and consequentialism"). In 1977, the Catholic Theological Society of America published a book called *Human Sexuality* (which I received when I was taking religious instructions from a priest at St. Patrick's Cathedral, prior to being received into the Church; I would be surprised if the book—or he—were still there). "Premarital sexual morality is largely a matter of drawing honest and appropriate lines . . . ," it said. "Is it self-liberating, other-enriching, honest, faithful, life-serving, and joyous? To what extent, if any, is there selfishness, dishonesty, disrespect, promiscuity, the danger of scandal or of hurting or shaming family and loved ones? Young people . . . should be challenged to question themselves as to whether they are not simply using each other to prove their respective masculinity, femininity, sexual attractiveness or prowess. To this should be added for young and old alike the question of willingness to accept a child if one is conceived. No contraceptive device thus far invented is altogether foolproof. Dishonesty is certainly involved when a man engages in sexual intercourse with a woman with whom he would not want to have a child. . . ."

Although not exactly an endorsement of free love, passages like this—which, all else aside, implicitly endorsed birth control—had the effect of enabling many Catholics to do what they were going to do anyway, but without soul-withering guilt. (For the majority of American Catholics, birth control is not an issue; they practice it as much as other Americans do, and in good conscience.) The authors of *Human Sexuality* were prudential—but, admittedly, less repressive than the authors of Antioch University's rules governing what it calls "interactions," rules that obviate any possibility of spontaneity in human affection during one's college years and that dichotomize love and sex in a way that the Church wouldn't in its worst dreams do. "Interactions," indeed. How utilitarian—how transactional—can anybody get? ("Please, ma'am, may I move an inch higher? lower?") A finger's breadth can mean, if Antioch's rules, which require verbal assent to each escalation of physical intimacy, are read literally—as they are meant to be read—the difference between grad school and expulsion.) The thing the Church has always had going for it was the conviction, and the insistence, that love is transcendent; it was not something you weighed and measured but was given freely, and it multiplied, of its nature, and expanded.

In 1968, Pope Paul VI issued the encyclical *Humanae Vitae,* which condemned artificial contraception . . . and it was hard to find an American Catholic who wasn't, as a consequence, glum—who wasn't, as Andrew Greeley wrote, traumatized. "Disaster," he said, "was the result of a single decision made because of the decrepit and archaic institutional structure of the church, a structure in which effective upward communication practically does not exist."

It occurs to me that for the Holy Father to position his arguments between relativity and absolutism is coarse. There is an organic, subtle interaction at the intersection between the ideal and the concrete, in which Christianity is rooted. It is at that intersection that life happens.

In the press room, I talk with Jackie Lyden, here for National Public Radio, and born and raised a Catholic, about the Holy Father and women: In July, the Pope called on American bishops to fight "a bitter, ideological" feminism among some Catholic women that led (he said) to "forms of nature worship and the celebration of myths and symbols" usurping traditional celebrations.

Although I'm not quite sure what John Paul II was so worked up about, I myself get a little tired of women lying down on bare earth and communing with the roots of trees and writing bad prose about it (in the Christian tradition, the earth is not our solemn mother but our delightful sister; that is what enabled St. Francis of Assisi to laugh at nature as well as to love it); a hundred thousand years ago, when I was an editor at *Ms.* magazine, I had no great enthusiasm for women who sent in stories about eating cookies made with menstrual blood or about baked umbilical cords served with postnatal tea. (A lot of these stories were written by women who liked to call themselves witches.)

I have with me in Denver the manuscript of a book of quotations by and about the saints — *A Splendor of Saints* — by my daughter, Anna Harrison. I am gratified to see that when one reads the stories of the saints — the gore and the self-flagellation and the mortification of the flesh — there is a point after which one finds one has stopped being appalled and stops perceiving the saints (in particular, women saints, and their obsessive concern with food and with fasting) as self- or flesh-loathing.

The cumulative effect of stories about the saints is exalting; cumulatively, these stories glorify and celebrate the body — and that is because, as medievalist Caroline Walker Bynum writes, their point "was ultimately not rejection of the physical and bodily, but a finding of the truly physical, the truly nourishing, the truly fleshly, in the humanity of Christ.... Physicality was not so much rooted out or suppressed as embraced and redeemed *at that point* where it intersected with the divine.... Women reached God, not by reversing what they were, but by sinking more fully into it." Blessed Angela of Foligno, for example, fantasized about parading around unclothed, garlanded with rotting fish and meat; she was a glutton.... The Church could just as well have made gluttony the great sin as sex, my daughter says, and one sees her point: we eat the body of Christ. One could make a case that eating too much chocolate cake — or eating blood pudding — is a greater slap in his face than committing adultery.

It is natural for a woman to see her body as her *self*. Think of the paradigms: Eve's *body* was the arena and origin of temptation and sin; Mary's body was the arena of redemption, the source of her personhood and her saintliness. She is depicted in medieval paintings as a priest. "The reverence for Mary that we find in thirteenth-century women mystics," Bynum tells us, "is . . . reverence for the bearer and conduit of the Incarnation. The ultimate identification was with Christ as human." And the flesh of Christ was regarded, in the fifteenth century, as both male and female. Popular piety has always adored flesh and representations of flesh. Flesh was the occasion of our salvation.

We are our bodies. Mary *was* her body. The only two infallible statements ever made were made about Mary, and one was that she—in her flesh—had been assumed into heaven. Bodily. The faithful had believed that for a thousand years; the infallible statement followed upon near-universal democratic practice and belief.

O my Lady, my life, O Queen of Heaven, O Mother of God, although I am certain that your glorious body is unceasingly praised in heaven with melodious jubilee by all the heavenly court, still I . . . desire with all my heart to render here on earth such praise and thanks as I can to all your precious limbs.

May your sweet nose glory! By the power of the Holy Spirit, it never drew or sent forth a breath without all your thought being ever present in the presence of the most High. . . . To that same nose of yours and to your most blessed nostrils be ever given an odor of sweetness, praise, and honor above the mingled odor of all the spices and all the herbs that habitually send forth a delightful fragrance. . . .

Your eyebrows and your eyelids . . .

May your neck, your shoulders, and your back be perpetually honored above the charm of the lilies. . . .

—ST. BIRGITTA OF SWEDEN

AUGUST 11

I order breakfast from room service. On morning TV, a black female fundamentalist invites me to "walk in the spirit and leave behind the lusts of the flesh. . . . Leave the natural realm," she says. I dive under the covers. . . . My lover's breath always smells like flowers, as the saints' are said to have done, though God knows he's no saint. Whenever he leaves me I solace myself with my own milky smell, which comes from his body and cannot be washed off. . . . The Pope is a fundamentalist. I wish he were not. I have had enough fundamentalism in my life.

Isn't it odd: Catholics are said, by psychologists, who ought to know, to have more fun in bed than non-Catholics. Greeley says that research done by the National Opinion Research Center and the Gallup organization indicates that Catholics have more sex, and sex more often, than Protestants do, and are more playful in their sex lives, and enjoy sex more than Protestants do, and are more tolerant of homosexuals. And yet so many Catholics — divorced Catholics, Catholics who are, as we used to say, living in sin — suffer spasms of guilt over what Europeans call "these little sins of the body." (I include myself; I am divorced, and I am joined in an irregular relationship with a man whom I entirely and forever love.)

"Pope John Paul II tries to understand . . . to convince," says Joaquin Navarro-Valls, director of the Holy See press office. "He will not excommunicate. That is not his way." Perhaps not. But the real question is, How many of the faithful — if the encyclical demands of Catholics what they cannot in honor or love or conscience do — will excommunicate themselves?

This terrifying dichotomy of body and soul. I watch Johnny Cash and June Carter Cash on early-morning TV; they are singing "Will the Circle Be Unbroken?" They have it all together, body and soul. John Donne had it all together; and we can, if we're lucky, remember a time when we were loved and in love and had it together, flesh and spirit one, the immortal glimpsed in the mortal.

AUGUST 11, LATER THAT NIGHT

Mass in the park: a sea of color in the dusk — a parade of smiling bishops in rosy *zucchetti*. Young people in saris and *salwar chamises* and silk kimonos (carrying oil-stained McDonald's bags) and Arsenio Hall porkpie hats. Vietnamese bearing soaring kites, and twelve children carrying a 16-foot rugged cherrywood cross (received by twelve

young pilgrims in Rome on Palm Sunday in 1992 and carried there-
after throughout America, from Los Angeles to Newark, San Antonio
to Portland, and anointed by the tears and prayers of the faithful). Bell
choirs and banners, nuns clapping to the Gloria. Clouds of incense:
"Come to me, all you who are weary." Organ and trumpet: "You have
turned my mourning into dancing." Archbishop Stafford of Denver
implores the kids to "make a difference." Well, who doesn't speak
Oprah-ese/Renaissance talk these days? But is this why Augustine
gave us his *Confessions* and God gave us Gerard Manley Hopkins? So
that an archbishop could speak in Oprah ese?

Each of them had been called to Denver for a purpose, the kids
were told: "*Ask, why? Why am I here? Why am I alive at all? What must
I do?*" The question spoke directly to teenage angst, giving it shape,
giving sadness a purpose (" *Why am I born? Why am I living? What do I
get? What am I giving?*"). Their faces and their bodies (crocodile lines,
nudgy nuns, good-natured jousting) affirmed for one another that
they were both normal and universal, and negated what they, ghetto-
ized in mass culture somewhere between Pat Robertson and Barney,
must often have occasion to fear: that they are freaks and marginalized
persons, suffering from a kind of social psoriasis. Here they can retreat
from their own cynicism; here it's cool to be Catholic.

On the short walk back to the hotel, I meet a con man. I do not
know at first that he is a con man, although a less preoccupied fool
would have known—his wife has died of cancer, he needs spiritual
support (and money), he needs friends (and money), he needs to know
where he can find a hotel room (and money). I have been walking in
the moonlight thinking that one thing or another was a con—my conscience or the Pope. And I meet a con man. I have been thinking of
Chesterton:

> "*The outer ring of Christianity is a rigid guard of ethi-
> cal abnegations and professional priests; but inside that in-
> human guard you will find the old human life dancing like*

children, and drinking wine like men; for Christianity is the
only frame for pagan freedom. But in the modern philosophy
the case is opposite; it is its outer ring that is obviously artistic
and emancipated; its despair is within. . . . We might fancy
some children playing on the flat grassy top of some tall island
in the sea. So long as there was a wall round the cliff's edge
they could fling themselves into every frantic game and make
the place the noisiest of nurseries. But the walls were knocked
down, leaving the naked peril of the precipice. They did not
fall over; but when their friends returned to them they were
all huddled in terror in the centre of the island; and their song
had ceased."

—CHESTERTON, *Orthodoxy*

I have wanted to be forever in a garden where the world was violently tamed and everything smelled sweet; I have wanted the walls
to close around me like a warrior's shield; I have wanted to be held so
tightly there was no room for a mouse or a free movement or a doubt; I
have wanted such support as would render vertigo of the body and the
mind impossible. . . . I have wanted, but only in dark dreams, what I
once had and threw away, in mingled gladness and disgust, to join the
large and terrifying, wonderful world.

I have been in that garden, and I know that its sweetness owes
nothing to life and everything to sterility; the shield is a shroud, and
without movement there is death, an icy splinter in the heart. This is
not a garden; this is the kingdom of the Snow Queen, whose wintry
kiss turns the heart into a frozen lump; this is the garden where wolves
clothed as lambs howl and ravens clothed as angels scream.

It is the garden from which one views the world with dread and
loathing and the assumption of spiritual superiority that is in fact a
form of acedia; it is the sanctuary of souls doomed to love and to court
the destruction of the astonishing world . . . the world they believe to
be the devil's playground, his orchard of poisoned sweets. The Snow

Queen is an apocalyptic bully. The lure of certainty — of everlasting
safety within the walls of immutable revealed truth — is very great.

Back in my hotel room: on the television there is a commercial pro-
moting safe sex. (Latex *gloves?*) It is so anti-erotic as to make one vow
never to have sex again. And they call the Church repressive.

Oh, I am so glad, so grateful, not to be in the icy garden I lived in
when I was a child. My mother combined the frankincense of martyrdom with the radiance of her beauty and the passion of her belief. After
she became a Jehovah's Witness, I had a nightmare that was to recur
until I left that sect: In the dream I stand in a walled garden; climbing
red roses shine like bright blood against a white-washed wall. An icy
creature, resplendent, of indeterminate sex, calls to me; I feel the voice
flowing through my veins. The creature extends its arms in a gesture
magisterial and maternal, entreating and commanding; I am without
will. I walk toward its embrace, fearful, unable not to abandon myself
to a splendid doom. I am seized in its arms and hurled out of the garden; I fly ravaged through dark and hostile space.

Tonight, after television (the grating invective of my co-
religionist Pat Buchanan the last voice I hear), for the first time in decades, I dream that dream again.

AUGUST 12

The air conditioner is blasting; I wake up icy cold. Only lottery-
winning journalists who have been credentialed by the Secret Service
are allowed anywhere near the tarmac when the Pope lands. I watch
what I have come to see on television: Church luminaries together
with President Clinton and his entourage (including Hillary Rodham
Clinton and Chelsea Clinton, in polka dots) are waiting in a light rain
for the Holy Father to arrive at Stapleton International Airport on an
Alitalia Boeing 747.

"I have met four presidents. I am an old Pope. You are a young

President." Was the President of what used to be called the Free World being rather clumsily complimented, or slyly condescended to?

Standing under a huge white umbrella under a lightning-streaked sky, the Pope defeats expectations and alludes to "the Subject" — abortion: "If you want equal justice for all and true freedom and lasting peace, then, America, defend life. All the great causes that are yours today will have meaning only to the extent that you guarantee the right to life." The President stands by impassively. They exchange gifts — a walking stick topped with an angel for the Pope, a Bible from the Pope to President Clinton.

A photograph of them walking together, each with hands locked behind his back and head down, is a study in maleness, a study in black and white, a study, ineffably, of narcissism. They look curiously compatible. And pale.

Two-hundred-foot-wide white streamers connect person to person when, later that afternoon, almost precisely on schedule, the Pope's motorcade emerges from the wings of Mile High Stadium, he in his white popemobile, a bulletproof modified Chevrolet Cheyenne four-wheel-drive pickup truck. Ninety thousand people pound their feet on the metal floor of the stadium. Seventy-five thousand more watch his image on Jumbo Tron TV screens at Celebration Plaza. The kids, and teary nuns, combine hothouse ardor with seemliness.

(From the notebook given to the press: "When the Holy Father reaches the top step and enters from stage right the trumpets will sound and white doves will be released. . . . 4:21:10 P.M. Drummer: Song — Ethnic Drumming 4 minutes. . . . 1. Look around and see who is here. 2. Raise your banners and see who is here. 3. Stand up and say hello . . ." Spontaneity is not left to chance.)

The Holy Father greets his young people in French, Italian, German, Portuguese, Lithuanian, Croatian, Polish. He evokes the intercession of the Black Madonna for the Polish nation and, in Spanish, greets, "with particular esteem," Latin Americans, "heirs of a vibrant

Catholic tradition, for which the Church is giving special thanks to God on the occasion of the Fifth Centenary of the Evangelization of the Americas."

Every time he utters the word "life" the crowd waves white handkerchiefs.

"We are in Denver! Denver, Colorado!" he exults, as if he can't quite believe it himself . . . as if the adulation and exaltation he elicits circle around and come back to reside in him.

He has come to listen, he says. What will he be able to hear above the sound of wild greeting and adulatory applause, the white noise of endorsing praise?

The Pope is perhaps, I think, a little mad, as people who are both extroverted and lonely frequently are. He has tics: when he reads a prepared speech, for example, he invariably, no matter how much he improvises, reads aloud the printed words THE END. John Paul II is an apocalyptic man; perhaps he savors the words THE END. Admit: it is by such measures that we determine whether someone is sane or insane, congenial or dangerous to our safety.

I don't get the point of this Pope. I do not love him, as I understand love, but then there are a lot of people I don't get the point of — Joan Crawford, Brooke Astor, Robin Williams, Janet Reno. I didn't get the point of Richard Nixon until the day of his wife's funeral: when he broke and sobbed, I saw, and perceived, a Richard Nixon utterly different from the one who had inhabited my imagination, and I was able to construct and assign a whole universe of motives and feelings to him that had hitherto escaped me. I keep waiting for a single gesture, one defining moment, that will allow me to love the Pope, who is the head of my spiritual family, the man who says, "The world will be what we want it to be."

The gesture never comes.

He says that moral evil flows from personal choice, "because conscience itself is losing the ability to distinguish good from evil. . . . In a culture which holds that no universally valid truths are possible . . . good comes to mean what is pleasing or useful at a particular moment. Evil means what contradicts our subjective wishes. Each person can build a private system of values."

This is an affirmation of natural law, which is at the heart of *Veritatis Splendor*. Natural law has been defined as a force working in history that tends to keep human beings human; it is the objective truth that is written on every human heart. One is capable of obscuring the writing by sin; natural law is, nonetheless, everlasting—a question not of opinion but of fact. Truth and morality are inseparable. Human reason cannot impose values on nature or create values of its own; humans must discover the values inherent in the universe and in the human heart.

"The Pope," said the Pope in Denver, "has not spoken against American civilization and television; he has spoken for an authentic promotion of what is civilization . . . of what is human dignity. . . . The root of violence is in the human heart, society will be condemned to housing it . . . even, to an extent, glorifying it, unless it reaffirms the moral and religious truths which alone are an effective barrier to lawlessness and violence."

The gesture I am waiting for will not come. In his encyclical—which he says was occasioned by "an overall and systematic calling into question of traditional moral doctrine"—the Holy Father, placing human dignity snugly and exclusively under the banner of non-negotiable Church teaching, says that morality is absolute and absolutely never a matter of subjective decision or the wisdom accrued from life experience or an educated conscience or a matter of intentions, circumstances, and consequences.

Sickened by the rotten fruits of determinism and relativity and individualism, one might well agree with Karol Wojtyla, in light of the Kevorkianizing of America, the cloning and the killing of embryos, that certain acts are "intrinsically evil." But agreement isn't likely to be the response to the Pope's demotion of the role of conscience, his assertion of the official Church's authority to determine in each and every case which acts are intrinsically evil.

The brilliance and beauty of Roman Catholicism, it has always seemed to me, was the autonomy granted one who allowed oneself to be held tightly by the core beliefs of the Church (as contained in the Creed) and wished to live without harm or damage to oneself or others or God: the Law, one felt, was indeed written not in stone or in encyclicals but in the human heart. And if, after scouring one's conscience and willing one's heart and mind to conform, one found oneself in legitimate disagreement over a specific Church teaching — well, the judgment call was left to the Highest Court of Appeal. The Holy Father would not have it so: "Polarization and destructive criticism have no place within the household of the faith," John Paul II said in Denver, with which no good family member could disagree — one may find oneself, has found oneself, in loyal opposition to the Church; one certainly didn't maliciously seek polarization. But the encyclical, 179 pages and more than 40,000 words long, makes it clear that external opposition to the central teachings of the Church — as defined, we are obliged to assume, by the Incumbent — is punishable by the purging of dissenting moral theologians and the condemnation of Catholic institutions that allow dissent to thrive. And so, God help us, is internal disagreement. (How will he police this?) Papal authority has become synonymous with Truth.

The Holy Father, choosing, apparently, to overlook ambiguity in Scripture and tradition, says that universal moral wrongs transcend eras and cultures. This is his list of "morally unacceptable" sexual sins: contraception, artificial insemination, homosexual acts, masturbation, premarital sex, abortion, adultery. (The word "contraception," incidentally, appears only once in the hefty encyclical.)

In Denver, and in *Veritatis*, the Pontiff often speaks of the human conscience as if it were a wild beast capable of being appeased, but capable also of turning on its owner with the ultimate betrayal—alienation from God. Conscience "is not exempt from the possibility of error." He is adamant that the magisterium—the authority of the Church to teach religious truth—is not an optional source for the formation of conscience but it is a paramount and absolutely necessary one.

AUGUST 13

At the Radisson, I see a young man running down the hall, flapping his arms. "He saw me! He saw me! He saw me!" he shouts. Some of the young people have the mystical belief that the Pope sought out and engaged their eyes and made contact with them among thousands.

I rummage through my files: "*We must feel the poverty of others as if it were our own, and convince ourselves that the poor cannot wait. Public authorities . . . must take on the unjust differences which offend the human condition of men and women who are . . . children of the same God.*"

Bravo, John Paul. This is the Church one loves. The Church that speaks for "*the sick, the elderly, the marginalized, the victims of violence, those who don't have work or decent housing, the displaced and the imprisoned; in a word, to those suffering in body or spirit . . . but especially for the most abandoned and dispossessed.*"

And *this* is the Church one loves: that evening at Mile High Stadium, something inexplicable, quirky, and, under the circumstances, bittersweet happens. The fourteen stations of the cross—the betrayal of Christ and his condemnation, his denial by Peter, his judgment at the hands of Pontius Pilate, and (scorned, rejected, spat upon, cursed, whipped, and crowned with thorns) his crucifixion, his promise to the good thief, his last words to Mary and the Beloved Disciple, his death, his entombment. After each station, moments of silence: meditation and prayer. This tableau is enacted by three people, the Fountain Square Fools, a Cincinnati theater group . . . and Jesus Christ, king of the world, is played by a woman, Christina Brown (twenty-three, sloe-eyed, olive-skinned, long crinkly hair parted in the middle). The Reverend Dan Anderson of Cincinnati says, in what appears to be a desperate attempt to sound casual, "[She] looks like Christ." Joaquin Navarro-Valls says, "A woman can represent all humanity and all humanity was represented by the death of Christ." Such pleasure to mull over that, and not a little pain. It seems so simple: if a woman can represent all humanity, can she not be a priest? Why not?

The Holy Father is absent in the flesh; his visage is beamed in by satellite to Mile High Stadium. He had spent the day at Camp St. Malo, a Catholic retreat in the Rockies, where he was resting—reading poetry, praying, hiking. The Holy Father is photographed walking in the woods, holding a knapsack, wearing sneakers (gold laces) and a long white robe, very Comme des Garçons.

Oh yes, I think, a little mad. He doesn't appear to find anything funny about wearing gold-colored shoestrings with his white sneakers in order for the pontifical colors to be correct.

"Do you think he's cuckoo?" I ask a colleague and a friend (male, gay, a kind man who feeds the hungry and clothes the poor, who believes that to leave the Church under present circumstances is a sin). "What if he is?" says my friend. "What is the Church?" he asks, and proceeds to define it—exactly what the Holy Father would call taking liberties with established truth. "The Church is the body of people struggling to live in the unity that was established by the Incarnation. We struggle constantly, constantly, constantly, against whatever odds and whatever forces, to help the community grow and flourish and survive. I refuse to leave. I'd have to be kicked out—but nobody's going to throw me out of my Father's house. I'd miss the tension too much."

As for me, I'd care nothing for a God who hadn't suffered; he'd be a bully. The only God I could believe in is fully God and fully human.

"The Church," my friend says, "has never really dealt with the implications of the Incarnation. Why did God choose to become a human being to effect the Redemption? He could have just said, Poof! you're redeemed. He ascended in the flesh; he still has a human nature. What are the implications of this? The Church has insisted that the liturgy have a sensory appeal — Hopkins calls the senses the inroads to the soul. It's been called idolatry, but candles and incense and music increase your spiritual susceptibility.

"But I find it difficult to give any thought to anything they say about sexuality because they've never really explored the role of sexuality and its relationship to the Incarnation . . . and at the same time they're preoccupied with sexuality. It's only within our lifetime — Vatican II — that the Church acknowledged that sex had a purpose other than procreation. Before that they never acknowledged that the sensory exchange, the act of love between two people, had not only a validity but a necessity. Look at what refusing to deal with the body leads to.

"The trouble the hierarchy has with women, and vice versa, rests on their being looked upon as subspecies — which again contradicts the Incarnation. . . . The inability to deal with the body led to the separation of men and women in the institutional Church. In the early Church there was no priesthood. The Eucharist was celebrated by equals. Over time, the eucharistic minister, the priest, the servant, became the master.

"Why should I leave? That would be fragmenting the community. Okay, the homily is boring, the music is bad. If you go to church anyway, you're making a statement: I can't worship by myself; I must worship in community as an expression of my belief that we are part of a larger community, holy and universal.

"God can do with nature anything he wishes — and there is homosexuality in nature. Let's acknowledge that sex is central — not something that should be indulged in at the least whim; you can't use people. No real systemic theology has been addressed to this. We say the body is holy and treat it as if it were poison. Jesus' humanity and ours are inseparable. . . .

"We were loved from the moment of conception. The rights of a fetus derive from the fact that the fetus is loved by God. But how can I invite others to act on what I take on faith and can't prove? Can I ask a woman to be constrained by something I can't prove in an area so central to her life?

"I would go to my cat before I would go to my cardinal for moral direction. I don't pay any attention to him or to the Pope. But I have no reason to leave the Church."

AUGUST 15

John Paul II traveled back to Rome on an American Airlines 767 (Shepherd One) from which four seats were removed to accommodate a custom-made curtained bed (between twin- and full-size) draped in Belgian linen sheets and a down comforter. He could have seen a Michael Jackson video, had he wished, or a Madonna movie. He enjoyed a choice of roasted veal, beef tenderloin pignoli, chervil chicken, salmon with linguine. Caviar. Godiva chocolates. Häagen-Dazs. When he is at home in the papal palace, he drinks one glass of dry white Latium wine at supper; cows that produce milk just for him range near Castel Gandolfo in the Castelli Romani. Can one begrudge him this? Poor unmarried man. It's silly to get exercised over caviar and Godiva—though the soapbox antipapists in Denver did, frothing. Asceticism doesn't endear itself to me as particularly adorable or ennobling. I used, when I lived in India, to step over the naked body of a Hindu holy man each day to get in and out of my Bombay flat. There he was, unmoving, eyes bloodshot and gazing straight ahead (his enormous member maintaining an enormous erection) among the weeds and rats and monkeys and passion flowers of my garden, as immovable, so far as I could see, as the sun. Sometimes my son, in whom the naked holy man occasioned no wonder, tried to share his banana-yogurt breakfast with him; the holy man—who subsisted on heat and dust and mortification—resisted my child's sunny claim on his attention. I used to wonder what was in his head; I still do.

I flew home from Denver through spectacular lightning, lightning like flowers, bursts of yellow, rose, blue, green. I fell asleep. (Whose was the nightlong breathing that kept my soul alive?)

The plane hit an air pocket and I awakened with a jolt, this conviction formed, born of a forgotten dream: I am not nervous about God. Where had my nervousness gone? The face staring back at me from the dark window—my own reflection—smiled a delphic smile.

"Even in our sleep," Aeschylus said, "pain that cannot forget falls drop by drop upon the heart, and in our own despair, against our will, comes wisdom to us by the awful grace of God."

I flew away from Denver, but Denver was not far from me.

"We Are One Body, One Body in Christ." The theme song, which in Denver I had considered musically insipid, anemic, played in my mind as I sailed in the dark through flowers of light.

I belong to a Church that takes its terrible and glorious kaleidoscopic 2,000-year-old inheritance seriously.

("Tradition," Chesterton wrote, "means giving votes to the most obscure of all classes, our ancestors. It is the democracy of the dead. Tradition refuses to submit to the small and arrogant oligarchy of those who merely happen to be walking about. . . . We will have the dead at our councils.") I belong to a Church that has survived Medicis and cretins and scandals and knaves. And who knows? Perhaps history will reveal that this Pope was a good Pope—or an irrelevant one. About one who commands and wishes to hold back the tide it is never easy to know.

It hardly seems to matter, in the flowers, in the dark.

"He receives every one of us," the Holy Father said. "We are accepted by Him. That is Communion. We receive Him and He receives us, and that is the full human life."

That is what matters: community, communion. Communion is the defining moment. We drink the wine; we eat the bread: we are one body.

A wall of orange lightning shrouds the throbbing plane, and I think of my last two days in Denver. . . .

They marched, thousands and thousands of them, to Cherry Creek State Park. They walked fifteen unshaded miles. Walkers and runners talk of suddenly entering a "meditative zone." The rhythm of walking is the rhythm of prayer.

It was bitterly cold at night. They sang hymns and played liars' poker deep into the night; unprepared for the cold, they slept in sleeping bags, body to body. They were awakened by mariachi music, to a spectacular sunrise and lauds at 6:30 A.M., after which it was horrendously hot; they were unprepared for the heat.

A headline in the Sunday *Rocky Mountain News* read: OFFICIALS FEAR MEDICAL CALAMITY TODAY. It seemed (suddenly) to have occurred to everyone that there would probably not be enough toilets, and there would almost certainly not be enough water; and there would almost definitely be too many people for emergency personnel to deal with. The Arapahoe County sheriff got on TV to say, almost before the sun came up, "People are dropping like flies."

The sheriff and Sister Mary Ann Walsh, World Youth Day communications director, had a TV face-off (much grinding of teeth) about the safety of the event and the efficiency of the planning. "This ain't no bingo game," the sheriff said.

A sixty-one-year-old man died of a heart attack. Eighteen thousand people sought medical aid, mostly for heat exhaustion and dehydration.

To the thousands and thousands who had walked on Saturday were added thousands and thousands more for Sunday Mass: estimates put them at half a million. All along the way of the march people offered them cups of water—the poor dopey kids were drinking Coke and eating candy bars and getting dehydrated and falling into prairie-dog holes, spraining ankles and suffering altitude sickness, bee stings and blisters, exhaustion. Bottles fell from nerveless fingers. It was weedy, polleny, and moldy along the way. And the sheriff was right: access to water and to portable toilets was not good. People with houses along the park sprinkled marchers with garden hoses to cool them off; later, firefighters did. The whole carried the halt. The Church is people, clergy and laity, moving, walking through life. Some of them are maimed.

Regarded in a certain light — the light that bathes and tickles the distant past — all of history, even and especially its tragedies and morbidities, consists of cosmic fun and games. The Church exists in time. In eternity there is no time. And God broods gently over us all.

1995

Dennis Covington's *Salvation on Sand Mountain* is one of the best books I know for teaching literary journalism, not because it's the final word but because for young writers it can be a boost toward the first one. It's a good book, a very good book, in part because the art of it is so plain. Covington had no choice if he was going to tell the truth, because it's a story about a subculture so exotic it has become a cliché. Covington has to break through the cliché to get to the power beneath. The real deal, not the worn-out representation.

About the cliché: It's snake handling. A tiny charismatic movement within American Christianity that looms large in the minds of the secular and even of those Christians who wonder if out there in the piney woods, beyond their suburban congregation, there might be something more old-timey, more *authentic*. What could be more authentic, faith-wise, than believing in God so much you'll pick up a rattlesnake without fear?

When I teach Covington, I pair it with Peter Adair's 1967 documentary film *Holy Ghost People*. I let my students know there'll be snakes, because there are people who really can't deal with snakes, and I don't want them to be surprised. But they always are, because the film — a handheld, cinema verité depiction of a single service at a Holiness church — doesn't rush the snakes. It lingers on the preaching, the singing, the voices of the believers. And when the snakes enter the picture, it's so casual you almost don't notice them. That's not what it's about. It never was.

Which is why, given the choice of one chapter from *Salvation on Sand Mountain*, I chose this one. Here's a spoiler: There aren't any snakes in "Under the Brush Arbor." The handlers forgot to bring them. "Well, we don't *have* to have serpents to worship the Lord," one of them declares. What they need — and don't take this as saccharine — is each other, the actual "I and thou" of church, people to perform and people to perform *for*, the roles rippling between them. That tension is drawn especially tight when one of those people is a writer. "The relationship between journalist and subject is often an unspoken conspiracy," observes Covington. "The handlers wanted to show me something, and I was ready to be shown." That's one way to begin writing: Get ready to be shown.

DENNIS COVINGTON
Under the Brush Arbor

The card he pressed into my hand read: "Charles McGlocklin, the End-Time Evangelist." "You can have as much of God as you want," he said. His voice was low and urgent. "These seminary preachers don't understand that. They don't understand the spirit of the Lord. They're taught by man. They know the *forms* of godliness, but they deny the *power.*"

Brother Charles was a big man in his early fifties with a full head of dark hair and hands the size of waffle irons. He didn't have a church himself, and he didn't particularly want one. He'd preached on the radio, he said, and at county fairs and trade days. In years past, he'd driven all over the South, conducting revivals under a tent he'd hauled in the back of his '72 Chevy van. He said he had even stood on the road in front of his house trailer in New Hope, Alabama, and preached at passing cars.

"I get a lot of stares," he added, and then he put his big hand on my shoulder and drew me toward him confidentially. "I have received visitations by angels," he said. "One of them was seven feet tall. It was a frightening experience."

I said I bet it was.

"And I'll tell you something else," he said. "One night I was fasting and praying on the mountain, and I was taken out in the spirit. The Lord appeared to me in layers of light." His grip tightened on my shoulder. "He spoke a twelve-hour message to me on one word: *polluted.*"

"Polluted?"

"Yes. Polluted. Now, you think about that for a minute. A twelve-hour message."

I thought about it for a minute, and then decided Brother Charles was out of his mind.

In time, I'd find out he wasn't, despite the fact that he kept four copperheads in a terrarium on his kitchen counter between the Mr. Coffee and the microwave. He said God moved on him one night to handle a big timber rattler right there in the kitchen. His wife, Aline, showed me a photo of him doing it. Aline was thirteen years younger than Charles, childlike and frankly beautiful, a Holiness mystic from Race Track Road who worked the night shift weaving bandage gauze. "I had just got up, getting ready to go to work," she said, "and my camera was just laying there." She pointed at the photo. "You see how the Holy Ghost moved on him?"

In the photo, Charles is standing in the kitchen in his white T-shirt and jeans. He has a rattlesnake in one hand, and he appears to be shouting at it as though it were a sensible and rebellious thing. "There's serpents, and then there's *fiery* serpents," Charles said. "That was one fiery serpent."

Another time, Charles said he wanted to take up a serpent real bad, but he didn't have one on hand. The Holy Ghost told him, "You don't have a snake, but you've got a heater." So Charles ran to the wood-burning stove in the living room and laid his hands on it. "Baby, that thing was hot," he said. But his hands, when he finally took them off the stove, weren't a bit burned. Instead, they were as cold as a block of ice, he said.

Aline reminded him that he *did* get a blister from a skillet once, but Charles said, "God wasn't in that. That was in myself. That's why I got burned."

"You were just thinking about that corn bread," Aline added with a knowing smile.

Long before I was a guest in their home, I'd seen the McGlocklins at services at The Church of Jesus with Signs Following in Scottsboro. We became friends, and then something more than friends, but that is a long and complicated story that began, I think, on the afternoon of my first brush-arbor meeting on top of Sand Mountain, when Aline was taken out in the spirit, and I accompanied her on tambourine.

I had never even heard of a brush arbor until J. L. Dyal built one in a field behind his house near the Sand Mountain town of Section in the summer of 1992. Brother Carl had invited me to the services, and J.L. had drawn a map. "You take a left at the Sand Mountain Dragway sign," he said. "We'll get started just before sundown."

I was pleased the handlers had felt comfortable enough to include me. It meant the work was going well. The relationship between journalist and subject is often an unspoken conspiracy. The handlers wanted to show me something, and I was ready to be shown. It seemed to me that the conviction of Glenn Summerford was not the end of their story, but simply the beginning of another chapter. I was interested in what would happen to them now that Glenn was in prison and The Church of Jesus with Signs Following had split. But I had a personal agenda too. I was enjoying the passion and abandon of their worship. Vicki didn't seem to mind. She encouraged me to go. So I told Brother Carl and J.L. I'd be there for the brush-arbor services, although I couldn't visualize what they were talking about. "Brush arbor" seemed a contradictory term. The word *arbor* suggested civilized restraint. The word *brush* didn't.

I did know that outdoor revivals had once been commonplace in the rural South. The most famous occurred in 1801, when thousands of renegade Presbyterians, in their rebellion against stiff-necked Calvinism, gathered in a field near Cane Ridge, Kentucky, for a week-long camp meeting. They were soon joined by Methodists and Baptists, until their combined ranks swelled to more than twenty-five thousand, a crowd many times greater than the population of the largest town in Kentucky at the time. Something inexplicable and portentous happened to many of the worshipers in that field near Cane Ridge. Overcome by the Holy Spirit, they began to shriek, bark, and jerk. Some fell to the ground as though struck dead. "Though so awful to behold," wrote one witness, "I do not remember that any one of the thousands . . . ever sustained an injury in body."

Cane Ridge set the stage for the dramatic events at a mission on Azusa Street in Los Angeles in 1906, when the Holy Ghost descended in power on a multiracial congregation led by a one-eyed black preacher named William Seymour, and the great American spiritual phenomenon of the twentieth century, Pentecostalism, began in a fury of tongue speaking and prophesying and healing.

Cane Ridge had been the prototype of revivalism on a grand scale. The crowd at J.L.'s brush arbor was somewhat smaller — thirteen of us altogether, plus a gaggle of curious onlookers who hid behind Brother Carl Porter's Dodge Dakota pickup. But the facilities at J.L.'s were top-notch. Traditional brush arbors had been small and temporary, primitive shelters usually built at harvest time from whatever materials might be at hand. Willow branches were especially prized because of their flexibility. Thick vines added strength. The idea was to give field hands a place to worship so they wouldn't have to leave the premises before all the crops were in. But J.L. had constructed his brush arbor out of sturdy two-by-fours over which he had stretched sheets of clear plastic so that services could be held even in a downpour. The vines and brush piled on top of the plastic appeared to be decorative rather than functional, yielding the impression of a brush arbor without all its inconveniences. J.L.'s father-in-law, Dozier Edmonds, had helped string electricity to the structure and had installed a length of track lighting. The place was perfect, except for one thing. There weren't any snakes.

"I thought you were going to bring them," said Brother Carl to Brother Charles.

"I thought Brother Willie was going to bring them," Charles replied. He was getting his guitar out of the car, an instrument the Lord, he said, had taught him to play.

"Brother Willie got serpent bit last night," Carl reminded him.

"I know, but he said he was going to be here today."

"Maybe I need to check on him after the service," Carl said. "It was a copperhead," he confided to me. "Over in Georgia. Bit him on the thumb, but it didn't hurt him bad."

"Well, we don't *have* to have serpents to worship the Lord," Charles finally said. He put his boot up on a pine bench that would serve as the altar and began strumming the guitar. When everyone had gathered around, he started to sing. "*He's God in Alabama. He's God in Tennessee. He's God in North Carolina. He's God all over me. Oh, God is God . . . and Jesus is his name. . . .*"

The service had begun at five o'clock to avoid the mid-afternoon heat. The light was low and golden over the field, and Charles's voice rose above it like a vapor, unamplified, snatched away by the breeze. Aline was there; Brother Carl and the old prophetess, Aunt Daisy; J.L. and his wife, Dorothea; one of their daughters-in-law and her baby; and Dorothea's father, Dozier, and her mother, Burma, who had a twin sister named Erma. Both Burma and Erma, sixty-eight, attended snake-handling services, usually in identical dresses, but only Burma actually handled.

I'd also brought photographers Jim Neel and Melissa Springer with me, and they moved quietly around the edges of the arbor as the service picked up steam. The choice of photographers had been simple. Jim was one of my oldest friends. In addition to being a sculptor and painter, he'd worked with me as a combat photographer in Central America during the 1980s. Melissa, whose work I'd first noticed when it was censored by police at an outdoor exhibit in Birmingham, had been documenting the lives of men and women clinging to the underbelly of the American dream—female impersonators, dancers with AIDS, women inmates in the HIV isolation unit at Alabama's Julia Tutwiler prison. When I told her about the snake handlers, she said she had to meet them, but unlike most people who say they want to, she kept calling and insisting that we set a time. She and Jim were an interesting study in contrasts: He was moody, private, and intense; Melissa was warm, expansive, and maternal. But both were obsessed with their work, easy to travel with, and open to possibilities.

Melissa had worn an ankle-length dress this time. At her first service in Scottsboro, she'd gotten the message when Aunt Daisy prophesied against the wearing of pants by women. Outsiders are bound to get preached at a little in Holiness churches. But the same Holiness preachers who draw attention to unorthodox details of behavior or dress inevitability hugged us after the service and invited us back.

Some preachers didn't take the Holiness prescriptions about dress quite as seriously as others. Charles McGlocklin's theory was simple: "You've got to catch the fish before you clean them."

His wife, Aline, didn't wear makeup or cut her hair, but she occasionally allowed herself the luxury of a brightly colored hair ornament. "God looks at the heart, anyway. He doesn't look on the outside," she said. She also drove a white Chevy Beretta with an airbrushed tag that read "Aline loves Charles." Charles's pickup had a matching tag, with "Charles loves Aline." Both sentiments were inscribed in the middle of interlocking hearts, like the brightly colored hearts on Aline's hair clasp.

Despite the empty chairs and lack of electric guitars or serpents, the worship at J.L.'s brush arbor followed the same pattern I'd experienced in Scottsboro. Without church walls, it seemed more delicate and temporal, though, and Brother Carl's sermon echoed the theme. He talked about the flesh as grass, passing in a moment, of earthly life being short and illusory. He talked about the body as "fleshy rags" that he would gladly give up in exchange for a heavenly wardrobe. But at the center of Carl's sermon was the topic of God's love, which he seemed to first discover fully even as he talked his way into it.

"It's got no end," he said, "no bottom, no ceiling. Paul says nothing can separate us from the love of God through Jesus Christ. And let me tell you, sometimes we find His love in the little things. The fact that we're here today is a sign God loves us." *Amen.* "The fact that we got a brain to think with, and a tongue to speak with, and a song to sing. I just want to thank Him for waking me up this morning," he said. "I want to thank Him for giving me food to eat and a roof over my head. Sometimes we ask Him to work big miracles, but forget to thank Him for the little ones." *Amen.* "But he's a great big God, and He never fails. His grace is sufficient to meet our every need. He's a good God, isn't He?" And everybody said amen.

Then Carl invited Brother Charles to give his testimony. In Holiness churches, a testimony is a personal story that reveals God's power and grace. It's not meant to exhort or instruct the congregation—that would be preaching—but simply to praise the Lord. In practice, though, the line between testifying and preaching is not so clear-cut.

Brother Carl and Brother Charles hugged, and after a few introductory comments about the beauty of the afternoon and the love he felt from everybody gathered there, Brother Charles began to testify. It was a story, both lurid and familiar, that could only have come from the South.

"Up until I was five years old," Charles said, "I lived in a tent on the banks of the Tennessee River at Old Whitesburg Bridge. Y'all know where that's at. Then my mother got remarried, and we moved to a houseboat at Clouds Cove."

Clouds Cove.

"My stepdaddy was a drunk."

"Amen," said J.L., who knew something about drunks himself.

"My real daddy lived to be eighty," Charles said. "He died in the Tennessee penitentiary, where he was serving a life sentence for killing his second wife. I was like a lamb thrown into a den of lions when we moved to Clouds Cove," Charles said. "In 1948, when I was six, we lived on nothing but parched corn for three weeks, like rats. We slept on grass beds. We didn't even have a pinch of salt. Now, that's poor."

Amen. They all knew what it was like to be poor.

"By the time I was eight, I'd seen two men killed in our house. I was afraid to go to sleep at night."

Help him, Jesus.

"I made it to eighth grade, but when I was just shy of turning thirteen years old, I got shot in the stomach with a twelve-gauge shotgun. That was the first time I heard the audible voice of God."

Praise His holy name!

"There I was, holding my insides in my hands. Them things, they really colored up funny, I thought to myself. Then I had the awfullest fear come up on me," Charles said. He was pacing back and forth by now, a loping, methodical pace, his huge, dog-eared Bible held loosely in one hand like an implement. "I saw a vision of my casket lid closing on me, and the voice out of heaven spoke to me and said, 'Don't be afraid, 'cause everything's gonna be all right,' and I felt that shield of faith just come down on me!"

Hallelujah!

"God's been good to me!"

Amen.

"He's been good to me!"

Amen.

"Doctors told my mother I had maybe fifteen minutes to live. 'There's no way he can make it,' they said. 'Almost all his liver's shot out, almost all his stomach.' I was on the operating table sixteen to eighteen hours. They had to take out several *yards* of intestines.

I stayed real bad for forty-two days and nights. I was one hundred twenty pounds when I got shot and eighty-seven when I got out of the hospital. But just look at me now!"

Praise His name!

Brother Charles was standing with his hands clenched at his side and a wild look in his eyes. He was a big man, an enormous man. It was not the first time I'd noticed that, but it was the first time I had considered the damage he might do if he ever had a reason.

"God's been good to me!" he said as he started pacing again.

Amen.

"I said He's been good to me!"

Amen!

He suddenly stopped in his tracks. "But I wasn't always good to Him."

"Now you're telling it," Brother Carl said.

"When I was sixteen, I went to live with my real daddy in Tennessee," Charles said. "He was one of the biggest moonshiners in the state, and I wanted to learn the trade. I dabbled in it a good long time. I was bad. I went up to Chicago and did some other things I shouldn't have."

Tell it. They'd all done things they shouldn't have.

"When I came back South, I drove a long-haul rig twice a week to New York City. Then I bought me a thirty-three acre farm in Minor Hill, Tennessee. Two-story house. Fine car. I had a still upstairs that could run forty to fifty gallons of whiskey, and in another room I stored my bales of marijuana. Pretty good for a boy who'd grown up picking cotton."

Amen. They knew about cotton.

He raised his Bible and shook it at us. "I don't have to tell you that's the deceitfulness of riches talking, boys."

Preach on.

"One day, things had really got bad on me. I had just got under so much that I couldn't go no further, and I was getting ready to kill myself. The devil spoke to me and said, 'Just go ahead and take that gun and kill yourself and get it over with.'"

No, Lord.

He walked to the edge of the arbor and pantomimed picking something up from the grass. "I went over there and got the gun and was fixing to put a shell in it, and when I did, this other voice came to me and said, 'Put that gun back down and walk back over in front of that wood heater.'"

Amen.

"I walked back over there in front of the wood heater, and suddenly that power from on high hit me in the head and knocked me down on my knees, and I said six words. I won't never forget what they was. I said, 'Lord, have mercy on my soul.'"

Amen. Thank God.

"He took me out in the Spirit and I came back speaking in other tongues as the Spirit gave utterance. The devil said, 'Look, look now. Now what are you going to do?' He said, 'Look at all that moonshine, all that marijuana you got. What are you going to do now? Ain't you in a mess now? Here you are, you've got the Holy Ghost, and you've got all *this* in your house.' And the Lord spoke to me and said, 'Just set your house in order.'"

Bless him, Lord!

"He said, 'Just set your house in order!'"

Amen!

"So that's what I did. I set my house in order. I got rid of that moonshine and marijuana. I told the devil to depart that place in the name of Jesus, and within a year I'd taken up my first serpent."

Amen.

"We've got to set our house in order!" Charles said, and now he was leaning toward us, red-faced, with flecks of white spittle in the corners of his mouth. "We're in the last day with the Lord, children! He won't strive with man forever! He's a merciful God, he's a loving God, but you better believe he's also a just God, and there will come a time when we'll have to account for these lives we've led! We better put our house in order!"

Amen. Thank God. Bless the sweet name of Jesus.

There were only thirteen people under that brush arbor, but it seemed like there were suddenly three hundred. They were jumping and shouting, and pretty soon Brother Carl was anointing Burma and Erma with oil, and Brother Charles had launched into "Jesus on My Mind" on his guitar, and J.L. and I had our tambourines going. There was so much racket that at first it was hard to hear what Aline was doing over in the corner by a length of dog wire that the morning glory vines had twined around. Her back was to us. Her hands were in the air, and she was rocking slowly from side to side, her face upturned and her voice quavering, "Akiii, akiii, akiii. Akiii, akiii, akiii. . . ."

It was the strangest sound I had ever heard. At first, it did not seem human. It sounded like the voice of a rare night bird, or some tiny feral mammal. And then the voice got louder, mounting up on itself, until it started to sound like that of a child who was lost and in great pain. But even as the hairs on my arms started to stand on end, the voice turned into something else, a sound that had pleasure in it as well as torment. Ecstasy, I would learn later, is excruciating, but I did not know that then.

"Akiii, akiii, akiii. . . ." The singing and praising elsewhere in the brush arbor had started to diminish. Brother Charles had stopped strumming his guitar. Brother Carl had put away his oil. Burma and Dorothea kept their hands raised, but except for an occasional amen or praise Jesus, the air fell silent around Aline's voice. Everyone was listening to her now. I could not disentangle myself from the sound of her voice, the same syllables repeated with endless variation. At times, it seemed something barbed was being pulled from her throat; at other times, the sound was a clear stream flowing outward into thin air. Her voice seemed to be right in my ear. It was sobbing. A panting after something she could not quite reach. And then it would be a coming to a rest in some exquisite space, a place so tender it could not be touched without "Akiii, akiii, akiii. . . ." The sun had set and the electric lights were not yet turned on, but the arbor seemed filled with a golden light. We were swaying in it, transfixed, with Aline silhouetted against the dog wire and the morning glory vines. All but her trembling voice was silent, or so it seemed, until I realized with horror that my tambourine was still going, vibrating against my leg, almost apart from me, as if it had a motive and direction of its own.

My hand froze. It was as though I had been caught in some act of indecency. But Aline's voice reacted with renewed desperation, "Akiii, akiii, akiii," and so I let the tambourine have its own way, now louder and faster, until it almost burst into a song, and then softer and more slowly, until it resembled the buzzing of a rattlesnake in a serpent box. It anticipated every move that Aline's voice made, and vice versa. The intimacy was unnerving: her voice and the tambourine, perfectly attuned to one another and moving toward the same end. I was unreasonably afraid that Charles would be angry with me. I didn't yet know the full dimensions of passion. It was much later that I would come to understand what had gone on in that moment. The tambourine was simply accompanying Aline while she felt for and found God. And I mean "accompany" in the truest sense: "to occur with." And nobody could predict when something like that might happen. Through the tambourine, I was occurring with her in the Spirit, and it was not of my own will.

I cannot say how long the episode lasted. It seemed to go on for a very long time. J.L. turned the lights on at the end. The men hugged the men. The women hugged the women. Aline and I shook hands. If the snake handlers found anything unusual about our curious duet afterward, they never spoke directly to me about it. But I do know one thing: It was after that brush-arbor meeting on Sand Mountain that they started to call me Brother Dennis.

1997

Maybe it's unfair to include this excerpt from Anne Fadiman's *The Spirit Catches You and You Fall Down,* the subtitle of which can only hint at the nuances of Fadiman's story: *A Hmong Child, Her American Doctors, and the Collision of Two Cultures.* By the time the reader comes to "The Sacrifice," the two cultures in question — those of traditional Laotian Hmong medicine and Western science — have not just collided but crumpled against one another in the broken body of a little girl named Lia Lee, who suffers from epilepsy so devastating that she falls into a vegetative state. Or so say her doctors. Her parents understand it differently, as a condition caused by *dabs,* spirits. The truth, it turns out, is more complicated than either doctors or parents initially comprehend. But all that is past by the time we come to "The Sacrifice," Fadiman's account of a healing ceremony conducted by a *txiv neeb,* a traditional Hmong shaman. A reader entering the story at this point catches only glimpses of the tragedy that has led to this moment. The emotional power of Fadiman's story, of Lia's story, is blunted. For the sake of *this* book, though, that may be for the best. Our eyes are unbothered by tears. We're not adding our own prayers or hopes to the *txiv neeb*'s ritual. It's sad, what has happened to this little girl, but we're merely observers — taking notes, like Fadiman. If there can't be a healing, perhaps there can at least be comprehension. That's the great strength of Fadiman's astonishing book: her dedication to understanding.

Such dedication is neither as basic nor as common as it sounds. Some writers see such understanding as impossible, while others are more interested in themselves. For a gonzo journalist such as Hunter Thompson, understanding was beside the point; for a *belle lettrist* such as Christopher Hitchens, being right, according to his own convictions, mattered more than inhabiting the beliefs of others. Fadiman is different. She doesn't need to own the story, to make it hers. Rather, she comes alongside the story, the *stories:* the supernatural within the natural, the ordinary beliefs of the Hmong within the mundane of Merced, California, converging at 37 East 12th Street, Apartment A, where Fadiman sits with her notebook, eyes, heart, and mind wide open.

ANNE FADIMAN
The Sacrifice

Long before Shee Yee turned into a tiny red ant and bit the evil *dab* on the testicle, he spent three years apprenticed to a sorcerer. He learned how to change himself into anything he wished, to kill *dabs*, to fly like the wind, to heal the sick, and to raise the dead. Shee Yee's services as a healer were sorely needed, because there was much illness in the world.

This is how the illness had come. The wife of a wicked god named Nyong laid an egg as large as a pig house. For three years, the egg did not hatch. Nyong's father chanted to the egg and, in response, heard the jabbering voices of many evil *dabs* inside it. He ordered Nyong to burn the egg, but Nyong refused. So the egg burst, and out swarmed the *dabs*. The first thing they did was to eat Nyong's wife, down to the last bone, hair, and eyelash. Then, still hungry, they came after Nyong. Nyong opened the door that led from the sky, where he lived, to the earth. Through it flew the *dabs*, as big as water buffalos and as red as fire, with showers of sparks in their wake. Nyong was safe, but from that day on, the people of the earth have known illness and death.

Shee Yee spent many years fighting the *dabs* and restoring sick people to health. He was assisted by a winged horse, a bowl of holy water, a set of magical healing tools, and a troupe of familiar spirits. One day Nyong murdered Shee Yee's infant son and tricked Shee Yee into eating the flesh. When Shee Yee realized what he had done, he was so stricken with grief and horror that he fled the earth and climbed the staircase up through the door in the sky. To avenge his son's death, he pierced both of Nyong's eyes. Nyong, blind and enraged, now lives at the foot of a mountain in the sky, and Shee Yee lives in a cave at its summit, surrounded by his familiar spirits.

Shee Yee never returned to earth, but he did not leave its people entirely at the mercy of illness and death. After he climbed the staircase through the sky, he poured the bowl of holy water into his mouth, and then he spat it, with great force, on his healing tools: a saber, a gong, a rattle, and a pair of finger bells. The tools broke into pieces and fell to earth. Anyone who was sprayed with holy water, or who caught a fragment of one of Shee Yee's tools, was elected to be a *txiv neeb*, a host for a healing spirit. The door in the sky is now closed to everyone but *txiv neebs*. When they pursue the lost soul of a sick person, they summon Shee Yee's familiar spirits and ride Shee Yee's flying horse up the staircase through the sky. In order to deceive any evil *dabs* they may meet en route, they pretend they *are* Shee Yee, and thus they partake of the first healer's cunning, courage, and greatness.

The *txiv neeb* who was to perform a healing ceremony for Lia brought his own tools: saber, gong, rattle, finger bells. He also brought his own flying horse. The horse was a board about ten feet long and ten inches wide which, when attached to a pair of sawhorselike supports that fitted into four slots, became a bench. To the people who filled the Lees' living room, the bench was not a piece of furniture. Nor was it a metaphor. It was truly a flying horse, just as to a devout Roman Catholic, the bread and the wine are not a symbol of Christ's body and blood but the real thing.

The Lees had risen well before dawn. Foua told me, "We must

have the *neeb* ceremony early in the morning, when it is cool, because
that is when the soul can come back better. Also, if it is hot, the pig will
get tired and die." (I thought: But the pig is going to get killed anyway! Then I realized that a dead pig cannot be sacrificed.) The sun was
rising when I arrived, sending pale shafts of light through the door that
opened onto East 12th Street. Two translucent plastic painter's tarps
had been laid over the threadbare brown wall-to-wall carpet to protect
it from the blood of the pig—or rather, pigs, since a small pig was to be
sacrificed for the whole family and a large pig was to be sacrificed for
Lia. The Lees had bought them the previous day at a local farm, paying
$225, which came partly from welfare savings and partly from relatives'
contributions, for the pair.

On the electric stove, three large aluminum pots, filled with
water that would be used to singe the pigs' bristles, had been set to
boil. Bags of fresh vegetables and herbs, grown by the Lees and their
relatives, rested next to the mortar and pestle Foua had brought from
Laos. They would be used in the preparation of the traditional festal
dishes: minced pork and vegetables rolled in rice wrappers; pig bones
and meat boiled with homegrown greens; chopped intestines, liver,
heart, and lungs (the dish May Ying called "doo-doo soup"); raw
jellied pig's blood; stewed chicken; two kinds of pepper sauce; and
steamed rice. A Hmong proverb says, "With friends, flavorless vegetables are as tasty as meat, and water is as good as wine." However, the
combination of friends and good food is better still. The feast, which
was to follow the *neeb* ceremony, would continue far into the night.

Early this morning, Nao Kao had used a special paper punch
to cut a stack of spirit-money, which would pay the pig for its soul
and settle other spiritual accounts. The spirit-money, thick and cream-
colored and pinked into scallops, lay on the carpet next to the *txiv
neeb*'s altar, which represented the cave of Shee Yee. In Laos, the altar
would have been made from one of a pair of identical trees; one would
have been left standing, and one would have been felled with an ax in
the direction of the setting sun. Here, the altar was a crude wooden

table that had been covered with the sports section of the *Merced Sun-Star*. Arrayed on top of a refrigerator ad that said NO DOWN PAYMENT FOR 90 DAYS! were the *txiv neeb*'s sacred tools, the same ones Shee Yee had used; a short saber ornamented with red and white streamers; an ancient iron gong; a monkey bone with a padded end wrapped in black cloth, which was used to beat the gong; a tambourine-sized iron ring strung with rattling metal disks; and two finger bells, which looked like bronze doughnuts and enclosed little tintinnabula made of jingling metal pellets. Next to the tools was a brown plastic bowl containing rice and a single uncooked egg, sustenance for the familiar spirits. Three Styrofoam coffee cups and a white china bowl—a lake into which the *txiv neeb*'s soul could plunge if he were pursued by evil *dabs*—were filled with holy water. A small candle at the front of the altar, not yet lit, would shed light on the unseen realm into which the *txiv neeb* was to travel.

I had read a number of ethnographic commentaries on the power and influence of *txiv neebs*. Somehow, I had never imagined that when I finally met the ultimate metaphysical interlocutor, the great plea-bargainer for the soul, the preeminent champion in the struggle for the demonic—to cite three of the many reverential epithets I had come across—he would be sitting in front of a television set, watching a Winnie-the-Pooh cartoon. The *txiv neeb* who was to perform today's ceremonies was named Cha Koua Lee. He wore blue flip-flops, black pants, and a white T-shirt decorated with dancing pandas. May Ying Xiong had told me all *txiv neebs* were skinny, because they expended so much energy in the shaking trance during which they traveled to the realm of the unseen, and indeed Cha Koua Lee, who looked to be in his late forties, was thin and muscular, with sharp features and a stern expression. It was against his code of honor to charge for his services—especially with the Lees, who were members of his clan—and although some families voluntarily paid him, he was forced to live on public assistance. However, he always received compensation in the form of the heads and right front legs of the pigs over whose sacrifices he presided. After eating the meat, he left the lower jaws to dry outside his apartment, and then added them to a collection he kept on a shelf, to be ritually burned at the end of the Hmong year. At that time the pigs' souls would be released from their duties as proxies for the souls of the people for whom they had given their lives, and allowed to be reborn. In Laos, Cha Koua Lee had burned his pig jaws in a fire pit. In Merced, he burned them in a disposable turkey-roasting pan. Then he placed the charred remains in the branches of a tree outside town, beneath the sky through which they had already journeyed.

After the smaller pig, a tan and white female, was carried into the living room and laid on one of the plastic tarps, the *txiv neeb* performed the day's first order of business: a ceremony to safeguard the health and well-being of the family for the coming year. The Lee family stood in a closely packed huddle in the middle of the living room. Wearing a black cloth headdress, the *txiv neeb* tied a cord around the pig's neck. The pig grunted softly. Then he ran the cord from the pig to the Lees, wrapping it tightly around the whole group. The pig's soul was thus bonded to the souls it would protect. The *txiv neeb* regarded each person's soul as a tripartite entity, composed of one part that, after death, would stand guard at the grave; one part that would go to the land of the dead; and one part that would be reincarnated. All three parts would be secured today. Then the pig's throat was slit — by a Lee cousin, not by the *txiv neeb*, who must always maintain good relations with the animals of whom he has requested such a priceless gift.

In Laos, this ceremony would have taken place in the Lees' house, which Nao Kao and Foua had built to shelter not only their family but also a host of kindly domestic spirits: the chief household spirit, who lived in the central pillar, above the place where the placentas of the Lee sons were buried; the spirits of the ancestors, who lived in the four side pillars; the spirits of wealth, who lived near the uphill wall; the spirit who watched over the livestock, who lived in the downhill door; and the spirits of the two fireplaces. The presence of these spirits would have been felt by everyone in the house. It seemed to me that at 37 East 12th Street, Apartment A—where there were no pillars, no fireplaces, and indeed, according to the Lees, no benevolent spirits, because it was rented—the maintenance of a sacred atmosphere was an uphill battle. The television was still on, though without sound. Winnie-the-Pooh had been succeeded by a wrestling match between Hulk Hogan and Randy "Macho Man" Savage, broadcast from Atlantic City. Five feet from the altar, on the other side of the wall, hummed a refrigerator that contained a case of Budweisers, one of which would later be consumed by the *txiv neeb*. To the left of the front door, through which the familiar spirits would pass, there was a king-size carton of Attends youth diapers. The door was open. This worried me. What if an American were to stroll past and see a dead pig on the floor and nine people tied up with twine?

While the *txiv neeb* prepared for the next ceremony, several of the Lees' male relatives carried the slaughtered pig to the parking lot, which, fortunately, was behind the apartment building and could not be seen from the street. First they poured scalding water over the carcass and scraped the hide with knives. Then they expertly gutted the pig, threw the offal in a Rainbow low-suds detergent pail, unfurled and re-coiled the intestines, and rinsed the abdominal cavity with a green garden hose. Rivulets of bloody water, dotted with bits of hair and pig flesh, flowed through the parking lot. Cheng, May, Yer, True, and Mai watched with interest but not surprise. Like children raised on a farm, they were familiar with death, and indeed could probably have done the job themselves. They had all learned how to kill and pluck chickens before they were eight, and the older ones had helped their parents butcher several pigs.

When we walked back inside the apartment, I could tell in an instant that there had been a sea change. By some unaccountable feat of sorcery—I was never able to figure out exactly how it had happened—the bathos had been exorcised from Apartment A. Everyone could feel the difference. The Lee children, who talked and giggled as they walked from the parking lot, fell silent as soon as they crossed the threshold. The television was off. The candle on the altar had been lit. A joss stick was burning, filling the apartment with smoke trails that would guide the familiar spirits. The *txiv neeb* had put on a black silk jacket with indigo cuffs and a red sash. His feet were bare. He had shrugged all the American incongruities off his outer aspect, and his inner aspect—the quality that had singled him out for spiritual election—now shone through, bright and hard. I saw that I had underestimated him. It was Lia's turn now. Foua and Nao Kao believed that her condition was probably beyond the reach of spiritual healing. Another *txiv neeb* had told them that medicines must have hurt her irreparably, because if the cause were spiritual, the frequency of their *neeb* ceremonies would certainly have restored her ability to talk. However, within her status quo, there were degrees of illness. They hoped this *txiv neeb* would make Lia happier so that she would stop crying at night. And there was still the faintest flicker of a chance, not altogether extinguished even after years of failed sacrifices, that Lia's soul would be found after all, that the *dabs* who were keeping it would accept the pig's soul in its stead, and that she would be restored to health.

Foua sat in the middle of the living room on a red metal folding chair, wearing black pants and a black-and-blue blouse: American clothes, but traditional Hmong colors, the same colors the *txiv neeb* was wearing. A yard of shining black hair fell down her back. Lia sat on her lap, bare-legged, wearing a striped polo shirt and a diaper. Foua nestled Lia's head in the crook of her neck, smoothing her hair and whispering in her ear. Lia fit into the curves of her mother's body as tightly as a newborn infant.

The *txiv neeb* placed a bundle of spirit-money—Lia's expired life-visa, which he would attempt to renew—on the shoulder of her polo shirt. A Lee cousin waved a live brown chicken in the air. It would be sacrificed for Lia's *hu plig*, her soul-calling: a version of the same ceremony had installed her soul in her body when she was an infant. After it was boiled, the chicken would be examined to find out if Lia's soul had returned. Tight feet, firm eyes, and upcurled tongue, and a translucent cranium would be good auspices. Of these, the most important sign was the feet. A toe which did not match its mates—which, like a Hmong who failed to conform to the group ethic, did not fit gracefully into its community—would signal disharmony and disequilibrium. The cousin chanted to the chicken:

> I hope your legs are good
> I hope your eyes are good
> I hope your tongue is good
> I hope your beak is good
> I hope your head is clear.

Lia was surrounded by her entire family and by more than twenty of her relatives. Their solicitude converged on her motionless form like sunlight focused by a magnifying glass until it burns. Dee Korda had once said, "Lia knew how to love and how to let people love her." Whatever else she had lost, Lia still knew how to be loved.

Foua kissed Lia's nose and said, "You look very happy!"

One of the cousin's sons took the chicken to the kitchen, quickly sliced its neck, and shook the spurting blood into a plastic garbage bag.

Lia's pig—a bigger, browner one—was carried into the living room, its trotters bound with twine. Because Lia was a girl, her pig was male; their soul-bond would be a kind of marriage. It lay, snorting and struggling, on a plastic tarp. The *txiv neeb* tied a cord around its neck, then wrapped it around the integral unit of Foua and Lia, linking Lia's soul to her mother's as well as to the pig's. He walked the circuit from the pig to Foua-and-Lia many times, shaking his rattle loudly so that Lia's soul, wherever it was, would hear it. Then he beat his gong, again and again, to summon his familiar spirits. Finally, he tossed the polished halves of a water-buffalo horn on the floor to divine whether the spirits had heard him. When both horns landed flat side up, the answer was no; when one horn landed flat side up and one horn landed flat side down, the answer was ambiguous; final, when both horns landed flat side down, he knew that his spirits had all heard their master's call.

The pig had to be paid for the great gift it was about to give Lia. So the *txiv neeb* took a thick sheaf of spirit-money from the floor next to the altar and placed it next to the pig. Squatting low, he spoke quietly to the pig, explaining that it would be well rewarded for its work and that at the end of the year its soul would be set free from its obligations. He threw the divination horns again to see if the pig had accepted. When they told him yes, he thanked the pig, unwound the cord from the pig's neck and from Foua-and-Lia, and brandished his saber to cut Lia's sickness away. Then he took one of the cups from the altar, poured some water in his mouth, and spat it out, as Shee Yee had done, making a trilling noise.

Prrrrrr.

Prrrrrr.

"These are waters of gold and silver," he said. "They will wash the sickness clean."

Prrrrrr.

From the kitchen came the sound of a knife being sharpened.

Two men lifted the pig onto a pair of folding chairs. Three men held it down. A Lee relative stuck it in the neck. It bellowed and thrashed. Another relative held a stainless steel bowl to catch the blood, but a good deal spattered on the plastic tarp, the carpet, and our bare feet. The *txiv neeb* took the pig's spirit-money and held it in the torrent. The blood would indelibly mark the money as belonging to the pig. Calling his familiar spirits, each by name, the *txiv neeb* touched Lia's back with a finger bell he had moistened with the bloody spirit-money. She, too, would now be marked, and any *dabs* who wished her ill would be barred from touching her.

The *txiv neeb* washed away more sickness.

Prrrrrr.

Then he took the spirit-money from Lia's shoulder and placed it on the flank of the sacrificed pig.

With the blood of the pig on her back, Lia could go anywhere in the world — even hundreds of miles away — and still be recognized as the child who needed healing. Since she no longer needed to be within sight of the *txiv neeb*, Foua carried her into the bedroom, laid her tenderly on the double bed, cushioned her legs with the blue blanket the family had brought from Laos, and turned on an electric fan. Lia's gaze, whatever it saw, was focused upward. Her glossy hair floated in the breeze.

Now the *txiv neeb* was ready for the most dangerous part of his mission. Standing in front of the bench, he flipped part of his cloth headdress over his face, completely blocking his sight. When the veil was down, he was blind to this world but able to perceive the realm of the unseen. The veil — along with the incense, the mesmeric iteration of the gong and the rattle, and the *txiv neeb*'s own repetitive movements — also helped him enter his ecstatic trance. In Laos he might have used opium, but it was not a necessity. When his familiar spirits were present, he could enter an altered state at will.

The *txiv neeb* sat on the Shee Yee's winged horse, crossing and uncrossing his feet on the carpet, doing a rhythmic tap dance as the rattle he held in his right hand and the finger bell he wore on his left hand echoed the sound of his horse's harness bells. Meanwhile, his assistant, a young man who wore black aviator sunglasses, beat the gong to tell the spirits that the journey was beginning. After a little more than half an hour, the assistant placed his hands around the *txiv neeb*'s waist. In a single movement, without missing a beat, the *txiv neeb* rose to his feet and jumped backward onto the bench. All his familiar spirits were in attendance. Without their aid, his body would have been too heavy for such a leap.

At this point, the *txiv neeb* was risking his life. During his trance, his own soul traveled far from his body, and if he fell before his soul returned, he would die. No one, not even the greatest *txiv neeb* in the world, could help him. Even if he did not fall, he might encounter *dabs* on his journey who wanted him dead, and it would take all his might and guile to fight them off.

The *txiv neeb* started to gallop. Sometimes he was on top of the horse, sometimes on the ground. Sometimes he *was* the horse, neighing and whinnying. He chanted loudly in a minor key, singing ancient incantations that were part Hmong and part Chinese. Even the Lees could not understand him, but they knew he was speaking to his familiar spirits and negotiating with the *dabs* for the release of Lia's captive soul.

The front door had been shut for some time, and the room was very hot and close. The air was thick with incense. The gong clanged. The rattle jangled. Someone poured water on the joints of the bench to cool them down. Now the horse was flying up the staircase to the sky. Now the door in the sky was opening. Now the *txiv neeb* was outside Nyong's home. Now he was climbing the mountain to Shee Yee's cave.

While the *txiv neeb* was on his journey, the cousin who had waved the chicken in the air — the soul-caller — opened the front door and stood facing the street. A small table at his feet held the sacrificed chicken, some rice, an egg, and a burning joss stick. In his right hand he held a pair of divination horns, and in his left hand he held a rattle. From time to time he tossed one or the other on the ground, judging the success of his work by the disposition of the horns or the lay of the metal disks.

> I am calling you
> I am calling you

He chanted to Lia's soul.

> I have an egg for you
> I have rice for you
> I have a chicken for you

I have everything waiting for you.

Inside the apartment, the spirit-money was burned and sent to the realm of the unseen. The gong sounded. The *txiv neeb*'s horse galloped faster and faster. The soul-caller looked out toward East 12th Street and chanted:

Where are you?
Where have you gone?
Are you visiting your brother?
Are you visiting your sister?
Are you visiting your cousin?
Are you looking at a flower?
Are you in Laos?
Are you in Thailand?
Are you in the sky?
Have you gone to the sun?
Have you gone to the moon?
Come home to your house
Come home to your mother
Come home to your father
Come home to your sisters
Come home to your brother
I am calling you!
I am calling you
Come home through this door
Come home to your family
Come home
Come home
Come home
Come home
Come home
Come home
Come home.

2004

I began writing about religion — or, at least, deliberately writing about religion — in 2000, when a writer named Peter Manseau proposed a collaboration. At first it was an online magazine, KillingTheBuddha .com, a name borrowed from a story about the ninth-century Buddhist sage Lin Chi, who advised a monk claiming to have met Buddha to kill him. The Buddha you meet, Lin Chi warned, was not the true Buddha but only an expression of your longing. You need to kill him so you can keep looking.

We took this as a parable about what religion could be: respectful but irreverent, more concerned with questions than with answers, an alternative to writing that presents religion as either "innocuous spirituality or dangerous fanaticism," as Peter wrote, "perfume or mustard gas." Our experiment became a book, *Killing the Buddha: A Heretic's Bible*, by way of the American method: a road trip. We bought a beat-up Ford Tempo for one dollar and set out wandering.

When we began we lamented the fact that the United States is not like some ancient, mythical land, a different god for every city. Soon, we discovered that in many ways it is, different gods everywhere, only most of them share the same name: Jesus. It's a Christian nation. And yet not in any way recognizable to journalists trained to seek out talking heads and "color" with which to illustrate the official stories of public religion. Candy Ayres, aka Elowen Graywolf, "senior crone" of the Fort Riley Dark Moon Coven Association — that's Fort Riley as in the massive army base in central Kansas — is certainly "colorful." But how would she register in a pollster's survey of American religion? If you asked her whether she's a Christian, she'd say yes. It'd be up to the pollster to think to ask whether she's also a witch and a Pagan, whether she dances in honor of "the horned one" and calls down the moon buck naked on a crisp Kansas summer evening — to which she'd say yes and yes and yes, a bit like Molly Bloom at the end of Joyce's *Ulysses*.

I was tempted to include an excerpt from one of Peter's later books, his investigative memoir *Vows* — perhaps the best book about American Catholicism in the new century. And I thought I might tuck in a piece from one of my books on the varieties of American fundamentalism. But this collaboration, this early experiment in how to write about religion — with recognition of our own questions and our own nervous giggles — kept coming back, a reminder of the gentle absurdity inherent to the documentation of things unseen.

PETER MANSEAU AND JEFF SHARLET

Heartland, Kansas

Pagans aren't supposed to tell their Craft names to strangers but Candy Ayres, also known as Elowen Graywolf, was a "crone," already a senior witch and a grandma at 47, which meant that even though she couldn't twiggle her nose to make the dinner dishes disappear, it was in her power to grant an exception with the help of a little magic.

"That's m-a-g-i-c-k," Elowen told us.

"What's the *k,* for?"

"Keep David Copperfield Away."

No hocus-pocus for her, no card tricks. To cast the spell needed to let us in on her magickal identity, Elowen simply shook her hands and shook our chakras and, presto change-o, right there in a Denny's in Durango, Colorado, we were initiated as observers into the outer edges of her witch group, the Salene Circle/Dark Moon Coven/Fort Riley Pagan Association.

Durango was not where Elowen lived, but that was where her husband had been transferred for Walmart management training, so that was where she was for the time being, and it suited her—there were nearly as many pagans in Durango as there were in her hometown, Miltonvale, Kansas, where twenty out of 240 families practiced a faith that monotheistic America might describe, at best, as "Other."

Elowen's daughter, Kim, worked at the Durango Denny's with an all-pagan waitstaff, their Mormon manager keeping an open mind so long as the witches kept the customers' coffee mugs full. There were gothic types with pale skin and pentagram necklaces, there was a gray-bearded regular at the counter who said he'd learned the Craft in the Navy during the Korean War, there was a clean-cut jock working the register who said he practiced "Syrian magick." When we asked him why, he shrugged. "I dunno. That's just what my family has always done." And there was Kim. Elowen had three children, but it was only her eldest who was her "witch daughter," just as Elowen had been witch daughter to Kim's grandmother, and her grandmother to her mother before her. It goes like that, generation to generation and, in Elowen's family, green eyes to green eyes. Elowen's own were emeralds set in rosy skin beneath platinum white hair, cropped to bangs in the front and falling like an avalanche over her shoulders. Kim had eyes of a darker shade, more like the green of a bottle. Her mother was stout and strong, but Kim still held the shape you could tell her mother had once owned: lean and smooth — which you'd better be if you're going to go around calling yourself Willowdancer, which Kim did. She had two names too.

Willowdancer was twenty-five, twice-married and twice-divorced with two kids, Zoe, two, and Ian, five. Magick, she said, was mostly just common sense. "Wear rose petals around your neck for thirty days" — a beginner's love spell — "and I don't care how ugly you are, *someone's* going to start associating you with sweet things." Most of the witches burned at the stake in the Middle Ages, she said, were just really good cooks. Or they were curious, like her: As a teenager, Willow had tried out Christianity only to be kicked out of three churches for asking too many questions. She'd run away from home, hit the other end of the virgin / whore spectrum — "literally," she said — and survived to join a religion that didn't bother with such distinctions. She'd made it to the promised land and found her mother there, waiting for her all along.

Naturally, she was a bit defensive, protective of her family and of their beliefs. She sat in on our lunch with Elowen as if she were a lawyer at a deposition. Were we trying to "save" her mother? she wanted to know. Elowen answered for us: "They can't, dear, I'm already Christian, in my way." Were we Catholics? Elowen answered again: "Kim, don't be rude. They clearly don't know what they are."

"Do you even know what a Pagan is?" Willowdancer asked.

"Of course they don't, dear," her mother said. "*Paganism* is kind of a silly term. There are too many different kinds of magick to use just one name."

Elowen proceeded to draw for us an umbrella labeled PAGANISM, with a spoke for each of its subsets: a curving line for Shamanism, another for Druidism, one for Wicca, one for witchcraft, and finally, confusingly, one for Paganism as well. She looked over her diagram, carefully rendered on a Denny's napkin, and then declared that it wouldn't tell us much.

"I guess you'll just have to see for yourself," she said.

Willowdancer groaned, rolling her eyes.

"Honey, they can't understand without seeing."

"There's nothing to see," Willowdancer said.

"I disagree, dear. There's lots to see."

Elowen shushed her daughter and insisted we be their guests at the Heartland Pagan Festival, an upcoming campout for witches and assorted other heathens in rural Kansas, on a big patch of land a group of Pagans owned collectively, a nation unto itself amidst miles of corn punctuated by equal numbers of grain silos and church steeples. Willowdancer agreed we could come, promising to show us around and make sure we saw the right things.

✦

This is what we saw: There were many, many witches, not to mention troll-people — those who believe they are "part troll," the way some people say they are "part Cherokee" — as well as vampires and half-lings and full-blood Vikings, radical faeries and mischievous elves and, strutting around in kilts and tartan, communicating by walkie-talkie, some big, bad-ass druids providing security. Some of the druids were bikers; many of the magick people were military: lifers and grunts and NCOs. There were also construction workers, Jiffy Lube mechanics, a major contingent from Kinko's. They came to the festival in campers and rusty RV's and souped-up Chevy two-tons; they camped in pup tents and under tarps and in some cases under trees; they brought tod-dlers and teenagers and their grandmothers.

All told, there were well over a thousand Pagans gathered for the festival's opening ritual, standing in a circle around the makings of a serious bonfire, a cabin-sized column of heavy timber which the "keepers of the flame" — sooty, muscular, bare-chested men with axes — had been hewing and stacking for days, and which they had topped with an enormous, hollowed-out log carved with a bearded face, a likeness of the "Horned One" to whom they prayed. There were also worshippers of the witch goddess Hecate, and of the Norse trickster god Loki, more popular among gay Pagans than his straight-arrow brother Thor. There were devotees of the Ancient Mother and of the Roman war god Mars, of the Green Man and of Isis, of Herne the Hunter and of the Bitch Goddess, she of uncountable mammaries. There were women in black velvet robes and men with great, gnarled staffs, and despite the mist of precipitation, the fog of cold breath, and the two days of rain and mud — a *lot* of mud — that had preceded the opening ritual, there were naked Pagans everywhere. Some whose nudity seemed like a gift to all who beheld them, others whose raw nakedness was just plain raw. There were drums, constant, unrelent-ing. And there was chanting, some like the barking of congested seals, some like the singing of drunk midwestern angels. Bells tinkled, a little boy riding on his mother's shoulders shouted "Yay!" with genuine joy, and through the throng of revelers the prayer of a man standing in front of the bonfire-to-be filtered out to the margins.

"Desire! Warmth! Light!" he called.

He waited, as if there was supposed to be a reply, but the crowd barely mustered a murmur, so he continued:

"Wisdom! Passion! Join us and protect us in this our rite!"

It was clear he wasn't talking to us, we of the great, half-nude army surrounding him; he was talking, actually, to the Horned One; but he wanted our help, our amplification. Despite the crowd's good intentions, though, this Pagan priest could not get an Amen. So a priestess took over, and directing the crowd like it was a grade school choir, coaxed out a chant:

Fire of passion,
fire of light,
fire of knowledge burning bright,
fire of heart, fire of mind,
fire of soul throughout all time.

The first time around, she was pretty much on her own. The second time wasn't much better. But by the third rep, most of the pagans were shyly following the words, as if in a contest to see who could say them the quietest, with the least inflection.

"Yay!" shouted the little boy, the only audibly eager heathen in the crowd.

Except, of course, for the loudmouthed woman next to us. She had a mane of red hair that drooped down to the middle of her back, and she wore a green robe with a gold belt beneath a patchwork parka. She had a lovely alto-soprano voice. What she didn't have was a spot close enough to hear the chant leaders. She kept trying to sing along with the priests and priestesses in the center, but she couldn't really make out what they were saying, so she fudged it: "Fire of passion, fire of light, fire of hmm-mm. Ooh, fire . . ."

When a group of Native American singers entered the circle and began a wailing, all-vowel song, she seemed relieved; as far as she was concerned, there were no words to this one, and she could wail with the best of them. But wailing, like ritual, is trickier than it seems; you can't just moan like a cat in heat and expect the Goddess to appear. On the edge of the great circle a small ring formed around the "ooh, fire" woman. She drowned out the Indians, and then, magickally, she mangled the next prayer, though it was the only one in the ritual everyone seemed to know. Even we understood that the words were "Earth my body, water my blood, air my breath, and fire my spirit," but still Ooh-Fire sang it as a litany of imperatives: "Lift my body! Water my brood! Hear my breath, fiery spirit!"

And then, as if in answer to her command, there *was* a fiery spirit. During the chanting and the prayers, the keepers of the flame had been getting busy with long metal prods and torches doused in gasoline, and now the fruit of their labor blossomed into the darkening sky; we felt its heat before we saw it, and then we saw it too, licking over the heads of the crowd.

"Yay!"

We wanted the fire as much as the nakedest Pagan, as much as the man with the biggest rack of antlers. He, we, all of us — we wanted the flames to transform this drizzly, shleppy event into something with heat, with energy, with the old, scary gods the Pagans kept insisting were coming to the party. The flames reached the hollowed-out log perched on top of the bonfire, and it exploded with light. The fire turned from yellow to deep, dark green, roaring through the log and around it, a trick devised by the keepers of the flame. It was an answer to our prayers: big flames, big logs, century-old wood sizzling and popping, calling out, crackle, crackle, boom, boom, boom. Even on the edge of the circle, we felt the reverberations in our sternums, and the heat washed our faces like a baptism.

Yay!

A chorus of drums leapt up to join the flames, bongos and

tablas and dhokals, bells and flutes and rain sticks and maybe some pots and pans. Cacophony. The man standing next to us—skinny, short, and sharp-faced, his head hairless but for a white goatee, a bit like an elvish Freud—began stripping off layer after layer, sweater after sweater, then his T-shirt and sarong, folding them neatly and piling them until he was down to nothing but bright red bike shorts. Then he peeled those off, too. Naked, he seemed less skinny; he was nothing but muscle and bone, powerfully built for his size. With his bike shorts folded and topping his pile of clothes, he leapt toward the flame like a white-tailed deer. No one knew who he was, but everyone stared. He may not have been a manifestation of the gods Loki or Thor, or of the Stag King, he may have been a bookkeeper from Wichita or a truck driver from Kansas City or a schoolteacher from Abilene, but something supernatural had to explain the—what else to call it?—the *broomstick* between his legs. We had never seen anything like it. No one had. "Yay!" The little kid shouted, and his mother's eyes grew wide; people laughed and put their hands to their mouths, delighted with this miracle, transfixed as Skyclad—so we named him, in honor of the pagan term for nudity—began dancing around the fire, dancing not with his hips nor his ass nor his shoulders but with his whole body, in the air as much as on the ground, his eyes black and huge, his arms akimbo and passing through the flames. Most of all, he danced with his penis, trailing behind him and swinging in front of him like a giant gong. Regardless of your sexual preference, regardless of whether you worshipped the Horned One or the Goddess whose flames engulfed him, regardless of what name you chose to call or not call the divine, it was amazing to behold.

There are many kinds of magick, Elowen had told us. Too many for just one name.

The altars at Heartland—some, smoothed-down tree stumps; others, half-buried circles of stones—were meant for leaving gifts to the gods, but kids at the festival insisted they were more like bartering tables. Leave a pretty rock, you can take a Sacajawea dollar. Leave a hemp necklace, you can take a rusty knife. Some of their parents liked to pretend magick was all goodness and light, but the kids knew otherwise. Make a bad trade, something bad will happen. Just look at the altar. Stacks of keys: Those are from people who'd left home and wouldn't go back. Dog tags: Those are for people who couldn't go back.

Later we joined the Salene Circle/Dark Moon Coven/Fort Riley Pagan Association at its camp, a dozen tents set apart from the crowd in an embrace of trees. We sat with a score of witches at Elowen's campfire, passing a bottle of mead, waiting for the dedication ceremony, or "wiccaning," of an infant girl named Aliyah. Her father, Kal-el, an artillery sergeant at Fort Riley, had missed the birth of his first child, Logan, because he'd been in the DMZ in Korea — "It's a live-fire area. No family allowed." — and now he was going to miss Aliyah's first year because he was about to be shipped back overseas. Kal-el sat by the fire wishing witchcraft was what outsiders imagined it to be. "But I can't stand up there popping off fireballs," he said. "I really wish I could. Yes, that would be really nice, because that would end a war really quickly, a guy blasting off fireballs, people running away, people saying, 'Okay, this is not good for our reality. We surrender.' Then I get to go home." He kissed Aliyah goodbye even as he dedicated her to the Goddess, rocking her in his arms.

A little bowling ball of a boy, black hair, a dragon on his T-shirt, a Charlie-Brown-striped sarong, rolled down the path toward us. There was a snake in the dirt but he stepped right over it and stomped up to us, fingering a kid's bowie knife, cheaply made but impressive-looking, with a serrated edge on one side and a compass in the hilt. He asked us if we'd seen any Dungeon Masters. "We're not Dungeon Masters," we answered. "I *know* that. That's not what I asked," the boy said, rolling his eyes. Later we spotted him showing off his knife to a smaller boy, running his finger down the dull blade, finding true north with the compass, expounding on the virtues of a leather grip. He had clearly earned his Pagan badge. "There's more than monsters out there," he counseled his younger friend. "You have to be prepared."

On a grassy peninsula reaching into Heartland's lake, the site of an altar to the hunter god Herne, the trickster god Loki, and the thunder god Thor, there was a man watching us who was so frail he looked like he might snap his fingers and disappear. Red goatee, pale skin, holding onto his cane even when he sat down on a stone. A sad, kind, quiet voice. He said he was admiring us in the sun. "Your sarongs are see-through when they're backlit, you know." He'd been a witch for twenty-five years and was the last one alive of his original coven. He talked to the dead, but they didn't answer.

"Frankly," he said, "it's not part of my craft to be all oogie-boogie. It's about recognizing the gods." He paused, reconsidering. "And it's about remembering the ancestors."

"The witches?" we asked, thinking of what we'd read about Paganism's fixation with the "Burning Time" when witches were burned at the stake.

He tilted his head and looked at us as if we were helplessly naïve, or just too young to understand.

"AIDS," he explained. "Queers. Remembering *them*."

There was a girl at Elowen's campfire named Mary Dragon, daughter of a witch called Crow Wolf and step daughter of a biker named Cat Johnson. Crow and Cat had not had an easy time of it in life. They were friendly but a little shy. Mary Dragon was smart as a whip, college-bound for sure; they let her do most of their talking. She explained their religion thusly: Monotheism is a mirror that offers only one reflection; Paganism is a spinning disco ball, a thousand glittering possibilities.

Not long after Skyclad began his dance at the opening ritual, storm clouds plowed in and spattered rain and hail down on the fire. The drummers didn't seem capable of tapping out "Yankee Doodle," much less a rhythm that could summon up gods, or forces, or just that feeling in the gut that makes you want to move or howl. Skyclad danced alone in the rain. Later that night, though, when the sky turned clear and cold as metal, when the drums thickened, when beautiful women unveiled themselves and old men hobbled around the fire like they were marking time, we stripped down to our sarongs and joined Skyclad and several hundred others weaving loopy circles around the fire. We dipped and twirled and skimmed the flames, shuffling in the mud and the heat to polytheistic polyrhythms. A couple of skeptics made to dance like holy fools. If that wasn't magick, it was a hell of a trick.

"What did you guys think of the opening ritual?" Elowen asked us. She meant the question pleasantly, but maybe because Willow muttered and rolled her eyes, and because we could still hear the herky-jerky bongos back up at the big circle, we told her the truth: We'd liked the fire but were disappointed with the words, the silliness of the chanting.

Elowen nodded. "That's alright," she said, "magick is individual. When we do our own rituals it's not like that at all. Would you like an example?"

A tall redhead called Velvet jumped up from beside the fire. "Ooh! Do we get to do an example?"

"Yes," Elowen said, and at her declaration several witches stood, pulling fleeces over their sarongs. A cold wind was blowing, pushing the clouds westward and making the evening even cooler. Only Elowen remained mostly naked.

"We're going to name the elements," Elowen explained. "By calling to the powers found in each direction, we invite the presence of the Goddess, who oversees them all."

Willow, who besides being a witch and a mother was also a belly dancer, was standing with her butt to the fire, casually twitching her hips and shaking her belly-dancing bells. Other than her chainmail skirt, she was naked, her stomach a tanning salon bronze.

Her bells trilled as she turned away. She disliked the talk, the explanations. She might be willing to act as a guide to the best Paganism had to offer, but she couldn't forget we were outsiders who were there to work magic of our own: the kind, she thought, who steal stories and make the world smaller than it is; the kind that scoffs at naked Pagans and their unsuspecting mothers; the kind that makes so many possibilities wear the same drab name.

"Kim, do you want to call North?" her mother asked.

"I'm not calling anything with them around."

"Suit yourself. Just stand back out of the circle then. We don't need your negativity."

Kim seemed to consider storming off but then decided to follow the group up to an empty field lit by a brilliant, nearly full moon. Her mother took up a position in the center of a circle made mostly of her fellow witches.

Velvet stood in the southern position. She'd come to Heartland this year to talk to a man named Owl, who besides being a Pagan was successful in business and knew how to get things done; he'd pledged to help Velvet win back custody of her baby son, granted to a fundamentalist uncle because the judge deemed Velvet Satanic. "As if I'd even talk to a Luciferian," she'd said. She was an elf witch.

In the west position stood Night, a raven-haired Latina who'd retired from the army and now worked for McDonald's and somehow managed to support several children. In the middle with Elowen stood Lady Keltic, who had asked Elowen for a spell to help her conceive. Elowen was the conductor; we were north and east.

One by one we called out the names of our elements—fire, water, earth, and air—and of our directions, free-associating on their attributes like we were gently speaking in tongues.

In the distance, a woman roared like a lion; a man walked by singing "Sitting on the Dock of the Bay"; the wind smelled like incense and PortaPotties; we were freezing. We looked at Elowen, her white mullet glorious beneath the moon, her naked torso seemingly impervious to the cold, her feet bare in the mud, and couldn't help ourselves: We laughed. She looked at us, in our muddy sneakers and double-knotted sarongs, shivering with notebooks in hand, and she laughed, too.

Willow didn't get the joke. "I can't believe you're showing them this. They just want to make you look stupid," she said. "To make fun of all of it. Can't you see that?"

We started to tell her she was wrong, but Elowen had a better answer. "Kimberly," she said. "They have no power over me. Over any of us. They've come here to learn about how we live and worship, and we are going to show them. What they do with that experience is on them. I don't believe they want to hurt me, or any of us, but they couldn't if they tried."

Willowdancer uncrossed her arms, then crossed them again, biting her lower lip to keep it from shaking in the cold.

On the far side of the field we could see torches being juggled over the heads of the crowd that had lingered at the opening ritual; a tipped-over trashcan added the sound of a cymbal to the drumming. The dancers still were circling the bonfire, all together, each alone.

Elowen took Willow by the shoulders and pulled her close. A mother warming a daughter with her heat, she swallowed Willow with her body like a flame wrapping a log.

"Do you really believe some silly book could have more power than we do?"

2004

✦

"Upon This Rock" begins with a joke—euphemism, in this case, for contempt. That's where Sullivan starts: with contempt for his assignment—an amiably bemused scene piece on a Christian rock festival for "a flash mag like *Gentleman's Quarterly*"—and his willingness to undertake it, for, what, three, four dollars a word? I don't think there's any condescension toward his future subjects because Sullivan knows he doesn't really need to consider them at all. They'll be props, the kids he plans to drive to the festival with. "We'd talk through the night, they'd proselytize me, and I'd keep my little tape machine working all the while," he writes. "Somehow I knew we'd grow to like and pity one another. What a story that would make—for future generations."

And that's pretty much what happens. Only the people, they're not props, and the plan goes wildly awry, and one can only imagine the face of Sullivan's editor at *GQ* upon learning that Sullivan would be filing something like twelve thousand words. And his face upon reading them, and realizing that *GQ* would be running them, that *GQ* was about to publish a story that would be, among other things, one of the best pieces of religion journalism in years, and the anchor of a collections of essays, *Pulphead*, that captures the first decade of the twenty-first century as Joan Didion's *Slouching Toward Bethlehem* captures the 1960s. Like Didion, Sullivan shifts between criticism, reporting, and memoir. Unlike Didion, he's funny. The real joke of "Upon This Rock" isn't the snark of its opening. That's a bait-and-switch. The snark is the bait. The switch comes when Sullivan finds a group of guys to talk with through the night, men who despite names like Pee Wee and Bub turn out to be so remarkably human that they move themselves around in the story, and move Sullivan, too, literally pushing him up a hill like he's the prop. It's their story, too, after all. Lucky for Sullivan, they're willing to share.

JOHN JEREMIAH SULLIVAN
Upon This Rock

It is wrong to boast, but in the beginning, my plan was perfect. I was assigned to cover the Cross-Over Festival in Lake of the Ozarks, Missouri, three days of the top Christian bands and their backers at some isolated midwestern fairground. I'd stand at the edge of the crowd and take notes on the scene, chat up the occasional audience member ("What's harder—homeschooling or regular schooling?"), then flash my pass to get backstage, where I'd rap with the artists themselves. The singer could feed me his bit about how all music glorifies Him, when it's performed with a loving spirit, and I'd jot down every tenth word, inwardly smiling. Later that night I might sneak some hooch in my rental car and invite myself to lie with a prayer group by their fire, for the fellowship of it. Fly home, stir in statistics. Paycheck.

But as my breakfast-time mantra says, I am a professional. And they don't give out awards for that sort of toe-tap, J-school foolishness. I wanted to know what these people are, who claim to love this music, who drive hundreds of miles, traversing states, to hear it live. Then it came, my epiphany: I would go with them. Or rather, they would go with me. I would rent a van, a plush one, and we would travel there together, I and three or four hard-core buffs, all the way from the East Coast to the implausibly named Lake of the Ozarks. We'd talk through the night, they'd proselytize at me, and I'd keep my little tape machine working all the while. Somehow I knew we'd grow to like and pity one another. What a story that would make — for future generations.

The only remaining question was: how to recruit the willing? But it was hardly even a question, because everyone knows that damaged types who are down for whatever's clever gather in "chat rooms" every night. And among the Jesusy, there's plenty who are super f'd up. He preferred it that way, evidently.

So I published my invitation, anonymously, at youthontherock .com, and on two Internet forums devoted to the good-looking Christian pop-punk band Relient K, which had been booked to appear at Cross-Over. I pictured that guy or girl out there who'd been dreaming in an attic room of seeing, with his or her own eyes, the men of Relient K perform their song "Gibberish" from *Two Lefts Don't Make a Right . . . But Three Do.* How could he or she get there, though? Gas prices won't drop, and Relient K never plays North Florida. Please, Lord, make it happen. Suddenly, here my posting came, like a great light. We could help each other. "I'm looking for a few serious fans of Christian rock to ride to the festival with me," I wrote. "Male/female doesn't matter, though you shouldn't be older than, say, 28, since I'm looking at this primarily as a youth phenomenon."

They seem like harmless words. Turns out, though, I had failed to grasp how "youth" the phenomenon is. Most of the people hanging out in these chat rooms were teens, and I don't mean 19, friends, I mean 14. Some of them, I was about to learn, were mere tweens. I had just traipsed out onto the World Wide Web and asked a bunch of 12-year-old Christians if they wanted to come for a ride in my van.

It wasn't long before the little fuckers rounded on me. "Nice job cutting off your email address," wrote "mathgeek29," in a tone that seemed not at all Christlike. "I doubt if anybody would give a full set of contact information to some complete stranger on the Internet. . . . Aren't there any Christian teens in Manhattan who would be willing to do this?"

"Oh, I should hope not," I blubbered.

A few of the children were credulous. "Riathamus" said, "i am 14 and live in indiana plus my parents might not let me considering it is a stranger over the Internet. but that would really be awsome." A girl by the name of "LilLoser" even tried to be a friend:

> I doubt my parents would allow their baby girl to go with some guy they don't and I don't know except through email, especially for the amount of time you're asking and like driving around everywhere with ya. . . . I'm not saying you're a creepy petifile, lol, but i just don t think you ll get too many people interested . . . cuz like i said, it spells out "creepy" . . . but hey—good luck to you in your questy missiony thing. lol.

The luck that she wished me I sought in vain. The Christians stopped chatting with me and started chatting among themselves, warning one another about me. Finally one poster on the official Re-lient K site hissed at the others to stay away from my scheme, as I was in all likelihood "a 40 year old kidnapper." Soon I logged on and found that the moderators of the site had removed my post and its lengthen-ing thread of accusations altogether, offering no explanation. Doubt-less at that moment they were faxing alerts to a network of moms. I recoiled in dread. I called my lawyer, in Boston, who told me to "stop using computers."

In the end, the experience inspired in me a distaste for the whole Cross-Over Festival, and I resolved to refuse the assignment. I with-drew.

The problem with a flash mag like the *Gentlemen's Quarterly* is that there's always some overachieving assistant, sometimes called Greg, whom the world hasn't beaten down yet and who, when you phone him, out of courtesy, just to let him know that "the Cross-Over thing fell through" and that you'll be in touch when you "figure out what to do next," hops on that mystical boon the Internet and finds out that the festival you were planning to attend was in fact not "the biggest one in the country," as you'd alleged. The biggest one in the country — indeed, in Christendom — is the Creation Festival, inaugurated in 1979, a regular Godstock. And it happens not in Missouri but in ruralmost Pennsylvania, in a green valley, on a farm called Agape. This festival did not end a month ago; it starts the day after tomorrow. Already they are assembling, many tens of thousands strong. But hey — good luck to you in your questy missiony thing. lol.

I made one demand: that I not be forced to camp. I'd be given some sort of vehicle with a mattress in it, one of these pop-ups, maybe. "Right," said Greg. "Here's the deal. I've called around. There are no vans left within a hundred miles of Philly. We got you an RV, though. It's a twenty-nine-footer." Once I reached the place, we agreed (for he led me to think he agreed), I would certainly be able to downgrade to something more manageable.

The reason twenty-nine feet is such a common length for RVs, I presume, is that once a vehicle gets much longer, you need a special permit to drive it. That would mean forms and fees, possibly even background checks. But show up at any RV joint with your thigh stumps lashed to a skateboard, crazily waving your hooks-for-hands, screaming you want that twenty-nine-footer out back for a trip to you ain't sayin' where, and all they want to know is: Credit or debit, tiny sir?

Two days later, I stood in a parking lot, suitcase at my feet. Debbie came toward me. She was a lot to love, with a face as sweet as a birthday cake beneath spray-hardened bangs. She raised a powerful arm and pointed, before either of us spoke. She pointed at a vehicle that looked like something the ancient Egyptians might have left behind in the desert.

"Oh, hi, there," I said, "Listen, all I need is, like, a camper van or whatever. It's just me, and I'm going 500 miles . . ."

She considered me. "Where ya headed?"

"To this thing called Creation. It's, like, a Christian-rock festival."

"You and everybody!" she chirped. "The people who got our vans are going to that same thing. There's a bunch o' ya."

Her husband and coworker Jack emerged—tattooed, squat, gray-mulleted, spouting open contempt for MapQuest. He'd be giving me real directions. "But first let's check 'er out."

We toured the outskirts of my soon-to-be mausoleum. It took time. Every single thing Jack said, somehow, was the only thing I'd need to remember. White water, gray water, black water (drinking, showering, le devoir). Here's your this, never ever that. Grumbling about "weekend warriors." I couldn't listen, because listening would mean accepting it as real, though his casual mention of the vast blind spot in the passenger-side mirror squeaked through, as did his description of the "extra two feet on each side"—the bulge of my living quarters—which I wouldn't be able to see but would want to "be conscious of" out there. Debbie followed us with a video camera, for insurance purposes. I saw my loved ones gathered in a mahogany-paneled room to watch this footage; them being forced to hear me say, "What if I never use the toilet—do I still have to switch on the water?"

Mike pulled down the step and climbed aboard. It was really happening. The interior smelled of spoiled vacations and amateur porn shoots wrapped in motel shower curtains and left in the sun. I was physically halted at the threshold for a moment. Jesus had never been in this RV.

What do I tell you about my voyage to Creation? Do you want to know what it's like to drive a windmill with tires down the Pennsylvania Turnpike at rush hour by your lonesome, with darting bug-eyes and shaking hands; or about Greg's laughing phone call "to see how it's going"; about hearing yourself say "no No NO NO!" in a shamefully high-pitched voice every time you try to merge; or about thinking you detect—beneath the mysteriously comforting blare of the radio—faint honking sounds, then checking your passenger-side mirror only to find you've been straddling the lanes for an unknown number of miles (those two extra feet!) and that the line of traffic you've kept pinned stretches back farther than you can see; or about stopping at Target to buy sheets and a pillow and peanut butter but then practicing your golf swing in the sporting-goods aisle for a solid twenty-five minutes, unable to stop, knowing that when you do, the twenty-nine-footer will be where you left her, alone in the side lot, hulking and malevolent, waiting for you to take her the rest of the way to your shared destiny?

She got me there, as Debbie and Jack had promised, not possibly believing it themselves. Seven miles from Mount Union, a sign read CREATION AHEAD. The sun was setting; it floated above the valley like a fiery gold balloon. I fell in with a long line of cars and trucks and vans—not many RVs. Here they were, all about me: the born again. On my right was a pickup truck, its bed full of teenage girls in matching powder blue T-shirts; they were screaming at a Mohawked kid who was walking beside the road. I took care not to meet their eyes— who knew but they weren't the same fillies I had solicited days before? Their line of traffic lurched ahead, and an old orange Datsun came up beside me. I watched as the driver rolled down her window, leaned halfway out, and blew a long, clear note on a ram's horn.

I understand where you might be coming from. Nevertheless that is what she did. I have it on tape. She blew a ram's horn, quite capably, twice. A yearly rite, perhaps, to announce her arrival at Creation.

My turn at the gate. The woman looked at me, then past me to the empty passenger seat, then down the whole length of the twenty-nine-footer. "How many people in your group?" she asked.

I pulled away in awe, permitting the twenty-nine-footer to float. My path was thronged with excited Christians, most younger than 18. The adults looked like parents or pastors, not here on their own. Twilight was well along, and the still valley air was sharp with campfire smoke. A great roar shot up to my left—something had happened onstage. The sound bespoke a multitude. It filled the valley and lingered.

I thought I might enter unnoticed—that the RV might even offer a kind of cover—but I was already turning heads. Two separate kids said, "I feel sorry for him" as I passed. Another leaped up on the driver's-side step and said, "Jesus Christ, man," then fell away running. I kept braking—even idling was too fast. Whatever spectacle had provoked the roar was over now: The roads were choked. The youngsters were streaming around me in both directions, back to their campsites, like a line of ants around some petty obstruction. They had a disconcerting way of stepping aside for the RV only when its front fender was just about to graze their backs. From my elevated vantage, it looked as if they were waiting just a tenth of a second too long, and that I was gently, forcibly parting them in slow motion.

The evangelical strata were more or less recognizable from my high school days, though everyone, I observed, had gotten better looking. Lots were dressed like skate punks or in last season's East Village couture (nondenominationals); others were fairly trailer (rural Baptists or Church of God); there were preps (Young Life, Fellowship of Christian Athletes—these were the ones who'd have the pot). You could spot the stricter sectarians right away, their unchanging antifashion and pale glum faces. When I asked one woman, later, how many she reckoned were white, she said, "Roughly 100 percent." I did see some Asians and three or four blacks. They gave the distinct impression of having been adopted.

I drove so far. You wouldn't have thought this thing could go on so far. Every other bend in the road opened onto a whole new cove full of tents and cars; the encampment had expanded to its physiographic limits, pushing right up to the feet of the ridges. It's hard to put across the sensory effect of that many people living and moving around in the open: part family reunion, part refugee camp. A tad militia, but cheerful.

The roads turned dirt and none too wide: Hallelujah Highway, Street Called Straight. I'd been told to go to "H," but when I reached H, two teenage kids in orange vests came out of the shadows and told me the spots were all reserved. "Help me out here, guys," I said, jerking my thumb, pitifully indicating my mobile home. They pulled out their walkie-talkies. Some time went by. It got darker. Then an even younger boy rode up on a bike and winked a flashlight at me, motioning I should follow.

It was such a comfort to yield up my will to this kid. All I had to do was not lose him. His vest radiated a warm, reassuring official-dom in my headlights. Which may be why I failed to comprehend in time that he was leading me up an almost vertical incline — "the Hill Above D."

Thinking back, I can't say which came first: the little bell in my spine warning me that the RV had reached a degree of tilt she was not engineered to handle, or the sickening knowledge that we had begun to slip back. I bowed up off the seat and crouched on the gas. I heard yelling. I kicked at the brake. With my left hand and foot I groped, like a person drowning, for the emergency brake (had Jack's comprehensive how-to sesh not touched on its whereabouts?). We were losing purchase; she started to shudder. My little guide's eyes showed fear.

I'd known this moment would come, of course, that the twenty-nine-footer would turn on me. We had both of us understood it from the start. But I must confess, I never imagined her hunger for death could prove so extreme. Laid out below and behind me was a literal field of Christians, toasting buns and playing guitars, fellowshipping. The aerial shot in the papers would show a long scar, a swath through their peaceful tent village. And that this gigantic psychopath had worked her vile design through the agency of a child—an innocent, albeit impossibly confused, child . . .

My memory of the next five seconds is smeared, but I know that a large and perfectly square male head appeared in the windshield. It was blond and wearing glasses. It had wide-open eyes and a Chaucerian West Virginia accent and said rapidly that I should "JACK THE WILL TO THE ROT" while applying the brakes. Some branch of my motor cortex obeyed. The RV skidded briefly and was still. Then the same voice said, "All right, hit the gas on three: one, two . . ."

She began to climb—slowly, as if on a pulley. Some freakishly powerful beings were pushing. Soon we had leveled out at the top of the hill.

There were five of them, all in their early twenties. I remained in the twenty-nine-footer; they gathered below. "Thank you," I said.

"Aw, hey," shot back Darius, the one who'd given the orders. He talked very fast. "We've been doing this all day—I don't know why that kid keeps bringing people up here—we're from West Virginia—listen, he's retarded—there's an empty field right there."

I looked back and down at what he was pointing to: pastureland.

Jake stepped forward. He was also blond, but slender. And handsome in a feral way. His face was covered in stubble as pale as his hair. He said he was from West Virginia and wanted to know where I was from.

"I was born in Louisville," I said.

"Really?" said Jake. "Is that on the Ohio River?" Like Darius, he both responded and spoke very quickly. I said that in fact it was.

"Well, I know a dude that died who was from Ohio. I'm a volunteer fireman, see. Well, he flipped a Chevy Blazer nine times. He was spread out from here to that ridge over there. He was dead as four o'clock."

"Who are you guys?" I said.

Ritter answered. He was big, one of those fat men who don't really have any fat, a corrections officer—as I was soon to learn—and a former heavyweight wrestler. He could burst a pineapple in his armpit and chuckle about it (or so I assume). Haircut: military. Mustache: faint. "We're just a bunch of West Virginia guys on fire for Christ," he said. "I'm Ritter, and this is Darius, Jake, Bub, and that's Jake's brother, Josh. Pee Wee's around here somewhere."

"Chasin' tail," said Darius disdainfully.

"So you guys have just been hanging out here, saving lives?"

"We're from West Virginia," said Darius again, like maybe he thought I was thick. It was he who most often spoke for the group. The projection of his jaw from the lump of snuff he kept there made him come off a bit contentious, but I felt sure he was just high-strung.

"See," Jake said, "well, our campsite is right over there." With a cock of his head he identified a car, a truck, a tent, a fire, and a tall cross made of logs. And that other thing was . . . a PA system?

"We had this spot last year," Darius said. "I prayed about it. I said, 'God, I'd just really like to have that spot again—you know, if it's Your will.'"

I'd assumed that my days at Creation would be fairly lonely and end with my ritual murder. But these West Virginia guys had such warmth. It flowed out of them. They asked me what I did and whether I liked sassafras tea and how many others I'd brought with me in the RV. Plus they knew a dude who died horribly and was from a state with the same name as the river I grew up by, and I'm not the type who questions that sort of thing.

"What are you guys doing later?" I said.

Bub was short and solid; each of his hands looked as strong as a trash compactor. He had darker skin than the rest—an olive cast—with brown hair under a camouflage hat and brown eyes and a full-fledged dark mustache. Later he would share with me that friends often told him he must be "part N-word." He was shy and always looked like he must be thinking hard about something. "Me and Ritter's going to hear some music," he said.

"What band is it?"

Ritter said, "Jars of Clay."

I had read about them; they were big. "Why don't you guys stop by my trailer and get me on your way?" I said. "I'll be in that totally empty field."

Ritter said, "We just might do that." Then they all lined up to shake my hand.

While I waited for Ritter and Bub, I lay in bed and read *The Silenced Times* by lantern light. This was a thin newsletter that had come with my festival packet. It wasn't really a newsletter; it was publisher's flackery for *Silenced*, a new novel by Jerry Jenkins, one of the minds behind the multi-hundred-million-dollar *Left Behind* series—twelve books so far, all about what happens after the Rapture, to people like me. His new book was a futuristic job, set in 2047. The dateline on the newsletter read: "March 2, 38." You get it? Thirty-seven years have passed since they wiped Jesus from history. *The Silenced Times* was laid out to look like a newspaper from that coming age.

It was pretty grim stuff. In the year 38, an ancient death cult has spread like a virus and taken over the "United Seven States of America." Adherents meet in "cell groups" (nice touch: a bit of old Commie lingo); they enlist the young and hunger for global hegemony while striving to hasten the end of the world. By the year 34—the time of the last census—44 percent of the population had professed membership in the group; by now the figure is closer to half. This dwarfs any other surviving religious movement in the land. Even the president (whom they mobilized to elect) has been converted. The most popular news channel in the country openly backs him and his policies; and the year's most talked-about film is naked propaganda for the cult, but in a darkly brilliant twist, much of the population has been convinced that the media are in fact controlled by . . .

Forgive me! That's all happening now. That's evangelicalism. *The Silenced Times* describes Christians being thrown into jail, driven underground, their pamphlets confiscated. A dude wins an award for ratting out his sister, who was leading a campus Bible study (you know how we do). Jerry Jenkins must blow his royalties on crack. I especially liked the part in *The Silenced Times* where it reports that antireligion forces have finally rounded up Jenkins himself—in a cave. He's 97 years old but has never stopped typing, and as they drag him away, he's bellowing Scripture.

Ritter beat on the door. He and Bub were ready to hear some Jars of Clay. Now that it was night, more fires were going; the whole valley was aromatic. And the sky looked like a tin punch lantern—thousands of stars were out. There were so many souls headed toward the stage, it was hard to walk, though I noticed the crowd tended to give Ritter a wider berth. He kind of leaned back, looking over people's heads, as if he expected to spot a friend. I asked about his church in West Virginia. He said he and the rest of the guys were Pentecostal, speaking in tongues and all that—except for Jake, who was a Baptist. But they all went to the same "sing"—a weekly Bible study at somebody's house with food and guitars. Did Ritter think everyone here was a Christian? "No, there's some who probably aren't saved. With this many people, there has to be." What were his feelings on that? "It just opens up opportunities for witnessing," he said.

Bub stopped suddenly—a signal that he wished to speak. The crowd flowed on around us for a minute while he chose his words. "There's Jewish people here," he said.

"Really?" I said. "You mean, Jew Jews?"

"Yeah," Bub said. "These girls Pee Wee brung around. I mean, they're Jewish. That's pretty awesome." He laughed without moving his face; Bub's laugh was a purely vocal phenomenon. Were his eyes moist?

We commenced walking.

I suspect that on some level—say, the conscious one—I didn't want to be noticing what I noticed as we went. But I've been to a lot of huge public events in this country during the past five years, writing about sports or whatever, and one thing they all had in common was

this weird implicit enmity that American males, in particular, seem to
carry around with them much of the time. Call it a laughable general-
ization, fine, but if you spend enough late afternoons in stadium con-
courses, you feel it, something darker than machismo. Something a
little wounded, and a little sneering, and just plain ready for bad things
to happen. It wasn't here. It was just . . . not. I looked for it, and I
couldn't find it. In the three days I spent at Creation, I saw not one
fight, heard not one word spoken in anger, felt at no time even mildly
harassed, and in fact met many people who were exceptionally kind.
I realize they were all of the same race, all believed the same stuff,
and weren't drinking, but there were also 100,000 of them. What's that
about?

We were walking past a row of portable toilets, by the food
stands. As we came around the corner, I saw the stage, from off to the
side. And the crowd on the hill that faced the stage. Their bodies rose
till they merged with the dark. "Holy crap," I said.

Ritter waved his arm like an impresario. He said, "This, my
friend, is Creation."

For their encore, Jars of Clay did a cover of U2's "All I Want Is You."
It was bluesy.

That's the last thing I'll be saying about the bands.

Or, no, wait, there's this: The fact that I didn't think I heard a
single interesting bar of music from the forty or so acts I caught or
overheard at Creation shouldn't be read as a knock on the acts themselves, much less as contempt for the underlying notion of Christians playing rock. These were not Christian bands, you see; these
were Christian-rock bands. The key to digging this scene lies in that
one-syllable distinction. Christian rock is a genre that exists to edify
and make money off of evangelical Christians. It's message music for
listeners who know the message cold, and, what's more, it operates
under a perceived responsibility—one the artists embrace—to "reach
people." As such, it rewards both obviousness and maximum palat-

ability (the artists would say clarity), which in turn means parasitism. Remember those perfume dispensers they used to have in pharmacies — "If you like Drakkar Noir, you'll love Sexy Musk"? Well, Christian rock works like that. Every successful crappy secular group has its Christian off-brand, and that's proper, because culturally speaking, it's supposed to serve as a stand-in for, not an alternative to or an improvement on, those very groups. In this it succeeds wonderfully. If you think it profoundly sucks, that's because your priorities are not its priorities; you want to hear something cool and new, it needs to play something proven to please . . . while praising Jesus Christ. That's Christian rock. A Christian band, on the other hand, is just a band that has more than one Christian in it. U2 is the exemplar, held aloft by believers and nonbelievers alike, but there have been others through the years, bands about which people would say, "Did you know those guys were Christians? I know — it's freaky. They're still fuckin' good, though." The Call was like that; Lone Justice was like that. These days you hear it about indie acts like Pedro the Lion and Damien Jurado (or people I've never heard of). In most cases, bands like these make a very, very careful effort not to be seen as playing "Christian rock." It's largely a matter of phrasing: Don't tell the interviewer you're born-again; say faith is a very important part of your life. And here, if I can drop the open-minded pretense real quick, is where the stickier problem of actually being any good comes in, because a question that must be asked is whether a hard-core Christian who turns 19 and finds he or she can write first-rate songs (someone like Damien Jurado) would ever have anything whatsoever to do with Christian rock. Talent tends to come hand in hand with a certain base level of subtlety. And believe it or not, the Christian-rock establishment sometimes expresses a kind of resigned approval of the way groups like U2 or Switchfoot (who played Creation while I was there and had a monster secular-radio hit at the time with "Meant to Live" but whose management wouldn't allow them to be photographed onstage) take quiet pains to distance themselves from any unambiguous Jesus-loving, recognizing that this is the surest way to connect with the world (you know that's how they refer to us, right? We're "of the world"). So it's possible — and indeed seems likely — that Christian rock is a musical genre, the only one I can think of, that has excellence-proofed itself.

It was late, and the Jews had sown discord. What Bub had said was true: There were Jews at Creation. These were Jews for Jesus, it emerged, two startlingly pretty high school girls from Richmond. They'd been sitting by the fire — one of them mingling fingers with Pee Wee — when Bub and Ritter and I returned from seeing Jars of Clay. Pee Wee was younger than the other guys, and cute, and he gazed at the girls admiringly when they spoke. At a certain point, they mentioned to Ritter that he would writhe in hell for having tattoos (he had a couple); it was what their people believed. Ritter had not taken the news all that well. He was fairly confident about his position among the elect. There was debate; Pee Wee was forced to escort the girls back to their tents, while Darius worked to calm Ritter. "They may have weird ideas," he said, "but we worship the same God."

The fire had burned to glowing coals, and now it was just we men, sitting on coolers, talking late-night hermeneutics blues. Bub didn't see how God could change His mind, how He could say all that crazy shit in the Old Testament — like don't get tattoos and don't look at your uncle naked — then take it back in the New.

"Think about it this way," I said. "If you do something that really makes Darius mad, and he's pissed at you, but then you do something to make it up to him, and he forgives you, that isn't him changing his mind. The situation has changed. It's the same with the old and new covenants, except Jesus did the making up."

Bub seemed pleased with this explanation. "I never heard anyone say it like that," he said. But Darius stared at me gimlet-eyed across the fire. He knew my gloss was theologically sound, and he wondered where I'd gotten it. The guys had been gracefully dancing around the question of what I believed—"where my walk was at," as they would have put it—all night.

We knew one another fairly well by now. Once Pee Wee had returned, they'd eagerly showed me around their camp. Most of their tents were back in the forest, where they weren't supposed to be; the air was cooler there. Darius had located a small stream about thirty yards away and, using his hands, dug out a basin. This was supplying their drinking water.

It came out that these guys spent much if not most of each year in the woods. They lived off game—as folks do, they said, in their section of Braxton County. They knew all the plants of the forest, which were edible, which cured what. Darius pulled out a large piece of cardboard folded in half. He opened it under my face: a mess of sassafras roots. He wafted their scent of black licorice into my face and made me eat one.

Then he remarked that he bet I liked weed. I allowed as how I might not not like it. "I used to love that stuff," he told me. Seeing that I was taken aback, he said, "Man, to tell you the truth, I wasn't even convicted about it. But it's socially unacceptable, and that was getting in the way of my Christian growth."

The guys had put together what I did for a living—though, to their credit, they didn't seem to take this as a reasonable explanation for my being there—and they gradually got the sense that I found them exotic (though it was more than that). Slowly, their talk became an ecstasy of self-definition. They were passionate to make me see what kind of guys they were. This might have grown tedious, had they been any old kind of guys. But they were the kind of guys who believed that God had personally interceded and made it possible for four of them to fit into Ritter's silver Chevrolet Cavalier for the trip to Creation.

"Look," Bub said, "I'm a pretty big boy, right? I mean, I'm stout. And Darius is a big boy"—here Darius broke in and made me look at his calves, which were muscled to a degree that hinted at defor-

mity; "I'm a freak," he said; Bub sighed and went on without breaking eye contact — "and you know Ritter is a big boy. Plus we had two
coolers, guitars, an electric piano, our tents and stuff, all" — he turned
and pointed, turned back, paused — "in that Chevy." He had the same
look in his eyes as earlier, when he'd told me there were Jews. "I think
that might be a miracle," he said.

In their lives, they had known terrific violence. Ritter and Darius
met, in fact, when each was beating the shit out of the other in middle-
school math class. Who won? Ritter looked at Darius, as if to clear his
answer, and said, "Nobody." Jake once took a fishing pole that Darius
had accidentally stepped on and broken and beat him to the ground
with it. "I told him, 'Well, watch where you're stepping,'" Jake said.
(This memory made Darius laugh so hard he removed his glasses.)
Half of their childhood friends had been murdered — shot or stabbed
over drugs or nothing. Others had killed themselves. Darius's grand-
father, great-uncle, and onetime best friend had all committed suicide.
When Darius was growing up, his father was in and out of jail; at least
once, his father had done hard time. In Ohio he stabbed a man in the
chest (the man had refused to stop "pounding on" Darius's grand-
father). Darius caught a lot of grief — "Your daddy's a jailbird!" —
during those years. He'd carried a chip on his shoulder from that.

"You came up pretty rough," I said.

"Not really," Darius said. "Some people ain't got hands and
feet." He talked about how much he loved his father. "With all my
heart — he's the best. He's brought me up the way that I am."

"And anyway," he added, "I gave all that to God — all that anger
and stuff. He took it away."

God had left him enough to get by on. Earlier in the evening, the
guys had roughed up Pee Wee a little and tied him to a tree with ratchet
straps. Some other Christians must have reported his screams to the
staff, because a guy in an orange vest came stomping up the hill. Pee
Wee hadn't been hurt much, but he put on a show of tears, to be funny.
"They always do me like that," he said. "Save me, mister!"

The guy was unamused. "It's not them you got to worry about," he said. "It's me."

Those were such foolish words! Darius came forward like some hideously fast-moving lizard on a nature show. "I'd watch it, man," he said. "You don't know who you're talking to. This'n here's as like to shoot you as shake your hand."

The guy somehow appeared to move back without actually taking a step. "You're not allowed to have weapons," he said.

"Is that right?" Darius said. "We got a conceal 'n' carry right there in the glove box. Mister, I'm from West Virginia—I know the law."

"I think you're lying," said the guy. His voice had gone a bit warbly.

Darius leaned forward, as if to hear better. His eyes were leaving his skull. "How would you know that?" he said. "Are you a prophet?"

"I'm Creation staff!" the guy said.

Jake stood up—he'd been watching this scene from his seat by the fire. The fixed polite smile on his face was indistinguishable from a leer. "Well," he said, "why don't you go somewhere and *create* your own problems?"

I admit that these tales of the West Virginia guys' occasional truculence might appear to gainsay what I claimed earlier about "not one word spoken in anger," et cetera. But it was playful. Darius, at least, seemed to be performing a bit for me. And if you take into account what the guys have to be on guard for all the time back home, the notable thing becomes how effectively they checked their instincts at Creation.

Whatever the case, we operated with more or less perfect impunity from then on. This included a lot of very loud, live music between two and three o'clock in the morning. The guys were running their large PA off the battery in Jake's truck. Ritter and Darius had a band of their own back home, First Verse. They were responsible for the music at their church. Ritter had an angelic tenor that seemed to be coming out of a body other than his own. And Josh was a good guitar player; he had a Les Paul and an effects board. We passed around the acoustic. I had to dig to come up with Christian tunes. I did "Jesus," by Lou Reed, which they liked okay. But they really enjoyed "Redemption Song." When I finished, Bub said, "Man, that's really Christian. It really is." Darius made me teach it to him; he said he would take it home and "do it at worship."

Then he jumped up and jogged to the electric piano, which was on a stand ten feet away. He closed his eyes and began to play. I know enough piano to know what good technique sounds like, and Darius played very, very well. He improvised for an hour. At one point, Bub went and stood beside him with his hands in his pockets, facing the rest of us, as if guarding his friend while the latter was in this vulnerable trance state. Ritter whispered to me that Darius had been offered a music scholarship to a college in West Virginia; he went to visit a friend, and a professor heard him messing around on the school's piano. The dude offered him a full ride then and there. Ritter couldn't really explain why Darius had turned it down. "He's kind of our Rain Man," Ritter said.

At some juncture, I must have taken up my lantern and crept back down the hill, since I sat up straight the next morning, fully dressed in the twenty-nine-footer. The sound that woke me was a barbaric moan, like that of an army about to charge. Early mornings at Creation were about "Praise and Worship," a new form of Christian rock in which the band and the audience sing, all together, as loud as they can, directly to God. It gets rather intense.

The guys had told me they meant to spend most of today at the main stage, checking out bands. But hey, fuck that. I'd already checked out a band. Mine was to stay in this trailer, jotting impressions.

It was hot, though. As it got hotter, the light brown carpet started to give off fumes from under its plastic hide. I tumbled out the side hatch and went after Darius, Ritter, and Bub.

In the light of day, one could see there were pretty accomplished freaks at this thing: a guy in a skirt wearing lace on his arms; a strange little androgynous creature dressed in full cardboard armor, carrying a sword. They knew they were in a safe place, I guess.

The guys left me standing in line at a lemonade booth; they didn't want to miss Skillet, one of Ritter's favorite bands. I got my drink and drifted slowly toward where I thought they'd be standing. Lack of food, my filthiness, impending sunstroke: These were ganging up on me. Plus the air down here smelled faintly of poo. There were a lot of blazing-hot portable toilets wafting miasma whenever the doors were opened.

I stood in the center of a gravel patch between the food and the crowd, sort of gumming the straw, quadriplegically probing with it for stubborn pockets of meltwater. I was a ways from the stage, but I could see well enough. Something started to happen to me. The guys in the band were middle-aged. They had blousy shirts and half-hearted arena-rock moves from the mid-'8òs.

What was . . . this feeling? The singer kept grinning between lines, like if he didn't, he might collapse. I could just make out the words:

> There's a higher place to go
> (beyond belief, beyond belief),
> Where we reach the next plateau,
> (beyond belief, beyond belief) . . .

The straw slipped from my mouth. "Oh, shit. It's Petra."

It was 1988. The guy who brought me in we called Verm (I'll use people's nicknames here; they don't deserve to be dragooned into my memory voyage). He was a short, good-looking guy with a dark pony-tail and a devilish laugh, a skater and an ex-pothead, which had got him kicked out of his house a year or so before we met. His folks belonged to this nondenominational church in Ohio, where I went to high school. It was a movement more than a church—thousands of members, even then. I hear it's bigger now. "Central meeting" took place in an empty warehouse, for reasons of space, but the smaller meetings were where it was at: home church (fifty people or so), cell group (maybe a dozen). Verm's dad said, Look, go with us once a week and you can move back in.

Verm got saved. And since he was brilliant (he became something of a legend at our school because whenever a new foreign student enrolled, he'd sit with her every day at lunch and make her give him language lessons till he was proficient), and since he was about the most artlessly gregarious human being I've ever known, and since he knew loads of lost souls from his druggie days, he became a champion evangelizer, a golden child.

I was new and nurturing a transcendent hatred of Ohio. Verm found out I liked the Smiths, and we started swapping tapes. Before long, we were hanging out after school. Then the moment came that always comes when you make friends with a born-again: "Listen, I go to this thing on Wednesday nights. It's like a Bible study — no, listen, it's cool. The people are actually really cool."

They were, that's the thing. In fifteen minutes, all my ideas about Christians were put to flight. They were smarter than any bunch I'd been exposed to (I didn't grow up in Cambridge or anything, but even so), they were accepting of every kind of weirdness, and they had that light that people who are pursuing something higher give off. It's attractive, to say the least. I started asking questions, lots of questions. And they loved that, because they had answers. That's one of the ways evangelicalism works. Your average agnostic doesn't go through life just primed to offer a clear, considered defense of, say, intratextual Scriptural inconsistency. But born-agains train for that chance encounter with the inquisitive stranger. And when you're a 14-year-old carting around some fairly undernourished intellectual ambitions, and a charismatic adult sits you down and explains that if you transpose this span of years onto the Hebrew calendar, and multiply that times seven, and plug in a date from the reign of King Howsomever, then you plainly see that this passage predicts the birth of Christ almost to the hour, despite the fact that the Gospel writers didn't have access to this information! I, for one, was dazzled.

But also powerfully stirred on a level that didn't depend on my naïveté. The sheer passionate engagement of it caught my imagination: Nobody had told me there were Christians like this. They went at the Bible with grad-seminar intensity, week after week. Mole was their leader (short for Moloch; he had started the whole thing, back in the '70s). He had a wiry, dark beard and a pair of nail-gun cobalt eyes. My Russian-novel fantasies of underground gatherings — shared subversive fervor — were flattered and, it seemed, embodied. Here was counterculture, without sad hippie trappings.

Verm embraced me when I said to him, in the hallway after a meeting, "I think I might believe." When it came time for me to go all the way — to "accept Jesus into my heart" (in that time-honored formulation) — we prayed the prayer together.

Three years passed. I waxed strong in spirit. Verm and I were sort of heading up the high school end of the operation now. Mole had discovered (I had discovered, too) that I was good with words, that I could talk in front of people; Verm and I started leading Bible study once a month. We were saving souls like mad, laying up treasure for ourselves in heaven. I was never the recruiter he was, but I grasped subtlety; Verm would get them there, and together we'd start on their heads. Witnessing, it's called. I had made some progress socially at school, which gave us access to the popular crowd; in this way, many were brought to the Lord. Verm and I went to conferences and on "study retreats"; we started taking classes in theology, which the group offered — free of charge — for promising young leaders. And always, underneath but suffusing it all, there were the cell-group meetings, every week, on Friday or Saturday nights, which meant I could stay out till morning. (My Episcopalian parents were thoroughly mortified by the whole business, but it's not easy telling your kid to stop spending so much time at church.)

Cell group was typically held in somebody's dining room, somebody pretty high up in the group. You have to understand what an
honor it was to be in a cell with Mole. People would see me at Central Meeting and be like, "How is that, getting to rap with him every
week?" It was awesome. He really got down with the Word (he had
a wonderful old hippie way of talking; everything was something
action: "time for some fellowship action . . . let's get some chips 'n'
salsa action"). He carried a heavy "study Bible"—no King James for
the nondenominationals; too many inaccuracies. When he cracked
open its hand-tooled leather cover, you knew it was on. And no joke:
The brother was gifted. Even handicapped by the relatively pedes-
trian style of the New American Standard version, he could twist a
verse into your conscience like a bone screw, make you think Christ
was standing there nodding approval. The prayer session alone would
last an hour. Afterward, there was always a fire in the backyard. Mole
would sit and whack a machete into a chopping block. He smoked
cheap cigars; he let us smoke cigarettes. The guitar went around. We'd
talk about which brother was struggling with sin—did he need coun-
sel? Or about the end of the world: It'd be soon. We had to save as
many as we could.

I won't inflict on you all my reasons for drawing away from the
fold. They were clichéd, anyway, and not altogether innocent. Enough
to say I started reading books Mole hadn't recommended. Some of
them seemed pretty smart—and didn't jibe with the Bible. The defensive theodicy he'd drilled into me during those nights of heady
exegesis developed cracks. The hell stuff: I never made peace with it.
Human beings were capable of forgiving those who'd done them terrible wrongs, and we all agreed that human beings were maggots compared with God, so what was His trouble, again? I looked around and
saw people who'd never have a chance to come to Jesus; they were too
badly crippled. Didn't they deserve—more than the rest of us, even—
to find His succor, after this life?

Everything about Christianity can be justified *within the context of Christian belief.* That is, if you accept its terms. Once you do, your belief starts modifying the data (in ways that are themselves defensible), until eventually the data begin to reinforce belief. The precise moment of illogic is hard to isolate and may not exist. Like holding a magnifying glass at arm's length and bringing it toward your eye: Things are upside down, they're upside down, they're right side up. What lay between? If there was something, it passed too quickly to be observed. This is why you can never reason true Christians out of the faith. It's not, as the adage has it, because they were never reasoned into it—many were—it's that faith is a logical door which locks behind you. What looks like a line of thought is steadily warping into a circle, one that closes with you inside. If this seems to imply that no apostate was ever a true Christian and that therefore, I was never one, I think I'd stand by both of those statements. Doesn't the fact that I can't write about my old friends without an apologetic tone just show that I never deserved to be one of them?

The break came during the winter of my junior year. I got a call from Verm late one afternoon. He'd promised Mole he would do this thing, and now he felt sick. Sinus infection (he always had sinus infections). Had I ever heard of Petra? Well, they're a Christian-rock band, and they're playing the arena downtown. After their shows, the singer invites anybody who wants to know more about Jesus to come backstage, and they have people, like, waiting to talk to them.

The promoter had called up Mole, and Mole had volunteered Verm, and now Verm wanted to know if I'd help him out. I couldn't say no.

The concert was upsetting from the start; it was one of my first encounters with the other kinds of evangelicals, the hand-wavers and the weepers and all (we liked to keep things "sober" in the group). The girl in front of me was signing all the words to the songs, but she wasn't deaf. It was just horrifying.

Verm had read me, over the phone, the pamphlet he got. After the first encore, we were to head for the witnessing zone and wait there. I went. I sat on the ground.

Soon they came filing in, the seekers. I don't know what was up with the ones I got. I think they may have gone looking for the restroom and been swept up by the stampede. They were about my age and wearing hooded brown sweatshirts—mouths agape, eyes empty. I asked them the questions: What did they think about all they'd heard? Were they curious about anything Petra talked about? (There'd been lots of "talks" between songs.)

I couldn't get them to speak. They stared at me like they were waiting for me to slap them.

This was my opening. They were either rapt or mentally damaged in some way, and whichever it was, Christ called on me to lay down my testimony.

The sentences wouldn't form. I flipped though the list of dogmas, searching for one I didn't essentially think was crap, and came up with nothing.

There could have ensued a nauseating silence, but I acted with an odd decisiveness to end the whole experience. I asked them if they wanted to leave—it was an all but rhetorical question—and said I did, too. We walked out together.

I took Mole and Verm aside a few nights later and told them my doubts had overtaken me. If I kept showing up at meetings, I'd be faking it. That was an insult to them, to God, to the group. Verm was silent; he hugged me. Mole said he respected my reasons, that I'd have to explore my doubts before my walk could be strong again. He said he'd pray for me. Unless he's undergone some radical change in character, he's still praying.

Statistically speaking, my bout with evangelicalism was probably unremarkable. For white Americans with my socioeconomic background (middle to upper-middle class), it's an experience commonly linked to one's teens and moved beyond before one reaches 20. These kids around me at Creation—a lot of them were like that. How many even knew who Darwin was? They'd learn. At least once a year since college, I'll be getting to know someone, and it comes out that we have in common a high school "Jesus phase." That's always an excellent laugh. Except a phase is supposed to end—or at least give way to other phases—not simply expand into a long preoccupation.

Bless those who've been brainwashed by cults and sent off for deprogramming. That makes it simple: You put it behind you. This group was no cult. They persuaded; they never pressured. Nor did they punish. A guy I brought into the group—we called him Goog—is still a close friend. He leads meetings now and spends part of each year doing pro bono dental work in Cambodia. He's never asked me when I'm coming back.

My problem is not that I dream I'm in hell or that Mole is at the window. It isn't that I feel psychologically harmed. It isn't even that I feel like a sucker for having bought it all. It's that I love Jesus Christ.

"The latchet of whose shoes I am not worthy to unloose." I can barely write that. He was the most beautiful dude. Forget the Epistles, forget all the bullying stuff that came later. Look at what He said. Read The Jefferson Bible. Or better yet, read *The Logia of Yeshua*, by Guy Davenport and Benjamin Urrutia, an unadorned translation of all the sayings ascribed to Jesus that modern scholars deem authentic. There's your man. His breakthrough was the aestheticization of weakness. Not in what conquers, not in glory, but in what's fragile and what suffers— there lies sanity. And salvation. "Let anyone who has power renounce it," he said. "Your father is compassionate to all, as you should be." That's how He talked, to those who knew Him.

Why should He vex a person? Why is His ghost not friendlier? Why can't I just be a good Enlightenment child and see in His life a sustaining example of what we can be, as a species?

Because once you've known Him as a god, it's hard to find comfort in the man. The sheer sensation of life that comes with a total, all-pervading notion of being — the pulse of consequence one projects onto even the humblest things — the pull of that won't slacken.

And one has doubts about one's doubts.

"D'ye hear that mountain lion last night?"

It was dark, and Jake was standing over me, dressed in camouflage. I'd been hunched over on a cooler by the ashes for a number of hours, waiting on the guys to get back from wherever they'd gone. I told him I hadn't heard anything.

Bub came up from behind, also in camo. "In the middle of the night," he said. "It woke me up."

Jake said, "It sounded like a baby crying."

"Like a little-bitty baby," Bub said.

Jake was messing with something at my feet, in the shadows, something that looked alive. Bub dropped a few logs onto the fire and went to the Chevy for matches.

I sat there trying to see what Jake was doing. "You got that lantern?" he said. It was by my feet; I switched it on.

He started pulling frogs out of a poke. One after another. They strained in his grip and lashed at the air. "Where'd you get those?" I asked.

"About half a mile that way," he said. "It ain't private property if you're in the middle of the creek." Bub laughed his high expressionless laugh.

"These ain't too big," Jake said. "In West Virginia, well, we got ones the size of chickens."

Jake started chopping their bodies in half. He'd lean forward and center his weight on the hand that held the knife, to get a clean cut, tossing the legs into a frying pan. Then he'd stab each frog in the brain and flip the upper parts into a separate pile. They kept twitching, of course — their nerves. Some were a little less dead than that. One in particular stared up at me, gulping for air, though his lungs were beside him, in the grass.

"Could you do that one in the brain again?" I said. Jake spiked it, expertly, and grabbed for the next frog.

"Why don't you stab their brains before you take off the legs?" I asked. He laughed. He said I cracked him up.

Darius, when he got back, made me a cup of hot sassafras tea. "Drink this, it'll make you feel better," he told me. I'd never said I felt bad. Jake lightly sautéed the legs in butter and served them to me warm. "Eat this," he said. The meat was so tender, it all but dissolved on my tongue.

Pee Wee came back with the Jews, who were forced to tell us a second time that we were damned. (Leviticus 11:12, "Whatsoever hath no fins nor scales in the waters, that shall be an abomination unto you.")

Jake, when he heard this, put on a show, making the demi-frogs talk like puppets, chewing the legs with his mouth wide open so all could see the meat.

The girls ran off again. Pee Wee went after them, calling, "Come on, they're just playin'!"

Darius peered at Jake. He looked not angry but saddened. Jake said, "Well, if he wants to bring them girls around here, they oughtn't to be telling us what we can eat."

"Wherefore, if meat make my brother to offend," Darius said, "I will eat no flesh while the world standeth."

"First Corinthians," I said.

"8:13," Darius said.

I woke without having slept — that evil feeling — and lay there steeling myself for the strains of Praise and Worship. When it became too much to wait, I boiled water and made instant coffee and drank it scalding from the lid of the peanut butter jar. My body smelled like stale campfire. My hair had leaves and ash and things in it. I thought about taking a shower, but I'd made it two days without so much as acknowledging any of the twenty-nine-footer's systems; it would have been stupid to give in now.

I sat in the driver's seat and watched, through tinted glass, little clusters of Christians pass. They looked like people anywhere, only gladder, more self-contained. Or maybe they just looked like people anywhere. I don't know. I had no pseudo-anthropological moxie left. I got out and wandered. I sat with the crowd in front of the stage. There was a redheaded Christian speaker up there, pacing back and forth. Out of nowhere, he shrieked, "MAY YOU BE COVERED IN THE ASHES OF YOUR RABBI JESUS!" If I were to try to convey to you how loudly he shrieked this, you'd think I was playing wordy games.

I was staggering through the food stands when a man died at my feet. He was standing in front of the funnel-cake window. He was big, in his early sixties, wearing shorts and a short-sleeve button-down shirt. He just . . . died. Massive heart attack. I was standing there, and he fell, and I don't know whether there's some primitive zone in the brain that registers these things, but the second he landed, I knew he was gone. The paramedics jumped on him so fast, it was weird — it was like they'd been waiting. They pumped and pumped on his chest, blew into his mouth, ran IVs. The ambulance showed up, and more equipment appeared. The man's broad face had that slightly disgruntled look you see on the newly dead.

Others had gathered around; some thought it was all a show. A woman standing next to me said bitterly, "It's not a show. A man has died." She started crying. She took my hand. She was small with silver hair and black eyebrows. "He's fine, he's fine," she said. I looked at the side of her face. "Just pray for his family," she said. "He's fine."

I went back to the trailer and had, as the ladies say where I'm from, a colossal fucking go-to-pieces. I kept starting to cry and then stopping myself, for some reason. I felt nonsensically raw and lonely. What a dickhead I'd been, thinking the trip would be a lark. There were too many ghosts here. Everyone seemed so strange and so familiar.

Plus I suppose I was starving. The frog meat was superb but meager —
even Jake had said as much.

In the midst of all this, I began to hear, through the shell of
the twenty-nine-footer, Stephen Baldwin giving a talk on the Fringe
Stage — that's where the "edgier" acts are put on at Creation. If you're
shaky on your Baldwin brothers, he's the vaguely troglodytic one who
used to comb his bangs straight down and wear dusters. He's come
to the Lord — I don't know if you knew. I caught him on cable a few
months ago, some religious talk show. Him and Gary Busey. I don't remember what Baldwin said, because Busey was saying shit so weird the
host got nervous. Busey's into "generational curses." If you're wondering what those are, apologies. I was born-again, not raised on meth.

Baldwin said many things; the things he said got stranger and
stranger. He said his Brazilian nanny, Augusta, had converted him and
his wife in Tucson, thereby fulfilling a prophecy she'd been given by
her preacher back home. He said, "God allowed 9/11 to happen," that it
was "the wrath of God," and that Jesus had told him to share this with
us. He also said the Devil did 9/11. He said God wanted him "to make
gnarly cool Christian movies." He said that in November we should
vote for "the man who has the greatest faith." The crowd lost it; the
trailer all but shook.

When Jake and Bub beat on the door, I'd been in there for hours,
rereading *The Silenced Times* and the festival program. In the program, it said the candle-lighting ceremony was tonight. The guys had
told me about it — it was one of the coolest things about Creation.
Everyone gathered in front of the stage, and the staff handed out a
candle to every single person there. The media handlers said there was
a lookout you could hike to, on the mountain above the stage. That was
the way to see it, they said.

When I opened the door, Jake was waving a newspaper. Bub
stood behind him, smiling big. "Look at this," Jake said. It was
Wednesday's copy of *The Valley Log*, serving Southern Huntingdon
County — "It is just a rumor until you've read it in *The Valley Log*."

The headline for the week read MOUNTAIN LION NOT BELIEVED TO BE THREAT TO CREATION FESTIVAL CAMPERS.

"Wha'd we tell you?" Bub said.

"At least it's not a threat," I said.

"Well, not to us it ain't," Jake said.

I climbed to their campsite with them in silence. Darius was sitting on a cooler, chin in hands, scanning the horizon. He seemed meditative. Josh and Ritter were playing songs. Pee Wee was listening, by himself; he'd blown it with the Jewish girls.

"Hey, Darius," I said. He got up. "It's fixin' to shower here in about ten minutes," he said. I went and stood beside him, tried to look where he was looking.

"You want to know how I know?" he said.

He explained it to me, the wind, the face of the sky, how the leaves on the tops of the sycamores would curl and go white when they felt the rain coming, how the light would turn a certain "dead" color. He read the landscape to me like a children's book. "See over there," he said, "how that valley's all misty? It hasn't poured there yet. But the one in back is clear   that means it's coming our way."

Minutes later, it started to rain, big, soaking, percussive drops. The guys started to scramble. I suggested we all get into the trailer. They looked at each other, like maybe it was a sketchy idea. Then Ritter hollered, "Get 'er done!" We all ran down the hillside, holding guitars and — in Josh's case — a skillet wherein the fried meat of a still-unidentified woodland creature lay ready to eat.

There was room for everyone. I set my lantern on the dining table. We slid back the panes in the windows to let the air in. Darius did card tricks. We drank spring water. Somebody farted; the conversation about who it had been (Pee Wee) lasted a good twenty minutes. The rain on the roof made a solid drumming. The guys were impressed with my place. They said I should fence it. With the money I'd get, I could buy a nice house in Braxton County.

We played guitars. The RV rocked back and forth. Jake wasn't into Christian rock, but as a good Baptist he loved old gospel tunes, and he called for a few, God love him. Ritter sang one that killed me. Also, I don't know what changed, but the guys were up for secular stuff. It turned out that Pee Wee really loved Neil Young; I mean, he'd never heard Neil Young before, but when I played "Powderfinger" for him, he sort of curled up like a kid, then made me play it again when I was done. He said I had a pretty voice.

We all told each other how good the other ones were, how everybody else should really think about a career in music. Josh played "Stairway to Heaven," and we got loud, singing along. Darius said, "Keep it down, man! We don't need everybody thinking this is the sin wagon."

The rain stopped. It was time to go. Two of the guys planned to leave in the morning, and I needed to start walking if I meant to make the overlook in time for the candlelighting. They went with me as far as the place where the main path split off toward the stage. They each embraced me. Jake said to call them if I ever had "a situation that needs clearing up." Darius said God bless me, with meaning eyes. Then he said, "Hey, man, if you write about us, can I just ask one thing?"

"Of course," I said.

"Put in there that we love God," he said. "You can say we're crazy, but say that we love God."

The climb was long and steep. At the top was a thing that looked like a backyard deck. It jutted out over the valley, commanding an unobstructed view. Kids hung all over it like lemurs or something.

I pardoned my way to the edge, where the cliff dropped away. It was dark and then suddenly darker—pitch. They had shut off the lights at the sides of the stage. Little pinpricks appeared, moving along the aisles. We used to do candles like this at church, when I was a kid, on Christmas Eve. You light the edges, and the edges spread inward. The rate of the spread increases exponentially, and the effect is so unexpected, when, at the end, you have half the group lighting the other half's candles, it always seems like somebody flipped a switch. That's how it seemed now.

The clouds had moved off—the bright stars were out again. There were fireflies in the trees all over, and spread before me, far below, was a carpet of burning candles, tiny flames, many ten thousands. I was suspended in a black sphere full of flickering light.

Sure I thought about Nuremberg. But mostly I thought of Darius, Jake, Josh, Bub, Ritter, and Pee Wee, whom I doubted I'd ever see again, whom I'd come to love, and who loved God—for it's true, I would have said it even if Darius hadn't asked me to, it may be the truest thing I will have written here: They were crazy, and they loved God—and I thought about the unimpeachable dignity of that love, which I never was capable of. Because knowing it isn't true doesn't mean you would be strong enough to believe if it were. Six of those glowing specks in the valley were theirs.

I was shown, in a moment of time, the ring of their faces around the fire, each one separate, each one radiant with what Paul called, strangely, "assurance of hope." It seemed wrong of reality not to reward such souls.

These are lines from a Czeslaw Milosz poem:

And if they all, kneeling with poised palms,
millions, billions of them, ended together with their
    illusion?
I shall never agree. I will give them the crown.
The human mind is splendid; lips powerful, and the
summons so great it must open Paradise.

If one could only say it and mean it.

They all blew out their candles at the same instant, and the valley—the actual geographical feature—filled with smoke, there were so many.

I left at dawn, while creation slept.

2006

This story is about religion and the way we talk about it, and it's also about events that defy documentation, and it's called "The Aftermath." So you don't really have to ask why it's here, at the (almost) end. The author, Matthew Teague, writes for magazines, including *Philadelphia*, where "The Aftermath" appeared, among luxury gift guides, in December 2006.

MATTHEW TEAGUE
The Aftermath

A woman walked through the valley, toward the funerals. She wore black. The field was harvested and empty, and she moved across it slow and straight, like an earthbound raven.

In the pale landscape, only she moved. She and a piece of caution tape, caught in the wind. Yellow. A color so familiar by now that it worked against its nature. Instead of warning the curious, it drew them in, promising that *Yes, it happened here*. Flickering in the wind. *Right here*.

Jack from Boston grinned. He flashed a little camera in his pocket. "How close can we get?" he asked. Jack from Boston was new.

We stood in a little patch of gravel, looking at our feet. I said, "I think it's up to you."

Jack had arrived moments ago, and introduced himself as a freelance writer and sociologist. From Boston. He had a theory. We stood together another moment, then without talking he trotted toward the yellow tape, crunching in the gravel.

A few days ago, television satellite trucks, scores of them, had populated this gravel patch at an intersection of two quiet roads out-

side Paradise. The television people had moved on, but a few strag-
glers remained in the area. A few journalists, many tourists of a peculiar sort, and one sociologist.

Jack hovered near the caution tape, snapped a picture, moved
a little closer, and thought better of it. He hurried back to the gravel.

"How did it go?"

"Good," he said. He seemed a little out of breath. "It was good."

He pulled a book from the trunk of his car. "My book," he said.
It was called *The Genocidal Mind*, by Jack from Boston. He flipped it
open to a section about chaos theory. "I'm here looking for this," he
said.

Chaos theory proposes order within apparent disorder. "The
crime here seems random," Jack said, "but there are patterns within it.
Things to find. Things to learn."

Behind Jack, the gravel announced the arrival of an enormous
and ancient American-made car, so long and heavy that it heaved on
the gravel like a ship on waves. It stopped a few feet away, idling. A
young man sat in the passenger seat and looked at us. He had the full
beard and smooth upper lip of a married Amish man. He gave a soft
smile, like a teacher to pupils. Then he lifted an enormous camera, an
antique Polaroid dug from some forgotten trunk in the back of a barn.
It held a massive flash unit.

Pop.

The car lurched and pulled away, leaving a wake of gravel. An
Amish drive-by. Jack grinned, still holding his book about patterns in
chaos.

The woman in black had moved on from the valley, and joined
the rest of her funeral party. Others came behind her, with bowed
heads and a measured gait. In the background, the Amish schoolhouse
stood perfect and serene. So familiar by now that it worked against its
nature: Instead of imparting knowledge, it offered only mystery.

✳

There's an old Amish saying about death. When the old and infirm pass away, survivors take comfort because they've passed "through the strait gate," into the New Jerusalem.

There's a second Amish saying about death. Not for the old or infirm, but for the martyrs: They pressed with such force through the strait gate, they left their flesh on the posts.

Death holds no secret from the Anabaptist people, and poses no questions. Their entire faith springs from physical destruction, beginning with persecution and slaughter for re-baptizing former members of the Roman Church. They assembled their stories in a book called *The Martyrs Mirror*, first published in 1660. The Amish still read it in their homes, alongside the Bible and the hymnbook. The full title is *The Bloody Theater or Martyrs Mirror of the Defenseless Christians Who Baptized Only Upon Confession of Faith, and Who Suffered and Died for the Testimony of Jesus, their Saviour, From the Time of Christ to the year AD 1660.*

They were "defenseless" because they clung to the Anabaptist belief of nonresistance to violence. Not just pacifism, but nonresistance altogether. Pacifism stands aside, cool and objective, and watches the world dash itself to pieces. Nonresistance means something more. It adds a layer of duty, and compassion.

An Anabaptist man named Dirk Willems, for instance, remains one of their most revered martyrs. He's the closest thing to an Amish hero. In the winter of 1569, Spanish inquisitors captured him outside a small Dutch village. They locked him in a palace used as a makeshift prison, and he lowered himself from a window with a rope of rags. He fled over the frozen landscape, pursued by palace guards, and when he came to a pond, he slid across a thin layer of ice. Then behind him he heard a splash and the cry of a palace guard, who had fallen through. Dirk Willems turned back and rescued the guard, who then arrested him and took him back to the palace.

According to *The Martyrs Mirror*, a strong east wind blew on the day Dirk Willems died, so that "the kindled fire was much driven away from the upper part of his body, as he stood at the stake; in consequence of which this good man suffered a lingering death."

The residents of the nearby Dutch village marveled, horrified. How on earth could anyone turn back to the aid of his persecutor?

Charlie Roberts drove a milk truck.

That's about it. People have said since then that they didn't notice anything dangerous about him in those final days. Didn't notice anything too odd, or strange. But then, they never really noticed him at all.

There's a certain distance between people, in this part of Lancaster County. The Amish and non-Amish live near each other, but not intertwined. So there's a formality, a clarity about one's role in society. You can see it in the space between houses, how they're not scattered across the countryside — that's not community — but they're not built close, either.

I understood this slowly, after becoming friends with an Amish man named Sam Fisher. He owns the Nickel Mines auction house, which sits just down the road from Charlie Roberts's house, and within sight of the Amish school. Sam is a warm, engaging man with an unexpected and wicked sense of humor; he never hesitated to make a joke about the nearby town of Intercourse. But I visited him many times at the auction house, where during the week he works alone, and each time he rose to greet me with, "Hello. Can I help you?"

"Hi Sam," I'd say. "It's just me."

But Sam knew his role, and mine. He was the auctioneer. I was the potential customer. And each meeting felt like the first, until conversation relaxed him, the roles eased, and he remembered this funny story or that dirty one.

I asked him one day if he knew Charlie Roberts from down the road.

"Oh, no," he said.

The milk-truck driver's role is this: In the middle of the night he enters a farm and pulls his truck near a barn or outbuilding. Amish farmers, having milked their cows during the day, keep the milk in tanks. The milk-truck driver empties them, records the amount in each, then drives away again. Sometimes at dawn he might see the farmer, or his children, standing against the new sun. A hand to shade the eyes, and a hand to say hello.

In a land where people stand some distance apart, Charlie Roberts slipped easily through the spaces between. He looked unremarkable. Medium height and build. Hair the color of the hay jutting from a thousand horses' mouths. His interests seemed simple. One day this autumn, for instance, he walked into the Valley Hardware store and bought two plain packages of plastic zip ties.

A few days later, on the morning of October 2nd, he walked his children to the school bus. He wore a baseball cap. As his children climbed aboard the bus, Roberts's wife, Marie, called out, "Hey kids, come back here, Dad wants to give you a hug."

The children stepped back down, and Roberts hugged and kissed them. He said, "Remember, Daddy loves you."

He had a plan by then, and weapons, and implements of evil. And no one saw it coming. They only knew Charlie Roberts drove a milk truck.

John Bachman made a little steeple with his forefingers and pressed them to his lips, trying to remember Charlie Roberts. Something. Anything.

"He and Marie called," Bachman said. "They needed help."

Bachman sat in a high-backed chair in the parlor of Bachman Funeral Home, an ancient brick home in the village of Strasburg. His family were Anabaptist immigrants who landed in Lancaster County long ago, and they have buried their neighbors for generations.

He remembered something. "It was 1997," he said. The Robertses had lost their baby, who lived just 20 minutes after her birth. They needed help arranging her burial.

Did he remember Charlie Roberts at all?

"No, not really," he said finally. "It was a hard time for them. They just seemed like a confused couple."

Somewhere along the way, the Bachman family drifted from the Anabaptist sect, but that mattered little. They were people of Lancaster. There are some people who don't fit in, John Bachman said. A family could live in the place for a lifetime and never be of it, so to speak.

Bachman fell silent. In the bookcase behind his chair, he still keeps an old and worn copy of *The Martyrs Mirror*.

The Amish own no church buildings. They meet in each other's homes, moving from pasture to pasture, never allowing pride to take root in the form of pillars, or façades, or elaborate crucifixes. So in Amish culture, the closest thing to a holy place, an altar, is the schoolhouse.

The building is almost supernatural in its austerity: architecture made perfect through practicality. One room. A door to enter and leave, windows for light. Wooden desks for sitting, and books. Within, children learn lessons up to an eighth-grade level, with little emphasis on science. Then they take jobs on the family farm, or in the community.

To outsiders, the Amish way seems backward: no electricity, the horse and buggy, plain clothing, no ornamentation and little formal education. But all their decisions revolve around community. A thing's effect on the community — to bring it together or pull it apart — determines whether the Amish accept or reject it. They believe that if a man spends half the night watching television, then fails to milk his cows in the morning, the community at large suffers. So they reject it. But that same man, in the half-light of dawn, might milk his cows better in the glow of a gas-powered lantern. So they accept it.

The needs of each individual are subsumed by the needs of the community. So the one-room schoolhouse serves as a preservation hall, where each generation hands down its values to the next. A sanctuary for community.

Charlie Roberts arrived at the schoolhouse door at mid-morning. Charlie the milk-truck driver. The man who had never caused suspicion, or even notice, and who still carried the warmth of his children's kisses at the top of his memory. He also carried zip ties, guns, ammunition, lubricant, a stun gun, and lumber to bar the door.

He approached one captive with a pistol in his hand. The Amish hunt frequently, and many men own rifles, but handguns are unfamiliar.

Roberts held it out to her. *Do you know what this is?*

She searched her mind for an answer. She said, *It is a horseshoe.*

Sam Fisher, the Amish auctioneer, was helping a friend repair a building that morning. The building had a phone, which is rare but not unheard-of among the Amish, and Sam heard it ring.

He answered it, listened a moment, then called out to his friends upstairs. "You should come down here," he said.

"We're almost finished," one called back.

"No," he said. "Come down."

Word spread that way across the entire community. A mysterious act, people said. Something horrible. Messengers ran across fields and delivered the breathless news: The milk-truck driver took over the school. He ordered the boys and teachers out, and kept the girls. He shot them.

How many? Still unclear.

Did anyone die? No one knew.

Across Lancaster County, the Amish withdrew into their community. They gathered in homes and businesses, and on the grass outside the school. They waited for some word of life or death, watching while helicopters touched down and took off again, collecting the girls like some terrible harvest machine. Television cameramen arrived and captured them in video footage that looked like still photography: people standing with hands in pockets, staring into the middle distance.

Details trickled out. Thirty-two-year-old Charlie Roberts had apparently planned to molest the 10 little Amish girls, but when police arrived he went ahead and shot them all, and then himself. Police had bashed their way into the building and found a scene of such horror that men's lives changed just from the sight. One officer had picked up a little girl and run outside with her, hoping for medical salvation, but she died in his arms. Word came that four of the girls had died. Then five. The other five suffered wounds of varying severity. Word came.

The media flattened the earth with enormous satellite trucks. The reporters and photographers moved together from this place to that, from the school to Roberts's house, to the restaurants and hotels, then back to the school, always together. The television crewmen started calling themselves "the Herd."

Sam Fisher arrived at his auction house to find it commandeered as a makeshift information headquarters. Officials and police made announcements at Sam's podium like auctioneers, rattling off life and death instead of quilts and chairs. Outside, the Herd gathered on the gravel patch. In a land where night comes down like a dark blanket, generators hummed, lights crashed onto pastureland, and reporters in makeup stood with microphones, speaking into thin air.

Amish buggies typically travel on the edge of the road, and in much of Lancaster County there is so little other traffic that the roads wear in a lopsided way. But in the days after the school shooting, the little winding byways looked like rush-hour Philadelphia. Trucks and vans and police cars and others jostled for position with horse-drawn buggies.

The out-of-town reporters seemed exceedingly polite, most people agreed. But there were so many. The attention bewildered the

Amish. Mail came from New York, from Germany. It came from the world, one piece from Australia simply addressed to "Amish Families USA."

People yearned for something the Amish appeared to embody, although no one seemed able to articulate it. Something about the chaos of our world intruding on their ordered world, a wicked hand reaching in to crush a pure heart. There must be some greater significance, a pattern in the chaos, as Jack the sociologist said. There must be some understanding. A lesson.

An act of such horror must surely have meaning.

John Bachman, the funeral director, received two calls. He expected the first one, from Marie Roberts. She wanted him to help bury her husband, the milk-truck driver.

He met with her, and saw a certain look in her face. She looked hollow. "After doing this job for so many years, you just know the look," he said. "You see it a lot when someone loses a child, for instance. I can walk into a room full of people grieving for a child, and without a word I can pick out which couple are the parents. There's just a look. Marie had that look."

Then Bachman received the second, less expected call. An Amish bishop had a request of his own. The victims' families hoped to attend Charlie Roberts's funeral. Bachman understood why. "They needed to forgive Marie at the first opportunity," he said. "It's their way."

Meanwhile, the world's thinkers searched for a larger importance to graft onto what had happened in Lancaster County. They struggled to explain the inexplicable, in the face of Charlie Roberts's apparent mental breakdown. "The horrific school shooting in the Amish community on Oct. 2 underscored the dangers that lurk in our educational institutions across the country," someone wrote in the *Seattle Post-Intelligencer*.

A writer for *U.S. News* magazine took a colder, more political

path. "In the horrific murder of the Amish schoolchildren in Pennsylvania, the crazed killer had an arsenal of guns and was prepared
for a siege," he wrote. "However, limiting guns is a taboo subject in
the White House and Congress. We certainly don't want to offend the
NRA."

And so forth.

A strange new tourism sprang up from all the coverage. Cars
and minivans from around the country suddenly appeared, looking for
the schoolhouse. They came from New York, Ohio, Colorado and further afield. Eventually, in the privacy of darkness, the Amish knocked
down the schoolhouse and replaced it with empty soil. But for now,
people came, seeking something they couldn't quite name. So many
came that police installed themselves in front of the school, where they
waved people along: Keep moving, nothing to see.

A burgundy Chevrolet van pulled to the side of the road one day,
and the driver stuck his head outside the window. He was Otis, who
had driven from Tennessee, and he had a couple of questions. "Are you
local?" he asked. "Can you tell me where the school is?"

Another middle-aged man in the passenger's seat gave a little
wave, and in the back I saw two older ladies craning their necks to see.
"This is my brother," Otis explained. "My mother. My aunt."

I pointed toward the school and asked why they felt compelled
to come see it. One of the ladies said, "We just want to know why."
Otis fumbled for his answer. After a while, his brother dug out his
wallet and flipped it open to show a Tennessee state trooper's identification. He offered it as an explanation, and said, "I guess that tells you
something right there." But after a moment he shook his head and replaced the wallet in his pocket.

The big Chevy van pulled away, and dropped down into the
shallow valley. When they reached the school they slowed almost to a
stop, until the policeman waved them along. They crested the next hill,
pulled into someone's driveway, and turned around for a second slow

pass. Maybe these tourists, like the television reporters, the thinkers and everyone else, hoped the schoolhouse might serve its old purpose one last time.

We hoped that if we listened hard enough, we might hear a whisper: *This is your lesson for today. This is who, and where, and why. You'll stay safe, if you can only understand.*

On a cool Saturday, Charlie Roberts's friends and family gathered under a green tent in a church cemetery. Amish men and women, scores of them, stood together outside the tent. Most of them had never attended such an event, and they stood apart, as always. Then, slowly, they moved together under the tent and joined the service. They mourned a man who had persecuted them for nonresistance, by killing their children.

It was awkward at first. The Amish didn't know where to stand, or where to cast their eyes. But then a sense of order descended on them, and they formed a silent line. John Bachman, the funeral director, recognized the dead girls' parents because they shared Marie Roberts's hollow-eyed expression. One by one they walked past her and reached to her, touched her, embraced her. They whispered to her.

Bachman, who has spent a lifetime under such tents, said, "I knew I was witnessing a miracle."

The Amish flabbergasted the world with their forgiveness. Their strange and unfamiliar forgiveness. How could they come out with it so soon, before they had even buried all the bodies of their children?

The Amish had no choice, in their minds. No more than old Dirk Willems had, when he turned back on that frozen pond so long ago. They are practical people, and theirs is a practical forgiveness. To outsiders, forgiveness implies a certain emotional resolution. But to the Amish it is a matter of nonresistance, and scriptural duty. Not resolution.

"We say we forgive them," an Amish woman explained to me.

She was a young woman, closely related to more than one of the children shot at the school. "And we do forgive. But the emotional part carries on."

"There is no way we can live up to what the people are saying about us," Sam, the auctioneer, said. He smoked cigarettes. He wasn't proud of it, but the strain and grief overwhelmed him, and he smoked. "We are not perfect. Some of us are bad." He thought a moment, and took a sorrowful drag on his cigarette. "I'm bad," he said.

The television news crews would soon disappear. The world's attention span is short, and we expect life's hardest questions to be answered on the evening news, if not sooner. We have become meaning-seekers, forever imposing pattern and significance on events we don't immediately understand.

The Amish, in contrast, have attention spans that reach centuries into the past, and infinitely into the future. On that October morning, God reached into their schoolhouse and enacted a mystery they may never understand, in this world. This eternal view gives them a sense of acceptance that puzzles the rest of us, and draws us to them.

After the Amish delivered their forgiveness to Marie, the widow of a milk-truck driver, they left the cemetery tent. They walked back across the fields in the direct Amish way, all dressed in black, looking down and walking with deliberate steps. A flock of earthbound ravens.

There remained only what happened. An event with no meaning. An event with no more or less importance than the passing away of five little girls: Naomi, Marian, Anna Mae, Lena and Mary Liz, aged seven to 13. They pressed with such force through the strait gate, they left their flesh on the posts.

2011

I couldn't bring myself to end a book that begins with Walt Whitman at the martyrdom of five little girls. So let us have "attention spans that reach centuries into the past," as Matthew Teague writes, and return to the beginning with this single, casual paragraph from the novelist and essayist Francine Prose, writing on her response to a political — and cultural, and, for some, religious — movement in the fall of 2011. The particulars — one's views on the regulation of finance or the electoral process or the place of protest — are not so important here as the moment evoked by Prose, and the last words, once a poem, here an American liturgy.

FRANCINE PROSE
Untitled

As far as I can understand it myself, here's why I burst into tears at the Occupy Wall Street camp. I was moved, first of all, by what everyone notices first: the variety of people involved, the range of ages, races, classes, colors, cultures. In other words, the 99 percent. I saw conversations taking place between people and groups of people whom I've never seen talking with such openness and sympathy in all the years (which is to say, my entire life) I've spent in New York: grannies talking to goths, a biker with piercings and tattoos talking to a woman in a Hermes scarf. I was struck by how well organized everything was, and, despite the charge of "vagueness" one keeps reading in the mainstream media, by the clarity—clarity of purpose, clarity of intention, clarity of method, clarity of understanding of the most basic social and economic realities. I kept thinking about how, since this movement started, I've been waking up in the morning without the dread (or at least without the total dread) with which I've woken every morning for so long, the vertiginous sense that we're all falling off a cliff and no one (or almost no one) is saying anything about it. In Zuccotti Park I felt a kind of lightening of a weight, a lessening of the awful isolation

and powerlessness of knowing we're being lied to and robbed on a
daily basis and that everyone knows it and keeps quiet and endures it;
the terror of thinking that my own grandchildren will suffer for whatever has been paralyzing us until just now. I kept feeling these intense
surges of emotion — until I saw a placard with a quote from Walt Whitman's "Song of Myself": "I am large, I contain multitudes." And that
was when I just lost it and stood there and wept.

NOTES

INTRODUCTION

1. I'm indebted for my reading of Moore to Jeff Allred, *American Modernism and Depression Documentary* (New York: Oxford University Press, 2009), 13–14. I've taken this passage of "On Poetry" from the version in Alfred Kreymborg, ed., *Others for 1919: An Anthology of the New Verse* (New York: Nicholas L. Brown, 1920), 131–32.

2. The shortest version of "On Poetry" may be found in Marianne Moore, *Complete Poems* (New York: Penguin, 1994), 36.

3. Angela Zito, "Religion Is Media," *The Revealer: A Daily Review of Religion and Media*, April 16, 2008, http://therevealer.org/archives/2853.

4. James Agee and Walker Evans, *Let Us Now Praise Famous Men* (Boston: Houghton Mifflin, 1941), 11.

5. Wendy Doniger, *The Implied Spider: Politics and Theology in Myth* (New York: Columbia University Press, 1998), 4.

6. Eugene Jolas, ed., *Transition Workshop* (New York: Vanguard, 1949), 29.

7. Matthew Arnold, "Up to Easter," *Nineteenth Century* 21 (1887), 638. Despite his praise, Arnold was not an admirer; he considered "new journalism" to be excessively democratic and thus *"feather-brained."*

8. John D'Agata, "Finding Love at Thirty: An Interview with Seneca Review on the Occasion of its Thirtieth Anniversary," *Seneca Review* 30, no. 1 (2000), 9.

9. Deborah Tall and D'Agata offered a more formal definition of the lyric essay in 1997: "These 'poetic essays' or 'essayistic poems' give primacy to artfulness over the conveying of information. They forsake narrative line, discursive logic, and the art of persuasion in favor of idiosyncratic meditation. . . . It might move by associa-

tion, leaping from one path of thought to another by way of imagery or connotation, advancing by juxtaposition or sidewinding poetic logic"; "New Terrain: The Lyric Essay," *Seneca Review* 27, no. 2 (1997), 7. John D'Agata, "Introduction," *Seneca Review*, 37, no. 2 (2007), 9; John D'Agata, ed., *The Lost Origins of the Essay* (Saint Paul, MN: Graywolf, 2009), 3.

10. Phillip Lopate, "The Essay, an Exercise in Doubt," *New York Times*, February 16, 2013, accessed February 17, 2013, http://opinionator.blogs.nytimes.com/2013/02/16/the-essay-an-exercise-in-doubt/; William Bentinck-Smith, *The Harvard Book: Selections from Three Centuries* (Cambridge: Harvard University Press, 1982), 98; Svetlana Alexievich, "A Search for Eternal Man," Svetlana Alexievich: Voices from Big Utopia, accessed March 1, 2013, http://www.alexievich.info/indexEN.html.

11. John Grierson, "Flaherty's Poetic *Moana*," *New York Sun*, February 8, 1926. William Stott, in his *Documentary Expression and Thirties America* (New York: Oxford University Press, 1973), wonders whether Grierson's coinage wasn't so much the translation he'd later cite as an appropriation of a sociological term, *documentary value*. Stott argues that Grierson's original, didactic ambitions for the genre as providing "the information necessary to organized and harmonious living" evolved away from a form for information alone. "The way of information will not serve," Grierson would conclude; "it is too discursive. And the way of rational explanation will not serve, because it misses the corporate life we are dealing with"; quoted in Stott, *Documentary Expression and Thirties America*, 9–11. Grierson refers to "shimmying exoticisms" in his essay "First Principles of Documentary," in Forsyth Hardy, ed., *Grierson on Documentary* (London: Faber and Faber, 1966), 145.

12. Peter Manseau and Jeff Sharlet, *Killing the Buddha: A Heretic's Bible* (New York: Free Press, 2004), 112–13.

13. John D'Agata, ed., *The Next American Essay* (Saint Paul, MN: Graywolf, 2003), 7.

14. Justin Kaplan, ed., *Whitman: Poetry and Prose* (New York: Library of America, 1996), 745.

15. Michael Taussig, *Shamanism, Colonialism, and the Wild Man: A Study in Terror and Healing* (Chicago: University of Chicago Press, 1987), 10.

16. Kaplan, *Whitman*, 713–14.

17. Peter Coviello, ed., *Walt Whitman's Memoranda During the War: Written on the Spot in 1863–'65* (New York: Oxford University Press, 2004), 4.

18. Joan Didion, *Slouching Toward Bethlehem* (New York: Noonday, 1990), 141.

19. Norman Sims, ed., *The Literary Journalists: The New Art of Personal Reportage* (New York: Ballantine, 1984), 8–22. Given the confusion over this mutant genre, anthologies and analyses that seek to identify distinct features are particularly valuable.

Among those I consulted are John S. Bak and Bill Reynolds, eds., *Literary Journalism Across the Globe: Journalistic Traditions and Transnational Influences* (Amherst: University of Massachusetts Press, 2011); Robert Boynton, *The New New Journalism: Conversations with America's Best Nonfiction Writers on Their Craft* (New York: Vintage, 2005); Patricia Foster and Jeff Porter, eds., *Understanding the Essay* (Buffalo, NY: Broadview, 2012); Lee Gutkind, ed., *In Fact: The Best of Creative Nonfiction* (New York: Norton, 2004); John C. Hartstock, *A History of American Literary Journalism* (Amherst: University of Massachusetts Press, 2000); John Hellman, *Fables of Fact: The New Journalism as New Fiction* (Urbana: University of Illinois Press, 1981); Kevin Kerrane and Ben Yagoda, eds., *The Art of Fact: A Historical Anthology of Literary Journalism* (New York: Scribner, 1997); Michael L. Johnson, *The New Journalism: The Underground Press, The Artists of Nonfiction, and Changes in the Established Media* (Lawrence: University Press of Kansas, 1971); Dwight McDonald, *Masscult and Midcult: Essays Against the American Grain* (New York: New York Review of Books, 2011); Bill Roorbach, ed., *The Art of Truth: Contemporary Creative Nonfiction* (New York: Oxford University Press, 2001); David Shields, *Reality Hunger: A Manifesto* (New York: Knopf, 2010); Norman Sims, *True Stories: A Century of Literary Journalism* (Evanston, IL: Northwestern University Press, 2008); Norman Sims and Mark Kramer, eds., *Literary Journalism: A New Collection of the Best American Nonfiction* (New York: Ballantine, 1995); Patsy Sims, ed., *Literary Nonfiction: Learning by Example* (New York: Oxford University Press, 2001); Ronald Weber, *The Literature of Fact: Literary Nonfiction in American Writing* (Athens: Ohio University Press, 1980); Mas'ud Zavarzadeh, *The Mythopoeic Reality: The Postwar American Nonfiction Novel* (Urbana: University of Illinois Press, 1976).

20. Tom Wolfe and E. W. Johnson, eds., *The New Journalism* (New York: HarperCollins, 1973), 31–32.

21. Ibid., 103.

22. Ed Burns, "The Dickensian Aspect," *The Wire*, season 5, episode 6, directed by Seith Mann, aired February 10, 2008.

23. Jeffrey Stout, *Democracy and Tradition* (Princeton: Princeton University Press, 2003), 9. I came to think about piety as a literary quality through a long series of conversations with the cultural critic Cornel West for a profile in *Rolling Stone*, mostly held in an office the bookshelves of which are lined with book covers featuring the faces of his heroes and inspirations. "Bessie Smith smiles between Herman Melville and Flannery O'Connor," I wrote then. "The radical black crime novelist Chester Himes looms beneath a tiny portrait of Le Corbusier, the Swiss-French pioneer of modern architecture." It was West who directed me to Stout's work; a similar concern, with reference to Whitman among others, pervades his *The American Evasion of Philosophy: A Genealogy of Pragmatism* (Madison: University of Wisconsin Press,

1989) and even more urgently his *Prophesy Deliverance! An Afro-American Revolutionary Christianity* (Louisville, KY: Westminster John Knox Press, 1982).

24. Ed Folsom, ed., *Democratic Vistas: The Original Edition in Facsimile* (Iowa City: University of Iowa Press, 2010); "Tiny ships": 51; "Old undying elements . . . regions": 46–47.

25. Ibid., 58.

26. Ibid., 16.

27. Ibid., 24.

CREDITS